Intelligent Technologies for Web Applications

Chapman & Hall/CRC
Data Mining and Knowledge Discovery Series

SERIES EDITOR
Vipin Kumar
University of Minnesota
Department of Computer Science and Engineering
Minneapolis, Minnesota, U.S.A.

AIMS AND SCOPE

This series aims to capture new developments and applications in data mining and knowledge discovery, while summarizing the computational tools and techniques useful in data analysis. This series encourages the integration of mathematical, statistical, and computational methods and techniques through the publication of a broad range of textbooks, reference works, and handbooks. The inclusion of concrete examples and applications is highly encouraged. The scope of the series includes, but is not limited to, titles in the areas of data mining and knowledge discovery methods and applications, modeling, algorithms, theory and foundations, data and knowledge visualization, data mining systems and tools, and privacy and security issues.

PUBLISHED TITLES

UNDERSTANDING COMPLEX DATASETS:
DATA MINING WITH MATRIX DECOMPOSITIONS
David Skillicorn

COMPUTATIONAL METHODS OF FEATURE SELECTION
Huan Liu and Hiroshi Motoda

CONSTRAINED CLUSTERING: ADVANCES IN ALGORITHMS, THEORY, AND APPLICATIONS
Sugato Basu, Ian Davidson, and Kiri L. Wagstaff

KNOWLEDGE DISCOVERY FOR COUNTERTERRORISM AND LAW ENFORCEMENT
David Skillicorn

MULTIMEDIA DATA MINING: A SYSTEMATIC INTRODUCTION TO CONCEPTS AND THEORY
Zhongfei Zhang and Ruofei Zhang

NEXT GENERATION OF DATA MINING
Hillol Kargupta, Jiawei Han, Philip S. Yu, Rajeev Motwani, and Vipin Kumar

DATA MINING FOR DESIGN AND MARKETING
Yukio Ohsawa and Katsutoshi Yada

THE TOP TEN ALGORITHMS IN DATA MINING
Xindong Wu and Vipin Kumar

GEOGRAPHIC DATA MINING AND KNOWLEDGE DISCOVERY, SECOND EDITION
Harvey J. Miller and Jiawei Han

TEXT MINING: CLASSIFICATION, CLUSTERING, AND APPLICATIONS
Ashok N. Srivastava and Mehran Sahami

BIOLOGICAL DATA MINING
Jake Y. Chen and Stefano Lonardi

INFORMATION DISCOVERY ON ELECTRONIC HEALTH RECORDS
Vagelis Hristidis

TEMPORAL DATA MINING
Theophano Mitsa

RELATIONAL DATA CLUSTERING: MODELS, ALGORITHMS, AND APPLICATIONS
Bo Long, Zhongfei Zhang, and Philip S. Yu

KNOWLEDGE DISCOVERY FROM DATA STREAMS
João Gama

STATISTICAL DATA MINING USING SAS APPLICATIONS, SECOND EDITION
George Fernandez

INTRODUCTION TO PRIVACY-PRESERVING DATA PUBLISHING:
CONCEPTS AND TECHNIQUES
Benjamin C. M. Fung, Ke Wang, Ada Wai-Chee Fu, and Philip S. Yu

HANDBOOK OF EDUCATIONAL DATA MINING
Cristóbal Romero, Sebastian Ventura, Mykola Pechenizkiy, and Ryan S.J.d. Baker

DATA MINING WITH R: LEARNING WITH CASE STUDIES
Luís Torgo

MINING SOFTWARE SPECIFICATIONS: METHODOLOGIES AND APPLICATIONS
David Lo, Siau-Cheng Khoo, Jiawei Han, and Chao Liu

DATA CLUSTERING IN C++: AN OBJECT-ORIENTED APPROACH
Guojun Gan

MUSIC DATA MINING
Tao Li, Mitsunori Ogihara, and George Tzanetakis

MACHINE LEARNING AND KNOWLEDGE DISCOVERY FOR
ENGINEERING SYSTEMS HEALTH MANAGEMENT
Ashok N. Srivastava and Jiawei Han

SPECTRAL FEATURE SELECTION FOR DATA MINING
Zheng Alan Zhao and Huan Liu

ADVANCES IN MACHINE LEARNING AND DATA MINING FOR ASTRONOMY
Michael J. Way, Jeffrey D. Scargle, Kamal M. Ali, and Ashok N. Srivastava

FOUNDATIONS OF PREDICTIVE ANALYTICS
James Wu and Stephen Coggeshall

INTELLIGENT TECHNOLOGIES FOR WEB APPLICATIONS
Priti Srinivas Sajja and Rajendra Akerkar

Intelligent Technologies for Web Applications

Priti Srinivas Sajja

Rajendra Akerkar

CRC Press
Taylor & Francis Group
Boca Raton London New York

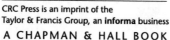

CRC Press is an imprint of the
Taylor & Francis Group, an **informa** business
A CHAPMAN & HALL BOOK

CRC Press
Taylor & Francis Group
6000 Broken Sound Parkway NW, Suite 300
Boca Raton, FL 33487-2742

Printed in the United States of America on acid-free paper
Version Date: 20120424

International Standard Book Number: 978-1-4398-7162-1 (Hardback)

Visit the Taylor & Francis Web site at
http://www.taylorandfrancis.com

and the CRC Press Web site at
http://www.crcpress.com

Dedication

To Srinivas and Abhignya

Priti Srinivas Sajja

To my parents, Ashalata and Arvind Akerkar

Rajendra Akerkar

Contents

Part III: Semantic web and web knowledge management

Preface

The Web is becoming the largest data repository in the world and presents a key driving force for a large spectrum of information technology (IT). To develop effective and intelligent web applications and services, it is critical to discover useful knowledge through analyzing large amounts of content, hidden content structures, or usage patterns of web data resources. To achieve such a goal, a variety of techniques in diverse research areas need to be integrated, including natural language processing, information extraction, information retrieval, information filtering, knowledge representation, knowledge management, machine learning, databases, data mining, web mining, text mining, agent, human–computer interaction, and the semantic web. These integrated techniques should address the key challanges from the heterogeneous and dynamic nature of web contents and usage patterns.

Within the past ten years, the Web research community has brought to maturity a comprehensive set of foundational technology components, both at the conceptual level and in the form of prototypes and software.

Intended readers

This book describes the basics as well as the latest trends in the area of an integrated approach instead of an edited volume of papers/chapters. The book provides a detailed review of issues for web researchers. With extensive use of examples and more than 100 illustrations, as well as bibliographical notes, end-of-chapter exercises, and glossaries, to clarify complex material and demonstrate practical applications, this book can serve as a senior undergraduate-level book. It can also serve as a good reference for researchers and practitioners who deal with the various problems involving semantics, intelligent techniques for web ontologies, and the semantic web.

Understanding web-related concepts, studying the underlying standards and technical components, and putting all of this together into concrete terms require a substantial amount of effort. This book provides comprehensive and easy-to-follow coverage on both the "what-is" and "how-to" aspects of web-related technologies.

In particular, this book is written keeping the following readers in mind:

- Software engineers and developers who are interested in learning the intelligent and semantic web technology in general
- Web application developers who are interested in studying the intelligent web technologies and in constructing web applications
- Researchers who are interested in the research and development of intelligent and semantic technologies

- Undergraduate and graduate students in computer science departments, whose main area of focus is the intelligent and semantic web
- Practitioners in related engineering fields

The prerequisites needed to understand the concepts in this book include the following:

- Working knowledge of a programming language
- Basic understanding of the Web, including its main technical components such as URL, HTML, and XML

Salient features

This book has the following salient features:

- Makes all fundamental as well as in-depth material available at one place in an integrated manner
- Provides a more concrete organization than an edited volume
- Incorporates new topics on artificial intelligence (AI), thus making the book more effective and helpful in solving problems
- Integrates illustrations and examples to support pedagogical exposition
- Equips the reader with the necessary information in order to obtain hands-on experience of the topics of discussion
- Facilitates experimentation of the content discussed in the book by making available fundamental tools, research directions, practice questions, and additional reading material
- Integrates all material, yet allows each chapter to be used or studied independently
- Supplies further tools and information at the associated website for instructors and students

Outline of the chapters

The book is organized into four parts. Part I provides an introduction to the Web, machine learning, new AI techniques, and web intelligence.

Chapter 1 describes introductory concepts such as a brief history of the Web and the Internet. It also discusses the latest trends on the Web such as blogs, tweets, wikis, etc. Collaborative mapping, aggregation technologies, open platforms, tools, and application programming interfaces (APIs) are discussed in this chapter. The chapter also describes the organization of the content.

Chapter 2 reviews machine learning that has made its way from AI into web applications and technologies. It presents the capabilities of machine learning methods and provides ideas on how these methods could be useful for web intelligence. The chapter establishes fundamentals such as linear regression, estimation, generalization, supervised learning, unsupervised learning, reinforcement learning, hidden Markov models, and Bayesian networks.

Chapter 3 covers the new AI and knowledge-based system (KBS) and discusses the limitations of the typical symbolic AI and the need of bio-inspired AI for the Web. The most essential and widely employed material pertaining to neural networks, genetic algorithms, fuzzy systems, and rough sets are discussed in brief with their possible advantages.

Chapter 4 explores the basic roles as well as practical impacts of artificial intelligence and advanced information technology for the next generation of web-based systems, services, and environments. The chapter also presents the concept of wisdom web.

Part II is dedicated to information retrieval, mining, and extraction of content from the Web.

Web information retrieval is another important aspect linked to web intelligence. Web spiders, distributed spiders, focused spiders, search engine mechanisms, personalized search techniques, and natural language processing (NLP) in conjunction with effective retrieval are discussed in Chapter 5. This chapter also presents architectures of knowledge-based systems for information retrieval from the Web.

Web mining is the application of machine learning (especially data mining) techniques to web-based data for the purpose of learning or extracting knowledge. Web mining methodologies can generally be classified into one of three distinct categories: web usage mining, web structure mining, and web content mining. Chapter 6 discusses these methodologies along with suitable applications.

Chapter 7 introduces the concept of information extraction to facilitate structured data extraction. Information extraction (IE) is a technology enabling relevant content to be extracted from textual information available electronically. It plays a crucial role for researchers and professionals as well as for other end users who have to deal with vast amounts of information from the Internet. This chapter focuses on wrapper induction as well as semiautomatic and automatic wrapper generation along with a suitable case study.

Part III is dedicated to the semantic web and web knowledge management.

Chapter 8 establishes the semantic web as an immediate extension of the Web in which the meaning (semantics) of content and services on the Web is defined along with the content. Embedding of such semantics makes it possible for the Web to "understand" the content and satisfy the requests of people and machines to use the Web. The chapter discusses metadata, metadata standards, layered architecture of semantic web, and tools and ontology constructs such as resource description framework (RDF), web ontology language (OWL), and extensible markup language (XML). Ontology spectrum, meta-ontology, editors, inference and annotation tools, etc., are also included. It also discusses web applications such as semantic search, social communities, and semantic web research issues.

The Web encompasses a large amount of content organized heterogeneously. For effective retrieval and better access of the content available on the Web, it is necessary to use suitable knowledge representation, knowledge use, and knowledge-sharing techniques. Chapter 9 discusses various knowledge management techniques for the Web. It also suggests a generic architecture on the top of the semantic web for knowledge management.

Chapter 10 combines the concepts and the methods of two fields, namely, the semantic web and social networks, which, together, aid in the analysis of the social web and in the design of a new class of applications that combine human intelligence with machine processing. The chapter presents the application of semantic web technologies to the social web that forms a network of interlinked and semantically enabled content and knowledge. It also provides readers with an understanding of the key concepts and methods of both the fields and describes a simple real-world application incorporating social and semantic metadata.

Part IV discusses additional topics such as agent-based web, security issues, and human–computer interaction.

An agent is an entity that is autonomous, independent, and cooperative. It does intended work on behalf of the user. To carry out various web activities and support web functionalities in a structured manner, one may take the help of agents. Chapter 11 discusses agent typology, intelligent agents, agents for the Web, web services, and case studies. Considering the technologies discussed within the aforementioned chapters, some agents can be designed to fit into the framework of a multi-agent web. One such possible framework of a multi-agent system is discussed in this chapter. The chapter also elaborates on applications suitable for the framework suggested.

Chapter 12 discusses issues related to web security. It reviews different AI and machine learning methods concerning security, privacy, and reliability issues of cyberspace. It also enables readers to discover the types of methods at their disposal, summarizes the state of the practice in this important area, and provides a classification of existing work. The topics include security management and governance, network security and authentication, intrusion detection, trust management, access control, and privacy.

The expectations from the Web are ever increasing, and the Web will also evolve accordingly. However, the facilities offered by such a giant organization would be made more effective with better interface. Chapter 13 focuses on human–web interactions. It defines web interaction and identifies interaction applications. Topics such as interactive information search/retrieval, interactive query expansion, personalization, user profiling, visualization, user interfaces, usability, web adaptation, and interactive authoring/annotation for the semantic web are discussed in this chapter along with other similar applications.

Use as a book

The book can be covered in a total of approximately 40–45 lecture hours (plus 20–30 hours dedicated to exercises and hands-on practice).

Parts I and II can be covered as a complete course in about 30 taught hours. Such a course requires a significant amount of additional practical activity, normally consisting of several exercises from each chapter and a project involving the design and implementation of a web application.

Parts III and IV can be covered in a second course. They can alternatively be integrated in part within an extended first course. In advanced, project-centered courses, the study of current technology can be accompanied by a project dedicated to the development of technological components. The advanced course can be associated with further readings or with a research-oriented seminar series.

Acknowledgments

The organization and the contents of this book have benefited from our experience in teaching the subject in various contexts. All the students attending those courses, dispersed over many schools and countries (Sardar Patel University, the International School of Information Management, Saint Mary's University, American University of Armenia, and SIBER-India), deserve our deepest gratitude. Some of these students have class-tested rough drafts and incomplete notes and have contributed to their development, improvement, and correction. Similarly, we would like to thank the staff from IT companies and government organizations who attended our courses for professionals and helped us learn the practical aspects that we have tried to convey in this book. We would also like to thank all the colleagues who have contributed, directly or indirectly, to the development of this book, through discussions on course organization or the actual revision of drafts. They include Pawan Lingras, Terje Aaberge, Svein Ølnes, David Camacho, Henry Hexmoor, and Darshan Choksi.

We thank the reviewers of this edition for a number of very useful suggestions concerning the organization of the book and the specific content of chapters.

We also thank Aastha Sharma, David Fausel, Sarah Morris, the staff at CRC Press, and Remya Divakaran (SPi Global) who have contributed to the birth of this book.

Finally, we express our gratitude to our families for their love, support, and patience during the preparation of the book. We also thank our families for reminding us that there are things in life beyond writing books.

Priti Srinivas Sajja

Rajendra Akerkar

Authors

Priti Srinivas Sajja joined the faculty of the Department of Computer Science, Sardar Patel University, Gujarat, India, in 1994 and is presently working as an associate professor. She received her MS (1993) and PhD (2000) in computer science from Sardar Patel University. Her research interests include knowledge-based systems, soft computing, multiagent systems, and software engineering. She has more than 100 publications in books, book chapters, journals, and in the proceedings of national and international conferences. Three of her publications have won best research paper awards. Dr. Sajja is the coauthor of *Knowledge-Based Systems*. She supervises the work of seven doctoral research students. She is also the principal investigator of a major research project funded by the University Grants Commission (UGC), India. She serves as a member on the editorial boards of many international science journals and has served as a program committee member for various international conferences.

Rajendra Akerkar is a professor/senior researcher at Western Norway Research Institute (Vestlandsforsking), Norway. His research and teaching experience includes over 20 years in academia, spanning different universities in Asia, Europe, and North America. As the founder of Technomathematics Research Foundation (TMRF), he is instrumental in ensuring that the organization lends a platform for research in India. Under his leadership, TMRF has become a well-known organization among the research community worldwide.

Akerkar's current research agenda focuses on learning and language—how each works in the human and how they can be replicated in a machine. He received a DAAD fellowship in 1990 and was also awarded the prestigious BOYSCASTS Young Scientist Award of the Department of Science & Technology, Government of India, in 1997. He is the editor in chief of the *International Journal of Computer Science & Applications* and an associate editor of the *International Journal of Metadata, Semantics, and Ontologies*. Akerkar serves as a member of the scientific committees of several international conferences and also serves on the editorial boards of international journals in computer science. He has authored 12 books, more than 90 research papers, and has edited 5 volumes of international conferences. He initiated the International Conference Series on Web Intelligence, Mining and Semantics (WIMS). Akerkar has been actively involved in many industrial research and development projects for more than 14 years.

part one

Introduction to the Web, machine learning, new AI techniques, and web intelligence

chapter one

Introduction to World Wide Web

1.1 Brief history of the Web and the Internet

The World Wide Web, abbreviated as WWW and commonly known as the Web, has been weaving a variety of solutions for different problems and meeting information requirements of a global audience. It is a system of interlinked hypertext documents in multimedia accessed via Internet, which is defined as network of networks. The dream was conceived by Tim Berners-Lee, who is now director of the World Wide Web Consortium and extending the dream project further in a form of semantic web by adding semantics to the existing web. The Web is developed to be a pool of information to allow collaborators from remote sites to share their ideas and information.

During the year 1980, Tim Berners-Lee built ENQUIRE as a personal database of people using hypertext and software utilities to access the database. The objective was to share data globally without common machines and presentation software. He implemented this system on a newly acquired NeXT workstation. After the invention of supporting hypertext transfer protocol (HTTP) and a web browser named World Wide Web, the first web server and page were created that described the project itself. It was further modified to be used on any machine rather than NeXT. On August 6, 1991, Berners-Lee posted a short summary of the World Wide Web project on the alt.hypertext newsgroup. This date also marked the debut of the Web as a publicly available service on the Internet. According to the summary, the World Wide Web (WWW) project aimed to allow all links to be made to any information anywhere. He invited high-energy physicists and other experts to share data, news, and documentation. Inspired from the message, university-based scientific departments and physics laboratories adopted the concept developed such as Fermilab (Fermi National Accelerator Laboratory for high-energy physics, Batavia, IL) and SLAC (Stanford Linear Accelerator Center, Stanford University, Menlo Park, CA).

There was still no graphical browser available for computers besides the NeXT. This gap was filled in 1992 with the release of Erwise (an application developed at Helsinki University of Technology, Finland) and ViolaWWW (created by Pei-Yuan Wei, which included advanced features such as embedded graphics, scripting, and animation). This gave rise to the development of different web browsers. Some prominent early browsers are Mosaic (now Netscape Navigator) and Cello. Immediately after that, in 1994, the World Wide Web Consortium was founded at Massachusetts Institute of Technology (MIT) with the support of Defense Advance Research Project Agency (DARPA) and European Commission. Berners-Lee made the Web available freely, with no patent and no royalties due. By the end of 1994, the total number of websites has increased, however, the increase is minute (in comparison with) the present standards of 15 million index pages approximately. However, by 1996, the usage of the Web was no longer optional. Earlier, people had identified the possibilities of free publishing and instant worldwide information, but, at present, the Web has opened up the possibility of direct web-based commerce and instantaneous group communications worldwide. The innovation of protocols, standards, and utilities like search engine and e-mail made the Web ubiquitous and fall within the reach

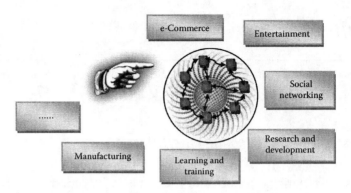

Figure 1.1 Ubiquitous applications of the Web.

of a common man. New ideas such as blogs and social networking are also welcomed in recent times. Some typical application areas of the Web include e-commerce, decision support in various businesses, e-learning, social networking, training, information repository services, manufacturing, and research and development. Figure 1.1 represents ubiquitous application of the Web. Some of the recent innovations are discussed in the next section.

1.2   Blogs

A blog, derived from the term web log (or weblog), is a type of website that is usually maintained by an individual to share details regarding personal views, events, or multimedia materials such as graphics or videos. The term weblog was coined by Jorn Barger on December 17, 1997, to describe the list of links on his Robot Wisdom website that "logged" his Internet wanderings. The short form "blog" was coined by Peter Merholz, who jokingly broke the word *weblog* into the phrase *we blog* in the sidebar of his blog Peterme.com in April–May, 1999. Blog entries are commonly displayed in reverse-chronological order, from most recent entries to the oldest. Blog can also be used as a verb, meaning to maintain or add content to a blog. Many blogs are interactive and allow visitors to leave comments and messages. Such instructiveness makes the blog different from other static websites. Further, a typical website encompasses plenty of web pages, each may have some subpages under a home page following a well-organized approach. A blog is normally a single page of entries by a single author in the most personalized way. There may be archives of older entries optionally to manage the large stuff in a well-organized way. A blog is normally public and accessible to anyone without any formality such as registration. However, to post a personal comment that may require to be processed (replied) further, there is a need of user information such as an e-mail ID. Figure 1.2 represents a typical blog.

Early blogs were simply manually updated components of common websites. However, the evolution of tools to facilitate the production and maintenance of blog is much easier and less technical. Blogs can be hosted by dedicated blog hosting services or on regular web-hosting services. Alternatively, a blog can be developed and maintained using blog software (also called as blogware) like Wordpress (which is a third-party software, see http://wordpress.org/) and Blogsmith (http://www.blogsmith.com/). The blog software supports the authoring, editing, and publishing of blog posts and comments, with special functions for image management, moderation of posts, and comments. All blog software support authoring, editing, and publishing of entries in the following format:

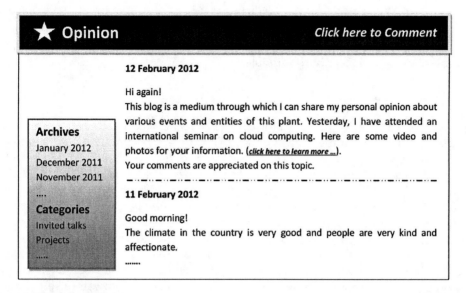

Figure 1.2 Example of a blog.

- Title or headline of the post
- Body, main content of the post
- Reference or link to other article
- Date and time on which the blog is published
- Blog entries can optionally include comments and categories (or tags)

Generally blogs publish focused content on a particular topic such as home design, sports, mobile systems technology, etc. However, there may be some blogs that provide a variety of content and links to plenty of other locations. Most of the blogs have a few things in common. These include

- Heading and main content
- Archives
- Facility for the readers to comment and contact
- Some useful related links (blogrolls)
- Feeds like really simple syndication (RSS), resource description framework (RDF), or atoms
- Excerpts (summary) and plugins for readymade additional functionalities

A blog may have features like trackbacks and pingbacks in order to allow users to comment on blog posts and link to the posts and comment on and recommend them further. Track back is a way to provide notification between different websites. If a person finds the specific blog content interesting, he may send trackback *ping* to the Web author. Pingback offers the advanced facility of automatically notifying the author that the other person referred the author's post. Pingbacks can be automated and do not send content, whereas trackbacks are manual and send an excerpt of the initiating post. The facility of trackback and pingback aim to provide some control on comments on blog content and hence help in extending authority to blog commenting. Some tools offer a feature of comment moderation to monitor and control the comments on the different article posts. Here authors (blog publishers) are given rights to manage the comment spam, delete harsh comments, and approve cool comments. Finally, it must be remembered that blogs require continuous, regular, and meaningful update.

1.3 Tweets

A tweet is a small message, post, or status update on some network. The size of a tweet is comparatively smaller than the typical e-mail. The "tweet" originally means a sound of a bird or whistle, which sweetly says something. Tweet is also considered as a real-time microblogging service. The term tweet became popular by a social networking website called Twitter (Twitter Inc., San Francisco, CA) created in 2006 by Jack Dorsey who is an American software architect and businessman. This site offers facility to send and receive tweets up to 140 characters. That is why it is sometimes described as the short message service (SMS) of the Internet. Generally, tweets are displayed on the user's home page or profile page of the website and are visible by default free of cost. However, it may be restricted to the user's friends list. Other users may choose to read and subscribe (opt) for some specific users tweets. These subscribers are known as followers. The process of subscribing a user's tweet is known as "following." Alternatively, such tweets can be followed on compatible external applications such as smart phones or by SMS available. It is reported that Twitter currently has more than 175 million users. The original project code name for the Twitter service was twttr, inspired by Flickr and the five-character length of American SMS short codes. Flickr is an image-hosting and video-hosting website for online community created by Ludicorp and later acquired by Yahoo! It is a popular website to share and embed personal photographs and images. The basic advantage of using the facility to tweet a message or an item is that one can "post once" and the service will redistribute the item to multiple followers.

Twitter's Application Programming Interface (API) is based on the representational state transfer (REST) architecture. REST is a collection of network design principles and guidelines that define resources and ways to address and access data. With the REST architecture, the Twitter works with most web syndication formats that help in gathering information from one source and sends it out to various destinations. Twitter is compatible with two of them—RSS and atom syndication format (atom). Both formats retrieve data from one resource and send it to another. A web page administrator can embed RSS/atom code into the code of his or her site. Visitors can subscribe to the syndication service—called feed—and receive an update every time the administrator updates the web page. Twitter uses this feature to allow members to post messages to a network of other Twitter members. In effect, Twitter members subscribe to other members' feeds. By allowing third-party developers partial access to its API, Twitter allows them to create programs that incorporate Twitter's services.

Current third-party applications include the following applications:

- *Twitterlicious* and *Twitterific*, two applications that allow users to access Twitter through desktop applications on PCs and MACs, respectively
- *OutTwit*, a Windows application that allows users to access Twitter through the Outlook e-mail program
- *Tweet Scan*, which allows users to search public Twitter posts in real time
- *Twessenger*, which integrates with the Windows Live Messenger 8.1 instant messenger program

- *Twittervision*, which integrates a Twitter feed into Google Maps
- *Flotzam*, which integrates Twitter with Facebook, Flickr, and blogs
- *iTunes to Twitter*, an application that broadcasts the title of the song currently playing in the user's iTunes to his or her network
- *TwitterBox*, a Twitter application that works inside the virtual community of Second Life

The ability to send and receive multiple tweets without any limit and sophisticated interface made twitter very popular in societies and industries. Tweeting is a tool for accessing opinions, decisions, and market information. Tweeting can be used as a very good communication and business tool. It can be used in the field of education for classroom community and collaborative writing within and across schools and institutes.

1.4   Wikis

A Wiki is a collaborative web platform that allows multiple users from different locations to add information at a centralized place in an interactive fashion. The interface for interaction is created in such a way that users do not require any training. The wiki concept was first introduced by Ward Cunningham as "the simplest online database that could possibly work" in the year 1995. This is also considered as writable web or open editing concept. Wiki looks like a simple website with an edit facility/link. Readers of the page can modify it or add content directly through this link. Wikis can be used as a centralized repository for many applications and provides efficient document management. Wiki can be used as a website, as a knowledge base for FAQ system, and as an information sharing utility. As many authors contribute and evaluate information for a specific topic, wiki can enhance the quality and quantity of information. Table 1.1 shows some typical applications that can be benefited by wikis.

On request, wiki shares available information and allows editing of the information through any browser. It also invites users to create new pages and promotes a specified topic. Wiki can create links to new empty pages that do not yet exist to invite users to share their opinion. There are many different ways in which users can edit the wiki content. Figure 1.3 gives an idea how users can work with wiki.

The content of wiki is normally specified with a simplified markup language, sometimes known as *"wiki text."* Some wikis allow dedicated content such as a repository of images or collections of audio. Common facilities that a wiki typically provides is creating new pages, editing content, navigation, and searching. Sometimes external search engine facility can be embedded within a wiki. Majority of wikis provide limited access to hypertext markup language (HTML) and cascade style sheet (CSS). This is the prime reason that generally wikis look simple. Many modern wikis are making "What You See Is What You Get" (WYSIWYG) editing available to users through scripts and controls

Table 1.1 Applications Benefited by Wikis

Project management and up-to-date project status information
Tutorials and e-learning
Internal notice board and institutional news circulation
FAQ management
Online document management and information sharing
Managing groups and social interactions

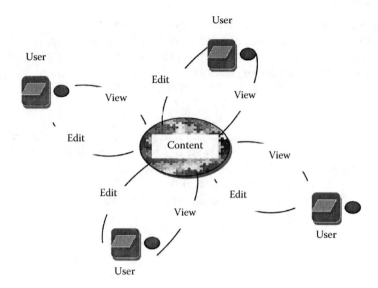

Figure 1.3 Working with wikis.

(like JavaScript or ActiveX controls). The scripts and controls translate the formatting instructions into appropriate wiki text. The translation is transparent and hidden from users to avoid complexity.

Most wikis maintain a log of changes made to wiki pages and maintain versions of the pages. The administrator or author may revert to the older version. With the help of such a revert facility, authors can revert to an older version of the page. Some wikis like MediaWiki insist contributors to provide separate edit summary when they edit a page. The edit summary is an important parameter that justifies the editing and helps in taking the decision whether the page is to be reverted back or not.

For implementation of such collaborative and sharable platform, wiki software is used. The wiki software is implemented on a server and can be executed on different web servers. The content is stored in file systems and changes are stored in a relational database for version management. Some software that are helpful in creating wikis are given in Table 1.2.

Wiki can be developed and used as a standalone system. Such wikis are known as personal wikis. The example of such a personal wiki is the Wikidpad.

1.4.1   Improving wiki content reliability, quality, and security

In spite of its simplicity and advantages, wiki is not considered a reliable source of information. As anybody can contribute in such a system, the content of the system is easily tampered. However, there are genuine contributors and editors, who catch such malicious tampering and correct the mistakes and destructive content for the benefit of others. Many times, users contribute the content that they thought correct and genuine, such as ideas, research information, and experiments. It is not advisable to change such information; however, in this situation, one or more versions showing suggestions and changes can be prepared and a link can be provided adjacent to this. This strategy is also applicable if contributor to wiki does not have rights to edit the content. To improve the reliability, the content pages are ranked by administrator, readers, and contributors. There are

Table 1.2 List of Software for Wiki

ConcourseConnect is a freely available J2EE application with social networking, online community, business directory, and customer relationship management capabilities. This tool supports features like wiki, blog, document management, reviews, online advertising, and project management modules
DokuWiki is a simple-to-use Wiki to facilitate documentation management needs within a small institution. It uses plain text files and has a simple but powerful syntax, which ensures the data files remain readable outside the Wiki
MediaWiki is a popular free web-based wiki software application. It is developed by, and it runs, all the projects of the Wikimedia Foundation, including Wikipedia, Wiktionary, and Wikinews. It is written in the hypertext processor (PHP) programming language and uses a backend database
TiddlyWiki is a HTML/JavaScript-based wiki in which the entire site/wiki is contained in a single file. This tool does not require any server support
Wikidpad is a freeware (open source) personal-use wiki with native support of international characters (Unicode). This software is executable on a single machine. It helps in the implementation of features like storing thoughts, ideas, to-do lists, contacts, and other notes with wiki-like linking between pages
Windows SharePoint Server 2010 has built-in Wiki support. It is built on ASP.Net, C#, and Microsoft SQL Server
Wikia (formerly known as Wikicities) is a free web-hosting service for wikis

sophisticated software programs that help in improving reliability, security, and quality of wiki content by checking and imposing constraints on content and contributors. Table 1.3 suggests some ideas to improve trustworthiness and quality of wiki content.

Wikis that allow only registered users are known as closed wikis. In general, wiki allows anonymous editing by just recording IP address of the machine from which editing is done. In closed wikis, only registered users, whose information (like name and biography) is formally recorded, can edit the wiki content. With this strategy, wiki content is reliable and controllable; however, growth of content on wiki is slower. The popular Wikipedia is an open wiki that allows anonymous editing and records only IP addresses. The countermeasures shown in Table 1.3 help in preventing attacks from malicious contributors, vandalism content, harmful code, and bugs. Besides these, an edit war may occur

Table 1.3 Improving Reliability, Quality, and Security of Wiki Content

Improvement	Countermeasures
Improving reliability of content	By correcting the content manually with the help of experts and administrators
	By providing links to the edited version of the content
	By accreditation of users as well as content
Improving quality	By frequent editing, ranking, and filtering the content
Improving security	By allowing only registered users to edit the content
	By imposing requirement of additional waiting period before allowing any edit
	By dedicated software support (such as JavaScript) to automatically find vandalism, bugs, and harmful content
	By preparing a list of malicious sites, if any, within the content pointing to any of the sites from the list

as contributors repetitively change the same wiki. Such edit wars can be easily identified by observing the time interval between reverts and administrator may lock the page or contributor for further change.

1.5 Collaborative mapping

Collaborative mapping is the aggregation of web maps and user-generated content in order to provide application-specific information and support decision making and problem solving. The content and maps utilized here are provided through users and other resources like websites. The processed content and maps can take different distinct forms to support the intended tasks. Any user with a location-aware device can create their personal map enriched with helpful contents. Collaborative mapping is an initiative to collectively produce models of real-world locations online for the benefit of people. Advances in technology for location-aware devices and emergence of the Web have changed the way people are interacting. With these technologies, any user can create a map, associate information related to that location, and share the collaborated content within a group and within communities through social networking means. Tools like GeoURL and Blogmapper help in finding the location of blogs all over the world, based on coordinates specified in latitude and longitude.

There are various techniques available through which content and maps are collaborated. The simplest way is to assign the content on the map itself. This technique is known as shared surface. Here content is created and associated with a map at the time of map creation by sharing a common surface. WikiMapia is an example for the same. WikiMapia adds user-generated place names and descriptions to locations. This technique is very simple and user friendly; however, it has limitations of revision control such as concurrent accessing and versioning.

1.6 Aggregation technologies

Aggregator is a special word coined for the website that aggregates a specific type of information from multiple online sources. There are websites for aggregate news, poll information, reviews, search results, and other multimedia information. An aggregator is a client software or a web application that collects the syndicated web content to a single location for ease of viewing and managing. It is a consolidated view of content from multiple locations. The major advantage of using such a syndication process is saving time and effort that are needed to check plenty of websites and to create unique customized presentation for information collected. The process is automatic and repeated according to user-determined intervals. Unlike the typical web surfing and e-mailing where content is pushed to the user, here content is considered as pulled toward the user. Users have to opt (subscribe or unsubscribe) for subscribing such aggregation facility. All websites may not contain the aggregation facility, as it requires building and embedding special features with the websites. Aggregator features are frequently built into portal sites, web browsers, and e-mail programs. The aggregation applications are also identified as RSS reader, feed readers, or feed aggregators. The syndicated content aggregator will retrieve and interpret the content usually supplied in the form of RSS or other extensible markup language (XML)-formatted data such as RDF or atom. Atom refers to a pair of related standards: the *atom syndication format* in XML along with a simple hypertext-based *atom publishing protocol* (*AtomPub* or *APP*) for creating and updating web resources.

There are a variety of software applications and components that act as aggregators and collect, format, translate, and republish the content. During the process of aggregation, the aggregator may resolve the semantic and contextual differences in the information. The aggregator exhibits two major characteristics such as transparency and ability to analyze the collected content. An aggregator is supposed to be transparent to the users seeking information to a resource. Further, it should resolve contextual differences for effective comparisons and aggregations of content from different resources. Aggregator is also required to synthesize collected information instead of simply presenting it. That is why the typical e-mail facilities and simple search engines do not fit into this category. Besides aggregation, a simple aggregator may combine several capabilities for a given application. These capabilities include post-aggregation analysis, synthesis, comparison, intra- and interorganizational relationships, and customized presentation. Table 1.4 provides example for each of the aforementioned capabilities.

The source (target) from which multiple individual entities are collected by an aggregator is known as aggregated. The individual items that are collected by an aggregator are known as an "aggregatee." There may be an aggregator that collects information and whereabouts of aggregators. In this case, the aggregators collected by the main aggregator program become aggregatees. The aggregator that collects the aggregators can be called as meta-aggregator. Once the job of aggregation is over, post-aggregation activities are started.

Majority of the aggregators seek information from the public resource. Further, the aggregated data sources cannot differentiate simple users and aggregator programs demanding and retrieving information. These types of aggregators are financially independent and require no formalities or permission to do so. Aggregators are spreading rapidly in many industries. To restrict the access of aggregators can be restricted by imposing some financial schemes that mutually help both the aggregator and aggregated. The aggregators pay a nominal amount of fees and get rights to access the information, including some special information that is not yet published publicly. On the other hand, the aggregated receives fees and gets control on the aggregator. Such agreement between both the parties (the aggregator and aggregated) may be temporary or permanent for a given period of time. Here the aggregation service provider comes into picture. The primary duty of the service provider is to facilitate selling or renting the aggregator facility with necessary license and support. This strategy will be helpful for companies that want to share their information to the aggregators and the developers that generate and maintain the aggregator programs.

The most commonly used web-based aggregators are reader applications on the Web. Aggregators that fall within this category are used at a personal level. Table 1.5 provides a brief list of some RSS readers that act as aggregators.

Table 1.4 Aggregator Capabilities

Capabilities	Explanation/example
Seeking	Locating resources such as websites from the network environment
Retrieving	Retrieving information from different resources/locations
Comparing	Compare prizes for products
Intra-organizational relationship	Integrate multiple separate departmental diaries and budgets
Interorganizational relationship	Consolidate information about a company from multiple sources such as news

Table 1.5 Aggregator Examples

Abilon	Abilon is comparatively smaller in size and easier to use freeware that displays headlines from different sources in an easy-to-read format
Awasu	Awasu is a free RSS client for Windows that monitors news sites, e-mail accounts, and other resources like databases
Bloglines	Bloglines is an integrated service for searching, subscribing, publishing, and sharing news feeds, blogs, and other web resources. It is free and easy to use
BlogMatrix Jäger	BlogMatrix Jäger is an extensible "one-panel" reader, taking up a very small amount of screen space and includes a synchronization feature (+ Mac)
NewsGator	NewsGator executes in Microsoft Outlook and collects news from various locations
Newz Crawler	Newz Crawler wanders through different news sites and collects feeds mainly in XML and RSS forms
Novobot	Novobot collects news from RSS and non-RSS sources and provides an interactive desktop newsreader environment
RSS Bandit	RSS Bandit is a free desktop news aggregator for Windows built on the .NET Framework
RSSOwl	RSSOwl gathers information from various sources and organizes the retrieved information in a friendly way. It is also a freeware and is user friendly
RssReader	RssReader automatically collects news at user configurable intervals and warns with a little alarm on update with a short description of update
SharpReader	SharpReader is another RSS aggregator for Windows

More advanced methods of aggregating feeds are provided via asynchronous JavaScript (AJAX) coding techniques and XML components known as web widgets. Web widgets are small utilities embedded with a web page. Such utilities allow users to aggregate various resources such as e-mail services, documents, or feeds into a single interface. Majority of aggregators are meant for personal use. However, there are web applications that can be used to aggregate several blogs into one such as *planet* sites, which are used by online communities to aggregate community blogs in a centralized location. They are named after the Planet aggregator, a server application designed for this purpose.

1.7   Open platforms, application programming interface, and programming tools

Open platforms are suits of software utilities that offer facilities to use, extend, and customize the platform to develop application-specific utilities. Open platform means the platform that is publicly available and has various rights of usage associated with it. The word open indicates the mechanism of accessing and using the platform, not in the predefined way but in a user-defined fashion. Open platforms can be compared with the telephone. The basic utilities of telephoning are provided to companies or to application developers by the government. Third-party application developers create facilities like touchtone dialing, caller ID, voice mail, conferencing, videophone, etc., on their own products using the platform of basic facilities provided. The features added on the basic communication facility make the platform more personalized, interactive, and user friendly. Open platform publishes external interfaces that allow the software to function in many different ways according to the users' perspectives without modifying the source. These programming interfaces are meant for user-defined applications, hence known as Application Programming Interface (API). An open platform consists of different modules and utilities. Some of these utilities may further expose their internal design and code (source) and let users edit the source to achieve a high level of customization. Availability of such internal code/source is known as open source. An open platform can consist of software modules or utilities that are either commercial or open source or both.

Most open platforms have some characteristics in common. These characteristics are given as follows:

- *APIs* to use, extend, and customize platform facility for real problem solving. These are external programming interfaces and readily available to users.
- *Tools, library, and documentation* to support application development. The API provided along with a development platform only provides interface to the application. The platforms as well as interfaces do not provide required tool, library, and documentation for the proper utilization of the tool. Along with the API, tools, library, and development facility are required. Interactive wizards and development manuals are advisable for noncomputer professionals to help application development using the platform and API.
- *Training and support* on how to use the facilities offered. Providing training to third-party programmers opens up new markets for the platform. Training enables users and vendors in efficient and effective use of the resources (APIs and tools) and development of APIs to integrate their applications.
- *Consulting and troubleshooting* to ensure quality integration and step-by-step assistance beyond the general guidelines available with the manuals and library.
- *Consistency in platform design* to ensure compatibility with different technologies and ever-increasing future customer demand.

These characteristics are presented in Figure 1.4.

The open platforms are beneficial to users as they provide access to third party for further development in a flexible customized way. By providing the API, an open platform provides an enormous marketplace of choices. The open platforms enable the users' and developers' platform to meet more specialized needs and serve a wider variety of purposes.

1.8 Web intelligence

From the discussion of the aforementioned topics, it is obvious that the Web has entered human lives and has its significant impacts in different areas through various technologies. Communication, social networking, information sharing and distributing, and searching are the different areas that are normally explored by users. Considering the ever-increasing users' requirements and evolving complexity and size of the Web, effective techniques are needed for the Web structurization, content management, and access. Some of the major challenges and limitations of the current web can be shortlisted as follows:

- Lack of knowledge-based searches
- Lack of effective techniques to access the Web in depth
- Lack of mechanisms to deal with dynamic requirements of users
- Lack of automatically constructed directories
- Lack of multidimensional analysis and data mining support

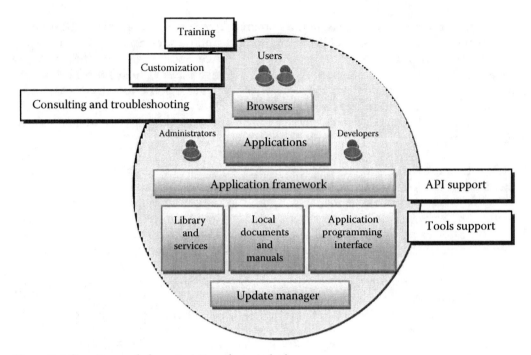

Figure 1.4 Structure and characteristics of open platform.

As stated earlier, to meet the challenges and needs of the future web, existing theories and technologies need to be enhanced intelligently to deal with the complexity of the Web. According to Lotfi Zadeh (2004), it is widely recognized that world knowledge plays an essential role in the assessment of relevance, summarization, search, and deduction. Artificial intelligence (AI) techniques are the computer-based techniques and/or approaches that make machines partly intelligent and understand the need and applicability of methods for effective utilization of resources. By employing the AI techniques for web applications, it is possible to impart some degree of intelligence in web-based business. Therefore, web intelligence (WI) is considered as an employment of AI techniques for the Web. Figure 1.5 highlights this hybridization.

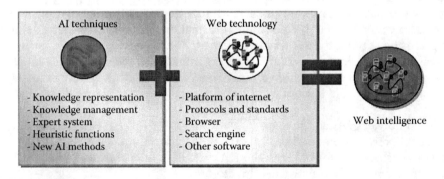

Figure 1.5 Hybridization of AI and web technology.

WI was first introduced by Yiyu Yao as a joint research effort in developing the next generation web-based intelligent systems by combining their expertise in datamining, agents, information retrieval, and logic. Yiyu Yao (2005) defined WI as follows:

> Web Intelligence exploits Artificial Intelligence and Advanced Information Technology on the Web and Internet.

The Web Intelligence Consortium (WIC) is an international, nonprofit organization dedicated to advancing worldwide scientific research and industrial development in the field of WI. According to WIC, IT promotes collaborations among worldwide WI research centers and organizational members and technology showcases at WI-related conferences and workshops. The consortium definition of WI is as follows:

> The Web Intelligence has been recognized as a new direction for scientific research and development to explore the fundamental roles as well as practical impacts of Artificial Intelligence (e.g. knowledge representation, planning, knowledge discovery and data mining, intelligent agents, and social network intelligence) and advanced Information Technology (e.g. wireless networks, ubiquitous devices, social networks, wisdom web, and data/knowledge grids) on the next generation of web-empowered products, systems, services, and activities. It is one of the most important as well as promising IT research fields in the era of web and agent intelligence.

Major aim of the WI is to utilize AI and Information and Communication Technology (ICT) on the Web. AI techniques can be helpful in knowledge acquisition, knowledge representation, and better management of knowledge on the Web. Hence, the AI techniques are helpful in meeting web challenges and needs. The Web has become an integral part of human life. Still the Web utilizes blind and dumb interfaces to the physical world, which makes web operations somewhat mechanical, tedious, and less human oriented. Hybridization of AI and web technologies help in simplifying complicated web operations in such a way that users remain transparent from the complex background operation and can enjoy friendly interface. Web techniques enriched with AI techniques make the environment not only friendly but also more human like. The simplest and still most useful example can be searching. Incorporating some simple heuristic filtering and ranking functions that determine quality and relevance of the search material can present the really required information in a friendly format instead of presenting a raw snapshot of the Web content. Further, this functionality can be developed as an independent, generic, and commercial agent. This increases modularity, increases friendliness, and provides a very effective result by adding just an extra little processing step.

1.9   Intelligence in web applications

Adding intelligence in web application increases value to the application. According to Surowiecki (2005), it is a step toward *wise crowds*. More formally, this is a collective or group intelligence (CI) to effectively use the information provided by others to improve one's application.

There are three components that need to harness collective intelligence:

1. Allow users to interact.
2. Learn about your users in aggregate.
3. Personalize content using user-interaction data and aggregate data.

Making a good use of a user's experience and personal taste is, therefore, one of the core ideas here. On the one hand, collective intelligence can be then described as the capacity of understanding, learning from, and reasoning about (intelligence) the data produced by groups of individuals (collective). On the other hand, it also comprises the emergence of intelligent behavior from the interaction of individuals in a group.

There are two forms of data representation that are used by learning algorithms. User interaction manifests itself in the form of the sparsely populated dataset.

There are a number of ways to transform raw ratings from users into intelligence. First, you can simply aggregate all the ratings about the item and provide the average as the item's rating. This can be used to create a top 10 rated items list. Averages work well, but then you are always promoting the popular content. A user is really interested in the average rating for content by users who have similar tastes. Clustering is a technique that can help find a group of users similar to the user. The average rating of an item by a group of users similar to a user is more relevant to the user than a general average rating. Ratings provide a good quantitative feedback of how good the content is. In addition, it is interesting to know how other forms of user-interaction get transformed into metadata. Basically, there are two main approaches to using information from users' interaction: content based and collaboration based.

The combination of group intelligence and social networks (e.g., Facebook, MySpace, and Google Buzz) is a particularly active research topic. Although everyone enjoys exchanging brief status updates of themselves and swapping photos with friends, social networks are undoubtedly moving toward the next level in order to fulfill a more active role in people's lives. By and large, networks themselves as well as the information within them remain rather passive in comparison with some examples given above. An example of a social network that is somewhat more active than usual is Digg.com, where users can share content from anywhere on the Web. In fact, users do not only share, but also organize the content dynamically by voting on the numerous contributions of other users. Therefore, the information is being organized by means of, what one could call, *collective filtering*.

It might be expected that in the near future such trends will continue, and social networks will progressively develop into collective intelligent ones that will have even greater impact on the everyday lives of their users.

1.10   Organization of this book

This book presents fundamental topics and further explores various advanced topics related to WI such as web knowledge management, semantic web, information retrieval, web mining, agent-based web, wrapper induction, and social networks. The book content is divided into four major parts. Part I introduces necessary fundamentals that are required to explore the WI in depth. These topics include introduction to the Web and current development, machine learning and necessary mathematical background, some bioinspired modern AI methods, and formal WI. In Chapter 1, introductory concepts such as brief history of the Web and the Internet are discussed. Chapter 2 highlights capabilities of machine learning methods and provides brief ideas on how these methods could be useful for WI. The chapter establishes background of fundamental concepts such as linear regression, estimation, generalization, supervised learning, unsupervised learning, reinforcement learning, hidden Markov models, and Bayesian networks. Chapter 3 provides foundations of the modern AI and knowledge-based system (KBS) by discussing limitations of the typical symbolic AI and the need of bioinspired AI for the Web. Most essential and widely employed concepts pertaining to neural networks, genetic algorithms, fuzzy systems, and rough sets are discussed in brief with their possible advantages. The perceptive levels, goals, and characteristics of WI are formally and thoroughly discussed in Chapter 4. This chapter also discusses challenges and issues of WI, future of WI, and establishes platform for the wisdom web.

Web information retrieval is another important aspect that needs to be enlightened with respect to WI. Part II is dedicated to information retrieval, mining, and extraction of content from the Web. Web spiders, distributed spiders, focused spiders, search engine mechanisms, personalized search techniques, and natural language processing (NLP) in conjunction with effective retrieval are discussed in Chapter 5. It also presents architecture of KBS for information retrieval from the Web. Web mining is the application of machine learning (especially data mining) techniques to web-based data for the purpose of learning or extracting knowledge. Web mining methodologies can generally be classified into one of three distinct categories: web usage mining, web structure mining, and web content mining. Chapter 6 discusses these methodologies along with suitable applications. Chapter 7 introduces the concept of information extraction (IE) to facilitate structured data extraction. IE is a technology enabling relevant content to be extracted from textual information available electronically. IE plays a crucial role for researchers and professionals as well as other end users who have to deal with vast amounts of information, for example, from the Internet. This chapter focuses on wrapper induction and semiautomatic and automatic wrapper generation along with a suitable case study.

Part III is dedicated to semantic web and web knowledge management. Chapter 8 establishes semantic web as an immediate extension of the Web in which the meaning (semantics) of content and services on the Web is defined along with the content. Embedding of such semantics makes it possible for the Web to "understand" the content and satisfy the requests of people and machines to use the Web. The chapter discusses metadata, metadata standards, layered architecture of semantic web, tools, and ontology constructs like RDF, web ontology language (OWL), and XML. Ontology spectrum, metaontology, editors, inference and annotation tools, etc., are also included. It also discusses web application–like semantic search, social communities, and semantic web research issues. Web encompasses a large amount of content organized in heterogeneous fashion. For effective retrieval and better access of the content available on the Web, it is necessary to use suitable knowledge representation, knowledge use, and knowledge sharing techniques. Chapter 9 discusses various knowledge management techniques for the Web. This chapter also suggests a generic architecture on top of the semantic web for knowledge management. Chapter 10 combines the concepts and the methods of two fields, namely, semantic web and social networks, which together have the power to aid in the analysis of the social web and the design of a new class of applications that combine human intelligence with machine processing. This chapter presents the application of semantic web technologies to the social web that forms a network of interlinked and semantically enabled content and knowledge. This chapter supplies readers with an understanding of the key concepts and methods of both fields and describes a simple real-world application incorporating social and semantic metadata.

Par IV discusses additional topics such as agent-based web, security issues, and human–computer interaction. An agent is an entity that is autonomous, independent, and cooperative. Agent does intended work on behalf of its user. To carry out various web activities and support web functionalities in a structured fashion, one may take the help of agents. Chapter 11 discusses agent typology, intelligent agents, agents for the Web, web services, and case studies. Considering the technologies discussed within aforementioned

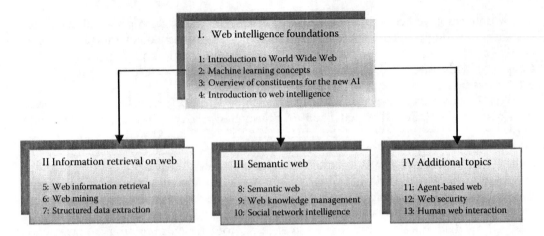

Figure 1.6 Organization of the book.

chapters, some agents can be designed and fit within a framework of a multiagent web. One such possible framework of a multiagent system is discussed in this chapter. The chapter also elaborates applications suitable for the framework suggested. Chapter 12 discusses issues related to the web security. It reviews different AI and machine learning methods in the security, privacy, and reliability issues of cyber space. It enables readers to discover what types of methods are at their disposal, summarizing the state of the practice in this important area, and gives a classification of existing work. The topics include security management and governance, network security and authentication, intrusion detection, trust management, access control and privacy, and privacy. Expectations from the Web are ever increasing and the Web will also evolve accordingly. However, the facilities offered by such a giant organization would be made more effective with better interface. Chapter 13 focuses on human–web interactions. It defines web interaction and identifies interaction applications. Topics like interactive information search/retrieval, interactive query expansion, personalization, user profiling, visualization, user interfaces, usability, web adaptation, and interactive authoring/annotation for semantic web are discussed along with other applications. Figure 1.6 illustrates the organization of the book content at a glance.

Reader and instructors may follow the organization shown in Figure 1.6 to design appropriate learning scheme.

Exercises

1.1 What are the four kinds of markup elements in HTML?

1.2 Use any search engine to find out about the semantic web project. What is the role of markup language within it?

1.3 Find a wiki site and study entries that people have made. If you find an entry on a current news item, you may actually catch it in the process of being updated!

1.4 Implement a single HTML5 page with one text box only (that is, no submit button). On enter or submission, display what was keyed beneath the text box in the following format inside <code></code>: My's log, date MM/DD/YYYY HH24:MI:SS—MESSAGE HERE. You must also display all historical messages in reverse order in the same format.

References

Surowiecki, J. 2005. *The Wisdom of Crowds*. New York: Anchor.
Yao, Y. Y. 2005. Web Intelligence: New frontiers of exploration. Paper presented at the *2005 International Conference on Active Media Technology*, pp. 3–8, Takamatsu, Japan.
Zadeh, L. A. 2004. A note on web intelligence, world knowledge and fuzzy logic. *Data Knowledge Engineering* 50(3):291–304.

chapter two

Machine learning concepts

2.1 Introduction

Artificial intelligence and machine learning (ML) techniques have been applied in many important applications in both scientific and business domains, and web data mining research has become a significant subfield in this area. ML techniques also have been used in information retrieval (IR) and text mining applications. The various activities and efforts in this area are referred to as web mining.

We begin with an overview of ML research and different paradigms in the field. This chapter presents the principles for applying ML to text, focusing on concrete techniques that range from various ways of representing documents and selecting features to particular classification and clustering algorithms.

Since the invention of the first computer in the 1940s, researchers have been attempting to create knowledgeable, educable, and intelligent computers. Many knowledge-based systems have been built for applications such as medical diagnosis, engineering troubleshooting, and business decision making (Akerkar and Sajja 2010). However, most of these systems have been designed to acquire knowledge manually from human experts, which can be both time consuming and labor intensive. ML algorithms have been developed to alleviate these problems by acquiring knowledge automatically from examples or source data. Simon (1983) emphasizes that ML is any process by which a system improves its performance. Similarly, Mitchell (1997) defines ML as the study of "any computer algorithm that improves its performance at some tasks through experience." ML algorithms can be classified as supervised or unsupervised learning. In supervised learning, training examples consist of input–output pair patterns. The goal of the learning algorithm is to predict the output values of new examples, based on their input values. In unsupervised learning, training examples contain only the input patterns and no explicit target output is associated with each input. The learning algorithm needs to generalize from the input patterns to discover the output values. This situation is presented in Figure 2.1.

ML techniques can be divided into four distinct areas: classification, clustering, association learning, and numeric prediction. Classification applied to text is the subject of text categorization, which is the task of automatically sorting a set of documents into categories from a predefined set (Sebastiani 2002, 2005). Basic classification of documents is employed in document indexing for information retrieval systems, text filtering (e.g. protection from e-mail spam), categorization of web pages, and other applications. Classification can also be used on paragraphs, sentences, and words depending on the particular application, like document segmentation, word-sense disambiguation, or topic tracking. In the ML methodology, classifiers (classification algorithms) are trained on earlier sorted (labeled) data, before being applied to sorting unseen texts.

Clustering text data deal with a number of challenges. Among others, the volume of text data, dimensionality and complex semantics are the most important ones. These characteristics of text data require clustering techniques to be scalable to large and high

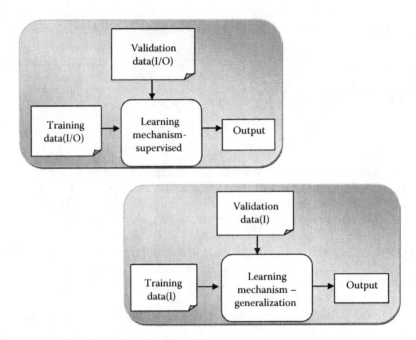

Figure 2.1 Supervised and unsupervised learning.

dimensional data, and able to handle semantics. Most of the existing text clustering methods use clustering techniques depends only on term strength and document frequency where single terms are used as features for representing the documents.

Association learning is a generalization of classification. The purpose is to capture relationships between arbitrary features (attributes) of examples in a dataset (Radovanovic 2006). In this way, classification captures only the relationships of all features to the one feature specifying the class. Direct application of association learning to text is not feasible because of the high dimensionality of document representations. Making use of association learning on information extracted from text (say, using classification and/or clustering) can yield numerous useful insights.

Numeric regression (prediction) is another generalization of classification, where the class feature is not discrete, but continuous. This slight change in definition results in differences in the heart of classification and regression algorithms. Nevertheless, by dividing the predicted numeric feature into a finite number of intervals, every regression algorithm can also be used for classification. The opposite is not typically feasible. As with association learning, straightforward application of regression on text is not useful, except for classification.

2.2   Linear regression

Prediction is used for a variety of types of analysis that may elsewhere be more precisely called *regression*. Regression is a data mining function that predicts a number. Profit, sales, mortgage rates, house values, square footage, temperature, or distance could all be predicted using regression techniques. For example, a regression model could be used to predict the value of a house based on location, number of rooms, lot size, and other factors.

A regression task begins with a dataset in which the target values are known. For example, a regression model that predicts house values could be developed based on observed data for many houses over a period of time. In addition to the value, the data might track the age of the house, square footage, number of rooms, taxes, school district, proximity to shopping centers, and so on. House value would be the target, the other attributes would be the predictors, and the data for each house would constitute a case.

In the model build (training) process, a regression algorithm estimates the value of the target as a function of the predictors for each case in the build data. These relationships between predictors and target are summarized in a model, which can then be applied to a different dataset in which the target values are unknown.

Regression models are tested by computing various statistics that measure the difference between the predicted values and the expected values. The historical data for a regression project are typically divided into two datasets: one for building the model and the other for testing the model.

Regression modeling has many applications in trend analysis, business planning, marketing, financial forecasting, time series prediction, biomedical and drug response modeling, and environmental modeling.

Regression analysis seeks to determine the values of parameters for a function, which cause the function to best fit a set of data observations that you provide. The following equation expresses these relationships in symbols. It shows that regression is the process of estimating the value of a continuous target (y) as a function (F) of one or more predictors $(x_1, x_2, ..., x_n)$, a set of parameters $(\theta_1, \theta_2, ..., \theta_n)$, and a measure of error (e):

$$y = F(x, \theta) + e.$$

The predictors can be understood as independent variables and the target as a dependent variable. The error, also called the residual, is the difference between the expected and predicted value of the dependent variable. The regression parameters are also known as regression coefficients. A linear regression technique can be used if the relationship between the predictors and the target can be approximated with a straight line.

2.3   Supervised learning: Classification

Training a classifier is the process of creating a function or data structure that will be used for determining the missing value of the class attribute of the new unclassified instances. There are numerous classifiers available. Each of them has a description about how it works and a reference for all parameters it uses. Some classification algorithms can distinguish between two distinct classes, making them two-class (or binary) classifiers, and others are naturally multiclass. However, this restriction may not be a problem, since there are ways to use binary classifiers for classification into more than two classes.

Binary classification can also be viewed as a one-class problem, where instances can be positive (belonging to the class) or negative. If a dataset contains both positive and negative instances, the view shift is a mere formality, but not if negative evidence is missing from the dataset—then the problem of separating the classes becomes a problem of describing the positive class.

There are classifiers that are able to give a real-valued estimate of their conviction about an instance belonging to a particular class (like the Naïve Bayes classifier), which may be valuable in some applications. Some offer classification decisions that are easy to interpret by a human (e.g., decision tree [DT] learners), while others output an answer that is not easy to trace (neural networks and support vector machines [SVMs]). The ability to learn online is also an important property a classifier can have, meaning that the learned model may be incrementally updated with each new training instance.

There are three different aspects of classifier performance:

- Training efficiency
- Classification efficiency
- Correctness of classification

Training and classification efficiency are measured in terms of execution speed and memory consumption and present very important factors in practical applications of classification. The end user will certainly be affected by low classification efficiency, and if online classifiers are used, by low training (i.e., "updating") efficiency as well. Nevertheless, the attention of the research community is dominated by the correctness aspect, often giving the other two only a passing glance.

The dataset used for classification is usually divided into the training set, used to train the classifier, and the test set, used for evaluating classifier performance. One widely used measure for evaluating classifier performance in ML is accuracy—the percentage of correctly classified examples from the test set. Sometimes, a third set is extracted from the dataset, called the validation set, which is used in the training phase to evaluate the classifier and help tune its parameters to yield optimal performance. It is important to separate the validation and test sets, because a classifier tuned on the test set would exhibit excellent performance when evaluated on it, which would in all probability be misleading.

The ratio between the training and test sets (the split) may depend on the amount of available data, the particular application, and many other factors—there are no firm rules. The usual splits include 2/1, 3/1, 4/1, and 9/1, and there are cases when test sets bigger than the training sets are used.

Several problems plague the singular split scheme. The first one concerns the distribution of classes in the original dataset, which may not be preserved in the training and test sets if they are generated randomly. Class distribution is an important property of datasets, and, practically, all classifiers either implicitly or explicitly use it while learning the model; therefore, a split that breaks the class distribution may also break classifier performance. A cure for this is stratification, the notion of preserving the class distribution in all datasets derived from the original.

The second, more serious problem lies in the arbitrariness of which examples end up in which set after the split (even with stratification). There are no guarantees that a particular split into a training and test set will yield a realistic evaluation of a classifier.

The problem is even more emphasized when the amount of available data is small. Then, the exclusion of the test set from training data may result in the generation of an inferior classifier. The solution to this problem is in cross-validation, a technique borrowed from statistics: the dataset is split into n subsets, one is declared the test set, the others are merged into the training set, and the classifier is evaluated. The procedure is repeated n times, every subset once being the test set, and the results are averaged. Each iteration is called a fold, and the whole process n-fold cross-validation. Stratification is also possible here, yielding stratified n-fold cross-validation. Even this may not be enough, so everything can be repeated k times, making sure that in each run the n subsets of the original dataset are sufficiently different. This is known as k runs of n-fold cross-validation, and the adjective "stratified" is also applicable.

As with the split, there are no firm rules for choosing the values of n and k. In ML, in general, there is some agreement that 10 as the value of both n and k is a satisfactory solution, but for applications on text these values may simply be too high for feasible training efficiency. For the same reason, leave-one-out cross-validation, the extreme case of n-fold cross-validation where n equals the total number of examples, is avoided on text. Many experiments in text categorization were performed on single splits; there are also examples of five runs of fourfold cross-validation.

But, having nk measurements means that a statistical test, usually the t-test, can be used to compare the performance of two classifiers and give more accurate estimates of the significance of the determined performance differences. Furthermore, in a scenario where, for example, multiple classifiers are being compared over multiple datasets, the number of statistically significant wins and losses can be counted for each classifier, and the subtracted value of wins–losses is used to rank the classifiers relative to one another.

2.3.1 Evaluation measures

Accuracy is a good measure for evaluating classifiers in a broad range of applications (Radovanovic 2009). However, consider a binary classification problem where examples from the negative class constitute 95% of the dataset. In this case, the trivial rejector, that is, the classifier that assigns all examples to the negative class, has an accuracy of 95%, but is totally unusable in practice if we care about the positive class at least a little. Such a dataset has an imbalanced class distribution, which is very common in textual domains. Class imbalance not only dismisses accuracy as an evaluation measure, but creates the need to fine-tune classifiers to assign an adequate importance to the minority class, in order to achieve desired performance.

Several evaluation measures that originated in IR are commonly used to evaluate text classifiers. IR is concerned with the relevance of documents retrieved from a database as a response to a user query, where "relevant" may now be considered as "belonging to the positive class." Then, precision is defined as the ratio of the number of relevant documents that were retrieved (the number of documents correctly classified as positive), and the total number of retrieved documents (the number of documents classified as positive). In terms of outcomes of binary classification summarized in Table 2.1, it is calculated as

$$\text{Precision} = \frac{TP}{TP + FP}.$$

Similarly, recall is the ratio between the number of relevant documents retrieved and the total number of relevant documents:

$$\text{Recall} = \frac{TP}{TP + FN}.$$

Table 2.1 Outcomes of Binary Classification

Actual class	Predicted class	
	Yes	No
Yes	True positive	True negative
No	True positive	True negative

For comparison, accuracy is given as

$$\text{Accuracy} = \frac{TP + TN}{TP + TN + FP + FN}.$$

Although they differ by just one term in the formula, precision and recall are really on the opposite sides of the spectrum—while precision characterizes the mistakes made in making the positive decision, recall expresses the coverage of the real positives by the decision, regardless of mistakes. The trivial acceptor has 100% recall and very low precision, while a classifier that makes only one positive classification, which happens to be correct, has 100% precision and very low recall. Therefore, these two measures are rarely used by themselves and may be combined to form the *F*-measure:

$$F_\beta = \frac{(\beta^2 + 1)\text{precision recall}}{\beta^2 \text{precision} + \text{recall}}.$$

When $\beta = 1$, *F*-measure represents the harmonic mean of precision and recall, taking both of them equally into account. For $\beta < 1$, precision is given more importance, ending with $F_0 = \text{precision}$, while $\beta > 1$ means recall gets the upper hand, with the other extreme at $F_\infty = \text{recall}$.

Classifiers can generally be tuned to favor precision or recall during training. The point where (averaged) precision and recall are equal for a particular test set is the break-even point (BEP) and is also used as a measure of classifier performance.

In the case of multiclass classification, all these measures can be considered for each class separately. If we denote the classification outcomes with regard to class i out of a total n by TP_i, TN_i, FP_i, and FN_i, then precision i and recall i calculated using them refer to classification performance on the ith class. There are two ways to express "global" precision and recall: microaveraging and macroaveraging. Microaveraged precision and recall are obtained by first summing up classification outcomes by class:

$$\text{Precision}^m = \frac{\sum_{i=1}^{n} TP_i}{\sum_i (TP_i + FP_i)},$$

$$\text{Recall}^m = \frac{\sum_{i=1}^{n} TP_i}{\sum_i (TP_i + FN_i)}.$$

while macroaveraging involves averaging of precision and recall calculated for each individual class:

$$\text{Precision}^M = \frac{\sum_{i=1}^{n} \text{precision}_i}{n},$$

$$\text{Recall}^M = \frac{\sum_{i=1}^{n} \text{recall}_i}{n}.$$

2.3.2 Decision trees

A DT is a tree whose internal nodes represent features, arcs are labeled with outcomes of tests on the value of the feature from which they originate, and leaves denote categories. The DT constructed from the weather dataset in Table 2.2 is shown in Figure 2.1.

Classifying a new instance using a DT involves starting from the root node and following the branches labeled with the test outcomes, which are true for the appropriate feature values of the instance, until a leaf with a class value is reached.

One of the widely used DT learning algorithms is Quinlan's C4.5 (Quinlan 1993). (An improved commercialized version C5.0 exists, which focuses on better generation of rules.) Learning a DT with C4.5 involves choosing the most informative feature using a combination of the information gain and gain ratio criteria described in Section 2.4, determining how best to split its values using tests, and repeating the process recursively for each branch/test, without considering features that were already assigned to nodes. Recursion stops when the tree perfectly fits the data or when all features have been used up. The tree in Figure 2.2 was generated using the C4.5 algorithm.

To avoid overfitting, pruning can be performed on the learned tree, which reduces its fit to the training data, at the same time attempting to improve its accuracy in the general

Table 2.2 Weather Data

ID	Outlook	Temperature	Humidity	Windy	Play
1	Sunny	Hot	High	False	No
2	Sunny	Hot	High	True	No
3	Overcast	Hot	High	False	Yes
4	Rainy	Mild	High	False	Yes
5	Rainy	Cool	Normal	False	Yes
6	Rainy	Cool	Normal	True	No
7	Overcast	Cool	Normal	True	Yes
8	Sunny	Mild	High	False	No
9	Sunny	Cool	Normal	False	Yes
10	Rainy	Mild	Normal	False	Yes
11	Sunny	Mild	Normal	True	Yes
12	Overcast	Mild	High	True	Yes
13	Overcast	Hot	Normal	False	Yes
14	Rainy	Mild	High	True	No

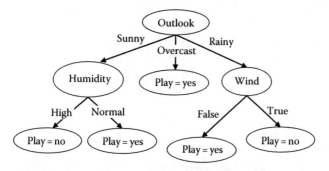

Figure 2.2 DT generated from the weather data.

case. In C4.5, it is done by converting the tree to an equivalent rule form (one for each path from root to leaf), estimating the general accuracy of each and improving it by removing some tests. Then, rules are sorted in decreasing order of estimated accuracy and used in this form for classification.

DTs (and rules) are especially useful when the workings of the classifier need to be interpreted by humans, offering insight into the structure of data. As for text, DTs may be unsuitable for many applications since they are well known for not being able to efficiently handle great numbers of features. Nevertheless, sometimes they do prove superior, for instance with datasets in which a few highly discriminative features stand out from the many.

2.4   Support vector machines

One of the most sophisticated and best performing classifiers ever applied on text is the SVM classifier. It is a binary classifier, and its main idea lies in using a predetermined kernel function, whose main effect is the transformation of the feature vector space into another space, usually with a higher number of dimensions, where the data are linearly separable. Quadratic programming methods are then applied to find a maximum margin hyperplane, that is, the optimal linear separation in the new space, whose inverse transformation should yield an excellent classifier in the original vector space. Figure 2.3 shows a graphical representation of the separating hyperplane for a two-dimensional (2D) space (after the transformation), where the class feature is depicted with labels + and ±. The hyperplane, in this case a line, lies in the middle of the widest strip separating the two classes and is constructed using only the instances adjacent to the strip—the support vectors (outlined by squares in Figure 2.3).

Although the theoretical foundations for SVMs were laid out by Vapnik in the 1970s, the computational complexity of various solutions to the quadratic programming problem restricted the use of SVMs in practice. Only relatively recently were approximate solutions derived that enabled feasible and, compared with some other classifiers, superior training times.

SVMs can handle very high dimensions and are not particularly sensitive to overfitting, making them highly suitable for application on text without dimensionality reduction. There is a wide consent that SVMs are one of the best performing text classifiers available today.

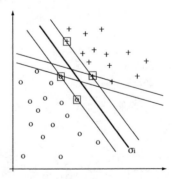

Figure 2.3 Maximum-margin hyperplane determined by the SVM, which separates the two classes, with highlighted support vectors.

2.5 Nearest neighbor classifiers

The training phase of nearest neighbor (also known as instance-based or memory-based) classifiers is practically trivial and consists of simply storing all examples in a data structure suitable for their later retrieval. Unlike other classifiers, all computation concerning the classification of an unseen example is deferred until the classification phase. Then, k instances most similar to the example in question—its k-nearest neighbor (kNN) —are retrieved, and its class is computed from the classes of the neighbors. The computation of the class can consist of just choosing the majority class of all the neighbors, or distance weighing may be used to reduce the influence on the classification decision of neighbors that are further away. The choice of k depends on the concrete data and application—there is no universally best value. The similarity function is usually the simple cosine of the angle between vectors; with richer representations of instances and more complex similarity functions, the issue moves into the field of case-based reasoning (Akerkar and Sajja 2010).

The major problem with applying kNN to text is the sheer volume of practical textual data, which consumes memory and slows down retrieval.

One of the first applications of the kNN classifier on text was by Yang and Liu (1999), who addressed this problem by organizing data into a three-layer network of weights, with one layer for words, one for documents, and one for categories. The same problem can be tackled by storing only the instances for which there is evidence during training that they would contribute significantly to classification.

2.6 Unsupervised learning: clustering

While classification is concerned with finding models by generalization of evidence produced by a dataset, clustering deals with the discovery of models that describe patterns in data, with little or no external guidance. Many algorithms for clustering data have been devised to date, but unlike classifiers, not many of them have been used in textual domains. One of the main reasons for this is certainly the high dimensionality of textual data, which not only hampers the less efficient algorithms, but makes evaluation more difficult as well, both for an expert analyzing the clusters and for automatic evaluation measures. Also, no clustering algorithm can perform well on every possible distribution of data, so naturally some algorithms are better on text than others.

Clustering is a convenient method for discovering data distribution and patterns in underlying data. The primary goal of clustering is to learn the dense as well as the sparse regions in a dataset. Clustering can be considered the most important unsupervised learning problem, which means it deals with finding a structure in the collection of unlabeled data.

There are two main types of clustering techniques, those that create a hierarchy of clusters and those that do not. The hierarchical clustering techniques create a hierarchy of clusters from small to big. The main reason for this is that, as was already stated, clustering is an unsupervised learning technique, and as such, there is no absolutely correct answer. For this reason and depending on the particular application of the clustering, fewer or greater numbers of clusters may be desired. With a hierarchy of clusters defined, it is possible to choose the number of clusters that are desired. At the extreme, it is possible to have as many clusters as there are records in the database. In this case, the records within the cluster are optimally similar to each other (since there is only one) and certainly different from the other clusters. But, of course, such a clustering technique misses the point in the sense that the idea of clustering is to find useful patterns in the database that summarize it and make it easier to understand. Any clustering algorithm that ends up with as many clusters as there are records has not helped the user understand the data any better. Thus, one of the main points about clustering is that there are many fewer clusters than there are original records. Exactly how many clusters should be formed is a matter of interpretation. The advantage of hierarchical clustering methods is that they allow the end user to choose from either many clusters or only a few.

The hierarchy of clusters is created through the algorithm that builds the clusters. There are two main types of hierarchical clustering algorithms:

- Agglomerative—Agglomerative clustering techniques start with as many clusters as there are records where each cluster contains just one record. The clusters that are nearest each other are merged together to form the next largest cluster. This merging is continued until a hierarchy of clusters is built with just a single cluster containing all the records at the top of the hierarchy.
- Divisive—Divisive clustering techniques take the opposite approach from agglomerative techniques. These techniques start with all the records in one cluster and then try to split that cluster into smaller pieces and then in turn to try to split those smaller pieces.

There are two main nonhierarchical clustering techniques. Both of them are very fast to compute on the database but have some drawbacks. The first are the single-pass methods. They derive their name from the fact that the database must only be passed through once in order to create the clusters (i.e., each record is only read from the database once). The other class of techniques is called reallocation method. They get their name from the movement or "reallocation" of records from one cluster to another in order to create better clusters. The reallocation techniques do use multiple passes through the database but are relatively fast in comparison to the hierarchical techniques.

2.6.1   k-Means clustering

The basic k-means clustering algorithm is one of the oldest and simplest clustering algorithms to be applied to text, which may still produce good results. It involves randomly choosing k points to be the centroids of clusters, and grouping instances around centroids based on proximity. Then, centroids are iteratively recomputed for each cluster, and instances regrouped until there is sufficiently little change in centroid positions. This algorithm depends heavily on the choice of k (which may not be obvious at all for a particular application) and the initial positioning of centroids (Akerkar and Lingras 2008). Having k-means generate empty clusters is not a rare occurrence at all.

The k-means method of cluster detection is the most commonly used in practice. This algorithm has an input of predefined number of clusters, which is called k. "Means" stands for an average: the average location of all the members of a single cluster. Let us assume that the data are represented as a relational table, with each object representing an object and each column representing a column. The value of every attribute from the table of data we are analyzing represents a distance from the origin along the attribute axes. Furthermore, to use this geometry, the values in the dataset must all be numeric. If they are categorical one, then they should be normalized in order to allow adequate results of the overall distances in a multiattribute space. The k-means algorithm is a straightforward iterative procedure, in which a vital notion is the one of centroid. A centroid is a point in the space of objects that represents an average position of a single cluster. The coordinates

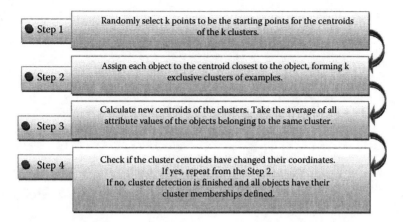

Figure 2.4 Broad steps of *k*-means algorithm.

of this point are the averages of attribute values of all objects that belong to the cluster. The iterative process of redefining centroids and reassigning data objects to clusters needs a small number of iterations to converge. The simple stepwise description of *k*-means can be given as shown in Figure 2.4.

Now, let us discuss the partitioning technique in detail.

The purpose of clustering is to obtain subsets that are more genuine than the initial set. This means that their elements are much more similar on average than the elements of the original domain. A partition $T_1, T_2, \ldots, T_k$ is represented by the centroids $z_1, z_2, \ldots, z_k$ such that

$$x \in T_i \Leftrightarrow \rho(x, z_i) \le \rho(x, z_j), \quad i, j = 1, \ldots, k.$$

One can see that even though no information about the classes has been used in this case, the *k*-means algorithm is perfectly capable of finding the three main classes.

The centroids are used for estimates of an impurity measure of the form

$$J(z_1, z_2, \ldots, z_p) = \frac{1}{N} \sum_{i=1}^{k} \sum_{x^{(j)} \in T_i} \rho\left(x^{(j)}, z_i\right) = \frac{1}{N} \sum_{j=1}^{N} \min_{1 \le i \le k} \rho\left(x^{(j)}, z_i\right).$$

The algorithms for partitioning (i.e., *k*-means and *k*-medoid) vary in the manner that they estimate the centroids. In the *k*-means algorithm, the mean of the real-valued observations in the cluster T_i is calculated as

$$z_i = \frac{1}{N_i} \sum_{x^{(j)} \in T_i} x^{(j)},$$

where N_i denotes the number of data points in T_i.

We can observe an interesting property in that the *k*-means algorithm will not increase the function *J*. On the contrary, if any clusters are changed, *J* is reduced. As *J* is bounded from below, it converges and, as a consequence, the algorithm converges. It is also shown that the *k*-means will always converge to a local minimum. The algorithm can be given as

Select k arbitrary data points $z_1, z_2, \ldots, z_k$.

repeat

$$T_i := \left\{ x^{(j)} \mid \rho(x^{(j)}, z_i) \leq \rho(x^{(j)}, z_s) \mid, \quad \text{where } s = 1, 2, \ldots, p \right\}$$

$$z_i := \frac{1}{|T_i|} \sum_{x^{(j)} \in T_i} x^{(j)}.$$

Until z_i do not change.

There are two key steps in the algorithm: the determination of the distances between all the points and the recalculation of the centroids.

Two disadvantages of the k-means method are that the mean may not be close to any data point at all, and the data are limited to real vectors.

An alternative algorithm is the k-medoid where the centroid is chosen to be the most central element of the set.

That is, $z_i = x^{(si)}$ such that

$$\sum_{x^{(j)} \in T_i} \rho\left(x^{(j)}, x^{(s_i)}\right) \leq \sum_{x^{(j)} \in T_i} \rho\left(x^{(j)}, x^{(m)}\right) \quad \text{for all} \quad x^{(m)} \in T_i.$$

Instead of explicitly assigning examples to clusters (hard assignment), each cluster can be represented by a vector of features and updated on witnessing an example (soft or fuzzy assignment), based on proximity. That way, representations of clusters are not limited to centroids and may fit some data distributions more naturally.

A close relative of the "soft" variant of the k-means algorithm is self-organizing maps (SOMs), a technique with strong origins in neural networks. While k-means is concerned with finding relations among examples in their own space, SOM projects them down to a 2D grid of interconnected points. Each example activates the point closest to its projection, and the activation is propagated through the grid in a neural network-like manner. Kohonen (1990, 1995) used a triangular grid SOM to organize a large collection of newsgroup documents.

2.6.2   *Difference between clustering and nearest neighbor prediction*

The main distinction between clustering and the nearest neighbor technique is that clustering is what is called an unsupervised learning technique, and nearest neighbor is generally used for prediction or a supervised learning technique. Unsupervised learning techniques are unsupervised in the sense that when they are run there is no particular reason for the creation of the models the way there is for supervised learning techniques that are trying to perform prediction. In prediction, the patterns that are found in the database and presented in the model are always the most important patterns in the database for performing some particular prediction. In clustering, there is no particular sense of why certain records are near to each other or why they all fall into the same cluster.

2.6.3   Probabilistic clustering

In the probabilistic clustering approach, instances are considered to be generated from a mixture model of k probability distributions, by first choosing model j with probability p_j, and then drawing an example adhering to the distribution. Each cluster corresponds to a distribution, with instances gathering around its mean at distances determined by variance. The likelihood that a particular dataset is drawn from a particular mixture model of k distributions is given by

$$L(X \mid R) = \prod_i \sum_i p_j P(x_i \mid r_j),$$

for instances x_i and clusters r_j. One probabilistic method, the expectation-minimization (EM) algorithm is based on alternatively estimating and maximizing the expected value of the log-likelihood function $\log L(X \mid R)$.

Benefits of probabilistic clustering include the ability to build the clusters using different datasets (because clusters are represented independently from examples), examining examples iteratively (the approach is online), and the generation of results that are easy to interpret.

2.7   Hidden Markov models

The Hidden Markov model (HMM) is one of the most important ML models in speech and language processing. In order to define it properly, we need to first introduce the Markov chain, sometimes called the observed Markov model. A Markov chain is a special case of a weighted automaton in which the input sequence uniquely determines which states the automaton will go through. Because they cannot represent inherently ambiguous problems, a Markov chain is only useful for assigning probabilities to unambiguous sequences. A Markov chain is useful when we need to compute a probability for a sequence of events that we can observe in the world. In many cases, however, the events we are interested in may not be directly observable in the world. For example, for part-of-speech tagging, we did not observe part-of-speech tags in the world; we saw words and had to infer the correct tags from the word sequence. We call the part-of-speech tags hidden because they are not observed.

An HMM is a finite set of states, each of which is associated with a probability distribution. Transitions among the states are governed by a set of probabilities called transition probabilities. In a particular state, an outcome or observation can be generated, according to the associated symbol observation probability distribution. It is only the outcome, not the state that is visible to an external observer, and, therefore, states are "hidden" to the outside; hence, the name HMM.

In order to define an HMM completely, the following elements are needed:

1. The number of states of the model, N.
2. The number of observation symbols in the alphabet, M. If the observations are continuous, then M is infinite.
3. A set of state transition probabilities $\Lambda = \{a_{ij}\}$

$$a_{ij} = p\{q_{t+1} = j \mid q_t = i\}, \quad 1 \le i, j \le N,$$

where q_t denotes the current state.

Transition probabilities should satisfy the normal stochastic constraints:

$$a_{ij} \geq 0, \quad 1 \leq i, j \leq N$$

$$\sum_{j=1}^{N} a_{ij} = 1, \quad 1 \leq i \leq N.$$

4. A probability distribution for the alphabets in each of the states, $B = \{b_j(k)\}$

$$b_j(k) = p\{a_t = v_k \mid q_t = j\}, \quad 1 \leq j \leq N, 1 \leq k \leq M,$$

where v_k denotes the kth observation symbol in the alphabet, and o_t denotes the current parameter vector.
Following stochastic constraints must be satisfied:

$$b_j(k) \geq 0, \quad 1 \leq j \leq N, \quad 1 \leq k \leq M$$

and

$$\sum_{k=1}^{M} b_j(k) = 1, \quad 1 \leq j \leq N.$$

5. If the observations are continuous, then we will have to use a continuous probability density function, instead of a set of discrete probabilities.
6. The initial state distribution $\pi = \{\pi_i\}$, where $\pi_i = p\{q_1 = i\}$, $1 \leq i \leq N$.

Therefore, we can use the compact notation $\lambda = (\Lambda, B, \pi)$ to denote an HMM with discrete probability distributions.

2.8 Bayesian methods

The probabilistic approach to modeling data has resulted in several useful ML techniques that can be applied on text. One of them is the simple, but effective, Naïve Bayes classifier, and the other is the more expressive but also more complex and still actively researched—Bayesian networks.

2.8.1 Bayes theorem

Let X be the data record (case) whose class label is unknown. Let H be some hypothesis, such as "data record X belongs to a specified class C." For classification, we want to determine $P(H \mid X)$—the probability that the hypothesis H holds, given the observed data record X.

$P(H \mid X)$ is the posterior probability of H conditioned on X. For example, the probability that a fruit is an apple, given the condition that it is red and round. In contrast, $P(H)$ is the prior probability, or a priori probability, of H. In this example, $P(H)$ is the probability that any given data record is an apple, regardless of how the data record looks. The posterior probability, $P(H \mid X)$, is based on more information (such as background knowledge) than the prior probability, $P(H)$, which is independent of X.

Similarly, $P(X \mid H)$ is posterior probability of X conditioned on H. That is, it is the probability that X is red and round given that we know that it is true that X is an apple. $P(X)$ is the prior probability of X, that is, it is the probability that a data record from our set of fruits is red and round. The Bayes theorem is useful in that it provides a way of calculating the posterior probability, $P(H \mid X)$, from $P(H)$, $P(X)$, and $P(X \mid H)$. The Bayes theorem is

$$P(H \mid X) = \frac{P(X \mid H)P(H)}{P(X)}.$$

2.8.2 Naïve Bayes

The Naïve Bayes model is a commonly applied method of text classification, which has been used for years in the field of IR. To see how the model works, let us assume that a given narrative consists of a vector of j words, $n = \{n_1, n_2, \ldots, n_j\}$. Also, assume that i possible event codes can be assigned resulting in a second vector $E = \{E_1, E_2, \ldots, E_i\}$. By making what is called the conditional independence assumption, the probability of assigning a particular event code category can then be calculated using the expression:

$$P(E_i \mid n) = \prod_j \frac{P(n_j \mid E_i)P(E_i)}{P(n_j)}, \tag{2.1}$$

where $P(E_i \mid n)$ is the probability of event code category E_i given the set of n words in the narrative. $P(n_j \mid E_i)$ is the probability of word n_j given category E_i. $P(E_i)$ is the probability of category E_i, and $P(n_j)$ is the probability of word n_j in the entire keyword list.

In application, $P(n_j \mid E_i)$, $P(E_i)$, and $P(n_j)$ are all normally estimated on the basis of their frequency in a training set. Also, $P(n_j \mid E_i)$ is normally smoothed to reduce the effects of noise. The approach we implemented was to add a small constant to the number of times a particular word occurred in a category, as shown in the following:

$$P(n_j \mid E_i) = \frac{\text{count}(n_j \mid E_i) + \alpha \times \text{count}(n_j)}{\text{count}(E_i) + \alpha \times N}, \tag{2.2}$$

where $\text{count}(n_j \mid E_i)$ is the number of times word n_j occurs in category E_i, $\text{count}(n_j)$ is the number of times word n_j occurs, $\text{count}(E_i)$ is the number of times category E_i occurs, N is the number of training narratives, and α is a smoothing constant. Larger values of α reduce the weight given to the evidence provided by each term. We chose to use a value of $\alpha = 0.05$, which corresponds to a small level of smoothing.

The conditional independence assumption is perhaps the most controversial aspect of the Naïve Bayes model. Informally, for the purposes of text classification, when this assumption holds, the probability of each index term (e.g., word or word sequence) being present depends on only the event code considered and is independent of the remaining terms in the narrative. The conditional independence assumption is almost always violated in practice. However, a long history of application shows that Naïve Bayes tends to work remarkably well even when this assumption is violated.

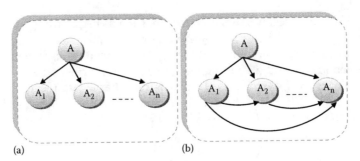

(a)   (b)

Figure 2.5 (a) Naïve Bayes classifier and (b) Bayesian network that captures interattribute dependencies.

2.8.3   Bayesian networks

Bayesian networks consist of nodes that are random variables, and vertices representing conditional probabilities between them. Their aim is to offer a computationally feasible and graphically representable way to express and calculate dependencies between events. The graphic in Figure 2.5a shows the Naïve Bayes classifier, with conditional probabilities $P(A_i|C)$ depicted as arcs from C to A_i. The dependencies between attributes, which are missing in Naïve Bayes, are added in the Bayesian network shown in Figure 2.5b.

Again, it would be computationally infeasible (and not even allowed in a Bayesian network) to calculate dependencies between all attributes, especially on high dimensional textual data. The trick with Bayesian networks is to express only the dependencies that are necessary (or strong enough to have an impact on the solution to a particular problem), under constraints that ensure the correctness and feasibility of computation.

This can be done manually, by supplying the structure of the network—then training a Bayesian network looks very much like training the Naïve Bayes classifier with conditionals being estimated from the dataset. If estimation of dependencies from data is not possible, training gets more difficult, and several solutions are available.

Learning the structure of the network presents a much bigger challenge and is still an area of active research.

2.9   Reinforcement learning

Reinforcement learning is a computational approach to understanding and automating goal-directed learning and decision making. Reinforcement learning is defined not by characterizing learning algorithms, but by characterizing a learning problem. Any algorithm that is well suited to solving that problem we consider to be a reinforcement learning algorithm. Reinforcement learning is different from supervised learning, the kind of learning studied.

Supervised learning is learning from examples provided by some knowledgeable external supervisor. This is an important kind of learning, but alone it is not adequate for learning from interaction. In interactive problems, it is often impractical to obtain examples of desired behavior, which are both correct and representative of all the situations in which the agent has to act. In uncharted territory—where one would expect learning to be most beneficial—an agent must be able to learn from its own experience.

One of the challenges that arise in reinforcement learning and not in other kinds of learning is the tradeoff between exploration and exploitation. To obtain a lot of reward, a reinforcement learning agent must prefer actions that it has tried in the past and found to be effective in producing reward. But to discover such actions, it has to try actions that it has not selected before. The agent has to exploit what it already knows in order to obtain reward, but it also has to explore in order to make better action selections in the future.

The dilemma is that neither exploitation nor exploration can be pursued exclusively without failing at the task. The agent must try a variety of actions and progressively favor those that appear to be best. On a stochastic task, each action must be tried many times to reliably estimate its expected reward. The exploration–exploitation dilemma has been intensively studied by mathematicians for many decades. Another key feature of reinforcement learning is that it explicitly considers the whole problem of a goal-directed agent interacting with an uncertain environment. This is in contrast with many approaches that address subproblems without addressing how they might fit into a larger picture. For example, we have mentioned that much of ML research is concerned with supervised learning without explicitly specifying how such ability would finally be useful. Other researchers have developed theories of planning with general goals, but without considering planning's role in real-time decision making, or the question of where the predictive models necessary for planning would come from. Although these approaches have yielded many useful results, their focus on isolated subproblems is a significant limitation. Reinforcement learning takes the opposite tack, by starting with a complete, interactive, goal-seeking agent. All reinforcement learning agents have explicit goals, can sense aspects of their environments, and can choose actions to influence their environments.

Moreover, it is usually assumed from the beginning that the agent has to operate despite significant uncertainty about the environment it faces. When reinforcement learning involves planning, it has to address the interplay between planning and real-time action selection, as well as the question of how environmental models are acquired and improved. When reinforcement learning involves supervised learning, it does so for very specific reasons that determine which capabilities are critical, and which are not. For learning research to make progress, important subproblems have to be isolated and studied, but they should be subproblems that are motivated by clear roles in complete, interactive, goal-seeking agents, even if all the details of the complete agent cannot yet be filled in.

2.10   Applications of machine learning

ML, as stated earlier, is the science to impart learning ability into machines with the help of fields such as computer science, mathematics, biology, cognitive science, and psychology. The major aim is to build machines that solve problems just like human beings. There are various applications of the ML, some of which are described in brief in this section.

2.10.1   Speech recognition

Most of the speech recognition software need to be trained from the domain terminology and pronunciation of the user in order to recognize speech and perform necessary actions. The software framework is developed with necessary utilities and learning algorithm. This is called development phase. However, the framework is made familiar with the probable owners by providing training of the user-specific content such as pronunciation at later phases, which is called training phase. This makes the software speaker-dependable systems. Speech recognition can be considered as pattern recognition and learning activities, where sound (audio) signals are examined and structured into a hierarchy of lower level units such as words and phrases. The features of the audio file are extracted by learning structure such as neural network. Patterns are found, analyzed, and classified from the

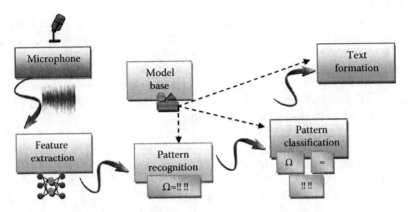

Figure 2.6 Speech recognition.

extracted features. Here, acoustic and linguistic models stored in the systems' model base help a lot. These units are mapped with appropriate text units and sentences are formed. Working of the system is illustrated in Figure 2.6.

2.10.2   *Computer vision*

Computer vision is the field that makes a machine see and identify images. Machine captures images through cameras from local or remote places and extracts information from the captured images. Computer vision is concerned with the theory of extracting useful information from the images. The image data can be simple stand-alone images, video sequences, views from multiple cameras, or multidimensional data from a medical scanner in offline or online manner. Typical application includes face recognition, gesture recognition, microscope image understanding and diagnosis, scan posted physical letters to sort according to the address written on them, handwritten character recognition, motion analysis, space applications, object recognition, embedded systems such as in cameras to detect human faces automatically, etc. Here, supervised and unsupervised learning can be applied for learning. Broad steps to be performed for the aforementioned applications are image acquisition noise clearing, image identification and learning through a technique like feature detection, and image representation. The models used for the same are bag of words (where each image is compared with a set of words), part-based models (where valid components of images are defined in a set and compared with image), and generative models (to regenerate image with known features using neural network).

2.10.3   *Robotics*

Robotics is a branch of science and engineering that deals with the guided machine that learns, reacts, and solves problems on behalf of human beings. A robot is a machine blessed with all efficiency-oriented parameters such as accuracy, speed, precession, and ability to perform mechanical tasks in repetitive manner. Imparting learning capabilities into the machines, robots can also achieve effectiveness. A robot can be equipped with human-like five senses with ML techniques for computer vision, mechanical motion, voice output, etc. Robots can be used in assembly line production, quality control, to classify drugs, accompanying blind humans, gaming, defense, disaster management, and training applications.

2.10.4 *Software engineering and programming language*

Cleverly designed systems through typical programming languages/environments cannot be made to learn not to repeat their mistakes. A manual effort is always needed to find a bug, repair it, and make the system executable. Instead of them, the idea is to try and make the program find a bug, fix it automatically, and ensure that the program runs forever. Fifth-generation programming languages employ intelligent techniques in order to facilitate user friendliness. Quick and automatic development and maintenance of software, automatic code generators, smart compilers, and visual development frameworks consider design specification in order to generate software on need. These categories of applications are further enhanced by providing intelligent test metrics to test quality factors of the software developed. Such new generation programming language also should support writing programs that are able to learn. In many current ML applications, standard ML algorithms are integrated with hard-coded software into a final application program, instead of the intelligent programming language directly supports writing program that have only framework and major components (subroutines) are to be learned automatically. This concept is visualized in Figure 2.7. With self-learning programming languages, bug identification and fixing, compilation help, automatic generation of code, software testing, and maintenance are much efficient.

Not only in automatic programming but ML can also be useful in different phases of software development. ML can be used in areas like model fitting and discovery; requirement discovery; and predication and estimation of software development activities, software testing, component reuse, and post implementation review.

2.10.5 *Computer games*

Most of the computer games utilize hard-coded intelligent techniques. However, there is an increasing demand from the audience for the games that are able to learn. ML helps the game program in learning the player's strategy and plans the machine strategy that has greater chances to win. Instead of offering fixed three to five generic levels (difficulty level feature) of the game to all the users, the game should match the player's ability by altering tactics and strategy. After playing a typical game in enormous fashion, the addicted players learn about the game's strategies and develop their own skills. On the other hand, the game should learn the users' favorite steps, patterns, loopholes, and playing style through ML. The games enabled with such feature may have

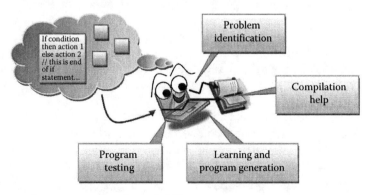

Figure 2.7 Automatic programming through ML.

longer life period and attract wide scope of players with different abilities. To impart ML, artificial intelligence (AI) agents can be planned. Such AI agents use reinforcement learning to automatically learn an opponent for games. Besides agent approach, other approaches are case-based learning, classification, and coaching feedback, where learning is facilitated by demonstrating how to play the game and feedback. The gaming also faces typical problems of ML such as

1. Mimicking the stupidity—as a novice player is playing, providing coaching, and demonstrating the game, the program may learn wrong things. Many times the program/agent sticks to the behavior that has been successful in the past and does not try a new strategy. Instead of that, the game program must try to check all major possible behaviors.
2. *Overfitting* the game for a particular portion of level—the techniques suitable at that portion/level are not necessarily the generalized techniques; however, the program has learned this as a generalized strategy and tries to apply them in general fashion. Similarly, one has to think about the local optimality problem.

There is great potential for ML application in the field of next generation games.

2.10.6   *Machine learning for web*

As we know, the Web is a huge resource of unstructured documents written in different ontologies. There are varieties of applications that involve multiple ontologies and require semantic mappings among the ontologies to ensure interoperability. Examples of such applications can be e-commerce, knowledge management, e-learning, information extraction, bioinformatics, web services, and tourisms. Instead of mapping the ontology in manual fashion, the ML utilities can be developed to learn semantic from the content represented in different ontologies and map them automatically. Similarly, ML can be used for web structure analysis, web mining, IR, and filtering.

2.11   *Conclusion*

ML usually refers to the changes in systems that perform tasks associated with artificial intelligence (AI). Such tasks involve recognition, diagnosis, planning, prediction, etc. The "changes" might be either enhancements to already performing systems or ab initio synthesis of new systems. We have written this chapter to give the reader sufficient preparation to make the extensive literature on machine learning accessible. However, the key to understanding the behavior of ML techniques in practice is to examine how a concrete problem was solved, and grasp the reasons why particular features, representations, and algorithms were chosen. Though the chapter does not explore deep into the details of how specific algorithms were employed, it gives the reader a general idea of possible uses of ML methods.

   The Web has become the largest knowledge base ever to have existed. However, without proper knowledge representation and knowledge discovery algorithms, it is just like a human being with extraordinary memory but no ability to think and reason. We believe that research in machine learning and Web are promising as well as challenging, and both fields will help create applications that can more effectively and efficiently utilize the Web of knowledge.

Exercises

2.1 Implement your own versions of Naïve Bayes and logistic regression. You may use whatever language with which you are most comfortable.

2.2 Construct a simple example (you can do this with four points) that shows that the cost of a clustering found by *k*-means by the cost of the optimal clustering (this ratio is called the approximation ratio for the approximation algorithm) can be arbitrarily high.

2.3 Could you use a kNN classifier with this dataset? If so, give the three nearest neighbors and resulting class for the following instance (explain your reasoning):

ID	Major	Project Score	Exam Score	Co-Op?	Employed?	Salary
6	Science	86	74	Y	?	27,000

2.4 Explain the advantages of *k*-means clustering.

2.5 Text mining commonly uses the vector space model. To represent a set of documents in a traditional "flat" format, each document is treated as a row. The words are the columns (attributes). For a given document, the value of an attribute is a weight, such as the number of times that word occurs in the document. Naïve Bayes has proven effective for text classification. However, Naïve Bayes has limitations.

    a. Give an example where Naïve Bayes would not be effective, but some other method would. (*Hint:* Naïve Bayes has a general limitation or assumption about characteristics of the data, which applies—you can describe this limitation as opposed to a specific example.)

    b. Describe briefly how another classification method would overcome the limitation you described.

2.6 Consider the following 1D dataset {10, 20, 30, 50, 90}. Perform *k*-means algorithm with two clusters, and initial centroids are 0 and 90. Compute (a) final centroids, (b) cohesion, and (c) separation.

2.7 Let us consider a simple HMM with three states ("*X*", "*Y*", and "*Z*") and two possible outputs ("*a*" and "*b*") with the following parameters:

- Initial vector $\pi = [1\ 0\ 0]^T$
- Transition probability matrix $A = [0.6\ 0.3\ 0.1;\ 0.0\ 0.6\ 0.4;\ 0.0\ 0.0\ 1.0]$
- Emission probability matrix $B = [0.9\ 0.1;\ 0.7\ 0.3;\ 0.2\ 0.8]$

Using the computations, draw the state transition diagram for the aforementioned model, labeling each arc with the probability of the transition.

References

Akerkar, R. A. and Lingras, P. 2008. *Building an Intelligent Web: Theory and Practice*. Sudbury, MA: Jones & Bartlett.

Akerkar, R. A. and Sajja, P. S. 2010. *Knowledge-Based Systems*. Sudbury, MA: Jones & Bartlett.

Kohonen, T. 1990. The self-organizing maps. *Proceedings of the IEEE* 78(9):1464–1480.

Kohonen, T. 1995. *Self-Organizing Maps*, 2nd extended edition, Springer Series in Information Sciences, Vol. 30. Heidelberg, Germany: Springer.

Mitchell, T. 1997. *Machine Learning*. San Mateo, CA: Morgan Kaufmann.

Quinlan, R. 1993. *C4.5 Programs for Machine Learning*. San Mateo, CA: Morgan Kaufmann.

Radovanovic, M. 2006. Machine learning in web mining. *Thesis*, Department of Mathematics and Informatics, Faculty of Science, University of Novi Sad.

Radovanovic, M., Ivanovic, M., and Budimac, Z. 2009. Text Categorization and Sorting Of Web Search Results, *Computing and Informatics*, Vol. 28, 861–893.

Sebastiani, F. 2002. Machine learning in automated text categorization. *ACM Computing Surveys*, 34(1):1–47.

Sebastiani, F. 2005. Text categorization. In *Text Mining and its Applications*, ed. A. Zanasi. WIT Press, Southampton, UK, pp. 109–129.

Simon, H. A. 1983. Why should machine learn? In *Machine Learning: An Artificial Intelligence Approach*, eds. R. S. Michalski, J. Carbonell, and T.M. Mitchell. Palo Alto, CA: Tioga Press, pp. 25–38.

Yang, Y. and Liu, X. 1999. A re-examination of text categorization methods. Paper presented at the *22nd Annual International ACM SIGZIR Conference on Research and Development in Information Retrieval*, pp. 42–49, Berkeley, CA.

chapter three

Overview of constituents for the new artificial intelligence

3.1 Foundations of the new artificial intelligence and knowledge-based system

Artificial intelligence (AI) is an area of computer science that deals with different techniques, which makes the machine intelligent. Human beings utilize intelligence to make their lives easy and achieve intended goals. The basic inspiration of the field of AI is to mimic human-like decision-making process. It is observed that natural intelligence has characteristics like responding quickly and flexibly, identifying similarity in dissimilar situation and vice versa, and following nonalgorithmic and symbolic approach of problem solving. The goal of AI is to achieve intelligence through machine-readable techniques. The field of AI has been an attraction for researchers since the evolution of computers and other machines. Various techniques have been identified that try to achieve natural intelligence. The majority of AI solutions offer good and acceptable solutions using practical heuristics instead of aiming toward best solution.

3.1.1 Knowledge-based systems

Knowledge-based systems (KBSs; Akerkar and Sajja 2009) are the artificial intelligent tools working in narrow domain. The major component of the KBS is a knowledge base. The knowledge base contains factual knowledge, information about rules and models, and procedural knowledge about a given domain. Control strategies and metaknowledge (knowledge about knowledge) are also part of knowledge base. Predicates, rules, scripts, frames, and semantic network as well as different mark-up languages (such as Artificial Intelligence Markup Language [AIML]) are tools through which knowledge is represented within the knowledge base. The process of collecting knowledge from experts and various sources is known as knowledge acquisition. The techniques that deal with representing knowledge within knowledge base are known as knowledge representation techniques. Other components of a typical KBS are inference engine, which provide capabilities of reference as well as inference; explanation and reasoning to provide brief reasoning and detailed explanation of the judgment provided through the KBS; self-learning to facilitate partial self-learning; and user interface for friendly and effective interaction with users. The general structure of a KBS is shown in Figure 3.1.

The KBSs support decision making, learning, and actions in various areas. These systems are useful in advisory systems, diagnostic systems, faultfinding systems, resource management, e-commerce, and computer gaming.

3.1.2 Limitations of symbolic systems

The KBSs as well as other traditional systems operate on knowledge base and database. Prime requirement to utilize such system is to construct and maintain knowledge and

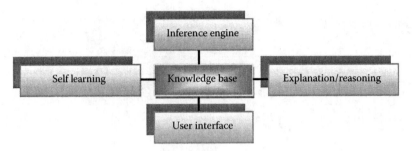

Figure 3.1 General structure of KBSs.

data in machine-readable form. Considering the nature of knowledge, which is abstract, voluminous, dynamically changing, and hard to characterize, the development of KBS is difficult. Besides the knowledge base, utilities like inference, explanation and reasoning, self-learning, and interface to the users need to be developed. Hence, the development of KBS requires high effort and time. Being an intelligent system, the major expectation from such system is learning from the environment itself. This problem is partially solved with empty KBS shells and systems that learn from cases in online fashion. However, there are fields where lot of data can be easily made available, but it is difficult to extract generalized rules from the lots. Furthermore, available information/data may be incomplete or imprecise and vague. To achieve human-like intelligent decision-making process, inspiration should be taken from human body itself. As a result, a new bioinspired computing term was coined and inspiration was taken from how a human routinely and subconsciously categorizes things into different classes and deals with incomplete and vague information, how one learns by experiments, and how the generation is becoming smarter every time. The new AI tools such as fuzzy logic, neural network, evolutionary techniques, and chaos theory help in moving a step ahead in achieving the goal of human-like processing and decision making. The next sections of the chapter elaborate these aforementioned topics in brief.

3.2   Fuzzy systems

Fuzzy systems are systems that utilize fuzzy logic. Humans routinely categorize different things into boundary-less classes. It is very common to judge things as good and bad, fine and rough, etc., to different extents. Humans loosely use words like low temperature, high speed, rich person, beautiful lady, young fellow, and luxurious car. However, a machine cannot understand such linguistic values. Furthermore, the meaning of "high speed" is different for different people. To impart the capability to deal with such vague and fuzzy variables that take different values at different intervals of time, fuzzy logic is used. Utilization of fuzzy logic makes a system very flexible and comparatively native in interaction with its users. Here are some fundamentals that may be helpful to the readers to understand the application of fuzzy logic in conjunction with the Web applications described in various chapters of the book.

3.2.1   Fuzzy set and fuzzy logic

The notion of set helps in categorizing things in a specific class where all members of the class satisfy common definitions and follow common characteristics. If definition of a non-fuzzy (crisp) set is provided, it is really very straightforward to check that a given number is a member of the set or not. If a number strictly follows the definition of class, then it is in the class. The possibility of a number to be in class is either totally "yes" or "no." Crisp sets strictly check the characteristics of an item and determine whether it is in the class or not. On the other hand, fuzzy sets introduced by Zadeh (1965) do not have clear boundaries and offer somehow kind and loose definition for the membership. Fuzzy sets allow an entity to be a member of class if it satisfies the set property to certain extent/grade. Fuzzy logic based on fuzzy sets offers graded membership and hence called multivalued logic between 0 and 1. Crisp logic works on binary values and cannot offer flexibility offered by multivalued logic.

3.2.2   Fuzzy membership function

To implement such multivalued logic, notion of fuzzy membership function is used. The fuzzy membership function takes an argument from the universe of discourse and generates grade by which the argument belongs to the fuzzy class. In other words, the membership function returns a fuzzy value between 0 and 1 to the given set for the given entity. The formal definition of fuzzy membership function is as follows:

Let X be a nonempty set. A fuzzy set A on X is characterized by its membership function $\mu A: X \rightarrow [0, 1]$, where $\mu A(x)$ is the degree of membership of element x in fuzzy set A for each x belongs to X.

Table 3.1 presents some fuzzy membership function definitions. First example in the table defines a fuzzy set FF for an integer number 4. Consider a singleton set F containing a

Table 3.1 Examples of Fuzzy Membership Function

Description	Fuzzy function
Fuzzy number x, where $x = 4$ • If the number is 3.3, then it does not belong to crisp set 4	
• If the number is 3.3, then it belongs to fuzzy set 4 with degree 0.8	
Fuzzy temperature • If temperature value is 18°C, which is less than 30°C, then it does not belong to crisp set hot temperature	
• If temperature value is 18°C, then it belongs to fuzzy hot temperature set with degree 0.75	

natural number 4. The number 4 is a natural number, and, henceforth, it is a member of set *F*. Other numbers such as 2, 4.2, 5.25, and 6 are obviously not a member of the set *F* as they do not fit into the definition of the set *F*. While dealing with such crisp sets (or machines operating on such crisp sets) like *F*, only number 4 is allowed to be a member of the set. Numbers like 4.24 or 3.56 are not allowed in the class. The later numbers are required to be rounded or trimmed to 4 to fit into the set. On the other hand, fuzzy set *FF* allows various forms of number 4 from 2 to 5 with a different degree of membership. That is, if the number is 2.6, then it is considered as number 4 with degree 0.38 and if the number is 4 then it is a member of a class with degree 1.

Similarly, fuzzy membership function for hot temperature is described in Table 3.1.

3.2.3 Forms and operations of fuzzy functions

Fuzzy membership functions can take many forms. Some popular types of fuzzy functions are triangular function, normal shape function, trapezoidal function, etc. The logical operators like AND, OR, and NOT are also applicable on fuzzy sets. Table 3.2 represents these operations of triangular fuzzy sets.

Most applications use minimum (or multiplication) operator for fuzzy intersection, maximum operator for fuzzy union, and $1 - \mu(X)$ for complementation. The operators used in Fuzzy Logic (*FL*), such as union, intersection, and complement, reduce to their crisp logic counterparts when the membership functions are limited to 0 or 1.

3.2.4 Fuzzy relations and operations on fuzzy relations

Fuzzy relations present a degree of association between the elements of two or more sets. Let *U* and *V* be two universes of discourse. A fuzzy relationship $R(U, V)$ is a set of product space $U*V$ and denoted by $\mu_R(x, y)$, where *x* is in *U* and *y* is in *V*. Being a fuzzy relation, the $\mu_R(x, y)$ maps on the closed interval [0, 1]. Let us consider a real-life situation to describe the notion of fuzzy and crisp relations. Consider the situation of an academic institute in which each student is assigned to a specific computer machine for practice. Let there be a set of students *S* containing some number of students as {*s1, s2, s3, s4*, …} and a set of machines *M* having equal number of machines such as {*m1, m2, m3, m4*, …}. The relation *A* on product set *S*M* named as "assigned to" between student and a machine is crisp. The individual relationship can be given as follows:

Table 3.2 Fuzzy Operations of Triangular Fuzzy Sets

Description	Fuzzy operation
Fuzzy AND operation between fuzzy sets A and B (also defined as intersection of two fuzzy sets A and B)	
Fuzzy OR operation between fuzzy sets A and B (also defined as union of two fuzzy sets A and B)	
Fuzzy NOT operation on fuzzy set A (also defined as complement of the fuzzy set A)	

$A = \{(m1, s1), (m2, s2), (m3, s3), \ldots\}$, where A is a crisp relationship and it always gives bivalue answer whether a machine is assigned to a person or not.

Consider another relationship R defines as "comfortable with" on set of machines and set of students. This relationship is fuzzy, and the comfort level of students can be measured with graded membership and takes the form $\mu_R(x, y) \rightarrow [0, 1]$. Here, it is not necessary that, if a person is assigned to a machine, he has to be totally comfortable with the machine.

3.2.5   Fuzzy rule–based systems

Fuzzy relations play an important role in fuzzy rule-based system. A fuzzy rule assumes the form "if x is A then y is B," where x is in U and y is in V. Some example rules for typical washing machines are as follows:

- If dirt type is greasy and dirt size is big, use long wash program.
- If dirt type is greasy and dirt size is small, use normal wash program.
- If dirt type is nongreasy and dirt size is small, use short wash program.

Fuzzy connectives are used to join simple fuzzy propositions or singleton fuzzy rules to make compound propositions. The examples of fuzzy connectives are negations ($\sim$), disjunctions ($\cup$), conjunctions ($\cap$), and implications ($\rightarrow$). Fuzzy rule-based systems use such multiple simple and complex fuzzy rules. The general structure of a fuzzy rule-based system is shown in Figure 3.2.

The human input is retrieved through an interface normally in fuzzy form, which is matched with the rules available in the rule base, conclusion is made and defuzzified if necessary. The machine operates on crisp value obtained from defuzzification, and appropriate action is performed through necessary action interface. Furthermore, on requirement, the computed output can be converted again in fuzzy form through fuzzy membership function definition and presented to the users.

3.2.6   Applications of fuzzy logic

Because of its ability to deal with partial and linguistic information, fuzzy logic-based systems act as good human-like interface with machines. The system offers opportunities of approximate reasoning and uncertainty management. Fuzzy logic-based system can be useful in the following way:

- Fuzzy control systems
- Robotics

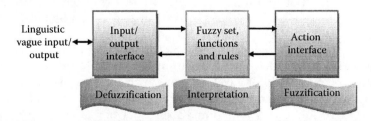

Figure 3.2 General structure of fuzzy rule-based systems.

- Pattern recognition and classification
- Image and speech processing
- Prediction and forecasting
- Planning, control, and monitoring
- Diagnosis and faultfinding
- Optimization and decision making
- Advisory systems

The Web technology can also be enhanced with fuzzy system as follows:

- Searching using modified Boolean operators such as diluted AND and OR
- Determining relevance of the content retrieved through typical search engine
- Web knowledge discovery
- Managing online information repositories by relevance
- Image compression and recreation to save bandwidth and reduce network traffic
- Fuzzy clustering and knowledge management of the Web
- Imparting reasoning and justification through XML and RDF like tools
- Decision support and advisory system on the Web
- Semantic web

3.3   Artificial neural networks

The major source of natural intelligence is biological brain and nervous system in human beings who have thinking abilities. The human brain and nervous system are made up of large number of processing units called neurons interconnected with each other. This biological network is known as neural network. Each neuron is having a limited processing power and contributes very little in decision making and solution providing. However, intelligence is generated from the parallel functioning and distributed asynchronous control of neurons in the network. Simple solutions from different neurons are worked out in parallel and contributed into a global solution. This makes the control of network distributed and provides degree of fault tolerance. Even if some neurons are not working, the network does not fail. Just as control is distributed, the storage capacity is also distributed. The item to be stored in memory is actually stored in the form of patterns, and each neuron is remembering a portion of the pattern. This is the reason that (why) with partial information human is able to retrieve full content. This feature is known as content addressable memory. Artificially generated network of simulation of biological neuron through combination of hardware and/or software is known as artificial neural network (ANN). The ANN is an effort toward simulating the biological neural network and henceforth generates human-like intelligence. Simple functionality that encompasses hardware and/or software (programming constructs), which mimic the properties of biological neurons, is called artificial neuron. Such multiple neurons are interconnected in a specific structure according to the application. ANNs are used for two basic purposes. The first one is to understand biological neural networks, and the second one is to solve AI problems without necessarily creating a model of a real biological system. Figure 3.3 introduces a biological neuron and a simulated artificial neuron. Figure 3.3 shows a biological neuron having cell body (cell composed of a cell body, an axon, and dendrites, forming a functional unit of the nervous system), nucleus (central part of a cell, containing the chromosomes), dendrite (extension of a nerve cell), and axon (extension of a neuron) in its first part. The artificial neuron shown in the second part of Figure 3.3 has functionality in its nucleus

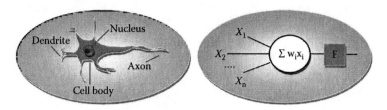

Figure 3.3 Biological and artificial neurons.

Table 3.3 Advantages of ANN Simulation

Capability simulated in an ANN	Advantages
Parallelism	Faster processing
Fault tolerance	Ability to work with partial infrastructure (hardware failure tolerance) as well as partial information and instrumental errors
Nonlinearity	Better interpretation and representation of data and information
Learning	Adaptivity and ability to modify the network structure on need and improve the performance
Generalization	Capability to solve unexpected data for which the network is not trained or experienced

(here Σ, or specifically $\Sigma\, w_i x_i$) and n number of sensory inputs. The inputs have different weights, which are utilized by the functionality at the nucleus along with the input values. The aggregated and processed input with weight is compared with a threshold value provided with the artificial neuron (here f). If the processed input is significant in comparison with the threshold value provided, the output is generated.

Characteristics like fault tolerance, distributed and asynchronous control, nonlinearity, high parallelism, learning, capability to handle imprecise and incomplete information, capability to generalize, etc., make the biological neural network robust and intelligent. Hence, similar capabilities are expected from an ANN. With simulation of such capabilities, an ANN allows noise sensitivity, provides better interpretation of information, learns from partial information, and provides effective solution. Table 3.3 provides summary of simulated capabilities and advantages achieved through the simulation.

3.3.1   Working of an artificial neuron

An artificial neuron can be considered as a device with many inputs and one output. Before using the neuron in real problem solving, it has to be trained. During the training period, the neuron can be trained to fire (or not), for particular input patterns. The output thrown by the neuron is compared with actual (desired) output, and modifications are made in the design of neuron. This is done frequently to train the neuron for most of the possible input patterns. At the time of actual usage when an input pattern is submitted to the neuron, actual output is calculated and provided. If the input pattern belongs to the taught list of input patterns, expected output is achieved. The singleton artificial neuron example is given in Figure 3.4. The figure describes the simulation of logical AND function with a single artificial neuron. The logical AND function is defined as follows:

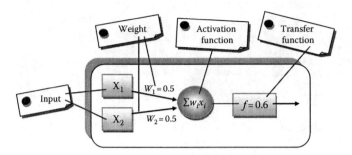

Figure 3.4 Artificial neuron for logical AND function.

Table 3.4 Truth Table for Logical AND Function

x_1	x_2	x_1 AND x_2
0	0	0
0	1	0
1	0	0
1	1	1

Let there be two inputs x_1 and x_2 that take values either 0 or 1. The AND operation between x_1 and x_2, denoted as x_1 AND x_2, provides output as shown in Table 3.4.

The singleton neuron that simulates the AND operation takes two inputs x_1 and x_2. Both the inputs have same importance, and, hence, their weights are similar, say 0.5. According to Table 3.4, the neuron should fire an output if both the inputs are 1. The functionality can be simulated with weighted sum, which is presented in Figure 3.4.

The nucleus of the neuron encompasses an arithmetic formula. This function simulated the work of nucleus and cell body. Many times the arithmetic formula selected to simulate functionality of a neuron results in null/zero value. To avoid that, a bias of fixed value is added to the neuron as an extra input, say X_0. The function f is known as threshold or cutoff value function. The threshold function used in Figure 3.4 is a hard limit function. If the output by the formula within the neuron is significant, that is greater than threshold value, then the neurons "fires." This threshold function is also known as transfer function. Instead of taking the arithmetic formula within a neuron, one may take different functions such as sigmoid and tangent functions. Similarly, instead of taking a straightforward linear transfer function, log-sigmoid, tan-sigmoid, etc., functions can be taken.

3.3.2   Architectures of artificial neural network

There are many real-life problems that cannot be solved with a single neuron. Single neuron can solve linearly separable problems. Other real-life problems, which are nonlinear in nature require use of multiple neurons working in parallel fashion. These multiple neurons can be arranged in a systematic architecture to solve complex problems and intelligent decision making. These architectures include multilayer perceptron, Kohonen, and Hopfield network.

3.3.2.1   Multilayer perceptron architecture

In the multiplayer perceptron architecture, neurons are arranged into various layers such as input layer, hidden layer, and output layer as shown in Figure 3.5.

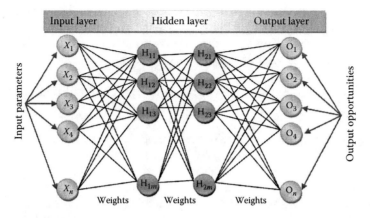

Figure 3.5 Multilayer architecture of neural network.

Neurons of the input layer directly take normalized environmental values and contain no processing function. Neurons in the output layer are enriched with application-specific output function. Similarly, neurons of a hidden layer have appropriate activation functions. Each neuron from a given layer is connected with every neuron of its adjacent layer in forward direction; hence, this architecture is also known as fully connected feed-forward architecture. Each connection has got some weight, which is assigned randomly at initial stage. Table 3.5 shows the simplified steps how the architecture works.

The discussed multilayer architecture requires the presence of sufficient number of training data (samples) that cover all categories including exceptional cases. This type of learning is known as supervised learning. The learning algorithm passes input values into forward direction (forward pass), compares the calculated output with the actual output provided in training set, calculates the error value, and propagates the error back

Table 3.5 Working of a Multilayer ANN

1. Determine parameters that affect the decisions. There should be sufficient number of neurons/nodes to accommodate these parameters
2. Determine all output opportunities. The number of neurons in the output layer is according to the output opportunities
3. Take one to two hidden layers containing average number (average of total input plus total output neurons) of nodes
4. Connect the network architecture properly (each neuron from a given layer is connected with every neuron of its adjacent layer in forward direction) and provide weights to every connections using a function that generates random numbers
5. Collect valid training datasets containing input as well as output
6. Repeat the following steps for all training datasets:
   a. Provide input from the environment and let the architecture calculate the output. This phase is known as a forward pass
   b. Compare the calculated output with actual output provided in the training data and find out the error (difference) according to the well-known back-propagation algorithm. Propagate the error back (backward pass)
   c. Adjust the weight and recalculate till you get correct output according to the training data
7. Use the architecture for the real input values for which output is required. As the weights are generalized according to the training set, the network is able to give meaningful output

(backward pass) in order to generalize the weights of the network. Quality of the network depends on the quality of the sample data provided. To test the network, similar dataset called validation set is used. The algorithm is known as back-propagation algorithm. If required training dataset as well as validation set is available prior to actual use of the network, the network is considered as trained in off-line manner. If the training data are coming in online fashion, it is considered as network trained in online fashion.

3.3.2.2   Kohonen architecture

The Kohonen ANN offers different approaches to model ANNs than the back-propagation method discussed earlier. This type of ANN is a basic "self-organizing" system, which is capable of solving problems in unsupervised fashion, where training set is not required. Here, it is not necessary to know in advance the possible input and output patterns that train the ANN. The Kohonen ANN automatically adapts itself in such a way that the similar input objects are associated with the physically close neurons in the ANN structure. The idea behind this is that the neurons that are physically located close to each other will react alike to similar inputs. The ability to self-organize provide adaptation to treat unknown input data without any training. This is just like an empty biological brain where patterns are not provided for training. Rather the patterns take shape while processing. The Kohonen ANN has only two layers of neurons as shown in Figure 3.6.

During the training in the Kohonen ANN, the m-dimensional neurons are "self-organizing" themselves in the 2D plane. Table 3.6 presents working of a self-organizing map.

3.3.3   Applications of artificial neural network

ANN can be applied in two broad situations such as (i) where there is high possibility of data availability and (ii) where it is very difficult to come up with the generalized

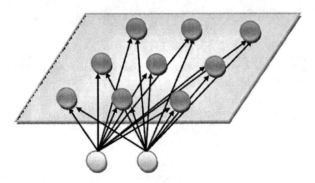

Figure 3.6 Kohonen architecture of neural network.

Table 3.6 Working of a Self-Organizing (Kohonen) Map

1. Input data are provided to the network architecture
2. The network operates on values and chooses the winning neuron. The winning neuron is the neuron that behaves (corresponds with input vector) in the best way. The winner node is often described as the most excited node to an input pattern or central node
3. Once winner is selected, the maximal neighborhood around this winner neuron is determined
4. Weight correction factor is calculated for each neighborhood
5. The weights of network are corrected

problem-solving model/rules. Because of fault tolerance, nonlinearity (parallel working), and learning capabilities, ANNs have been applied in several areas. Some applications include the following:

- Learning
- Pattern recognition
- Classification
- Forecasting
- Planning, control, and monitoring
- Optimization
- Advisory systems
- Speech recognition and synthesis
- Image processing and filtering
- Network routing
- Character recognition
- Machine control and robotics
- Operating system and multiprocessor scheduling
- Financial and business problem-solving applications

The Web technology can also be enhanced with ANN as follows:

- Data mining and information retrieval
- Web knowledge clustering and management
- Web traffic management
- e-Commerce security
- Image compression and recreation to save bandwidth and increase network speed
- Advisory and selection of desired web services
- Page ranking
- Personalized information management
- Web firewall and security algorithms

3.4   Genetic algorithms and evolutionary computing

Genetic algorithms (GAs) are adaptive heuristic search algorithm based on the evolutionary ideas of natural selection and genetic. Because of its basis on the principle of evolution, it is also known as evolutionary computing. The basic concept of GAs is to simulate processes in natural evolution based on Charles Darwin's survival of the fittest for problem solving. The basic working unit of all living organisms is cell. Within each cell, there are strings of deoxyribonucleic acid (DNA, made up of different amino acid units, that is, protein) and serve as the basic model of life in organisms. These DNA strings are based on chromosomes (protein structure to hold coil of DNA containing genes [DNA blocks]). Each gene encodes a particular protein. A few genes together in a group encode different characteristics such as eye color, skin color, height, etc. The group of genes is known as genotype. Complete set of genetic material (all chromosomes) is called genome. A genome may have a particular set of genes, that is, genotype. Figure 3.7 represents this biological background.

Applications of GAs were introduced by John Holland and developed by him, his students, and colleagues. In 1992, John R. Koza used GA to evolve programs to perform certain tasks. He called his method "genetic programming" (GP). GA has been widely

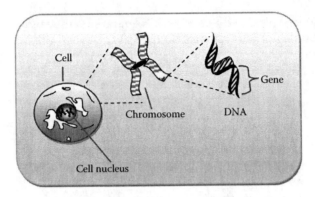

Figure 3.7 Cell, chromosome, DNA, and gene.

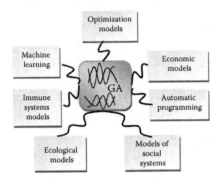

Figure 3.8 Applications of GAs.

studied, experimented, and applied in many fields in business and engineering applications. GAs are useful for the real-world problems where there is no formal model or for the problems that might prove difficult for traditional methods. GAs can be used as problem solvers, searching techniques optimizer, trainer, demonstrator, and bases for machine learning and provide computational model of innovation and creativity. Figure 3.8 demonstrates various applications of GAs.

3.4.1 Basic principles of genetic algorithms

GAs work on some basic principles as follows:

1. Encode problem into bit strings
2. Generate initial population by randomly considering encoded individuals
3. Recognize fitness values for acceptable individuals
4. Eliminate invalid elements from the population, which are not acceptable according to the fitness function
5. Modify the individuals by changes in individual bit string or by exchanging group of bits between two selected individuals

Prior to the application of a GA to solve a problem, the way to encode candidate solutions must be determined. The encoding can be binary number scheme, alphabets, tress, and

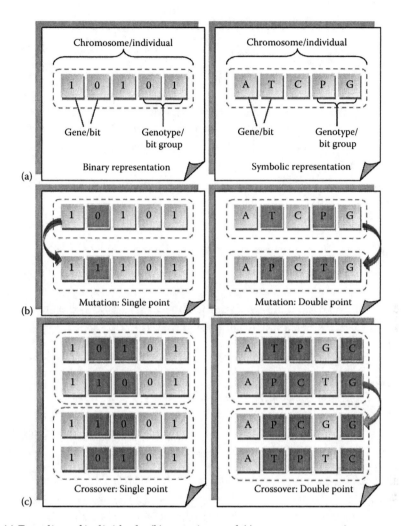

Figure 3.9 (a) Encoding of individuals, (b) mutation, and (c) crossover operations.

symbols. Each digit of the encoded individual refers to a gene; group of bits refers to a genotype; and full individual refers to a chromosome. A typical chromosome may look like as shown in Figure 3.9a.

Once the individuals in initial population are selected, the next step is to check the strength of the individuals. For this purpose, specific fitness function is applied on each individual and fit elements are allowed into the populations. The fitness function is defined over the genetic representation and measures the *quality* of the represented solution. The fitness function is application specific. One or more bit(s) in an individual is mutated to another possible bit representation or groups of bits are interchanged between two selected individual. The first operation is called mutation and later called crossover between two selected mates at given position. The new generated individuals after such reproduction are further tested for fitness. The process continues till desired solution automatically evolves. These steps are broadly known as initialization, selection, reproduction, and termination. Figure 3.9b and c represents mutation and crossover operations on the individuals.

3.4.2 An example of genetic algorithm to optimize a function

To clearly demonstrate how the GA works, let us take a classic example of a function optimization as follows:

The objective of an optimization function is to find the optimum value(s) of one or more parameters for a given function. Let us consider a function $y = f(x) = x^2$. Range for the function is $[0, 7]$. The objective is to find the value of "x" that maximizes the function y within the given range. The initial population by considering the binary encoding scheme is given as follows:

$I_1 = \{000, 010, 011, 101\}$

By applying the mutation and crossover functions, the population would have new members as shown in the following:

$\{100, 010, 011, 101\}$	(First element's first bit is mutated)
$\{100, 110, 011, 101\}$	(Second element's first bit is mutated)
$\{100, 110, 011, 101\}$	(Last two elements' last two bits are crossovered)

The new population will look as follows:

$I_2 = \{100, 110, 001, 111\}$

The fitness values of individual elements in the above population I_2 is as follows:

Fitness $I_2 = \{(\text{fitness}(100), \text{fitness}(110), \text{fitness}(001), \text{fitness}(111)\}$
Fitness $I_2 = \{(4*4), (6*6), (1*1), (7*7)\}$
Fitness $I_2 = \{(16), (36), (1), (49)\}$

Removing the candidate solutions (by percentile or roulette wheel selection) that are weak according to the fitness test, the new population can be given as follows:

$I_3 = \{110, 111\}$

After decoding the strong elements evolved in the third population, we get x values as 6 and 7. Since our aim is to maximize the function, we select 7 among both the values. The value 7 yields maximum result. To check the validity of the evolution, we may try the traditional method of optimization, which gives the same result.

GA is one of the efficient tools in searching required solution. The space in which the solutions may spread is called search space. Search space is a collection of all feasible solutions that may solve the problem to some extent. To understand the working of GA, schema (set of strings) theory is proposed by John Henry Holland and popularized by D.E. Goldberg and John Koza. The objective of this theory is to provide a formal model for the effectiveness of the GA search process. In schema theory, the search space is partitioned into smaller parts (subspace), and mathematical models are constructed on behavior of the subspace. The knowledge of pattern of individuals on a subspace helps in estimating how the individuals in the population belonging to certain schema can be expected to grow in the next generation. Taking this as a base, the building block hypothesis (BBH) is explored. The BBH theory explains how a GA solves a problem by evolving short, low order, and highly fit schema are sampled, recombined [crossed over], and resampled to form strings of potentially higher fitness.

3.4.3 Applications of genetic algorithms

GA can be applied in variety of areas. However, the prime candidates for a GA application are those that lack a formal model to compute solution. In general, some areas where GA can be applied are as follows:

- Searching
- Function optimization
- Game playing
- Commuter automated design
- Evolving rules/rule bases
- DNA, RAN, and protein structure prediction
- Security, encryption algorithm, and code braking (ethical hacking)
- Configuration application at molecular level in physics
- Molecular optimization in chemistry
- Control engineering
- Faultfinding systems
- Advisory systems
- Scheduling and sequencing problems
- Robotics
- Natural language processing (grammar induction and word sense disambiguation)
- Market analysis
- Multidimensional systems
- Recurrent neural network
- Quality control
- Parallel programming
- Software engineering
- Medical science, cloning, and applications like human genome project
- Social problems, biological, ecological, and mental models

GAs are also applied to the Web in the following manner:

- Swarm optimization for data clustering
- Automatic web data extraction
- Speech archiving on the Web
- Web content analysis
- Web content searching
- Security in web operations and e-commerce
- E-learning (e.g., scheduling classes and resources)
- Weather forecasting
- Online stock market prediction
- Evolving rules for data mining

3.5 Rough sets

The rough set theory was introduced by Zdzistaw Pawlak in 1970s while studying logical properties of information systems at Polish Academy of Sciences and the University of Warsaw, Poland. Rough sets deal with the classificatory analysis of imprecise and uncertainty of data and/or information. Rough set is considered as formal approximation of a simple crisp set. The approximation is provided in the form of approximation space and lower and upper approximations of the given set. The lower and upper approximation sets of a given set are crisp sets. However, the approximation set may be fuzzy. Rough sets and fuzzy sets are complementary generalizations of classical sets. The approximation spaces of rough set theory are sets with multiple memberships, while fuzzy sets are concerned with partial memberships. The approximation space classifies domain of interest into

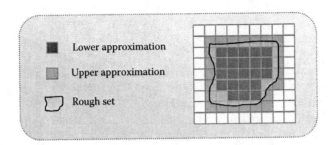

Figure 3.10 Rough sets.

some disjoint categories. Some objects belonging into same category are not distinguishable. When such unique and disjoint membership status is not identified, the notions of lower and upper approximation help. Figure 3.10 illustrates the concept of a rough set with upper and lower approximations.

The lower approximation is description of the domain objects, which certainly belong to the subset of interest, whereas the upper approximation is a description of the objects, which may possibly belong to the subset. The actual rough set is the subset defined through its lower and upper approximations.

3.5.1   Applications of rough sets

The problems that can be addressed by the theory of rough set are representation of uncertain data and information, analysis of data and information, analysis of conflicts, evaluation of data dependencies, and knowledge acquisition and discovery, etc. Some of the specific applications of rough sets are listed in the following:

- Data analysis
- Identification and evaluation of data dependencies and relationships
- Approximate reasoning or reasoning with uncertainty
- Data mining
- Automated knowledge acquisition
- Knowledge discovery
- Approximate pattern classification
- Image segmentation
- Granular computing
- Fuzzy-rough hybridization

Particularly for the Web, rough sets can be utilized as follows:

- Feature selection for web usage mining
- Grid service discovery
- Web content precashing
- Web content clustering
- Granular computing
- Ontology management
- Social networking framework for user centric information management

3.6 Soft computing

The formal methods and models may not be much helpful for many of the real-world problems. Some problems can be solved conceptually on paper; however, they result in impractical solution. Consider some simpler examples of searching for a mobile phone, selection of right template for website, or taking admission in a suitable course needs solutions in a limited time. Traditional methods offer best possible solutions in infinite time. Unfortunately, what we lack is time. We are interested in good as well as acceptable solution for real-life problems. For such problems, methods inspired by nature sometimes work very efficiently and effectively. Furthermore, these bioinspired methods have their own strengths and limitation. Real-life problem may be embedded with characteristics that need application of more than one such bioinspired method. This fact inspired many researchers to use hybrid some bioinspired methods. The field that deals with application of one or more such bioinspired methods and their hybridization at different levels are known as soft computing methods. The major constituents of soft computing methods can be named as (i) fuzzy logic, (ii) ANN, (iii) GAs, (iv) rough sets, etc. Figure 3.11 presents the constituents of soft computing.

3.6.1 Applications of soft computing

Soft computing techniques can be used in a large variety of realistic applications to consumer products and industrial systems. Application of soft computing has provided the opportunity to integrate human-like vagueness, real-life uncertainty handling, self-learning, and bioinspired mechanism for problem solving that otherwise very difficult for hard computing techniques. The contribution of soft computing has been experimented in various fields such as

- Automatic classification with explanation
- Robotics and artificial muscle
- Neuro-fuzzy advisory systems
- Design and tuning of mechanical systems through neuro-fuzzy approach

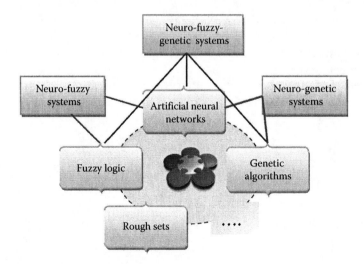

Figure 3.11 Constituents of soft computing.

- Neurogenetic systems to evolve weight metrics
- Neuro-fuzzy-generic systems for learning, evolving, and explanation
- Automatic fault diagnosis and advisory for repairing
- Determination of the parameters for an application from the data in interactive fashion

3.7   Benefits of the new AI to World Wide Web

Modern AI deals with techniques of connecting physical world to the computing world. It provides mechanism to integrate people and machine for mutual benefits. New AI offers ways to connect people to people, people to computer, and computer to computer. The step toward this goal of human computer connection is initialed with the invention of the Internet and the Web, which efficiently connect machines with machine and hence provide a basic platform for new AI methods. Through platforms like the Internet and the Web, the scope of AI application is enlarged. Rather, the new AI is enabled through technical advancement and infrastructural advancement like the Internet and the Web. The standard AI had ambitious goals and objectives, which were difficult to achieve. One of the original goals of AI was to automate applications where people are better. New AI goal is to exploit opportunities to perform tasks that people (neither machines) cannot do alone. Modern AI is capable of approximating many human cognitive abilities and partially or fully automating some of them through bioinspired computing. Here, efficient machines are blessed with the added effectiveness and hence can perform better than what humans can do in some fields. New AI makes it possible for organizations to make better decisions, connect people in more natural way, and help users to find complete solutions on need. The new AI aids more computational power to infrastructure and problem-solving strategies, which may increase the level of intelligence in various fields. Some broad categories of application areas include communication and network, information retrieval, extraction and filtering, natural language processing, game playing and entertainment, data and web mining, multiagent system for e-businesses and e-commerce, knowledge management and accounting framework, semantic web, etc.

Exercises

3.1   What are the advantages and disadvantages of neural networks?
3.2   What is a fuzzy set? What is a membership function?
3.3   What are the components of a fuzzy system?
3.4   Explore the use of GA to cluster data.
3.5   Why are learning algorithms important to ANNs?
3.6   (Project) Design a GA to construct a simple neural network.

References

Akerkar, R. and Sajja, P. S. 2009. *Knowledge-Based Systems*. Sudbury, MA: Jones & Bartlett.
Zadeh, L. A. 1965. Fuzzy sets. *Information and Control* 8:338–353.

chapter four

Web intelligence

4.1 Internet, web, grid, and cloud

The advancements of the Internet and wireless networks have made users of information and communication technology (ICT) do everything in a differently efficient way. Their business became e-business, entertainment became e-entertainment, learning became e-learning, and so on. Such advances offer new opportunities and challenges for many areas, such as business, commerce, marketing, finance, publishing, education, research, and development.

Modern ICT uses hybridization of computer networks, Internet, databases, protocols, browsers, search engines, programming languages, and other tools along with variety of agents for different tasks. It is not wrong to state that another virtual world exists in parallel on the World Wide Web (WWW), also known as the Web.

The Web assumes Internet as a communication network platform. Historically, the Internet was started as a military project (ARPANET) for controlling and monitoring the military activities of a U.S. project in the year 1969. The Internet is a *network of networks* that consists of plenty of private, public, academic, business, and government networks that are linked by a broad array of electronic and optical networking technologies. Typical services provided by the Internet are information storage and sharing, communication, accessibility, and social interaction. It is a global system of interconnected computer networks that use the standard Internet protocol suite transmission control protocol/Internet protocol (TCP/IP) to serve users worldwide. This protocol permits various components of the network to be interconnected and allowed communicate with each other.

The WWW is considered as interlinked set of documents and services. It is a wide-area hypermedia information retrieval (IR) mechanism on the platform of Internet aiming to provide universal access to a large universe of documents. According to Jacobs (2004), the Web is an information space in which the items of interest, referred to as resources, are identified by global identifiers called uniform resource identifiers (URIs) and used to find resources. Uniform resource locator (URL) encompasses a request to URI in view of retrieving the resource with the associated protocol. Besides the TCP/IP protocol, hypertext transfer protocol (HTTP) identifies how messages are formatted and transmitted.

According to Zeltser (1995), people have dreamt of a universal information database since the late 1940s. Such databases share information and provide platform to establish links between various components like organizations and user groups. As a result of popularity of the Internet, WWW technology on the Internet platform is established.

The WWW began in March 1989 at CERN (Conseil Europeen pour la Recherche Nucleaire, which is now called as European laboratory for particle physics) under the leadership of Berners-Lee (Zeltser 1995). The WWW is an Internet-based computer network that allows users on one computer to access information stored on another through the worldwide network. The Web consists of pages on the Internet that can be accessed using a web browser. As stated earlier, with the help of the protocols such as HTTP, the content of the Web can be accessed. With hypertext, which also allows multimedia content, an entity can contain a link to another website. Most of the web pages are written in the hypertext markup language (HTML), which works in conjunction with HTTP.

Grid is a flexible, secure, and coordinated collection of resource sharing among dynamic collection of resources and individuals. The grid computing assumes secured and interconnected infrastructure along with management and access techniques to utilize the resources. Grid computing provides a platform to write an application, which is independent of physical resources. The applications, which were specifically designed to use multiple processors or other federated resources, are the candidate of this approach. Grid computing helps in exploiting underutilized resources, increases efficiency and capacity by parallel utilization of multiple additional resources and hence provides cost-effective solution. Computational facility, storage, software, hardware, and special equipments, etc., are the major resources that applications would like to share through a common grid platform. Grid can be used for querying for information, planning, security, certification, resource management, and problem solving. There are many products and toolkits available that enable different aspects of grid computing. One of the most well-known toolkits is the Globus Toolkit (Bart et al. 2005).

Grid computing can be further enhanced to the so-called knowledge grid in order to deal with knowledge to impart intelligence in grid computing (Sajja 2011). The knowledge grid is designed as a multilayered software system based on a set of services for knowledge discovery on the grid. This knowledge grid platform and services enable the usage of a knowledge management system operating on several data warehouses located at different geographic locations.

Cloud computing is another new trend in the area. It is considered as a mechanism that let you share resources, software, and hardware over a distributed environment. There are three main cloud stacks known as (i) infrastructure as a service (IaaS), (ii) platform as a service (PaaS), and (iii) software as a service (SaaS).

IaaS is the base layer of the cloud stack. It serves as a foundation for the other two layers, for their execution. PaaS layer serves as a platform facilitator to execute different tasks. SaaS layer provides different documents and software on request. These services may be free or available on commercial bases. Most of the cloud computing infrastructures consist of services delivered through shared data centers and appearing as a single point of access for consumers' computing needs. The cloud may be further private, public, community, or hybrid cloud.

4.1.1   Components of typical web

As stated earlier, web is a centralized dynamic repository of content for people by people. People are contributors and users of the content available on web. Hence, the prime component of the Web is the content represented on it. Besides the content, it also requires the mechanisms to upload, access, update, and control the content. For smooth administration of such a huge entity, there is a requirement of standards and protocols.

Figure 4.1 shows the relationship between URI, resource, representation, and developer for web content representation.

Typically, the Web consists of the following things:

- Content to be shared in the form of text, images, animation, and graphs
- Web browsers and media players to enable presentation of the content stored
- Assistive technologies like screen readers, switches, scanning software, etc.

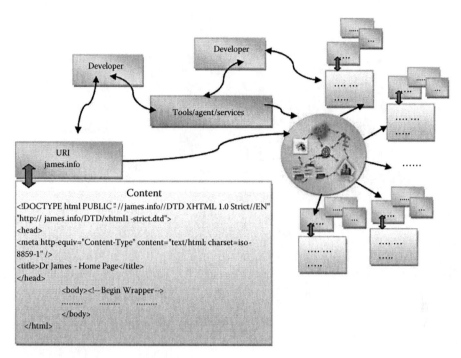

Figure 4.1 Representing content on the Web.

- Tools like developer tools and evaluation tools like validators, etc.
- Developers and users to contribute and use content

These components together build a framework of the Web, which is illustrated in Figure 4.2.

4.1.2   *Characteristics and benefits of the Web*

The Web consists of an immense and dynamic collection of data and information. However, working with such huge, unstructured, and dynamic collection is difficult. The Web possesses the following characteristics:

- Large volume and unbounded in space/time
- High complexity
- Highly dynamic information
- Users' participation
- Unstructuredness
- Distributed
- Nonhierarchical

The Web offers new means of storing, sharing, and transmitting the content to user's finger tips. There are plenty of advantages that the Web offers such as high degree of availability of content, any time access to a large group of users, and many more. To summarize, the Web provides benefits such as

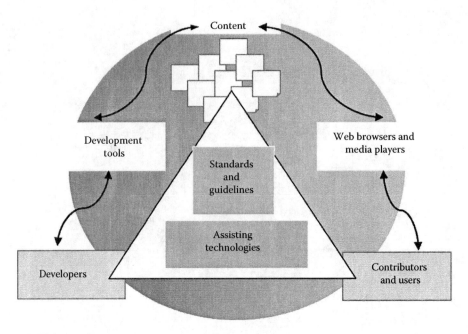

Figure 4.2 Web components.

- Online repository of content
- Sharing of resources
- Provide business assistance and services
- Provides documents downloading
- Opportunity for remote access
- Community support and social networking

4.2   Introduction to web intelligence

The size and complexity of the Web are the key elements that lead to the need of better environment and/or techniques to effectively utilize the Web. The size of the indexed WWW is more than 55 billion web pages in April 2010.*

Generally, to search the content from the Web, users may follow approaches like key word-based searching through search engines, querying directly the Web sources, or randomly surfing following the pointers and links. According to Chakrabarti et al. (1999) and Han and Chang (2002), the success of these techniques, especially with the more recent page ranking in Google and other search engines, shows the Web's great promise to become the ultimate information system. Furthermore, Han and Chang (2002) highlight the challenges and factors that lead to the need of more sophisticated and intelligent web. Some of the limitations and challenges are as follows:

- *Lack of knowledge-based searches*
  There are many search engines that return a large amount of information that are too general. Commercially used ranking and filtering algorithms are limited to popular/standard keyword-based results. Interpretation of a keyword filtered from

---

* *Source*: www.worldwidewebsize.com

the users' query is not specific as there is a little knowledge that the Web knows about the user. Furthermore, the search algorithms present information that consists of the given keyword directly within itself. There is a requirement of application of artificial intelligence (AI)-based search techniques that know the content as well as users' requirement so as to satisfy users' need effectively. Besides providing high-quality keyword-based search, there should be provision of possible combination of keyword options.

- *Lack of effective techniques to access the Web in depth*
  The Web is highly enriched with the valuable information and data; however, all the content cannot be explored by users. One of the possible reasons is that these sources are beyond search engine capabilities; hence, the information can never be presented to the users. Another reason is that tremendous information is being presented to the user, among which some of the data are very general and the user cannot explore all the result sets that are presented. Besides personalizing the search results, as stated in previous point, there is a need to make the resources accessible and available.
- *Lack of mechanisms to deal with users' dynamic requirements*
  While accessing the Web, generally users are lost into ocean of information and change objective/interest of search. The Web links may not be updated to reflect these trends. For the dynamic and automatic adjustment of the Web information services, AI techniques might be utilized.
- *Lack of automatically constructed directories*
  To organize the content of the Web, dozens of online tools are available. Some examples can be given as wikis, social bookmarking sites, web information directories, and really simple syndication (RSS) feed readers, etc. Unfortunately, developers must construct initial versions of such structures manually. This task is tedious and requires more time and effort. AI techniques might help in evolving suitable directory structure to support automatic generation of such supporting documents.
- *Lack of multidimensional analysis and data mining support*
  The Web supports search engine, developers' tools, and browsers' tools. These tools, especially the search engines, do not support multidimensional analysis and data mining support.

To meet the challenges and need of the future web, existing theories and technologies need to be enhanced intelligently so as to deal with complexity of the Web.

According to Zadeh (2005), it is widely recognized that world knowledge plays an essential role in the assessment of relevance, summarization, search, and deduction. AI techniques are the computer-based techniques and/or approaches that make machines partly intelligent and understand the need and applicability of methods for effective utilization of resources. By employing the AI techniques for web functions, it is possible to partly impart intelligence to the Web-based business. Web intelligence (WI) is therefore considered as employment of AI techniques for the Web.

WI was first introduced by Yao et al. (2001), as a joint research effort in developing the next-generation web-based intelligent systems, through combining their expertise in data mining, agents, information retrival (IR) and logic. According to Yao et al (2001), the formal definition of WI can be given as follows:

> Web Intelligence exploits Artificial Intelligence and Advanced Information Technology on the Web and Internet.

The Web Intelligence Consortium (WIC) is an international, nonprofit organization dedicated to advancing worldwide scientific research and industrial development in the field of WI. According to WIC, information technology (IT) promotes collaborations among worldwide WI research centers and organizational members, technology showcases at WI-related conferences, and workshops. The generic model showing hybridization of web and AI (as in Figure 1.5) as well as the W3C consortium definition of WI is given in Chapter 1.

The major aim of WI is to utilize AI and ICT on the Web. Figure 4.3 illustrates relation between the fields of AI, ICT, and WI. Each section included in this section introduces an area in brief. The content will be further elaborated in individual chapters.

4.2.1   Semantic web

Intelligence can be achieved by making the Web to know its own structures and content and by applying intelligent techniques to effectively access the resources. Semantic web was the first step toward WI.

The semantic web, as envisioned by Berners-Lee et al. (2001), is a huge collection of formalized knowledge and agents that are capable of understanding these formalizations and acting upon them. The formalized knowledge is available in ontologies that use logic- or graph-based formalisms on top of unambiguous pointers to web resources in order to

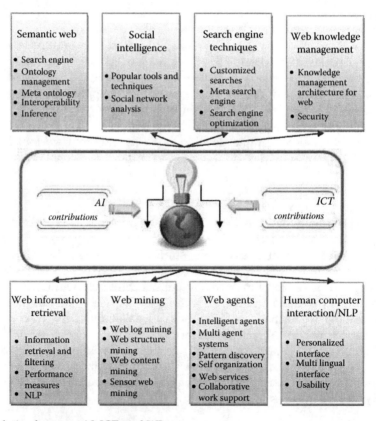

Figure 4.3 Relation between AI, ICT, and WI.

represent knowledge in a computer accessible manner. The semantic web paradigm is in some sense perpendicular to that of the Web 2.0 onward collections of human-generated networks and tags that are ambiguous, arbitrary, and chaotic. These tags and connections are created on-the-fly, reflecting the taggers' associations. Web 1.0 is considered as mostly read-only web and static HTML pages. Web 1.0 is used for information reference, advertizing, and home pages. Web 2.0 is considered as widely read–write web. This includes blogs, collaborative platforms like wikis, and applications like Google. Web 3.0 is conceived as portable personal web. This web version is more focused on users (personalization) and consolidates dynamic content with semantics.

The first incarnation of the semantic web was meant to address this problem by encouraging the creators of web pages to provide some form of metadata (data about data) to their web page, so simple facts like identity of the author of a web page could be made accessible to machines. This approach hopes that people, instead of hiding the useful content of their web pages within text and pictures that was only easily readable by humans, would create machine-readable metadata to allow machines to access their information. To make assertions and inferences from metadata, an inference engine is used. The formal framework for this metadata, called the resource description framework (RDF), was drafted by Hayes, one of the pioneers of AI. RDF is a simple language for creating assertions about propositions. The basic concept of RDF is that of the "triple": any statement can be composed into a subject, a predicate, and the object. The framework was extended to that of a full ontology language as described by description logic. This web ontology language (OWL) is thus more expressive than RDF. Please refer Chapter 8 for detailed discussion on these topics. The semantic web paradigm made one small but fundamental change to the architecture of the Web: a resource (i.e., anything that can be identified by a URI) can be about anything. This means that URIs that were formerly used to denote mostly web pages and other data that have some form of byte code on the Web can now be about anything from things whose physical existence is outside the Web to abstract concept.

The semantic web represents a powerful new technology but it does not provide a magic solution to all the Web intelligence community's problems. It is a new and robust weapon in the arsenal of tools that web developers can use to build new systems and improve existing systems. One of the most promising applications of semantic web technology is in providing a top-level view into the vast amount of existing information currently residing in isolated and proprietary databases containing data that is very difficult to fuse and share. The real power of the emerging semantic web is in providing information in a machine-readable and machine-understandable form for access by software agents. Once the infrastructure of semantic representation is in place, linked to huge sources of instance data, the doors will be opened for the innovative development of software agents. Some types of agents come easily to mind, such as agents to identify subtle inheritance relationships and agents to highlight information about individuals using pseudonym to hide their real identity. Nevertheless, agents will be built to perform tasks to support analyst that we cannot begin to imagine today. One of the most powerful evolving concepts is that these agents can be developed independent of the underlying distributed semantic web representation of information. New agents may be conceived that need new types of information not currently represented, or available, in the semantic web environment. In those cases, the semantic web environment can be expanded as dictated by business case decisions.

The concept of the semantic web is discussed in Chapter 8.

4.2.2   Social intelligence

Social intelligence is one of the multiple intelligences identified by Gardner's (1983) theory of multiple intelligences and closely related to the theory of mind. Social intelligence, according to the original definition of Thorndike (1920), is

> The ability to understand and manage men and women, boys and girls, to act wisely in human relations.

To impart human-like intelligence and to utilize the Web for routine business transactions, principles and algorithms of the social intelligence should be augmented with web management activities. By adding social intelligence, web activities may be focused on well-structured, goal-oriented groups. Social intelligence techniques help in managing collective knowledge processes in informal, loosely coupled groups. According to Nishida (2002), such hybridization focuses not only on technological development for WI but also on the design and analysis of a social framework for embedding WI into everyday life.

4.2.3   Search engine techniques

A search engine is an entity that searches information on the Web. The search results, also called hits, are collected from various locations (web pages, directories, databases, and other sites) using techniques like indexing, crawling, and searching. Web search engine stores useful information about the pages and locations on the Web. These pages can be retrieved by an algorithm (spider or crawler). Furthermore, for any search engine, it is desired to provide more relevant set of results to the user. Then the retrieved content is indexed. More the relevance of the content presented to the user, the search engine is more useful. Most search engines employ methods to rank the results to provide the suitable results first. Some search engines provide an advanced feature called proximity search, which allows users to define the distance between keywords. Also, language-integrated queries, queries in natural language, or fuzzy logic-based queries allow the user to type a question in the same form one would ask it to a human.

Generally, it is considered to be a solitary activity for satisfying users' individual needs. All mainstream search engines like Google, Yahoo, etc., and web browsers are designed for solo use. However, many tasks in both professional and casual settings can benefit from the ability to jointly search the Web with others. Collaborative web search often occurs in some search tasks, such as travel planning, literature search, technical information, and so on. The majority of these tasks were complex information seeking tasks that require comparisons and synthesis. The result shows that richer tasks benefit from collaborative search. Recently, some research efforts have focused on this area and some systems have developed. Moreover, there have been a few attempts to design search interfaces specifically for collaborative search. Foley et al. (2005) designed a collaborative video search system in which still images of retrieved videos are shown on a computerized table display. Morris (2008) and his colleagues developed a tool to make interactions with other searchers a collaborative activity. The main idea was to make the queries and results from one user's search visible to other users who had joined a search task. Pickens et al. (2008) took this idea further. They described an algorithm that combines multiple interactions of queries from multiple searchers during a single search session, by using two weighting variables called "relevance" and "freshness," where both are functions of the ranked list of documents returned for a given query. It is becoming a staple way to improve search quality by users' collaboration.

4.2.4   Web knowledge management

In order to use and manage the content/knowledge on the Web, one needs a machine understandable representation of such statements as well as powerful techniques for creating, retrieving, accessing, and manipulating the content. Plenty of unstructured knowledge is stored on the Web. Before utilization of knowledge for problem solving, there is need to present/convert it into suitable ontology according to the purpose. The techniques like ontology mapping, merging, and integration may help in better management of the Web content. Artificial intelligent techniques for knowledge representation and management help in this area.

4.2.5   Web information retrieval and filtering

IR is the science of searching for documents, part of documents, from given source/domain in order to retrieve content that is relevant to user's information need. According to DeClaris et al. (1994), IR experiences significant change in users' queries during a single session, where the source of information/domain to be searched is relatively static. According to DeClaris et al. (1994), in information filtering, the users' interests are nearly static; however, the interests are matched against a dynamic stream of content. The job of IR/filtering becomes more challenging on the Web because of large amount of content, existence of noise, complexity of the Web, dynamic nature of the Web, and multiuser environment. Different techniques available for the retrieval and filtering job are search by example, collaborative filtering, and filtering with help of metatags. Furthermore, it is to be noted that IR may contain unwanted information. To avoid this, one may use proper filtering techniques to eliminate noise from the result set.

4.2.6   Web mining

Web mining utilizes data mining techniques to discover and extract information from the Web resources. Locating resources, preprocessing, generalized pattern finding, and further analysis are the major activities of web mining process. Web mining can be further categorized into web content mining, web structure mining, and web usage mining. Web content mining describes the techniques required to mine the content from the Web. In web structure mining, emphasis is given on structure of the content to discover specific types of content. Typically, the Web structure mining utilizes hyperlink structure of the Web to analyze the Web content. Web usage mining focuses on users' interest and user behavior in order to study, develop, and use the new/existing techniques for web usage.

4.2.7   Web agents

An agent is an entity (software, person, or hardware) that performs the intended tasks on behalf of its user. The major characteristics of an agent are its autonomy, cooperation, and ability to learn. Web agents paradigm deal with the development of such agents for different functionalities of the Web. The objective of web agent is to enable agent technologies in order to improve the Web operations. This field includes study of intelligent agent, automatic computing, agent-based knowledge discovery, standards for web agents, agents for ontology engineering, self-organization of agents on network platform, personalized interface agents, search agents, retrieval agents, middleware and security agents, agent-mediated markets, grid intelligence and computing, information gateway, etc.

4.2.8   Human–computer integration

The acceptance of a good product depends on many factors. Friendly interface and ease of use is one of the most crucial success factors. Technology alone may not win user acceptance and subsequent marketability. Better user interface or, in other words, the human–computer interaction increases efficiency and cost-effectiveness. This becomes more important when the target users are the noncomputer/nontechnical professionals. Web contains a lot for everybody. Hence, it is required to have a friendly and easy to use interface to increase the scope/utilization of the content stored in the Web.

Furthermore, the systems that learn from its interaction and talk to the users naturally increase the power of WI. Application of AI techniques helps to improve the interface by considering the following points:

- Clear and efficient interaction
- Knowing users plans, goals, and needs through user profile and interaction
- Better representation of the content along with justification
- Better design, development, and quality control techniques for the development of interfaces for the Web
- Improving usability

Application of AI makes accessing the large amounts of content on the Web to be conveyed, manage, and understood. Also, it is easy to manage complex task structures related to the applications and to optimize real-time performance characteristics regarding the application.

4.3   Perspectives of WI

As stated earlier, major contributions for WI are coming from ICT and AI. ICT contributes mainly in database and information-based systems. ICT enables creation of a base structure of the Web and web content accessing mechanisms. It helps in data mining, IR, and knowledge discovery on web-based environment. ICT also contributes in the development of agents, security and quality standards, and protocols for two main aspects, namely, networking and accessing content. Table 4.1 describes the contribution of various fields of ICT.

AI systems are inspired from natural intelligence and try to mimic intelligent behavior observed commonly in human being. According to Rich and Knight (1991), the goal of AI is to make machines to do the things at which, at the moment, people are better. AI systems can be classified in many ways. According to Russell and Norvig (2010), AI systems can be classified into four major categories such as cognitive modeling approach (thinking humanly), turing test approach (acting humanly), laws of thought approach (thinking rationally), and rational agent approach (acting rationally).

Also, artificial intelligent systems do consider and related with fields like Mathematics, Statistics, Linguistics, Psychology, Neuroscience, and Biology. Table 4.2 presents the contributions of the aforementioned related fields.

Every field of ICT and AI contributes a little to make the online repository of content called the Web for a specific task. Contribution of the ICT is to provide base platform and AI is to impart intelligence. Figure 4.4 shows contributory field from ICT and AI.

Table 4.1 Contribution of Various ICT Fields

ICT field	Contribution
Networking	Contributes for hardware engineering, connecting devices, etc., for resource sharing
Information systems	Contributes by providing principles and concepts regarding information systems (like transaction processing systems, DSSs, and expert systems) development, databases, etc.
Protocols and security	Protocols for information/resource sharing such as FTP, HTTP, TCP/IP, etc., and security mechanisms and algorithms (encryption/decryption, etc.)
Software engineering	Contributes in terms of guidelines to develop software systems and modeling approaches (waterfall model, prototype model, etc.)
Tools	Contributes by providing tools like programming languages, packages, data collection and presentation tools, and personal computers
Quality standards	Contributes by providing models for quality measurements and quality standards

Table 4.2 Contributions of Various AI Fields

Fields	Contribution to AI
Mathematics	Contributes bases of logic, probability, and computing (e.g., number theory and memory management)
Statistics	Contributes bases of uncertainty, multivalues logic, algorithms, and approximate reasoning
Linguistics	Contributes bases of machine translation, natural language theory, and user-friendly interactions with systems
Psychology	Contributes in cognitive science, human–machine interaction, and development of heuristics functions
Biology and neuroscience	Contribute in understanding how natural intelligence works to develop bioinspired computing systems

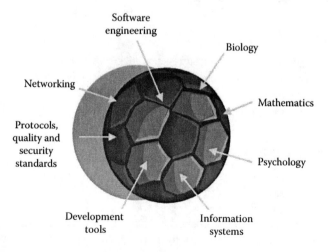

Figure 4.4 Perspectives of WI: role of ICT and AI fields.

4.4   Levels of WI

Intelligence can be imparted on the Web at different levels. Starting from the basic infra-structure to the application techniques, utilizing the Web resources can be made intel-ligent. According to Liu et al. (2003), WI can be studied at four different levels such as network level, interface level, application level, and knowledge level. According to Yao (2005), intelligence can be applied by exploring and expanding intelligent techniques to support retrieval, reading, analyzing, and writing activities on the Web. Further data, information, knowledge, and wisdom (DIKW) hierarchy is another aspect of categorizing the Web activities and systems. First level consists of systems and techniques that access and deal with simple data management. Second level considers systems and techniques that deal with information. Third is at knowledge level by making the Web enriched with meaningful content as well as knowledge-based accessing mechanism. The third knowl-edge level is further enhanced and considered as a kind of wisdom web. This section categorizes employment of intelligence at four different levels such as intelligence at basic infrastructure level, knowledge level, interface level, and application level.

4.4.1   Imparting intelligence at basic infrastructural level

In this level, basic infrastructure that enables web operations is considered. With the help of intelligent techniques, following can be done:

- Device and infrastructure can be reengineered
- Hardware embedded with AI techniques can be realized
- New routing and content accessing algorithms can be developed
- Efficient and secured built-in security and protocol can be designed, which may be embedded within machines

4.4.2   Imparting intelligence at knowledge level

Besides the intelligent transmission and effective interface, another prime factor that imparts intelligence in web operations is the high-value content. The content offered by the Web must be of high value in the sense of usefulness and applicability. This can be done by the following:

- Acquiring better content by knowledge acquisition methods
- Utilizing suitable knowledge representation scheme that enables easy access and operations on the content
- Addition of "semantic" on the Web

4.4.3   Imparting intelligence at interface level

Here, one may plan for the customized utilization of the Web content by effective presenta-tion of it. This can be achieved through the following:

- Multimedia utilization and customized presentation according to target audience
- Developing methods and algorithms that change the style of presentation based on application history and customer profile
- Intelligent human–computer interaction

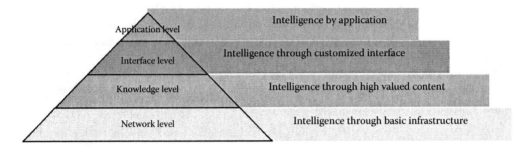

Figure 4.5 Levels of WI.

4.4.4 Imparting intelligence at application level

It is equally important to know the users and their requirements for utilizing WI. Candidate applications can be short-listed by studying interactions and behavior of web users/communities. For such application, generalized commercial product may be planned. These four levels are demonstrated in Figure 4.5.

4.5 Goal of WI

The overall goal and objective of WI are design and implementation of intelligent web systems at various levels. The goal of network level intelligent systems is to facilitate basic infrastructure for storage and transmission of the content on the Web. Network level systems are generally distributed systems sharing resources from a variety of platforms.

The systems at knowledge level facilitate utilization of the knowledge offered by such distributed resources at lower level. This may include conceptual formation and math-ematic modeling of the content.

The interface level systems are aimed to provide user-friendly environment through intelligent techniques like natural language processing (NLP), linguistic variables, and approximate reasoning. The application level systems map the models and sys-tems available to one/more suitable target groups of users. WI is applied here for social intelligence.

4.6 Characteristics of web intelligence

4.6.1 Openness

The Web is available to all. The most common ways to restrict users are usage of pass-word, defining various access levels, and security techniques like firewall and encryption of the content on the Web. Unfortunately, these techniques have their own limitations. Instead of making all the content available for all the time, the Web should use some intelligent mechanism, which is always open and accessible to selective users. This virtue can be achieved by WI.

4.6.2 Intelligent

The use of AI techniques enables the "knowledge" factor available on the Web; hence, the Web "knows" not only the meaning of the content it posses, but also be able to identify the right opportunities for better utilization. The usage of intelligent techniques saves the Web storage space, deals with complex unstructured environment of the Web, and infers new knowledge from the exiting knowledge. In this way, it is more than just a semantic web.

Furthermore, the usage of artificially intelligent techniques helps the Web to identify "right" audience of the intended content, and hence, the content never goes to the wrong hands.

4.6.3   Secured

The techniques and content available on the Web emphasize on wise (effective) utilization of its resources. This also includes identification of proper user and content linkage. Only the content/part of content for which users are eligible is allowed to be assessed. Metaknowledge embedded in resources improved artificially intelligence security techniques like encryption to access material and specially designed protocols according to the nature of application make the Web more secured.

4.6.4   User friendly

The creditability of an intelligent system lies on its ability to justify and explain its own decisions. Interface systems used for the Web can explain to the decisions suggested or taken. The interface also learns about target users and tries to customize the output according to users' style. The AI techniques like NLP further enhance the user friendliness of the Web access mechanisms.

4.6.5   Agent based

The Web is a complex and large repository of content and techniques. The activities/ functionalities of the Web can be divided into modules. These modules are handled by intelligent agents having characteristics such as autonomous, cooperation, and self-learning. This approach gives advantages of modularity, reusability, parallel use of multiple modules (cooperation), and learning.

4.6.6   Interoperability

The Web contains heterogeneous type of knowledge. The Web is for everybody. Anybody can access the content of the Web and contribute to the Web by adding content in any format/ontology. The techniques for ontology merging, mapping, and integrating help in increasing the interoperability of the Web content.

4.6.7   Global knowledge base

Along with the repository of meaningful content, the Web also serves as repository of intelligent techniques for various jobs like searching, filtering, and application of the content. The whole repository can be considered as a global online ever available knowledge base. AI techniques like evolution and inference further continuously update the knowledge base. Such knowledge base can be utilized for problem solving, documentation, training, and learning in various fields.

4.7   Challenges and issues of WI

4.7.1   Nature of knowledge

Intelligence requires knowledge. It is necessary to deal with knowledge component to be handled while imparting intelligence on the Web. However, knowledge is very difficult to define, collect, and record. There are a few guidelines available for knowledge acquisition, knowledge representation, and knowledge inference. Furthermore, successful acquisition and representation of the required knowledge are not enough as knowledge is continuously changing. Moreover, it is required to collect and manage a large amount of knowledge to solve a small problem in intelligent fashion.

4.7.2   Volume, complexity, and unstructured environment of web

The Web offers a voluminous repository of variety of contents on different fields. Since the Web is open for everybody, anybody can manage information in their own personalized way using different ontologies. This makes the Web more unstructured. Big size and unstructured environment increase the level of complexity, which reduces the efficiency of web operations.

4.7.3   Development methods, protocols, security, and quality standards

Even to develop a simple information system, we have a few guidelines available from the disciplines like systems analysis and design and software engineering. To develop an AI-based system, we need specific approaches and methods. Automatic knowledge acquisition, new methods for knowledge representation and inference, protocols for knowledge access, and standards to measure/compare quality of the system are still big challenges for the developers. When intelligence is freely encoded on platform like the Web, it can be easily shared by anybody. In this situation, intellectual copyright acts and quality standards play an important role. Protocols and techniques must be developed to authenticate the users and websites that are requesting and sharing information from remote locations.

4.7.4   Weak support from AI

The source and inspiration of AI system, the biological human brain, is still a mystery. Very little things we know about how human brain works; hence, it is difficult to mimic the functionalities of the biological brain. AI discipline provides weak guidelines in this direction. Furthermore, techniques that are suitable for the biological systems may not be fully fit into the Web environment.

4.8   Wisdom web

According to Data Information Knowledge Wisdom (DIKW) chain, data and information are needed to be renewed as knowledge and wisdom. From the simple web, a semantic web was extended. According to Berners-Lee et al. (2001), the semantic web is an extension of the current web enabling machines and humans to work in cooperation. The aim is to enrich the Web with the meaningful content where software agents roaming from page to page can readily carry out sophisticated tasks for users.

In a similar way, we may state that the next immediate transformation of the current web is the renewal of the Web into the wisdom web. The quality of acting wise and taking wise decision/judgment is enhanced in this next generation web. According to Liu et al. (2003) and the DIKW hierarchy stated earlier, the next obvious extension of the Web is the wisdom web. Liu et al. (2003) state that the new generation of the Web will enable the users to gain new *wisdom* of living, working, playing, and learning, in addition to information search and knowledge queries.

According to Liu et al. (2003), the fundamental capabilities of the wisdom web are autonomic web support, semantics, metaknowledge, planning, personalization, and sense of humor. Three basic capabilities of wisdom web are described in the following.

4.8.1 Autonomic regulation of functionalities between the resources

To automatic regulation of web functionalities in order to make the Web wise, the first need is to configure the server in such a way that it "knows" the Web. Such knowledgeable server must be able to find and utilize appropriate resources automatically in wise fashion. Furthermore, the Web is an ever-increasing repository of heterogeneous content; hence, this must be done in dynamic manner.

This can be done in an independent, transparent, and cooperative fashion. Such learning, automation, and cooperation properties are the basic characteristics of an agent. Hence, the server can act as an agent to perform the aforementioned activities in dynamic fashion. With the learning capabilities, the agents may evolve to new specific agents according to need.

4.8.2 Embedding knowledge into the Web

As stated in the Section 4.8.1, the web server should "know" the resources and wisely use the resources through automatic knowledge-oriented fashion. One of the prime requisites for this is to embed knowledge as well as wisdom (processed and matured knowledge) in the Web. Special markup languages and specialized ontology [like fuzzy extensible markup language (FXML)] may be utilized to embed knowledge into the Web to make the Web more informative (Sajja 2007).

4.8.3 Improving access mechanisms

Besides enriching the Web by adding knowledge component into the repository itself, there is a need to improve the surfing/accessing mechanisms to efficiently locate the useful resources according to the application perspectives. This includes improved security mechanisms, user-friendly interface, and efficient knowledge-based searching of the content. Still, it seems difficult for a machine to read between the lines and behave as exactly as user expectations.

Besides the previous mechanisms, some techniques like annotation, tagging, intelligent extraction of facts, quality control, etc., can be developed to aid transactions of wisdom web. Another aspect that aids the wisdom web concept is the wisdom of crowd and collective intelligence. Techniques that help in managing the collective intelligence, trust network, and crowd information management can also be helpful in managing the wisdom web.

4.9 Web-based support systems

Web-based support systems (WSSs) concern multidisciplinary investigations, which bring together different computer technologies, the Web, and domain-specific studies. Domain-specific studies focus on the investigation of activities in a specific field. Computer technologies are used to build systems that support these activities. The Web provides the platform for such systems.

There are two key features of WSS. They can be understood as extensions of existing research in two dimensions. In the application dimension, WSSs cover support systems in many different domains. They can be viewed as natural extensions of decision support systems (DSSs). In the technology dimension, WSSs use the Web as a new platform for the delivery of support. Along the application dimension, the knowledge from DSS can be easily applied to other domains. Along the technology dimension, the new advances in technology can lead to further innovations in support systems.

4.10   Designing an intelligent web

Defining how to design an intelligent web presents a foremost research challenge. Realizing our vision of the Web's potential requires overcoming two primary problems. First, at the abstraction level, the traditional schemes for accessing the immense amounts of data that reside on the Web fundamentally assume the text-oriented, keyword-based view of web pages. We trust a data-oriented abstraction will enable a new range of functionalities. Second, at the service level, we must replace the current primitive access schemes with more sophisticated versions that can exploit the Web totally.

4.11   Future of WI

Internet and web have proved themselves as the most promising platforms to offer effective problem solutions irrespective of time and location. However, with the time spans, gradually the expectations and demands of users are increasing. On the other hand, volume of content stored on the Internet and the Web platforms is also increasing exponentially. To meet such ever-increasing demands and to handle the large and increasing content, WI becomes essential.

We can see two ways in which WI research can be characterized. The first one is by adding "web" as a prefix to an existing topic. For example, from "digital library," "IR," and "agents," we can obtain "web digital library," "web IR," and "web agents." On the other hand, we can add "on the Web" as a postfix. For example, we can obtain "digital library on the Web," "IR on the Web," and "agent on the Web." Thus, the interdisciplinary field of WI can be applied to commercial and academic world. Special tools, methods, protocols, quality standards, and systems design approach might be considered for the WI field. Some dominant approaches can be observed and are briefly reviewed in this section.

WI presents ample opportunities and challenges for the research and development of new generation web-based applications, as well as for exploiting business intelligence. We believe that more attention will be focused on WI in the coming years. Recently, several specific applications and systems have been proposed.

E-commerce is one of the most important applications of WI. Web mining and web usage analysis play an important role in e-commerce for customer relationship management (CRM) and targeted marketing. Web mining is the use of data mining techniques to automatically discover and extract information from web documents and services. Text analysis, retrieval, and web-based digital library are other fruitful research areas in WI. Topics in this area include semantics model of the Web, text mining, and automatic construction of citation.

Web-based intelligent agents are aimed at improving a website or providing help to a user. We think that web agents will be a very vital issue. The Web itself has been studied from two aspects, the structure of the Web as a graph and the semantics of the Web. Studies on web structures investigate several structural properties of graphs arising from the Web, including the graph of hyperlinks, and the graph induced by connections between distributed search servants. The study of the Web as a graph is not only appealing in its own right, but also harvests valuable insight into web algorithms for crawling, searching, and community discovery, and the sociological phenomena that characterize its evolution. Studies of the semantics of the Web were initiated by Tim Berners-Lee, the creator of the WWW. The semantic web requires interoperability standards that address not only the syntactic form of documents but also the semantic content. A semantic web also lets agents utilize all the data on all web pages, allowing it to gain knowledge from one site and apply it to logical mappings on other sites for ontology-based web retrieval and e-business intelligence. Ontologies and agent technology can play a crucial role in enabling such web-based knowledge processing, sharing, and reuse between applications.

Exercises

4.1   Give your definition for a term "WI," with justification.
4.2   Discuss how e-commerce impacts on your daily life as an individual consumer. Is the overall impact on you positive or negative? Why?
4.3   Discuss the benefits of using intelligent shopping agents and their relative disadvantages.
4.4   What is wisdom web? Is it the same as wisdom of crowd?
4.5   Explore in detail the use of semantics in building an intelligent web.

References

Bart, J., Brown, M., Fukui, K., and Trivedi, N. 2005. Introduction to grid computing. http://www.redbooks.ibm.com/redbooks/pdfs/sg246778.pdf (accessed on September 14, 2011).

Berners-Lee, T., Hendler, J., and Lassila, O. 2001. Semantic web, a new form of Web content that is meaningful to computers will unleash a revolution of new possibilities. *Scientific American* 284:34–43.

Chakrabarti, S., Dom, B., Kumar, R., Raghavan, P., Rajagopalan, S., Tomkins, A., Gibson, D., and Kleinberg, J. 1999. Mining the web's link structure. *Computer* 32(8):60–67.

DeClaris, N., Harman, D., Faloutsos, C., Dumais, S., and Oard, D. 1994. Information filtering and retrieval: Overview, issues and directions. Paper presented at the *International Conference of the IEEE Engineering in Medicine and Biology Society*, Baltimore, MD.

Foley, C., Gurrin, C., Jones, G., Lee, H., McGivney, S., O'Connor, N. E., Sav, S., Smeaton, A. F., and Wilkins, P. 2005. TRECVid 2005 experiments at Dublin City University. Paper presented at the *14th Text REtrieval Conference (TREC'05)*, Gaithersburg, MD.

Gardner, H. 1983. *Frames of Mind: The theory of Multiple Intelligences*. New York: Basic Books.

Han, J. and Chang, K. 2002. Data mining for web intelligence. *Computer* 35(11):64–70.

Jacobs, I. 2004. Architecture of the world wide web. W3C Recommendation. http://www.w3.org/TR/webarch/ (accessed on September 14, 2011).

Liu, J., Zhong, N., Yao, Y., and Zbhigniew, W. 2003. The wisdom web: New challenges for web intelligence (WI). *Journal of Intelligent Information Systems* 20(1):5–9.

Morris, M. R. 2008. A survey of collaborative web search practices. Paper presented at the *Sigchi Conference on Human Factors in Computing Systems (CHI'08)*, New York.

Nishida, T. 2002. Social intelligence design for the web. *Computer* 35(11):37–41.

Pickens, J., Golovchinsky, G., Shah, C., Qvarfordt, P., and Back, M. 2008. Algorithmic mediation for collaborative exploratory search. Paper presented at the *31st Annual International ACM SIGIR Conference on Research and Development in Information Retrieval (SIGIR'08)*, pp. 315–322, New York.

Rich, E. and Knight, K. 1991. *Artificial Intelligence.* New Delhi: Tata McGraw-Hill.
Russell, S. J. and Norvig, P. 2010. *Artificial Intelligence: A Modern Approach.* New Jersey: Pearson Education.
Sajja, P. S. 2007. Knowledge representation using fuzzy XML rules for knowledge-based adviser. *International Journal of Computer, Mathematical Sciences and Applications* 1(2–4):323–330.
Sajja, P. S. 2011. Multiagent knowledge-based system accessing distributed resources on knowledge grid. In *Knowledge Discovery Practices and Emerging Applications of Data Mining: Trends and New Domains*, ed. A. V. Senthil Kumar. Hershey: IGI Global Book Publishing, pp. 244–265.
Thorndike, E. L. 1920. Intelligence and its use. *Harper's Magazine* 140:227–235.
Yao, Y. Y. 2005. Web intelligence: New frontiers of exploration. Invited talk at the *International Conference on Active Media Technology*, Kagawa, Japan.
Yao, Y. Y., Zhong, N., Liu, J., and Ohsuga, S. 2001. Web intelligence (WI), research challenges and trends in the new information age. Paper presented at the *First Asia-Pacific Conference on Web Intelligence*, Maebashi, Japan.
Zadeh, L. A. 2005. Web intelligence, world knowledge and fuzzy logic. In *Soft Computing for Information Processing and Analysis*, eds. M. Nikravesh, L. A. Zadeh, and J. Kacprzyk, Chapter 1. New York: Springer, pp. 1–18.
Zeltser, L. 1995. The world-wide web: Origins and beyond. http://zeltser.com/web-history/#About_WWW (accessed on September 14, 2011).

part two

Information retrieval, mining, and extraction of content from the Web

chapter five

Web information retrieval

5.1 Introduction

Information retrieval (IR), as its name denotes, is a systematic way of searching desired information in a given source. This source list includes a set of documents, a database, or a network environment like the Web. The term *IR* was coined by Mooers (1950). The meaning of the IR is very broad and includes wide applications starting from basic procedures such as finding a person by scanning through a document like a business card to a complex procedure such as collecting information from distributed databases on the Web. The IR has become a routine procedure from a common person to a spectacular field expert in order to carry out their business transactions. The IR becomes easy when the source follows homogeneous formats and structured environment from a small heap of content. High volume of the content and low degree of structuredness increases the complexity and difficulty in IR. The IR can be divided into three broad categories: (i) web search, which only searches documents from a really big source on web; (ii) searching and presenting documents from intranet; and (iii) personal domain-specific retrieval that considers searching from a given source, filters information, and presents the same effectively.

The process of IR, regardless of its categories, is divided into three main phases, namely (i) search, (ii) selection, and (iii) presentation of collected information. For efficient IR, these three basic components must be strengthened. Search is defined as an activity to look/locate for something. Many times the search is considered as an IR.

Searches on local repositories of documents containing databases, files, and other documents use traditional search algorithms like simple sequential search, quick search, index search, and binary search from sorted or unsorted files. Obviously, sorting makes searching more efficient as it provides clustering of the search space into multiple and easy to manage partitions to narrow the search domain. Using the facility like Unix's grepping command "grep", a word or an entity can be found through the traditional algorithms and techniques. Unlike traditional sources, to search from knowledge base (which is a repository of acquired knowledge), a special utility called inference engine is provided. The inference engine is a software program that infers new knowledge from the existing chunks of the knowledge available in the knowledge base, and it is also enriched with the searching strategy to search within the knowledge base.

To search from large distributed environment like the Web, a simple search becomes inefficient as it needs to process large amount of content quickly from a really big repository. Another demand is flexibility for searching on such platform. Additionally, the typical techniques may not allow relevant and/or rank-based retrieval of the content. Other issues are described below.

5.1.1 Managing web data

Another important issue related to the Web data is that search engines need to store and manage. Document identifiers are usually assigned randomly or in some order with which uniform resource locators (URLs) are crawled. Numerical identifiers are used to represent

URLs in different data structures. In addition to inverted lists, they are also used to number nodes in web graphs and to identify documents in search engines' repositories. A precise ordering of documents leads to an assignment of identifiers from which both index and web graph storing methods can benefit.

Thirty billion URLs require at least 1 TB of storage to hold all the metadata on the corresponding web pages, using a compressed format. Managing this amount of information effectively implies an extremely fast and space-efficient database, which consecutively implies in the availability of an efficient file system. Google's BigTable is possibly the best example of a type of database personification at the Web scale. BigTable is currently used to store data in a distributed system, which is usually generated and modified using the Map-Reduce paradigm. As a database, BigTable shares characteristics of both row-oriented and column-oriented databases. Every table has multiple dimensions, the values are kept in a compacted form, and it is optimized to the underlying file system, which is the Google file system (GFS).

HBase is an open source distributed database written in Java. HBase runs on top of the Hadoop distributed file system (HDFS). HBase provides BigTable-like capabilities to Hadoop,* the open source version of Map-Reduce. HBase is column-oriented and features compression, in-memory operations, and Bloom filters.

How to deal with duplicate data is another major concern. To detect multiple URLs, those represent exactly the same page and would add redundant and noisy information if they were displayed (e.g., mirrors). Furthermore, to detect multiple URLs that point to partially duplicated contents, partial reduplication can be used to improve ranking and spam detection. Spotting duplicates too reduces the size of the collection that needs to be searched. Defining a duplicate page is not obvious. To illustrate, two pages that contain the same text but differ on their hypertext markup language (HTML) formatting [or cascade style sheet (CSS)] have distinct layouts. Thus, they will not be considered as duplicates if we require that all the contents be the same in duplicated pages. Indeed, most mirroring systems implement similar requirements.

Near duplicates are more complex to handle. An example of a near duplicate can be a mirror page, which differs only by a date change or a footnote that was automatically added; neither of which would be detected using hashing. One method to identify near duplicates is to use the cosine distance as the similarity measure.

Web graph compression is another key problem. Web graphs may be represented using adjacency lists. They are basically lists that contain, for each vertex v of the graph, the list of vertexes straight by reachable from v. It has been observed that almost 80% of all links are local, which means that they point to pages of the same site. Therefore, it is apparent that assigning closer identifiers to URLs referring to the same site will result in adjacency lists that will contain very close IDs. Representing these lists using a d-gapped representation will thus lead to d-gapped adjacency lists having long runs of 1's.

Exploiting such redundancies of the Web graph makes it possible to reach extremely high compression rates. The intention of web graph compression schemes is not only to offer empirical concise data structures but also to allow fast access, as the graph will be needed for link analysis and related applications.

5.1.2 Context and web IR

Although a web search engine returns search results, which expand utility across all the users who submit their query, a few individuals may be inadequately served. For instance,

---

* http://hadoop.apache.org/

those searching for information on a "George Bush" other than the "former U.S. president." *Contextualization* of search results can be applied by web search engines to focus on this kind of situation. Major search engines usually detect the country from which each search originates (based on IP address) and use the information to

- Set the language of the interface
- Present advertising appropriate for the local promotion
- Recommend spelling suggestions proper to the language
- Bias search results toward sites operating in that country

In each case, the search interface assumes that the searcher communicates in the major language of that country and is most interested in advertisements targeting that market. This is called *localization*.

Personalization of search attempts to provide search results tailored for an individual rather than a realm. A search engine can keep track of a user's interactions (e.g., the queries they issued and the results they clicked on) using cookies and search logs and can potentially use these data to disambiguate or expand queries based on inferred interests or preferences. Nevertheless, much of the research on web search personalization assumes that the personalization context is deduced at the client side and is communicated to the search engine in the form of an expanded or transformed query. Personalization at the client side means that all of a person's local electronic information (e.g., documents, emails, and web pages downloaded) as well as a full record of their web interactions can be mined for personalization context. Personalization and localization can make things worse if faulty assumptions are made about the searcher's preferences or tasks. A decent search engine will allow searchers to override automated personalization and localization.

5.2   Typical web search engines

Search engines on web are the sites enriched with facility to search the content stored on other sites. There is difference in the way various search engines work, but they all perform three basic tasks:

1. Finding and selecting full or partial content based on the keywords provided
2. Maintaining index of the content and references to the location they find
3. Allowing users to look for words or combinations of words found in that index

An IR process begins when a user enters a query (statement) into the system through the interface provided. It is obvious that the result of search matches with plenty of content and a lot of matched content is presented to the users. Many search techniques extend this mechanism by ranking the content according to relevance to the query. Similarly, the content found by the search mechanism may not be stored directly but represented through reference or metadata associated with it (Figure 5.1).

Due to exponential increase in size of web, the search mechanism needs to handle millions of index pages. Earlier, the search mechanism had to deal with an index of only a few hundred thousand pages and documents, and enquiries received per day were 1000–2000. Today, this number increases from a few hundred thousand to millions of index pages.

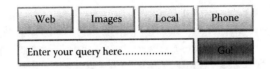

Figure 5.1 Typical interface for searching.

5.2.1   Introduction to web crawler

Historically, programs like "Gopher," "Veronica," and "Archie" have kept indexes of files stored on Internet. After emergence of the Web on the Internet platform, most of the search mechanism was generally applicable to the Web. To find the locations that hold the required content, which matches the user's query, a search engine is required to visit plenty of pages. For this purpose, the search mechanism employs special software robots, called spiders or crawlers. In their infancy, such programs were also called as wanderers, robots, spiders, fish, and worms, which retrieve web content (pages) and add them or their representations to a local repository. These crawlers/spiders built list of the words found on websites. The process of building list by such automatic process is known as crawling. The first real search engine Wanderer, in the form that we know search engines today, was developed by Matthew Gray in 1993. He initially wanted to measure the growth of the Web and created this program to count active web servers. He soon upgraded the program to capture actual URLs.

In order to build and maintain a useful list of words, a search engine's spiders have to search a lot of pages. The spider may start its search from the predefined list of locations/ sites, which are very popular, frequently used, and renown. The spider begins its search from a given location/site and follows every link of the sites given within the main site. The spider automatically shifts to the next specified sites in the list once the whole site/ location is traversed. During this process, building the list of words with its reference continues. The process repeats till a sufficient number of pages are identified. Behind this simple procedure, there are many hidden complications, which are transparent form users. To name a few, network connectivity, spider traps, canonicalizing URLs, parsing HTML pages, authenticity, and the ethics of dealing with remote web servers are common causes, which increase the complexity. According to Brin and Page (1998), the current generation web crawler can be one of the most sophisticated yet fragile parts of the application in which it is embedded. The typical abstracted process of a crawler is shown in Figure 5.2.

Once the crawler completes its job, that is, a snapshot of the Web content is taken and stored locally; conceptually, there is no need to go for further crawling. However, the Web is an ever-evolving dynamic entity and new content is uploaded with a high rate. Hence,

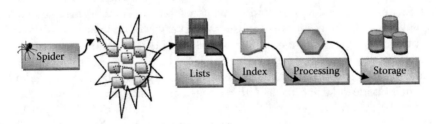

Figure 5.2 Web crawler process.

it becomes necessary to repeat the crawling procedure frequently. In order to achieve flexibility, a crawler needs to be exhaustive and generic to fulfill all search needs.

In general, a web crawler/spider should exhibit characteristics such as

- Efficiency to search required content from web with proper use of resources like memory and time
- Robustness to handle dynamic pages and spider traps like cycles
- Extensibility as the number of machines as well as representation style (like extensible markup language [XML]) is always increasing on the Web
- Frequency and continuity to handle new content
- Quality to search the most useful and relevant pages, etc.

5.2.2   Some early work in the area of web crawlers

Some early work in the area of web crawlers can be short-listed as follows (Wall 2010):

- *Archie*: The first search engine created in 1990 by Alan Emtage, a student at McGill University in Montreal, was Archie* ("archives," which was shortened to Archie). It was a kind of a database of web filenames, which it would match with the users' queries.
- *Veronica and Jughead*: Veronica[†] was developed by the System Computing Services Group at the University of Nevada in 1993. Veronica served the same purpose as Archie, but it worked on plain text files. Another user interface name Jughead appeared with the same purpose as Veronica soon. Both were using files sent via Gopher, which was created as an Archie alternative by Mark McCahill at the University of Minnesota in 1991.
- *File transfer protocol*: File transfer protocol (FTP) is a standard network protocol used to copy a file from one host to another over a transmission control protocol (TCP)-/IP-based network, such as the Internet. FTP is built on a client–server architecture and utilizes separate control and data connections between the client and server. FTP is used with user-based password authentication or with anonymous user access.
- *World Wide Web Wanderer*: As stated earlier, in June 1993, Matthew Gray introduced the World Wide Web Wanderer with an initial goal to measure the growth of the Web and then succeed to capture actual URLs.
- *ALIWEB*: In 1994, Martijn Koster presented Archie-like indexing of the Web (ALIWEB), which allowed users to submit the locations of index files on their sites, which enabled the search engine to include web pages and add user-written page descriptions and keywords. However, it was less user-friendly and many people did not know how to submit their site (Wall 2010).
- *Robots exclusion standard*: Martijn Koster also contributed standards for how search engines should index or should not index content. This allows webmasters to block bots from their site on a whole site level or page-by-page basis.
- *Primitive web search*: Programs like JumpStation, the World Wide Web (WWW) Worm, and the repository-based software engineering (RBSE) spider were introduced. JumpStation gathered information about the title and header from web pages and retrieved these using a simple linear search. The WWW Worm indexed titles

---

* http://archie.icm.edu.pl/archie-adv_eng.html
† http://www.encyclo.co.uk/define/Veronica

and URLs. Both the JumpStation and the WWW Worm were not ordering their listed results. However, the RBSE spider did implement a ranking system.

- *Excite*: Excite was the side product of the project Architext, which was started by six Stanford undergraduate students in February 1993. Excite utilized statistical methods for efficient searching.
- *EINet Galaxy web directory*: The EINet Galaxy web directory was built in January 1994. It was organized similar to how web directories are today. The biggest reason the EINet Galaxy became a success was that it also contained Gopher and Telnet search features in addition to its web search feature.
- *Yahoo*: Yahoo was conceived by David Filo and Jerry Yang as a collection of some web pages in April 1994. As their number of links grew, they had to reorganize and become a searchable directory. Unlike other programs listed earlier, along with each URL, a description is provided.
- *WebCrawler*: Brian Pinkerton of the University of Washington released the WebCrawler on April 20, 1994. It was the first crawler, which indexed entire pages. Soon it became so popular that during daytime hours it could not be used. America online (AOL) and Excite eventually purchased WebCrawler and ran it on their network.
- *Lycos*: Lycos was designed at the Carnegie Mellon University by Michael Mauldin. On July 20, 1994, Lycos went public with a catalog of 54,000 documents. In addition to providing ranked relevance retrieval, Lycos provided prefix matching and word proximity bonuses. Lycos, Tripod, Angelfire, HotBot, Gamesville, WhoWhere, and Lycos Mail are different integrated sites help individual users to retrieve, manage, consume, and create information tailored to meet users' need. Spiders from system like Lycos keep track of the words in the title, subheadings, and links, along with the 100 most frequently used words on the page and each word in the first 20 lines of text.
- *AltaVista*: AltaVista, which means "a view from above," was designed and developed by a team of experts at Digital Equipment Corporation's Research lab in Palo Alto, CA, in 1995. It shows a way to store every word of each HTML page on the Internet in a fast and searchable index. This led to AltaVista's development of the first searchable, full-text database on the World Wide Web. It has offered first-ever multilingual search capability on the Internet and the first search technology to support Chinese, Japanese, and Korean languages. The Web's first Internet machine translation (MT) service *Babel Fish* that can translate words, phrases, or entire websites to and from English, Spanish, French, German, Portuguese, Italian, and Russian was introduced by AltaVista.
- *HotBot from Inktomi*: The Inktomi Corporation came on May 20, 1996, with its search engine Hotbot as a service of an electronic magazine called *Wired* magazine. It was launched using a "new links" strategy of marketing, claiming to update its search database more often than its competitors. It also offered free web page hosting for short duration. It was one of the first search engines to offer the ability to search within search result. HotBot provides easy access to the Web's three major crawler-based search engines: Yahoo, Google, and Teoma.
- *LookSmart*: LookSmart was founded in 1997 and claimed to be the first consumer-facing search sites, utilizing a directory model. Their main business focus is to serve advertisers via a syndicated network. To do this job efficiently, they optimize traffic from other people's published sites and networks to the benefit of the advertisers.
- *Ask or Ask Jeeves*: Ask Jeeves was launched as a natural language search engine in April 1997. Ask Jeeves used human editors to try to match search queries. Earlier, the Ask Jeeves assigned rank to the results based on their popularity, and then it

switched over to the usage of clustering to organize sites by subject-specific popularity. In 2001, Ask Jeeves bought Teoma to replace the DirectHit search technology. In
2006, Ask Jeeves was renamed to Ask, and they killed the separate Teoma brand.
- *Google*: In 1998, Google was launched. It decided to rank pages using an important
  concept of implied value due to inbound links. This makes the Web somewhat demo-
  cratic as each of going link is a vote. Google has become so popular that major portals
  such as AOL and Yahoo have used Google. Eventually, it leads to the development of
  Google Advertising Professional program and Google Scholar search program. On
  January 21, 2005, Google opened up a free cross-platform ad tracking system. Section
  5.2.3 discusses the Google search process in detail.

5.2.3   Google searching

Larry Page and Sergey Brin started Google* with the goal to develop an efficient search
engine that gives users relevant links in response to search requests. Today, Google is one
of the most visited sites on the Web. Besides search engine, Google also provide facilities
like mail, social networking, and video content sharing. Google first acquires the keyword
from the user's query and searches the pages that contain these words. It then assigns
a rank to each page searched and stores the content into the search engine result page
(SERP). The rank is generally given according to the frequency of the keyword within the
content. The content with higher count appears early in the presentation. Google has taken
patent for its page rank technique. The major components of the techniques can be given
as follows:

- Searching the keywords within the content, including heading
- Assignment of rank to the page according to the count of given keyword appears
  within the content as well as number of other links that points to the target page.
  Google is counting each additional link referring the target page as vote. Votes from
  a higher ranked page value more than the votes from a lower ranked pages. Again
  more outgoing links dilute the rank of the page
- Finding relative importance of words present within the title, subtitles, metadata,
  and other positions for rank assigning procedure. Here, metatags or metadata allows
  the owner of the page to specify keywords and concepts under which the page will
  be indexed. To avoid careless and wrong (misfit) metadata, spider may take additional burden to correlate the metadata, with the page content
- Building an index of every significant word on a page

5.3   Architecture of a web crawler

The architecture of a typical web crawler includes components like domain name system (DNS) resolver, fetch and parse functionalities, URL filter, duplicate URL management utility, robot templates, and URL frontier. The process of conversion of IP address
that uniquely identifies a machine from a given URL is known as DNS resolution or DNS
lookup. The URL frontier consists of list of URLs required to be fetched. The operation
of fetching is done with the help of queuing using different priorities. A URL frontier
manages URLs and returns this list to the crawler. The URL list is finalized based on the

---

* http://computer.howstuffworks.com/internet/basics/google.htm

quality of the URL content and frequency of the update. That is, the frontier decides the priority of the page to be returned to the main thread of the crawling process by measuring quality and content change rate. The frontier should also consider the time difference between successive requests for content to the same host. One may insert a fixed time gap through timer thread to introduce sufficient gap between requests. This job can be managed efficiently by queuing with priority.

The fetch module retrieves content from web using typical hypertext transfer protocol (HTTP) protocol into buffer. This buffer is generally identified as a RewindInputStream (RIS). The content is stored temporarily for preprocessing. DNS resolver utility helps in determining the location of the web server from which the content is to be retrieved. Parsing module is used to extract links and text.

All the extracted links are converted into absolute URLs and run through the URL filter. Link information and keywords are passed to the indexer after passing tests that verify whether the links should be added to the URL frontier or not. The URL stream is redirected to the host splitter for local crawling process. On need, it can be sent to different peer crawling processes. The streams of URLs flow to duplicate URL eliminator process. Special utility called duplicate URL management helps in avoiding duplication in the retrieved links and contents within the URL frontier. For this purpose, the duplicate URL management utility maintains set of URLs discovered so far, which obviously requires high amount of memory. To check the duplication of the content (mainly web page), simple fingerprint mechanisms like checksum or shingles are performed. Optionally, a cache is added to the duplicate URL management utility (as well as to the host splitter, in case of distributed crawler, discussed later in this chapter). Addition of such cache into the duplicate URL management utility stores incoming URLs in cache instead of memory and saves time to store and merge every URL entry into the buffer. To host, this approach reduces network traffic by discarding incoming duplicate URLs instead of sending them further. When network connectivity is poor, this approach is quite useful. Figure 5.3 shows a typical architecture of a web crawler.

The URL frontier in Figure 5.3 encompasses two major components, namely (i) priority management and (ii) politeness management. To manage priority for the URL frontier, priority management uses queuing technique. The component mainly consists of priority queues that manage quality. Quality can be determined by parameters like frequent

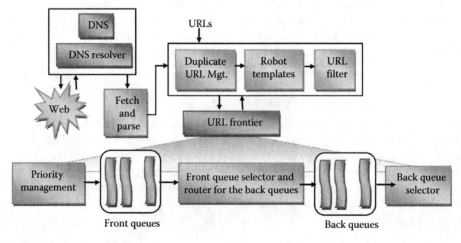

Figure 5.3 Web crawler architecture.

update, services, header data, date of creation, etc. Second component also uses queuing technology to manage time difference to avoid frequent requests to the host. It is obvious that a web crawler should impose a limit on the web server resources to avoid multiple simultaneous downloads. For such a "politeness," it is important to manage time difference.

Conceptually, there may be multiple threads performing such iterative process in simple or distributed environment. URL filter then modifies the list of URL in URL frontier. Some authors would not like spiders to access the temporarily generated (or restricted) content. In this situation, spiders are told through the metatag facility within the content to avoid indexing the document. For this situation, the robot exclusion protocol was developed. This protocol checks the metatags for any such information and tells a spider to leave the location/page without indexing and further following the links available within the content.

Depending on the robot templates and special instructions given by the author of the content, such filtering is done using metatags. See Table 5.1 for an example of such robot.txt file. This robor.txt file may be fetched prior from the Web and kept inside the URL frontier for easy access. Filtering should be done frequently at some predefined interval or at least before adding any URL to frontier.

Table 5.1 Robot Exclusion Protocol

The Robot Exclusion Standard is also known as the Robots Exclusion Protocol or robots.txt. This protocol prevents web spiders and other programs (robots) from accessing all or part of the website, which is published on web

The robot.txt file must be placed at the root of the website hierarchy. The example of such text file is given as follows:
   User-agent: *
   Disallow: /

According to the aforementioned robot.txt file, any user agent (mentioned by the wildcard character "*") is not allowed to consider the content for indexing

To specify limited access, one may mention specific directories/reference as follows:
   User-agent: *
   Disallow: /cgi-bin/
   Disallow: /images/
   Disallow: /tmp/
   Disallow: /private/

The aforementioned file does not allow the spider or any robots to access the specified directories

Similarly, to avoid specified crawler to index the content, one may write
   User-agent: user_def_bot #
   Disallow: /private/

The user defined robot or crawler cannot access the content
For websites with multiple subdomains, each domain must have its version of the robots.txt file. If *sample.com* has a robots.txt file but *first.sample.com* does not, the *first.sample.com* will be indexed.

Also many major crawlers support a little bit delay to wait between successive requests to the same server. For this purpose, the following instructions are included within the *robot.txt* file as follows:
   User-agent: *
   Crawl-delay: 10

To implement a simple web crawler, following steps can be performed:

Step 1 Start interaction with user and seek keywords and URL to start with
Step 2 Add the URL to list to search for
Step 3 Repeat while list is not empty
    Step 3.1 Consider the first URL and mark with appropriate flag
    Step 3.2 If the protocol of the selected URL is not HTTP, then break
    Step 3.3 Follow the robot.txt file, if any
    Step 3.4 Open the URL
    Step 3.5 If the URL is not an HTML file, then break else add the file into list of files found
    Step 3.6 Extract links by traversing the file
    Step 3.7 Repeat this procedure for every link within the file

While implementing crawler, it is to be remembered that both the network connectivity and users' time are precious. Hence, it is necessary that the implemented crawler work with efficiency. That is, the crawler must carefully choose the next page to visit. For efficient behavior of a crawler, an algorithm needs to decide, which page is to be downloaded, strategy for revisiting and load of website. To avoid frequently updated pages or visiting often such (frequently updated) pages may be a good strategy to revisit web content. Above all, the crawler must manage the cost recourse like network resources, server overload, and multiple usage of the crawler. To some extent, the robot.txt file (discussed earlier) solves the problem.

5.4   Distributed crawling

The crawling may be distributed within several machines on the Web. The process of crawling operation can be performed by several dedicated threads in parallel. Such parallel crawling can be distributed over nodes of a distributed system with the host splitter that manages list of URLs to the corresponding crawling node. Hashing technique is used for dividing and redirecting a list of URLs (from URL filter) that physically fall to the nearest host. However, it is difficult to find such location reference from the URLs. The special utility called host splitter dispatches each URL to a crawler thread on distributed platform. This distributed approach is shown in Figure 5.4. One has to manage redundancy of content appearing under different names and URLs and frequent update of the content.

5.5   Focused spiders/crawlers

As stated earlier, the typical crawlers are somewhat blind and carry out exhaustive searches frequently in order to serve multipurpose search queries. However, crawlers can be selective about the pages they fetch and are then referred to as *preferential* or heuristic-based crawlers (Cho et al.1998). That is, a crawler can focus on the Web area where only "relevant" and "required" content is available. These features make the crawler procedure customized and hence such crawlers are known as customized or focused crawlers. Content retrieval from web can be customized in order to get "required" (relevant) web pages on a given topic in traversing the Web. There are mainly two parameters that affect working of such focused crawlers: (i) relevance and (ii) quality or depth. Both these parameters allow a crawler to consider required content even if the content falls in low-rank category by the typical ranking procedure. Different preferential functions and/or

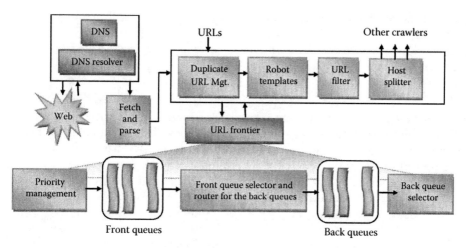

Figure 5.4 Distributed web crawler architecture.

heuristics are used to determine the relevance and quality of the content explored. Hence, other names of such crawlers are topical crawlers, preferential crawlers, or heuristic crawlers. All these crawlers are dedicated to search relevant and quality content from the Web. The resulting local repository (search database) contains maximum homogeneously semantic content.

In spite of the development of an efficient crawler, the whole web cannot be explored within a short duration as most of the crawlers try to cater every possible (and general) content that matches the keyword provided by the searcher. However, the keyword queries cannot naturally locate resources relevant to specific topics. Multiple crawling and crawling on indexes again are infeasible approaches in terms of effort and time. Furthermore, the crawlers may not be refreshed frequently. The basic functionalities of a crawler like seeking, acquiring, indexing, and maintaining can become more efficient if the crawler has to explore relatively less for specific area only. This leads to the development of customized crawlers that crawl the Web for the specific content only. Figure 5.5 demonstrates the scope of a typical focused crawler in comparison with the typical crawler. The focused crawler may continuously keep an eye for a change within selected web pages coming under its focus.

Focused crawling, proposed by Chakrabarti et al. (1999), is designed to narrow the acquisition to web segments that represent a specific topic. Arasu et al. (2001) proposed their own focused experimental search engine named testbed. Pant and Menczer (2002) introduced a

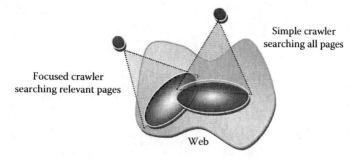

Figure 5.5 Scope of focused crawler.

web tool called MySpiders, which implements an evolutionary algorithm managing a population of adaptive crawlers who browse the Web autonomously. Tao et al. (2006) introduced a novel framework of focused crawling with a relevance matrix and rank calculation.

5.5.1   Architecture of the focused crawler

To accomplish its job, a crawler needs typical URL management having URL list, URL filter, frontier, and duplicate management functionalities. Robot templates for necessary customization to guide crawling process are also required. All these URL-related functionalities are grouped into a layer called URL management. Every customized crawler needs to focus on a specified narrow area instead of the whole web. For this purpose, the crawler is supported and guided by classification functionality, known as classifier. This classifier functionality helps in learning reliance and quality of the content. To learn the quality of content, it is needed to enrich the crawler with the example taxonomies and classifier needs to be trained with the example taxonomy. For any focused crawler, it is necessary to maintain harvest rate, which is defined as the maximum content/pages that are really of good quality and relevant with the users' need. All these functionalities are grouped into crawling layer. Similarly, an interface layer encompasses searching, browsing, third-party services, and local documents including users' profiles. These layers are shown in the architecture demonstrated in Figure 5.6.

5.5.2   Operational phases for the focused crawler

With the assumption that the classifier is pertained with a canonical taxonomy (such as Yahoo, The Open Directory Project, The Virtual Library, or The Mining Co.) and a corresponding set of examples; following main steps can be carried out.

Step 1 The user collects URLs that are examples of his interest. These are considered as seed URLs and submitted to the system, specifically to the Crawler frontier. This phase is known as collection of examples.

Step 2 The system proposes the most common classes where the examples fit best. The user may choose and mark some of these classes as *good* if taxonomy is clear and not too coarse for classification. This phase is known as taxonomy selection and refinement.

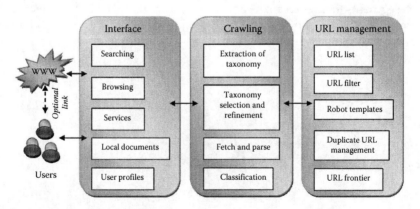

Figure 5.6 Focused crawler architecture.

Step 3 The system may provide additional URLs in a small neighborhood of the examples by considering depth and threshold (that determines the content is on *topic* by
using some methods like centroid). The user may inspect these examples, if needed.
Classification and extraction of content is done here. This phase is known as interactive exploration and classification.

Step 4 Appropriate content is fetched from the link provided by the frontier. Again, there
is a need to check the relevance of the new content and process may be continued.

Users may wish to inspect the system at specified time interval. Users may want to provide
their feedback by marking the useful content provided by the crawler.

5.5.3   Measuring relevance of the focused crawlers

As stated earlier, relevance of the content is determined using the depth and threshold
value. The classifier tree contains different categories as nodes say c. Relevant function
c returns a true value to indicate the given category is relevant to the topic provided.
For any content d, which is directly linked to the good and relevant category c, d is also
good and relevant. Chakrabarti et al. (1999) defined the following function to measure
the relevance:

$$P[c|d] = P\big[\text{parent}(c)|d\big].P\big[c|d.\text{parent}(c)\big] \tag{5.1}$$

Using the Bayes rule, it can be derived that

$$P\big[c|d,\text{parent}(c)\big] = P[c|\text{parent}(c)]P\big[d|c\big]/\sum P\big[d|c'\big] \tag{5.2}$$

$$C':\text{parent}(c') = \text{parent}(c),$$

where the sum ranges over all siblings c' of c.

Furthermore, two modes of focusing are possible with the classifier, namely, hard
focus rule and soft focus rule (Chakrabarti et al. 1999). According to the hard focus rule,
while fetching a document d, the aforementioned formulation is used to find the leaf node
c^* with the highest probability. If some ancestor of c^* has been marked *good,* then the future
visits of URLs found on d is *allowed*; otherwise, the crawler is pruned at d. According to soft
focus rule, it is believed that the priority of visiting each neighbor of the current page d is
the relevance of d. Its score is updated when a neighbor actually visits.

5.6   Collaborative crawling

Crawling can be done in collaborative fashion to support a number of users simultaneously browsing the Web through proxy servers. The focused crawling assumes narrow
domain topical localities on the Web. There may be multiple crawlers each focusing on
different areas of the Web. These crawlers can work in parallel and distributed fashion
in order to explore different topical localities of web. A collaborative focused crawler
with a controlling metacrawler is proposed by Jung (2009) on semantic web can be considered as an example of the same. There is another category of crawlers in which the
crawling process is enhanced by artificial intelligence (AI) techniques. These intelligent

crawlers consider arbitrary queries and keywords, their combinations, and constraints on meta-information about the Web content for flexible and efficient crawling. The focused, distributed, and intelligent crawlers use link information in order to find the content. According to Aggarwal (2002), the collaborative crawling can be considered as an intelligent process, which identifies the importance of different users during the simultaneous crawling process in order to bias the crawl toward those web pages, which are most likely to belong to the predicate provided as keyword or queries. Here, crawler is implemented as an iterative search process, which manages the set of web pages and corresponding priorities calculated with statistical measures and heuristics like intellectual distance from the keyword/predicate assigned by the user. When crawler assesses a page, corresponding priority is modified by the process. Such multiple processes execute together and collaboratively update their web page sets along with corresponding priorities.

5.7   Some tools and open source for web crawling

- Heritrix* is the Internet Archive's open-source, extensible, web scale, archival-quality web crawler project.
- WebSPHINX† (website-specific processors for HTML INformation eXtraction) is a Java class library and interactive development environment for web crawlers that automatically browse and process web pages.
- A highly configurable and customizable web spider engine JSpider,‡ Developed under the Lesser General Public License (LGPL) Open Source license using pure Java.
- Web-Harvest§ is an open source web data extraction tool written in Java. It offers a way to collect desired web pages and extract useful data from them. In order to do that, it leverages well-established techniques and technologies for text/xml manipulation such as extensible style sheet language transformations (XSLT), XQuery, and Regular Expressions. Web-Harvest mainly focuses on HTML/XML-based websites, which still make vast majority of the Web content. On the other hand, it could be easily supplemented by custom Java libraries in order to augment its extraction capabilities.
- WebEater,¶ which is a pure Java program for website retrieval and offline viewing.
- Bixo** is an open source web mining toolkit that runs as a series of cascading pipes on top of Hadoop. By building a customized cascading pipe assembly, you can quickly create specialized web mining applications that are optimized for a particular use case.
- Java Web Crawler†† is a simple web crawling utility written in Java. It supports the robots exclusion standard.
- WebLech‡‡ is a fully featured website download/mirror tool in Java, which supports many features required to download websites and emulate standard web browser behavior as much as possible. WebLech is multithreaded and will feature a graphical user interface (GUI) console.

---

* http://crawler.archive.org/
† http://www-2.cs.cmu.edu/~rcm/websphinx/
‡ http://j-spider.sourceforge.net/
§ http://web-harvest.sourceforge.net/
¶ http://sourceforge.net/projects/webeater
** http://openbixo.org
†† http://java.sun.com/developer/technicalArticles/ThirdParty/WebCrawler/
‡‡ http://weblech.sourceforge.net/

- Arachnid* is a Java-based web spider framework. It includes a simple HTML parser object that parses an input stream containing HTML content. Simple web spiders can be created by inheriting features of Arachnid with additional code after each page of a website is parsed.
- JoBo† is a simple program to download complete websites to your local computer. The main advantage to other download tools is that it can automatically fill out forms (e.g., for automated login) and also use cookies for session handling. In spite of its simple interface, JoBo is enriched with strong internal features. These features include flexible rules to limit download by URL, size, and/or multipurpose Internet mail extension (MIME) type.

5.8   Information retrieval: beyond searching

IR is a science of information finding, acquiring, storing, and utilizing the information for problem solving. IR is also known as information storage and retrieval. Information retrieved from collection of documents, reordered data, log, and history records generated from business transactions is presented in user-friendly way through an IR mechanism. These collections may be available at one place or distributed among several locations. Earlier, IR was considered as an area of information science and library science. However, statistics, linguistic, cognitive psychology, and computer science also claim IR to be a part of them.

According to Singhal (2001), the practice of archiving written information can be traced back to around 3000 BC, when the Sumerians designated special areas to store clay tablets with cuneiform inscriptions. Shakespeare, a well-known author, described seven stages of human life from infancy to senility. According to Lesk (1995), the history of IR parallels such a life and may undergo different stages. During 1890, Hollerith presented an idea to use tabulating machines to analyze U.S. census. After long time, the idea of utilizing computer to search and retrieve data and/or information begun with the legendary article, As We May Think, by Bush (1945). According to Bush, the current rate of progress seems to be finished by 2015 or so, and that time, most research tasks would be performed on screen instead of papers. He also talked about intellectual analysis of content by human being and by machine. The word "IR" was coined by Mooers (1950). Weaver (1955) has explored the possibility of automatic translations and opened up an area of machine translations. Luhn (1957) proposed utilization of words as indexing units for documents and measuring word overlap as a criterion for retrieval. During 1958, an International Conference on Scientific Information held at Washington, DC, considered action of IR systems as a solution to problems identified. Maron and Kuhns (1960) published an article focusing on indexing techniques to be utilized for IR. The Weinberg Report, issued in 1963 and entitled "Science, Government, and Information," was named after Alvin Weinberg articulated crisis of scientific information. Wiley came up with a publication on the subject (Becker and Hayes 1963). During the mid-1960s, scientists like Karen Sparck Jones, Gerard Salton, J.C.R. Licklider, and W. Sammon published meaningful work in the area, and at the same time, the National Library of Medicine develops Medical Literature Analysis and Retrieval System (MEDLARS), first major machine-readable database and batch retrieval system. Massachusetts Institute of Technology (MIT) had also started a project Intrex. During the late 1960s, Lancaster (1968) completed evaluation studies of the MEDLARS system and

---

* http://arachnid.sourceforge.net/
† http://www.matuschek.net/software/jobo/index.html

publishes the first edition of his text on IR. A few online systems such as NLM's AIM-TWX, MEDLINE; Lockheed's Dialog; SDC's ORBIT came into existence. At the same time, Theodor Nelson promoted the concept of hypertext. Jardine and Van Rijsbergen introduced the use of hierarchic clustering for IR in 1971. Three highly influential publications by Gerard Salton fully articulate his vector processing framework and term discrimination model: (i) a theory of indexing, (ii) a theory of term importance in automatic text analysis, and (iii) a vector space model for automatic indexing.

Initial text retrieval systems are comparatively simple and used for "small" corpora of scientific abstracts, law, and business documents. It can be considered as more data retrieval instead of IR. Data retrieval systems consider only keywords and retrieve content with the statistical and regular expression methods. Data retrieval systems just search documents that contain keywords provided by users, which in most of the time do not satisfy the user's requirements. Users are interested in meaningful information about subjects and less interested in only facts and/or data. Data retrieval systems retrieve facts and do not process them. Data retrieval systems deal with well-defined structure and semantics and do not allow an error within the retrieved content. IR systems retrieve documents, which may not necessarily be exactly matching with the keywords. Rather, emphasis is given on the retrieval of documents that are in relevance with the query. That is, an IR system needs to consider the relevance and quality of the retrieved content. For this purpose, it should know its users and semantic of the information. Above this, information may be further processed to present it in a friendly and natural form to increase its effectiveness. It also allows small errors and partial information. That is, an IR system needs to understand the content on repository, filter them according to relevance, and order (rank) for the content presentation.

After the explosion of information on web, automatic IR has become a crucial task. Manually searching such a large repository is practically impossible. For example, to explore the site of youtube* fully, it may take few thousand hours. While doing so, some more videos as a bonus would be uploaded on the site. Eventually, nobody can see full content of the site. One must consider a strategy that automatically explores and goes through the content and extracts only relevant content.

IR system initiates the retrieval process by accepting and formatting the query (keywords) by user and indexing the content on the resources in repetitive fashion. After matching the representation, retrieved documents are presented to the user. The user selects the required results from the content presented. To some extent, keywords that help in distinguishing the relevant content from the irrelevant one, that is, uniquely identifying the content, might help in increasing relevance and quality of the search. The formal steps are given as follows:

- Indexing
- Query formulation
- Matching query representation
- Selection
- Relevance feedback and interactive retrieval

For IR, different models are used. Some of the major models are Boolean retrieval, vector space model, probabilistic model, and latent semantic-based model. Next section introduces these models in brief.

---

* http://youtube.com/

5.9   Models of information retrieval

5.9.1   Boolean model and its variations

The very preliminary model of IR can be considered as exact match using statistical and logical expression. This model is also known as Boolean model of IR. Queries consisting of keywords are fired through a proper interface. Boolean operators like AND, OR, and NOT are applied to retrieve content. This methodology is simple, easy to implement, and enables users to form the structural and conceptual requirements. Obviously, it is very effective for ambiguous and exhaustive problem. However, it may not fit and directly applicable to the way in which human interacts. People normally consider A AND B as more As and less Bs. In Boolean terminology, A's and B's should be coexisting and hence exactly same. That is, the Boolean model treats all the keywords equally with giving them priorities and weights. AND is too rigid (strict) for retrieval in comparison with humans' natural process of retrieval, and OR is too diluted and cannot differentiate content effectively. The Boolean model is somehow blind and finds content that exactly matches the given keywords. Additionally, this model does not provide facility to rank (according to relevance) and arrange the retrieved content. However, modern Boolean approaches can make use of the degree of coordination, field level, and degree of stemming present to rank them (Fox and Koll 1988; Marcus 1991). Fox (1983) proposed to use weights to be given along with the keywords and query terms in normalized fashion (*P*-norm). These normalized weights can be used to rank the documents in the order of decreasing distance from the point $(0, 0, \ldots, 0)$ for an OR query and in the order of increasing distance from the point $(1, 1, \ldots, 1)$ for an AND query. *P* range (from 1 onward) is considered as a coefficient to indicate the degree of strictness of the operator. The *P*-norm uses a distance-based measure and the coefficient *P* determines the degree of exponentiation to be used. This approach requires an extract effort for expression evaluation in order to achieve flexibility. Furthermore, Fox and Sharan (1986) proposed "Mixed Min and Max" model, where the Boolean operators are softened by considering the query–document similarity to be a linear combination of the min and max weights of the documents. The weight of an indexed term is fuzzy (multivalued logic between 0 and 1) and specifies graded membership to the content. That is, the content is totally relevant to the keyword (with value 1) or generally related with the keyword (say with value 0.6). The standard definition of fuzzy intersection and union functions (minimum and maximum) had utilized in this approach.

5.9.2   Vector space model

The vector space model represents the documents and queries as vectors in a space having more than one dimension. Dimensions are defined by the keywords provided by the users (Salton and McGill 1986). The significant terms are identified by constructing an index. A morphological analysis is carried out to reduce different synonyms to a common term. Salton and McGill (1986) have given a special name "Stems." The document that has high occurrence of such stems is more relevant. That is, the content vector and query vector are prepared and compared. Similarity of content vector and query vector implies high degree of relevance. The model is very calculation intensive and slow. It also needs frequent recalculation on a little change in keywords. Furthermore, vector requires access to every content (document) term to calculate the length of query (Lee et al. 1997).

5.9.3   Probabilistic models

An IR system may assign ranks to the retrieved content based on their probability of relevance to the query, given all the evidence like statistical distribution of terms is available (Belkin and Croft 1992). This model considers the fact that there may be uncertainty in the representation of the information need and the documents. Turtle and Croft (1991) used Bayesian inference networks to rank documents by using multiple sources of evidence to compute the conditional probability P (ratio of information need by the content retrieved) that an information need is satisfied by a given document. This model provides opportunity to consider the retrieved content according to some rank based on some probability. It also offers flexibility in comparison with the Boolean model. However, the statistical approaches like probability model have a limited expressive power (Spoerri 1995), and it is required to choose proper keyword as in the Boolean model. Furthermore, a good amount of knowledge is required to estimate needed probabilities.

5.9.4   Latent semantic indexing

The techniques of IR in future can be used in conjunction with the domain semantics. Latent semantic indexing (LSI) considers associations among terms and documents to retrieve required content. LSI adds an important step to the document indexing process. In addition, to consider the existence of the keywords within content, the method examines the document collection as a whole, to see which other documents contain some of those words. In other words, besides matching keywords with content, the model also seeks for the contents that are semantically close. According to this model, the documents that contain many words common among them are semantically close; and the documents that contain very few common words are semantically distant. This is more human oriented and natural way of comparing semantics between two documents. A major advantage of this approach is that queries can retrieve documents even if they do not contain keywords.

5.10   Performance measures in IR

According to the definition, IR quality depends on how efficiently the relevant content is retrieved from given resources. All retrieved documents are not necessarily relevant as shown in Figure 5.7. Hence, it is necessary to recall relevant content from the retrieved one. The measures of recall can be defined as the proportion of relevant items in the entire repository which have been retrieved. Another parameter that measures effectiveness of the IT process is *precision*, which is defined as the proportion of relevant retrieved items. Both the relevance and precision are used to evaluate the overall IR process.

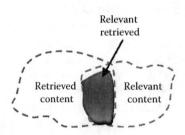

Figure 5.7 Relation between retrieved and relevant content.

The formal definition of the relevance and precision can be given as follows:

Recall = relevant retrieved content / relevant content...........................(1)

Precision = relevant retrieved content/retrieved content....................(2)

Another measure named discriminator is also considered to measure performance of the IR system. This measure identifies the role of irrelevant documents for rejection to evaluate performance of an IR system. The definition of the discriminator measure can be given as follows:

Discrimination = currently rejected irrelevant content/all irrelevant content.........(3)

Fall out can be measured by considering the proportion of nonrelevant content that is retrieved, out of all nonrelevant content available. The fall out can be considered as the probability of retrieving nonrelevant content retrieved by the query. The definition can be given as follows:

Fall out = intersection of nonrelevant and retrieved content / nonrelevant content·····(4)

The aforementioned measures of performance give broad guidelines to evaluate the process of IR. However, it is also to be noted that the judgment regarding relevance is carried out in a mature (genuine) way. Additionally, the reliance must consider the users' context (which also may change during the course of time, while interaction) and need. Above this, web is dynamically increasing and it is really difficult to judge the total number of relevant items for any given information problem.

In spite of the techniques to evaluate the performance of IR, new evaluation techniques are needed that do not considers the accuracy of a retrieval system but also provide emphasis on their interactive abilities and ease of use. A system that measures poorly in recall and precision, but provides good browsing and iterative querying facilities may be more successful and effective.

5.11   Natural language processing in conjunction with IR

Idea of utilizing computers to understand and operate on orders issued through human language is one of the prime expectations since the time of computer invention. In current era for any reference and problem solving in all disciplines, human depends on the Web. Obviously, the Web is expected to understand human language and refers content in a better way. Many language processing tasks are related to the Web, including web question answering, which may be considered as generalization of simple web search. Instead of providing keywords, questions in natural language are fired to the search engine. Some examples of such questions are as follows:

- What does search engine optimization (SEO) mean?
- How many bones are there in a human body?
- Where can the pH indicators be found?

It is important for any search mechanism to understand these questions/request first using a set of theories and a set of technologies. Using the systematic computational techniques that are inspired by linguistic technology for analysis, noise removal, partitioning the request into tokens, and understanding, such natural request can be handled automatically. However, fully understanding of such natural language requires intelligence, and is yet not fully automated. "Human-like language processing" reveals that natural language processing (NLP) is considered a discipline within area such as AI, psychology, and linguistic science. Some methods of question answering or any interface based on natural language use keyword-based techniques to locate required content from the given resources and filter them on need. After then, ranking is optionally based on syntactic criteria like word order and location or based on relevance defined. Some systems may use templates for locating and generating answers of the users' query. Templates are specifically useful for the factual type of questions. These keyword-based methods are also known as shallow methods.

Historically, the MT was the first computer-based application related to natural language. Weaver (1955) started one of the earliest MT projects in on computer translation based on expertise in breaking enemy codes during World War II. Such system used simple dictionary lookup for translation of given words and reordered them according to target output language, without considering lexical ambiguity inherent in natural language. This poor performance was improved slightly when Chomsky (1957) published syntactic structures introducing the idea of generative grammar. This also provided inspiration to the speech recognition research in parallel with the language processing. In the year 1966, Automatic Language Processing Advisory Committee of the National Academy of Science—National Research Council (ALPAC) reported that the MT was not immediately achievable.

Majority of NLP search engines in use today are on publicly searchable websites, that is, web. The most common example of NLP search engine is Ask Jeeves,* which uses a natural language search program to search for the users answer. It identifies the keywords in the given sentence. The search program will then search for those keywords just like any other search engine.

5.11.1   Generic NLP architecture of IR

For utilization of natural language interface along with the Web search, NLP functionalities like preprocessing, grammar handling, tokenizing, parsing, and interpretation mechanism needed to be incorporated with the search mechanism. Query provided by the user is received by the dialog processor and preprocessed first. The dialog will be interpreted by machine, and the formal query is sent to the search mechanism. The retrieved content is sent to the dialog processor and the result is sent to the users. Besides NLP functionalities, the dialog processor is also enriched with the dialog generator, analyzer, domain terminology, context model, and users' profiles. Figure 5.8 abstracts this procedure. One may add plug-ins like application filtering and formatting the search results within this architecture. It would be appreciable if some general purpose and reusable plug-in's library is made available centrally.

Implementation of NLP-based search engine requires an algorithm for searching a set of dictionaries, relationship among the entities (words) within the dictionary. Alternatively, a readymade NLP search engine can be purchased and customized for the dictionary and relationship between dictionary entities.

---

* http://www.ask.com

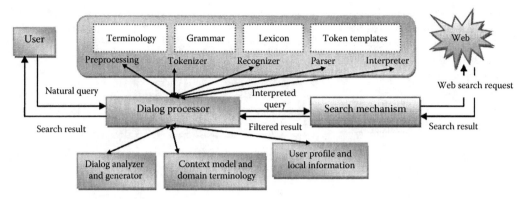

Figure 5.8 Generic NLP architecture.

An algorithm abstract can be given as follows (Bajwa et al. 2009):

Step 1 Reading and tokenizing the dialog provided by user.

Step 2 Analyzing the text to define its structure and transformation of the words. Recognition and interpretation of the terminology are controlled by modules for semantic and pragmatics analysis, which process linguistic knowledge. Local information, user profile, context model, and domain terminology helps in this process.

Step 3 Validation is carried out according to grammatical rules and main parts of the sentence such as verb, noun, action, etc., are identified.

Step 4 Associations are identified and relationships between the parts of sentence are defined.

Step 5 One may use proposition for identifying relationships and associations.

Step 6 After this lexical analysis, recognition and parsing processes are carried out.

Step 7 At last, dialog is generated for presentation, or search process is activated according to need.

5.12 Knowledge-based system for information retrieval

The process of IR mainly concerns with finding relevant documents and determining quality of the documents by giving appropriate rank. The rank to restrict the bulk of information and provide only relevant information can be determined by one or more proper heuristic function(s). Heuristic is nothing but practical application solution offered by field of AI, which does not provide any guarantee of success; however, in most of the cases, it gives good acceptable results. The heuristic for rank determination process may consider attributes like degree of usage, frequency of use, representation media, etc., along with the user's profile. The search strategy might determine the rank dynamically, and information having high rank value is extracted and presented. Minimum acceptable rank along with some infrastructural attributes like memory capacity, communication channel capacity, etc., can be designed to cut off and filter out unnecessary bulk information (Sajja 2008). Figure 5.9 shows the proposed generic model of the heuristic-based IR.

The knowledge base of the architecture shown in Figure 5.9 contains entities like crawling algorithms, general problem solving strategies, and integrated heuristics besides additional utilities. The knowledge base is connected with typical facilities such as inference engine, temporary workspace (if needed), self-learning and explanation, and reasoning

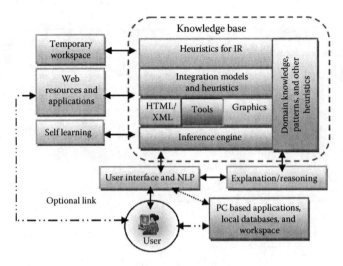

Figure 5.9 Framework of the proposed KBS.

modules. The heuristic functions are also part of the knowledge base. The user interface may be aided with NLP and/or multimedia support facilities for effective usage of the system. The user interface may reside at client machine or may be an independent component. This system must have connections to other information resources reside at the network to work as a gateway. Instead of presenting retrieved information directly, it is filtered by the heuristic functions within the system. Besides these, representation tools (may be in multimedia), XML, HTML, and other tools work with the knowledge base. While passing a query to the Internet (forward direction), the query can undergo a variety of verifications and validation checks to avoid syntactical errors, representation formats, etc. On the client side, the local applications and resource databases are also available for additional computing. In other words, this structure presents advantages of centralization and decentralization at any given point of time in an intelligent fashion. For each WWW page/link, it is assumed that information like the document title (header), summary, set of keywords, set of user profiles, information type (product data, technical publication, news, project data, etc.), universal resource locator (URL), etc., is available, which can be utilized by the system for filtering. Optionally, there may be a direct link available to applications and resources offered by the net. An example frame of a heuristic functions to be used can be given as follows:

All the information extracted from the user's query forms a keywords set I. Let I' be the set of all possible subsets of the elements of I. A heuristic function can be developed from I' to different weight factors between 0 and 1. So, conceptually, the design of such heuristic can be

$$R(i) : I' \rightarrow [0, 1] \text{ for } \forall i \in I,$$

where
    R is a heuristic function giving rank between 0 and 1
    I is the set information retrieved in the environment
    i is a piece of information considered for evaluation, $\forall i \in I$

It is obvious that if the system knows more about user's information needs, it can provide more accurate results for the users' search queries. For this purpose, the knowledge base keeps information about context, which is the description of user's search objective, besides list of keywords and user's profile. All these may be more personalized by interacting with users and may be with predefined set of questions. There should be a temporary workspace for enhanced storage to organize downloaded documents.

To present the filtered information to user, the following list of steps can be considered:

1. Read the query, validate it syntactically, and filter the keywords from the query. This can be aided with a set of predefined questions asked interactively to the user related to the purpose and objective of query. This phase is a preprocessing phase.
2. Parse the query, and information can be extracted from resource scanning.
3. Determine the rank factor with the help of proper heuristic for extracted information. Some interactive questions might be asked to the user at this level to effectively design the rank by considering customized attributes. An alternative approach is to check user's profile. The rank is considered as nonnegative priority number between 0 and 1.
4. Determine the cutoff rank, and check the infrastructural attributes to what extent information would be filtered.
5. Present the filtered information to the user.
6. Evaluate user's satisfaction level (for self-learning) from the responses. If necessary, update user's profile.
7. As it is necessary to respond gradual changes in user's interest, it is required to repeat the aforementioned steps till user's satisfaction, otherwise go to the next step.
8. Evaluate temporary workspace entry for self-learning, other modifications, and update knowledge base.

Figure 5.10 describes aforementioned steps.

Knowledge-based approach for filtering helps in reducing the information overload by excluding repetitive information and presenting the highly needed information instead of bulky presentation of information items. With the help of heuristic functions,

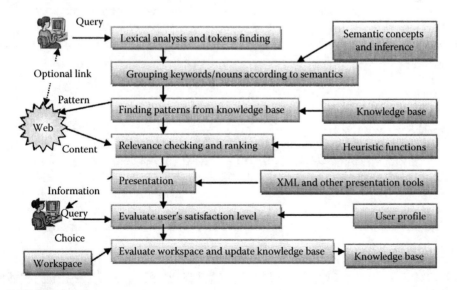

Figure 5.10 Filtering process.

the quality of the system can be increased, time and efforts would be minimized, and system works in a more effective manner. Additionally, the proposed model also offers advantages of knowledge-based system (KBS) like explanation, reasoning, NLP, self-learning, and knowledge management along with intelligent data/IR. For different categories of business, some generalized heuristics can be designed and reused many times. Specific and customized heuristic can also be developed for fine-tuning. The proposed KBS also has an optional link with the network environment to directly receive unfiltered data and hence provides mechanism of comparison. Utilization of information and knowledge gives its utmost benefits when used for real business in effective way. The timely and effective retrieval of information allows automatic resource integration and provides interoperability between heterogeneous systems. At present, still a significant amount of the Web resources are meant to be contributed and consumed by humans only and have usually human-oriented representation. Besides adding semantic to the content/information (as in the semantic web), the knowledge-based retrieval of information becomes important.

The KBS can also be utilized for special user group. That is, for visually challenged users, the output can be filtered out and represented into the voice media. Also, technology should reach out to common people who live in remote and rural areas. With the help of the proposed system, the required information is identified, extracted, ranked, and represented in natural language/translated form to rural people. The KBS capabilities of self-organization and reasoning with incomplete information are essential and useful features for corporate and development-oriented application. As knowledge-based ontology and population grow over time, the knowledge base becomes an increasingly rich and accurate representation of the user's interests. The proposed system has advantages like documentation of domain knowledge, explanation/reasoning, self-learning from the extracted information from the net, inference of knowledge and filtering, and presenting the required knowledge from the distributed environment.

5.13   Research trends

There are many diverse trends in web IR, and each one opens up interesting research problems. What follows is an overview of the upcoming sources of data that should become increasingly available, as well as a compilation of the major trends and challenges to be addressed for better web retrieval.

5.13.1   Semantic information

The key problems with semantic information are standards for metadata that describe the semantics and the quality or degree of trust for a given information source. The W3 Consortium is working extensively on standards, while the second requires authorization schemes that have not been developed yet. Other problems are common issues, namely scaling, rate of change, lack of referential integrity, distributed authority, heterogeneous content and quality, and multiple sources. One of the on-going efforts today is the Open Linking Data initiatives, which tries to add and improve links among semantic resources already available on the Web.

Semantic search engines represent a more recent development. These engines search semantic web data. A more pragmatic approach to semantic search is discussed by Aaberge et al. (2011).

5.13.2   Multimedia data

Multimedia data include images, animations, audio, and video. None of them have unanimously agreed standard formats. Popular formats are GIF, JPG, and PNG for images, MP3 for music, Real Video, or QuickTime for video, etc. The standard way out is to search any sort of data, including text, using the same model and with a single query language.

For a specific data type, we can develop a similarity model, and depending on the type, the query language will change. Examples include query by example for images or query by humming for audio. All this area belongs more to image and signal processing, rather than to IR. Searching for nontextual objects will be an important area of research in the near future.

5.13.3   Opinion retrieval

Social Software applications allow users to create and modify web pages very easily. Such systems enable users to quickly publish content and share it with other users. The success of social systems encouraged millions of users to become members of social networks and led to the creation of a large amount of user-generated content. Users create huge amounts of text in blogs. Many blogs contain personal information; others are dedicated to specific topics. The huge interest in blogs has also led to blog spam. In order to explore searching in blogs, *Text REtrieval Conference* (TREC) initiated a blog track in 2006. A collection was created by crawling well-known blog locations on the Web. More than 3.2 million documents, in this case, blog entries from more than 100,000 blogs were collected (Ounis et al. 2006).

One of the most fascinating and blog-specific issues is the subjective nature of the content. It is very likely to find opinions on topics. Several companies are beginning to exploit blogs by looking for opinions on their products. Consequently, a very natural retrieval task regarding blogs is the retrieval of opinions on a given topic. Typical approaches for opinion retrieval include list-based and machine learning approaches. List-based methods rely on large lists of words of a subjective nature. Their occurrence in a text is seen as an indicator of opinionated writing. Machine learning methods are trained on typically objective texts like online lexical documents and on subjective texts like product review sites. Systems learn to identify texts with opinions based on features like individual words, the number of pronouns, or adjectives.

5.14   Conclusion

The large size and the dynamic nature of the Web highlight the need for continuous support and updating of web-based IR systems. Search facilities like search engine, crawlers, and spiders facilitate the process of IR in different capacities by offering a variety of variation. This chapter introduces background of the domain of IR in context with the latest development and literature survey. Various models of web search facilities such as search engine, crawler, spider, etc., are elaborated in depth by providing detail methodology, architecture with a case of Google search engine. The chapter also highlights the use of AI area called KBS and heuristic filtering functions for the field of IR.

Exercises

5.1   List different ways in which web search is more difficult than traditional IR.
5.2   Select an information need. The information need should require gathering information about a subject from several websites with good information. You should

choose an information need that you think is neither too easy nor too difficult for a search engine. Write a description of your information need that can be used to judge whether any given web search result is relevant or not. Once you have your information need described, write *one query* that you will use on both search engines to capture the information need. The query should have the following properties:

- The query should be constructed to avoid anticipated ambiguity. Use several search terms if necessary.
- Do not use advanced search operations for either search engine.
- Make sure you use the same query for both search engines.

Run your query on each of Google and Bing.

5.3   Write a web crawler that collects the URL of web pages from any domain (say, vestforsk.no). Your crawler will have to perform the following tasks:

a. Start with http://www.vestforsk.no
b. Perform a web traversal using a breadth-first strategy.
c. Keep track of the traversed URLs, making sure they are part of the domain, and they were not already traversed (i.e., avoid duplicates and cycles)
d. Stop when you reach 700 URLs.

5.4   Draw an architecture diagram of a breadth-first web crawler. How could a depth-first crawler work?

5.5   Discuss four magic parameters that Google uses (a magic parameter is a number that needs to be set by Brin & Page—or their underlings).

References

Aaberge, T., Akerkar, R., and Boley, H. 2011. An intensional perspective on the semantic and pragmatic web. *International Journal of Metadata, Semantics and Ontologies* 6(1):74–80.

Aggarwal, C. 2002. Collaborative crawling: Mining user experiences for topical resource discovery. Paper presented at the *8th ACM Knowledge Discovery and Data Mining*, pp. 423–428, Edmonton, Alberta, Canada.

Arasu, A., Cho, J., Garcia-Molina, H., Paepcke, A., and Raghavan, S. 2001. Searching the web. *ACM Transactions on Internet Technology* 1(1):2–43.

Bajwa, I. S., Samad, A., and Mumtaz, S. 2009. Object oriented software modeling using NLP based knowledge extraction. *European Journal of Scientific Research* 35(1):22–33.

Becker, J. and Hayes, R. M. 1963. *Information Storage and Retrieval: Tools, Elements, Theories.* New York: Wiley.

Belkin, N. and Croft, B. 1992. Information filtering and information retrieval: Two sides of the same coin. *Communication of the ACM* 35(12):29–38.

Brin, S. and Page, L. 1998. The anatomy of a large-scale hypertextual web search engine. *Computer Networks and ISDN Systems* 30(1–7):107–117.

Bush, V. 1945. As we may think. *Atlantic Monthly* 176:101–108.

Chakrabarti, S., van-den Berg, M., and Dom, B. 1999. Focused crawling: A new approach to topic-specific web resource discovery. *Computer Networks* 31(11–16):1623–1640.

Cho, J., Garcia-Molina, H., and Page, L. 1998. Efficient crawling through URL ordering. *Computer Networks and ISDN Systems* 30(1–7):161–172.

Chomsky, N. 1957. *Syntactic Structures.* Hague, the Netherlands: Mouton & Co.

Fox, E. and Koll, M. 1988. Partial enhanced Boolean retrieval: Experiments with the SMART and SIRE systems. *Information Processing & Management* 24(3):257–268.

Fox, E. and Sharan, S. 1986. A comparison of two methods for soft Boolean interpretation in informa-tion retrieval. Technical Report TR-86-1, Virginia Technical Department of Computer Science, Blacksburg, VA.

Fox, E. 1983. Extending the Boolean and vector space models of information retrieval with P-norm queries and multiple concept types. PhD dissertation, Cornell University, Ithaca, NY.

Jung, J. J. 2009. Using evolution strategy for cooperative focused crawling on semantic web. *Neural Computing and Applications* 18(3):213–221.

Lancaster, F. W. 1968. *Evaluation of the MEDLARS Demand Search Service*. Bethesda, MD: National Library of Medicine.

Lee, D. L., Chuang, H., and Seamons, K. 1997. Document ranking and the vector-space model. *IEEE Software* 14(2):67–75.

Lesk, M. 1995. The seven ages of information retrieval. http://archive.ifla.org/VI/5/op/udtop5/udtop5.htm (accessed September 05, 2011).

Luhn, H. P. 1957. A statistical approach to mechanized encoding and searching of literary informa-tion. *IBM Journal of Research and Development* 1(4):309–317.

Marcus, R. S. 1991. Computer and human understanding in intelligent retrieval assistance. Paper presented at the *54th American Society for Information Science Meeting*, pp. 49–59, Washington, DC.

Maron, M. E. and Kuhns, J. L. 1960. On relevance, probabilistic indexing and information retrieval. *Journal of the ACM* 7(3):216–244.

Mooers, C. 1950. The theory of digital handling of non-numerical information and its implications to machine economics. Paper presented at the *Meeting of the Association for Computing Machinery*, Rutgers University, Newark, NJ.

Ounis, I., Rijke, M., Macdonald, C., Mishne, G., and Soboroff, I. 2006. Overview of the TREC-2006 Blog Track. Presented at the *15th Text Retrieval Conference*, pp. 17–31, Gaithersburg, MD.

Pant, G. and Menczer, F. 2002. MySpiders: Evolve your own intelligent web crawlers. *Autonomous Agents and Multi-Agent Systems* 5(2):221–229.

Sajja, P. S. 2008. Utilizing information resources by effective information retrieval through knowledge-based filtering, clustering, and presentation. *Sajosps* 8(2):99–101.

Salton, G. and McGill, M. 1986. *Introduction to Modern Information Retrieval*. New York: McGraw-Hill.

Singhal, A. 2001. Modern information retrieval: A brief overview. *IEEE Data Engineering Bulletin* 24(4):35–43.

Spoerri, A. 1995. Infocrystal: A visual tool for information retrieval. PhD dissertation, Massachusetts Institute of Technology, Cambridge, MA.

Tao, P., Fenglin, H., and Wanli, Z. 2006. A new framework for focused web crawling. *Wuhan University Journal of Natural Sciences* 11(5):1394–1397.

Turtle, H. and Croft, B. 1991. Efficient probabilistic inference for text retrieval. Paper presented at the *3rd International Conference on Computer-Assisted Information Retrieval*, pp. 644–661, Paris, France.

Wall, A. 2010. History of search engines: From 1945 to Google today. http://www.searchenginehis tory.com/ (accessed September 5, 2011).

Weaver, W. 1955. Translation. In *Machine Translation of Languages*, eds. W. N. Locke and A. D. Booth. New York: Wiley, pp. 15–27.

chapter six

Web mining

6.1   Introduction to web mining

World Wide Web (WWW or web) facilitates an unlimited access to the ocean of information in almost every aspect of life. The Web also provides platform to store many online libraries, large document repositories, content of various businesses/products, and personal information. The content on the Web is rapidly and exponentially increasing. Due to the size and volume of the Web, it has become increasingly difficult and costly to identify and categorize the relevant pieces of information. To aid the surfing of the Web effectively, utilities like search engine, agent like Softbot, and customized interfaces to the Web are used. These utilities help in finding, sorting, and filtering appropriate information on demand. However, these utilities are limited in scope and cannot help much in effective utilization of the Web. Web mining is the key solution for efficient web access and web component management. The emerging field of web mining aims at finding and extracting relevant information on the Web. Web mining is an automatic discovery of interested information from huge bulk of web components like documents, logs, linkage structures, users' transactions, and web semantics. Web mining is also known as web data mining, screen scraping, web scraping, and data extraction. To access the Web component effectively, various data mining techniques help a lot. The data mining techniques are applied on the Web components instead of applying on the known data sources. That is why the Web mining is referred as application of data mining techniques to the Web. Besides typical data mining techniques, the Web mining utilizes various techniques from fields like information retrieval, statistics, machine learning, NLP, and AI.

The Web mining includes (i) web content mining, which refers to actual data and/or information stored on different locations of the Web. These include every resource on the Web that users can visit fully or partially; (ii) web structure mining, which examines organizations of the content through tags defined in hypertext markup language (HTML), extensible markup language (XML), or resource description framework (RDF); and (iii) web usage/log mining, which describes behavior of the Web users, references of pages and location, browser information, agents mobility, if any, as well as internet protocol (IP)-address-related information. Web mining helps in managing large volume of web content efficiently, finds appropriate content intelligently, and analyzes web usage patterns for future use.

The key objective of web mining is to discover and utilize intelligent tools for information retrieval, which help users in various activities like surfing the Web, finding appropriate information, analyzing, extracting, filtering, evaluating, and presenting the information to the users. The chapter describes history and evolution of the field web mining and presents details about three basic aspects of the Web mining—web content mining, web log mining, and web structure mining.

6.1.1 Web as a graph

We view the Web as a directed graph, where the nodes represent pages, and the directed edges between node pairs represent links between pages. The notation $q \rightarrow p$ denotes that page q links to page p. In this notation, p is an outlink of q and q is an inlink of p. The adjacency matrix A of a graph of n nodes is an $n \times n$ matrix with $A(p, q) = 1$ if and only if $p \rightarrow q$. The number of pages that point to p is the in-degree of p and is denoted indeg(p), and the number of pages that p points to is called its out-degree, denoted by outdeg(p). Visualizing the Web as graph will be helpful for web structure mining. This is further discussed later in this chapter.

6.2 Evolution of web mining techniques

As mentioned in the previous section, the Web mining is a multidisciplinary effort to mine the Web for required and relevant information using techniques from various fields. The data mining techniques are dedicated techniques that extract patterns and useful information from the existing known sources of data. The data mining techniques are a step ahead from querying databases or files and retrieving the information. Instead of just retrieving information, the data mining techniques can observe pattern from the data sources and identify useful information from the sources. Similar mining methods can be applied on text and information chunks, which is thus called information/text mining and information retrieval. Text mining is formally defined as techniques to find, organize, and discover information from the textual resources. The domain/sources of the text mining system may be natural language and unstructured form. The typical data retrieval and mining techniques may not work efficiently for such unstructured resources. The text mining also involves the text preparation in order to apply computational algorithms on the mined text. Enhancing the data and text mining techniques with techniques of other fields and utilizing them for web component access and management is one of the key objectives of the Web mining field. As we know, the Web is huge, diverse, unstructured, and dynamic and thus raises problems of accessing and management. Cope up with automatic accessing and management techniques for the Web have been the prime interests of scientists and researchers. Web mining was started in the early 1990s when people had started taking interest in operations such as browsing history and book marking. Due to low precision/relevance of search results and inability of indexing all information available on the Web (low recall), knowledge extraction becomes a necessity. Above this, personalization and learning of the Web are also desired for many noncomputer professionals in different business support systems. The summary of challenges of mining on the Web is shown in Table 6.1. Because of these limitations, the typical data mining techniques may not be suitable for the Web. Here, web mining can help a lot. Besides only focusing on gaining business information, the Web data mining also supports making the right predictions and decisions for business.

As stated earlier, the Web mining is an application of mainly data mining and intelligent techniques to manage and access different types of web components like documents, logs, linkage structures, users' transactions, and web semantics. The relation between the Web mining along with different related activities for retrieval and mining is presented in Figure 6.1.

Table 6.1 Challenges of Mining the Web

Size	The amount of information on the Web is tremendous
Dynamic	The Web is dynamic and increasing exponentially. Anything can be found on the Web
Coverage	The coverage of the Web information and the geographic scope of the Web are very wide and diverse
Accessibility	Anybody can access and contribute to the Web from any location of the world
Unstructuredness	Different types of data, information, and knowledge exist on the Web. These types include multimedia (voice, text, graph, animation, and sound) in different representation schemes
Nested structure	Web content is represented through different representation schemes in multimedia fashion simultaneously. Furthermore, the Web can be accessed through links (surface web) and through parameterized query interfaces (deep web)
Redundant	The Web contains similar information in different forms by different authors and publishers. This includes same information at multiple locations in different representation schemes
Noise	The Web may retain virus, unwanted harmful data, and mixture of unnecessary garbage. This list includes virus, worms, Trojan, malware, spyware, advertisement (adware), uncensored data, outdated notices, etc. The mining technique must consider eliminating such noise

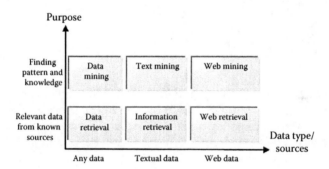

Figure 6.1 Web mining and other related activities.

6.3   Process of web mining

The general process of mining involves activities such as resource finding, information selection from the resources, processing on the resources, and analysis of the extracted knowledge. The Web components like documents, users' transactions, web log, and various repositories are scattered on the Web in distributed and unstructured fashion. The first job of a web mining technique is to find appropriate web components that can act as good resource of the required information. The resource can be any document, newsletter, website, blog, files, databases, etc. The second action is to select and extract information and content from the selected resources. To automatically select the required information from plenty of information is really a complex task that requires a significant effort. After selection, the collected content needs preprocessing. The typical preprocessing includes

Figure 6.2 Generic process of web mining.

deleting repetitive items, streaming, finding particular phrases from the text found, changing representation schemes, etc. Preprocessing of the retrieved content is advisable because real-life data and information are incomplete, inconsistent, and noisy. The standard techniques of the preprocessing are cleaning, transformation, reduction, parsing, and integration. Third job of the Web mining technique is to discover pattern from the extracted and preprocessed content across the Web. This is the phase where the data mining methodology can be utilized. At last, the Web mining technique needs to validate and process discovered pattern and extracted knowledge. During the last two phases, the human control becomes critical and can drastically improve the results. However, the modern web also provides interaction facility to overcome this requirement. The ultimate goal is to eliminate human interference with the help of intelligent techniques. The generic process of web mining is illustrated in Figure 6.2.

Web mining can be done with different objectives. The most common objective is mining the available content on the Web. Some are interested in learning about structure of the Web, usage pattern, and log of the Web. According to these objectives, the Web mining can be divided into three broad categories as follows:

- Web content mining
- Web usage mining
- Web structure mining

The Web content mining attempts to mine content of the Web and discover useful patterns through hyperlinks. In other words, the Web content is the process of extracting useful content from the Web. The content may consist of text, images, audio, video, and structured data like tables and graphs. The Web content mining goes beyond keyword extraction and requires advanced techniques such as NLP and AI. Web content mining strategies are of two groups—one that directly mines the content of documents and second that improves on the content search of other tools like search engines.

Web usage mining highlights the behavior of users on the Web and understands access patterns and trends. The Web usage mining deals with web log and accumulated data on web servers in order to understand the user behavior and the Web structure. There are two main purposes for web usage mining. The first one is to track general access pattern and second is customized usage tracking. The result of web usage mining can be used to restructure sites in a more efficient grouping, pinpoint effective advertising locations, and target users of specific audience. Customized usage tracking analyzes individual trends to customize websites to specific users.

Web structure mining extracts patterns from the links provided on the Web. It mines the structure of a document as well as relationship between categories of such documents and provides useful information about the Web structure beyond the content. This is helpful for publishers, readers, and researchers to develop content that suits the Web platform and directly or indirectly ease the Web content usage and management. Figure 6.3 illustrates the broad categories of web mining.

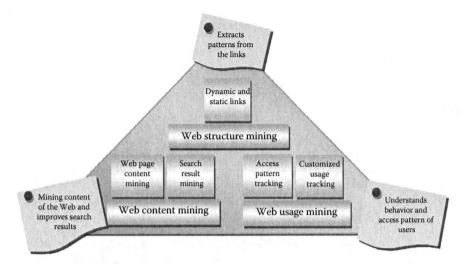

Figure 6.3 Categories of web mining.

6.4   *Web content mining*

The process of web content mining deals with mining useful content from the Web. The process involves mining; extraction; and integration of useful data, information, and knowledge. The process of web content mining utilizes techniques for text mining as most of the data are in text form. However, the content mining has its own unique approach in addition to borrowing techniques from data mining, text mining, NLP, and information retrieval. The Web content mining includes classification, clustering, structured data extraction, knowledge synthesis, information integration and schema matching, opinion mining and template detection, and page segmentation. Topics on web content mining are shown in Table 6.2.

Some of these techniques are discussed in the following sections.

6.4.1   *Classification*

Classification method for web mining is applicable to set of records or web components possessing different sets of attributes. The goal is to classify components into various groups as accurate as possible. The training sets and test (validation) sets are provided to the classification algorithm to build and to test the classification model, respectively. Typical classification techniques include the following:

- Decision tree–based methods
- Rule base classification
- Supervised learning through artificial neural network
- Evolutionary techniques
- Support vector machines, etc.

The classification follows supervised learning approach as the required classes and their definitions are given prior to the classification algorithm. The supervised learning allows us to take advantage of human knowledge about the classification problem. Once class

Table 6.2 Web Content Mining Techniques

Structured data extraction	Structured data extraction deals with extraction of important information about product, services, and data records that are available in structured form on host pages. The extraction can be done in manual or automatic fashion
Unstructured content extraction	The unstructured content (mainly text) extraction considers text mining, information retrieval, and extraction techniques to extract text from the Web pages. As most of the Web pages contain unstructured text, such extraction has high degree of utility
Web information integration	Web host similar information in different representation scheme or syntax. There are many information chunks that have same semantics, which are redundantly hosted on the Web using different syntax. To extract useful information from multiple sites and to avoid redundancy, information integration is desirable
Building concept hierarchies	Lot of information is available on the Web in unorganized way. It is necessary to organize the Web content according to some concept or categories. Technique of clustering and classification may be used here
Segmenting web pages and detecting noise	Web pages within the scope of extraction may be traversed through for a particular segment such as advertisement or content area for better extraction. Unnecessary adware and facilities like contact or help can be removed automatically while extracting information from the pages
Opinion mining	The customer surveys, opinion, and review information collection are specifically considered. Opinion mining deals with three main phases, namely (i) development of linguistic resources, (ii) classification of text by their opinion content, and (iii) extraction of opinion from the content
Template (schema) detection and matching	Many websites have large collection of pages generated dynamically from an underlying structured source like a database or follow a templatized format for better control and ease of development. The underlying homogeneous structure can be identified and matched for similarities. Such schema help in matching two documents that are semantically similar
Knowledge synthesis	Knowledge synthesis is the aggregation of extracted content by applying explicit and reproducible methods to identify, appraise, and then synthesize studies relevant to the users' query. The standard procedures for the knowledge synthesis are systematic reviews and meta-analyses
Classification and clustering	Classification technique of web mining related with classifying the Web content into different clusters and groups. Some standard methods for classification are decision tree–based methods, rule base classification, supervised learning, and evolutionary techniques
Association mining	Association mining is a popular method for discovering interesting relations between variables in large databases. This technique finds rules that will predict the occurrence of an entity based on general pattern exists in the given datasets

definitions and examples are available, the supervised learning algorithm extracts the important features in the examples.

6.4.2   Cluster analysis

Cluster analysis is related with the classification analysis in the sense that it involves finding groups of similar objects based on information found from the data and related sources. Here, the training set is not available; hence, it is known as unsupervised classification.

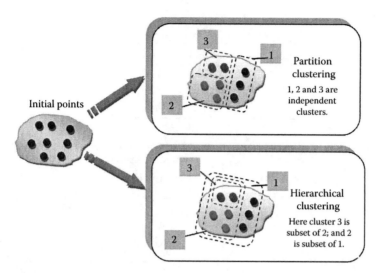

Figure 6.4 Partition and hierarchical clustering.

Web components are divided into groups using similarity metrics. Like classification, supervised learning simple segmentation, web content retrieved through query, and graph partitioning cannot be considered as clustering. Particularly, clustering is used for understanding and summarization of the Web content in order to provide short and abstract view of the Web. Furthermore, clustering can be "partitioned" where web components are divided into nonoverlapping subsets (clusters) such that each component is in exactly one subset, or it can be hierarchical where a set of nested clusters organized as a hierarchical tree. Other types of clustering can be probability clustering where clustering takes completely probabilistic approach. Typical clustering scenario is illustrated in Figure 6.4.

Besides the aforementioned general techniques, specific techniques like *k*-means (exclusive clustering), fuzzy *c*-means (overlapping clustering), and mixture of Gaussians (hybrid probabilistic technique) are available for clustering.

6.4.3 Association mining

Association mining is a popular method for discovering interesting relations between variables in large databases. This technique finds rules that will predict the occurrence of an entity based on general pattern exists in the given datasets. Agrawal et al. (1993) introduced association rules for discovering regularities between products in large-scale transaction data recorded by point of scale systems in supermarkets. According to them, for example, those who buy bread and cheese will prefer to purchase sauce also. This can be written in the form {bread, cheese} → {sauce}. Such information can be used as the basis for marketing decision or introduction of schemes like with bread and cheese, sauce pouch is free. Such technique is also applicable to areas like web mining, intrusion detection, and bioinformatics. The problem of association rule mining is defined as follows:

Let $I = \{i_1, i_2, i_3, \ldots i_n\}$ be a set of n items.

Let $D = \{d_1, d_2, d_3, \ldots d_m\}$ be a set of transactions. Usually, the set D is called the database. Each transaction (d_i) has unique transaction identification code and contains a subset of the items in I.

A *rule* is defined as an implication of the form $X \to Y$ where X and Y are two different subsets of I. Here, X is antecedents and Y is consequent of the rule $X \to Y$.

Table 6.3 Transaction Database for
Association Mining

Transaction ID	Bread	Cheese	Sauce
1	Yes	Yes	Yes
2	No	No	Yes
3	No	Yes	Yes

Let the set of items I = {bread, cheese, sauce} and a small database containing the item transactions. A sample transaction database is given in Table 6.3.
Alternatively, 0 and 1 can be written instead of yes or no.

Constraints on various measures of significance and interest can be used on set of all possible rules to select strong rules. The best-known constraints are minimum thresholds on support and confidence. Furthermore, we require the support of an item set, which is the proportion of transactions in the dataset that contains the item. In the example database, the item {bread, cheese, sauce} has a support of $1/3 = 0.3$ since it occurs in 30% of all transactions (one out of three transactions). Similarly, some other measures like confidence (also called strength), lift (also called improvement or interest), and conviction of a rule can be defined as shown in Table 6.4.

6.4.4 Structured data extraction

While publishing content on the Web, most of the authors take care of structurizing content. That is, content in a single document repository or file is generally homogeneous. Examples for such content are all files containing music, retrieved records from databases and images. These items are known as regularly structured objects (or records). These objects present valuable information about their owners, services, and products. Such structured objects are useful in extracting information from them to provide value-added services. This can be done through automatic techniques like supervised learning or hardcoded in the form of scripts written manually. However, it is practically impossible to carry out this task manually because of size and nature of the Web. The list of issues and challenges of the tasks are given in Table 6.1. Supervised learning method involves creation of architecture, learning algorithm, and large amount of training data. The hybrid automatic methods involve studying and observing likely locations and their structure in order to find out some pattern manually. These patterns are hardcoded by the programmers in the form of executable agents and executed on the Web for extraction. Another way is to build domain ontology. An ideal web data extraction system should automatically extract data from web pages with changed content and deliver the extracted data to use, database, or other application(s). The hybrid approach can be successfully implemented with wrapper induction or wrapper learning. In the wrapper learning, formal rules are generated from manually labeled locations/pages by user. The generated rules are further applied to extract target items from web pages.

6.4.5 Unstructured content extraction

Unstructured data exist in two main categories: bitmap objects and textual objects. Bitmap objects are nonlanguage-based files such as image, audio, or video files. Majority of the websites/pages contain textual information. Text mining is the automatic discovery

Table 6.4 Measures of Association Rule Mining

Support	Support is defined on item sets and gives the proportion of transactions, which contains the item
	Support of an item is used to find frequent (significant) items exploiting its downward closure property. That is, it measures how often a rule $X \rightarrow Y$ is applicable in a database
	It is also known as coverage
confidence$(X \rightarrow Y) =$ support$(XUY)/$ support(X)	Confidence is defined as the probability of seeing the rule's consequent under the condition that the transactions also contain the antecedent
	The measure of confidence is traduced by Agrawal et al. (1993)
	The confidence is used to produce rules from the frequent items that exceed a minimum confidence threshold
	It is also called strength
lift$(X \rightarrow Y) =$ support$(XUY)/$ {support(X) * support(Y)}	Lift measures how many times more often X and Y occur together than expected if they are statistically independent
	It is introduced by Brin et al. (1997)
	It is also called improvement or interest
conviction$(X \rightarrow Y) = 1 -$ support$(Y)/$ {$1 -$ confidence$(X \rightarrow Y)$}	Conviction compares the probability that X appears without Y if they were dependent with the actual frequency of the appearance of X without Y
	Conviction is a directed measure since it also uses the information of the absence of the consequent. It was developed as an alternative to confidence, which was found to not capture direction of associations adequately
	It is introduced by Brin et al. (1997)
leverage$(X \rightarrow Y) =$ support $(XUY) - ($support(X) * support$(Y))$	Leverage measures the difference of X and Y appearing together in the dataset and what would be expected if X and Y where statistically dependent
	It is introduced by Piatetsky-Shapiro (1991)
	The rational in a sales setting is to find out how many more units (items X and Y together) are required/sold than expected from the independent sells

of required information or concepts from text files from several resources using computer software. Unstructured text is usually in the form of blog content, personal websites, summaries, notes, memos, user groups, and product reviews, whereas structured text consists of text that is organized usually within professional and template websites or databases. Above this, the unstructured data also occur within documents that follow a defined format, which converts the structured documents into semistructured document. One technique to extract useful information from such unstructured content is enhanced searching. Search assisted with metadata or metaknowledge, natural language search, information extraction, and text mining algorithms, etc., can be used in this context. Beyond search, classification, taxonomies, intelligent content management techniques, etc., are also useful in mining unstructured content. Above these, the techniques like visualization and text analysis are also useful for unstructured content mining. Figure 6.5 illustrates component techniques that play key role in unstructured content mining on web.

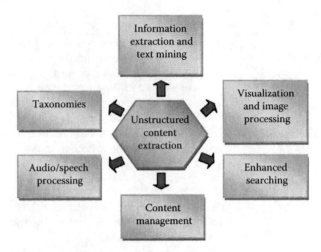

Figure 6.5 Techniques for unstructured content mining.

Besides the text mining, the unstructured text mining, content in alternative media like image, sound, graph, and animation can also be mined for useful information. The application benefited from such mining can be as follows:

- Junk removal from web content
- Automated text analysis, classification, and synthesis
- Discovering domain-specific items such as opinions
- NLP

6.4.6   Template matching

Many web pages have been developed using readymade template facility. That is, all the pages of a website follow common template structure to share a common administrative authority and uniform look and feel. Many time pages that share a template also share some common links. These links include links to websites, links to advertisement banners, links to the frequently asked questions (FAQ) and help pages, and links to the website's administrator page. From this information, it is easy to find out mirrors (total duplication of pages/site) and independent pages that share common items/links. The template detection follows following broad steps:

1. Consider a given set of hyperlinked documents as *D*.
2. Find out mirrors, if any.
3. Find out duplicate pages in *D*.
4. Identify, sort, and categorize the pages in set *D*. Each such category can be thought as a template.
5. Output the blocks/elements belonging to each such group.

After detecting the suitable templates, they are matched for similarities.

Finally, while presenting extracted content to user, it is desired that the content looks systematic and in good format. Representation of the extracted content in a good fashion is an important quality criterion for web content mining. The process of the Web content mining can be enhanced by predicting the information need of users. Here, the Web usage mining helps. The field of the Web usage (web log) mining deals with identifying behavior of web users, summary of references of pages and location, and providing other useful information such as browser information, agents mobility, if any, and IP-address-related information.

6.5   Web usage mining

The Web usage mining provides the collection of information accessed so far to its users. This usage data provide references to accessed web pages and locations. The objective is to collect web log automatically through suitable mining techniques for users. Such information mainly consists of references to the accessed pages, refereed locations, user subscription information, marketing strategies, promotional campaigns, and surveys. Optionally, the collected information is further processed for better presentation and use through software. With such information, more effective results can be produced to improve business. Web usage mining provides following advantages to a typical business:

- Improves quality of all electronic business by providing useful information and improving services to its customers
- Introduction and evaluation of market strategy
- Product promotion
- Training and learning
- Provides information about users' need and help in new product development
- Provides good knowledge about mistakes, loopholes, and forgeries in existing business strategies
- Improved communication with vendors, suppliers, and users and providing easier access paths for the business company as well as users.

6.5.1   Activities in web usage mining

The typical activities in the Web usage mining involves the following steps:

1. Retrieval of the log through automated techniques from different sources such as server log, proxy log, and client log
2. Identification of possible data abstraction in order to provide consistency
3. Cleaning noise and malwares from the retrieved log
4. Identification of the target information such as transaction data
5. Integration of various chunks of information and finding patterns from the collection
6. Analysis and use of the retrieved information

Figure 6.6 illustrates typical activities in the Web usage mining.

6.5.2   Retrieval sources for web usage mining

Data for web usage mining is collected from various levels of the Web such as server level, client level, and proxy level. Each level has its own characteristics and parameters that affect the process of web usage. These parameters include type of connection between two given points of locations, traffic between the points, and the navigation patterns between the points.

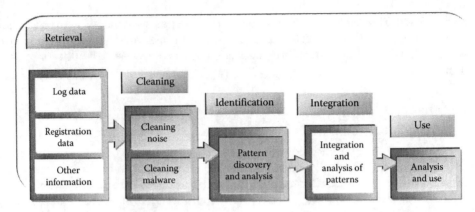

Figure 6.6 Activities for web usage mining.

Server log is an explicit collection of browsing history by multiple users for multiple sites in the form of typical log formats. This format consists of fields such as log sequence number, IP address, site/location reference, user ID, time duration, size of the item/document, cookies and session data, and agent/browser through which the location is accessed. Instead of directly accessing the web server log, there are agents called packet sniffers that capture all the data "packets" that transfer through the Web. Effectively used, the packet sniffer can act as network monitor or network analyzer.

Client-side log aggregation for mining is done through remote agents, embedding scripts within the browsers with concerns of users. The user's hold is maximum on his local machine; hence, it is very important to have such permission to use agent or script that collects data at backend while user surfs the Web. This causes additional steps for taking permission and then developing agent and/or script that collects the log for mining. However, by this way, only single user log is collected in this fashion. A mobile agent that moves from one host to another host might be helpful to find useful information from multiple users. Each such mobile agent has to possess "ticket" for authentication and security purposes.

At intermediate level, log can be collected by tracking business at proxy servers. Proxy logs highlight the actual hypertext transfer protocol (HTTP) requests from multiple clients of a similar type to multiple web servers. This may be useful to collect log for a limited domain users or a group that shares common proxy server.

6.5.3   Cleaning and data abstraction

After collection of data from different levels such as from server log, client-side log, and proxy server log, there is a need to convert the retrieved content into a common format and filtered from noise. This includes identifying and defining various terms such as valid users, server sessions, episodes, input–output streams, and view of a page. One may take help of standards defined by W3C such as web characterization activities. The Web characterization activity is concerned with looking at the overall patterns of web structure and usage.

6.5.4   Identification of required information

After the data abstraction and noise cleaning, preprocessing at various levels can be considered. Many times, the content that is available for mining has IP address, session information, user information, and agents used. To find exact correlation who has used which agent, which machine, and which session is difficult task. Preprocessing involves identifying the exact user's transaction including user information, IP address, agents, and sessions.

6.5.5 Pattern discovery and analysis

After identification of required information from the usage data, patterns are discovered using techniques like statistical analysis, clustering, classification, and association mining algorithms. Through proper usage of the discovered patterns, the Web usage mining has valuable offerings to a business with high impact on business product quality and effectiveness of the services.

6.6 Web structure mining

Web does not follow a strict and unified semantic model, but mixture of unstructured, semistructured, and structured elements. However, different objects are placed on the Web and linked with each other using HTML links. That is, the Web can be considered as a web page as a node and links between them as directed edges of the network posed by the structure of a directed graph. This situation can be represented as a huge directed graph structure G, where $G = (V, E)$, node $v \in V$ represents a web page, edge $(p, q) \in E$ from node p to point on behalf of node q's hyperlink. The Web actually behaves like a hypertext document information system. The Web objects such as pages and sites are generally exist between the numbers of links. Web structure mining focuses with structure of such hyperlinks on the Web. The objects of the Web are web pages and various links such as incoming links, outgoing links, and cocitation links. Based on the type and nature of links, possible tasks of the Web structure mining can be link-based classification, link-based clustering, etc. The attributes like link type (purpose and representation scheme such as HTML), link strength (can be fuzzy), and link cardinality (number of links between objects) play important role in these activities. The primary objective of the Web structure mining is to study and understand the organization of the Web through network of links. This is the reason why the area of web structure mining can be called area of link analysis. There are two basic techniques to analyze the network of links on the Web. These methods are (i) hyperlinked induced topic search (HITS) concept and (ii) PageRank method. These techniques are described in following sections.

6.6.1 HITS concept

HITS introduced by Kleinberg (1998) concerns with HITS algorithm for determining importance and ranking a set of documents accordingly. In HITS concept, Kleinberg identifies two kinds of pages from the Web hyperlink structure: authorities, pages with good source of content, and hubs, pages with good sources of links. For a given requirement of user, the algorithm finds authorities and hubs. According to Kleinberg, these two measures—authorities and hubs—are mutually reinforcing each other. That is, a good hub is a page that points to many good authorities, and a good authority is a page that is pointed to by many good hubs. However, the situation where a host points to a single document on a second host, or sometimes, a single document on one host points to a set of document on a second host. Manipulation of dynamically and automatically generated link also disturbs the prediction of authorities and hub calculations. Furthermore, all these authorities and hub content of reference may have misleading vocabularies, following which one may end up with nonrelevant document/page.

Outline of HITS algorithm is as follows:

```
1. Initialize all weights to 1
2. Repeat until the weights converge
3. For every hub i ∈ H, h_i = ∑_{j ∈ F(i)} a_j
4. For every authority i ∈ A, a_i = ∑_{j ∈ B(i)} h_j
5. Normalize
```

HITS sometimes tends to generalize to a nearby topic, particularly when hubs cover diverse topics. In order to address such issues, many researchers introduced variants to the basic HITS algorithm. Chakrabarti et al. (1998) compare the query term with the text surrounding a hyperlink, called the anchor text, to obtain a weighted version of the update rule. Chakrabarti et al. (1998) also uses the tags on a large hub page to break it into smaller hublets so that the links within a hublet stay topically focused. Moreover, if several pages from a single domain participate as hubs, Chakrabarti scales down their weights to prevent a single site from becoming dominant. These heuristics utilize page content while retaining the clean mathematical properties of HITS in terms of convergence.

In another development, Bharat and Henzinger (1998) conducted a user study that substantiated the improvements associated with several extensions to the basic HITS algorithm. Some of their heuristic improvements included weighting pages on the basis of their similarity to a given query topic and averaging the contribution of multiple links from any given site to a specific page.

The *Hub-averaging-Kleinberg algorithm*, modification to HITS, is designed to overcome its drawback of "topic drift." The heuristic is that if a hub is pointing to a large number of pages and therefore receiving a high hub score, it is not likely that all these pages are relevant to the search subject. Therefore, adjustment needs to be made to minimize the impact of irrelevant links. Instead of assigning to each hub the combined score of all authorities it points to, it is proposed to assign to the hub an average score of all the authorities it points to. Another implication of this is that a hub is of better value if it points to good authorities only.

6.6.2 PageRank method

The PageRank is introduced by Page et al. (1998). The PageRank algorithm calculates importance of web pages by analyzing the link structure of the Web. The broad steps of the algorithms are given as follows:

1. The PageRank algorithm assumes a page A having pages $T_1, \ldots, T_n$, which point to it (called citations).
2. The algorithm also uses a damping factor, which can be set between 0 and 1 (usually set to 0.85).
3. The number of outgoing links $C(A)$ is calculated after setting the damping factor.
4. The PageRank of a page A is calculated using the following formula:

$$PR(A) = (1 - d) + d(PR(T_1)/C(T_1) + \cdots + PR(T_n)/C(T_n)) \tag{6.1}$$

PageRank is also considered as a probability distribution over web pages. The sum of all the ranks becomes 1. PageRank became the basis of the Google (http://www.google.com) search engine.

The main benefit of PageRank comes from its static ordering, which allows the pages that contain a given query term to be retrieved using a traditional text-based indexer and to be displayed in the PageRank order.

6.7   Sensor web mining: architecture and applications

The idea of sensor web was conceived at the NASA/Jet Propulsion Laboratory (JPL) by Kevin Delin in 1997 to take advantage of data collected from different sensors through consumer-market chips. These data are analyzed and used to provide platform to share resources and control them in remote fashion. This is the approach that provides opportunity for efficient georeferencing in remote fashion. The acquired information can be further used to react intelligently and provide adaptive solution to its surroundings. The sensor web is a macroinstrument consisting of a number of sensor platforms called pods. Pods can be fixed, or mobile. Each pod senses some dynamic environmental data in real-time fashion. This gives realistic and spontaneous data for coordination. Pods developed with scripting enable users' access through the Web. Unlike the transmission control protocol (TCP)/IP, the sensor web is router free and synchronous. In the sensor web, each pod is aware of the status of other pods. Due to such pod-to-pod communication, between different types of pods (fixed, mobile, orbital, and terrestrial), communication is both omnidirectional and bidirectional.

Radio is used to connect the pod with its local neighborhood. The NASA/JPL sensor web pods use radios operating in the 900 MHz license-free ISM band with an upper range of ~200 m or more. Along with the radio, there is a microcontroller, which encompasses protocols and memory to hold the data and instructions. Instead of consuming battery or electricity, the components take energy from solar panel and micro power electronic system, which make the system self-sufficient in terms of energy. On the top of these component sets, application-specific sensor suits are installed. The typical architecture of a pod is described in Figure 6.7.

The sensor web is suitable for large-scale environmental information, aids geographic information system (GIS) applications, and environmental control and monitoring. Depending on application, multiple dedicated sensor webs can be established on various areas. These applications include weather forecasting, costal area monitoring, communication and education, and ecosystem information and management. This situation

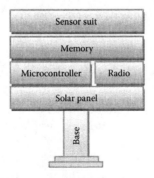

Figure 6.7 Architecture of a sensor platform—Pod.

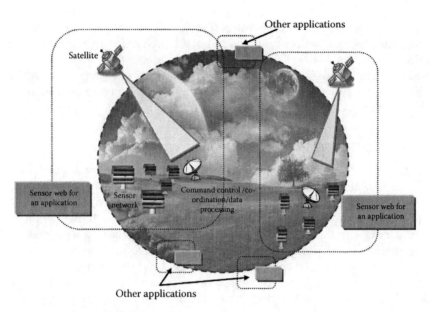

Figure 6.8 Scenario of multiple sensor web applications.

is illustrated in Figure 6.8. Such a scenario may include a series of event-responsive and multinode sensor webs dedicated to monitoring change factors within the domains of geologic, ecologic, meteorological, and oceanic studies.

The Huntington Gardens staff has used the sensor web to remotely monitor the state of its greenhouses and to ensure that watering (from both sprinkler and rainfall patterns) is uniform across various areas. Wetlands on the Florida coast at the Kennedy Space Center, remote eastern ice sheets of Antarctica, desert areas of Central New Mexico and Tucson, and a greenhouse simulation of an Amazonian rainforest have also utilized the sensor web. Details about these projects and real output can be seen at http://sensorwebs.jpl.nasa.gov/.

Mining useful content from raw sensor data is challenging due to massive quantity, high dimensionality, and distributed nature of data. The conventional data analysis may not be suitable here. It requires preprocessing of the collected data, predicative modeling based on collected data, data analysis, and extraction. According to Pang-Ninh (2006), preprocessing of data includes the following:

- Feature extraction to identify relevant attributes for a data mining task using techniques such as event detection, feature selection, and feature transformation
- Data cleaning to resolve data quality issues such as noise, outliers, missing values, and miscalibration errors
- Data reduction to improve the processing time or reduce the variability in data by means of techniques such as statistical sampling and data aggregation
- Dimension reduction to reduce the number of features presented to a data mining algorithm, principal component analysis (PCA), isometric mapping (ISOMAP), and locally linear embedding (LLE) are some examples of linear and nonlinear dimension reduction techniques.

Predicative modeling deals with classification for discrete valued attributes and regression for continuous valued attributes. The typical methodologies used for such modeling are supervised learning, decision tree classification, rule-based learning, graphical methods, logistic regression, and support vector machines. Cluster analysis and rule mining are also used to mine the processed and modeled data to extract useful information. Anomaly detection is also used optionally. Anomaly detection is a kind of deviation detection from usual pattern of the data. Unusual pattern of data occurrence can be found by statistical techniques like charting and histograms. Furthermore, the sensor data can be mined at a central place at a given time interval or in online real-time fashion on the network command control station. The later is desirable if the sensor data are application and area specific and affect a limited geographical area as well as bounded by scope of the application.

6.8   Web mining software

Web mining software are of variety of flavors. Some of the open source software for web mining includes RapidMiner (http://rapid-i.com/content/view/181/196/). The RapidMiner supports all steps of the data mining process from data loading, preprocessing, visualization, interactive data mining process design and inspection, automated modeling, automated parameter and process optimization, automated feature construction and feature selection, evaluation, and deployment. RapidMiner can be used as stand-alone program on the desktop with its graphical user interface (GUI), on a server via its command line version, or as data mining engine for the products and Java library for developers.

Another such tool is AlterWind Log Analyzer Lite (http://www.alterwind.com/loganalyzer/log-analyzer-lite.html), which is a free web analyzer report generator. This utility supports more than 430 search engines from 120 different countries.

One more utility called Analog (http://www.analog.cx/) is a free and fast program to analyze the web server log files in different formats.

To mine content from any java site JWAnalytics (http://code.google.com/p/jwanalytics/) is used. JWAnalytics stands for Java web analytics. It allows real-time storage of web analytics data from any Java site.

To analyze web logs such as mining unique visitors, their behavior, information regarding sessions, transactions and to organize the collected data for future use, htMiner (http://www.htminer.org/en/) is used. The resulting information through an automatic procedure by htMiner is stored in a PostgreSQL database for further analysis and reporting operations.

Visitator (http://www.fh54.de/visitator/home/1About/index.php) is the utility that performs analysis of web server log files in order to reveal information about the kinds of interests and behaviors of the site visitors. This software allows clustering and visual presentation of visitor groups based on access patterns.

Web Utilization Miner (WUM) is an integrated, java-based web mining environment for web mining activities such as log file preparation, basic reporting, discovery of sequential patterns, and visualization. It is an open source project that aims to knowledge discovery and knowledge management.

6.9   Opinion mining

Opinion mining or sentiment analysis refers to an area of text mining, NLP, and computational linguistics. The objective of opinion mining is to extract the opinion of author of a published literature and learn attitude of the author. Opinion mining plays an important role in mining applications for customer relationship management, consumer attitude detection, brand and product positioning, product reviews, and market research.

The opinion can be decision, judgment, evaluation, or appraisal. The facts available are different from opinion and fall within the scope of a typical search engine. However, opinion searching does not fall within the scope of a typical search engine or text retrieval system; rather it requires dedicated techniques. The rise of social networking platform gave encouragement in the field of opinion mining. By considering techniques such as text mining, deep parsing, machine learning, and NLP, opinion mining can be performed. The opinion mining would be helpful in following situations:

- To recommend and/or evaluate product or scheme
- To share brand experience and opinion
- Product and service bench marking
- New product design and introduction of new market strategy
- To locate target audience for a product
- In business and government intelligence
- Feedback and appraisal of employees
- Legal advisory
- Public thesaurus of different languages
- Political campaigning
- Advertisement and marketing (placing an advertisement where there is a positive opinion about the product, product comparison, etc.)

Typical opinion search includes finding opinion about a person, product, or an organization, aggregation of positive and negative opinions for a given object, finding how general opinion about an object is changing, etc. The methodology used for this is ranking, user interaction by question answering, and traditional surveys. The basic components of opinions are opinion holder, object for which opinions are collected, objectives of an opinion, and opinion itself. According to Bing Liu (2010), an *object O* is an entity that can be a product, topic, person, event, or organization. It is associated with a pair, *O*: (*T, A*), where *T* is a hierarchy or taxonomy of *components* (or *parts*) and *subcomponents* of *O*, and *A* is a set of *attributes* of *O*. Each component has its own set of subcomponents and attributes. Illustration of the object, opinions, and features relationships are shown in Figure 6.9.

Using the aforementioned concept (definition) and structure object as shown in Figure 6.9, a model of feature-based opinion mining is presented by Liu (2010), which is described in the following section.

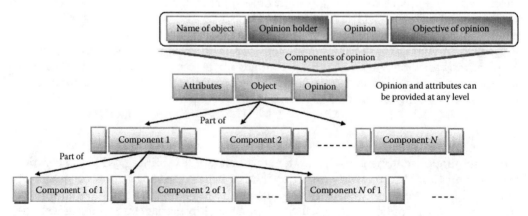

Figure 6.9 Relationships between object, opinions, and features.

6.9.1 Feature-based opinion mining

An object O is represented with a finite set of features given as $F = \{f_1, f_2,..., f_n\}$, which includes the object itself. Each feature $f_i \in F$ can be expressed with a finite set of symbols (words or phrases) Wi, which are *synonyms*. That is, there is a set of corresponding synonym sets $W = \{W1, W2,..., Wn\}$ for the n features. Every opinion holder has to select one or more synonyms from the set W about the features defined as in F for a given object. Let the document contains set of such opinions is d. The opinion mining task is the task to discover the synonyms about a particular feature for a given object from the document d. The major tasks of the feature-based opinion mining are as follows:

1. Identify the objective of opinion mining.
2. Identify objects, their attributes, and their subcomponents. Also determine the objects' hierarchical structure.
3. Identify the object features, prepare list of feature in a form of set F.
4. Determine the possible opinions, their synonyms, classify them into groups, and prepare set W.
5. Identify target opinion holders.
6. Collect opinions and compare them.

Once the opinions are collected, they are further grouped and analyzed (Sajja 2011). This process would not be easy if the opinions are not given using the predetermined synonyms. Instead of providing predetermined vocabularies, if loose and/or comparative statements are provided as feedback, it is difficult to extract opinions from the same. In this case, one has to go for extra processing steps such as parsing the statements and extracting required vocabulary (and all their synonyms) through proper extraction technique. One has to compare superlative and comparative statements, consider cross-lingual adaption, and domain-specific jargons. The feature-based mining is also considered as topic-based mining. Here, document or object topics are considered as component and features, and the aforementioned broad steps are applied for mining.

6.10 Other applications using AI for web mining

The modern web is considered as not only repository of the content but also thought as repository of services of all kinds. Web is actually thought as another virtual world where people, organizations, and systems are interacting for the day-to-day transaction to spectacular situations and problems. Typical tasks involved in web mining are as follows: (i) to retrieve useful information from web, analyze it, and use it (web content mining); (ii) to discover knowledge from hyperlinks and to identify web pages that meet users needs (web structure mining); and (iii) to learn about behavior or users and web usage history (web usage mining). All these tasks require methods and techniques that are beyond traditional computing (non-AI) techniques and typical mathematical model because of the nature of the Web. To perform the Web mining activities in efficient manner for the modern unstructured and huge web, AI techniques need to be utilized. Some of the useful techniques that help are listed as in Table 6.5.

Support of the AI techniques as mentioned in Table 6.5 enhances the process of mining by adding human-like intelligence in a different way. The conjunction of AI and web mining techniques evolves to an area of web intelligence (WI). According to Zhong et al. (2000), WI is defined as the study and research of the application of AI and information and communication technology (ICT) on the Web in order to create the next generation of

Table 6.5 AI Techniques for Web Mining

AI technique	Utilization
Multiagent systems	One or more independent and cooperative agents to perform various tasks of web mining. These agents are proactive and able to learn in order to perform the intended tasks
Swarm intelligence	Collective behavior of a swarm (agents, programs, and units) can lead to the emergence of an apparent intelligent behavior needed for the Web mining activities. The idea of such smaller working units (swarms) is taken from the natural examples such as ant colonies, bird flocking, herding, and fish schooling
Artificial neural network	An empty structure of input/output opportunities that has the capability of learning either by data (supervised) or by experience/problems (unsupervised) in a more human fashion. The suitable application can be classification, ranking the content, etc.
Fuzzy logic	Fuzzy logic allows utilization of uncertainty and vagueness in various activities and techniques while dealing with machines. Utilization of such loose as well as linguistic words makes system user friendly and provides high-level flexibility. Techniques that deal with user interactions and uncertain data are candidates of the FL application
Evolutionary systems	The candidates from given search space are encoded, and strong candidates are evolved through genetic operations like natural selection, mutation, and crossover, which may solve the problem
Heuristic-based techniques	The traditional web mining techniques and models may be enriched with the rule of thumb called heuristic. Heuristic is a practical solution of the problem, which is applicable in the general situations. Heuristic-based search and filtering function while retrieving content from the Web are examples of the same

products, services, and frameworks based on the Web. Chapter 4 of this book discusses the fundamental concepts of the WI.

6.11   Future research directions

As the Web and its usage increase, it will continue to produce more and more content, structure, and usage data, and the value of web mining will keep increasing. Outlined here are a number of research directions that should be pursued to guarantee that we continue to develop web mining technologies that will enable this value to be realized.

Market-basket analysis has been one of the evident accomplishments of data mining. Nonetheless, these data provide only the final result of the process, and that too decisions that ended up in product purchase (Akerkar and Lingras 2008). Clickstream data provide the opportunity for a detailed look at the decision-making process itself, and knowledge extracted from it can be used for optimizing the process, influencing the process, etc. There are research opportunities in extracting process models from usage data, understanding how various parts of the process model impact different web metrics of interest, and how the process models change in response to various changes that are made—altering stimuli to the user.

Furthermore, there is a scope for further research in extracting temporal models of how web content, web communities, web structures, authorities, and hubs are evolving. Large organizations generally archive usage data from their websites. With these sources of data available, there is a great scope of research to develop techniques for analyzing of how the Web evolves over time.

As services over the Web continue to expand, there will be a need to make them robust, scalable, and efficient. Web mining can be applied to better understand the behavior of these services, and the knowledge extracted can be useful for various kinds of optimizations.

There are many imminent research challenges related to privacy and security and to develop methodologies and tools that can be used to verify and validate that a web service is really using an end-user's information in a manner steady with its stated policies. The anonymity provided by the Web has led to a considerable increase in attempted fraud, from unauthorized use of credit cards to hacking into credit card databases for blackmail. Web mining is the perfect analysis technique for detecting and preventing such frauds. Research issues include developing procedures to recognize known frauds, and characterize and then recognize mysterious frauds, etc.

Exercises

6.1 How is web structure mining different from web usage mining and web content mining?

6.2 How PageRank is computed?

6.3 What is the difference between an *authoritative* page and *hub* page? How do they affect the weighting of a page?

6.4 (Project) Develop a desktop application (e.g., for the Google Desktop, the Yahoo Desktop, Windows Desktop, or Apple Dashboard Widget) that implements any version of the HITS algorithm.

6.5 (Project) Develop a machine learning method to classify an arbitrary web page as blog or not blog, for crawling purposes.

6.6 In PageRank, when a page links to itself, is the link counted? Is it sensible to assume that a page cannot vote for itself and that such links are not counted?

6.7 Discuss various approaches used by websites to perform personalization.

6.8 How does web mining differ from traditional data mining?

References

Agrawal, R., Imielinski, T., and Swami, A. 1993. Mining association rules between sets of items in large databases. Paper presented at the *1993 ACM SIGMOD Conference*, Washington, DC.

Akerkar, R. and Lingras, P. 2008. *Building an Intelligent Web: Theory and Practice*. Sudbury, MA: Jones & Bartlett.

Bharat, K. and Henzinger, M. 1998. Improved algorithms for topic distillation in hyperlinked environments. Paper presented at the *21st Annual International ACM SIGIR Conference*, pp. 104–111, New York.

Brin, S., Motwani, R., Ullman, J., and Tsur, S. 1997. Dynamic itemset counting and implication rules for market basket data. Paper presented at the *ACM SIGMOD International Conference on Management of Data*, pp. 255–264, Tucson, AZ.

Chakrabarti, S. et al. 1998. Automatic resource compilation by analyzing hyperlink structure and associated text. *Computer Networks and ISDN Systems* 30(1–7):65–74.

Kleinberg, J. M. 1998. Authoritative sources in a hyperlinked environment. Paper presented at the *ACM-SIAM Symposium on Discrete Algorithms*, pp. 668–677, San Francisco, CA.

Liu, B. 2010. Sentiment analysis and subjectivity. In *Handbook of Natural Language Processing*, eds. N. Indurkhya and F. J. Damerau. Goshen, CT: Chapman & Hall.

Page, L., Brin, S., Motwani, R., and Winograd, T. 1998. The PageRank citation ranking: Bring order to the web. Technical Report, Stanford University, Stanford, CA.

Pang-Ninh, T. 2006. Knowledge discovery from sensor data. http://www.sensorsmag.com/da-control/knowledge-discovery-sensor-data-753?page_id=1 (accessed September 2, 2011).

Piatetsky-Shapiro, G. 1991. Discovery, analysis, and presentation of strong rules. Paper presented at the AAAI Workshop on *Knowledge Discovery in Databases*, pp. 229–248, Anaheim, CA.

Sajja, P. S. 2011. Feature-based opinion mining. *International Journal of Data Mining and Emerging Technologies* 1(1):8–13.

Zhong, N., Jiming, L., Yao, Y. Y., and Ohsuga, S. 2000. Web intelligence. Paper presented at the *Computer Software and Applications Conference*, Taipei, Taiwan.

chapter seven

Structured data extraction

7.1 Preliminaries

Web information extraction (IE) is the problem of extracting target information from web pages. It is an important task for information identification and integration, because multiple web pages may present the same or similar information using completely different formats or syntaxes, which makes integration of information a challenging task. Due to the heterogeneity and lack of structure of web data, automated discovery of targeted information becomes a complex task. In order to provide value-added services, by extracting and making use of information from multiple sites, one needs to semantically integrate information from multiple sources. This problem has been studied by researchers in artificial intelligence (AI), database and data mining, and web communities. There are several approaches for structured data extraction, which is also called wrapper generation (WG).

This chapter focuses on extracting structured data from web pages. A computer program for extracting such data is called a *wrapper*. In the 1990s, research community started taking interest in the field of IE. Roughly, there are three basic approaches for IE. These are as follows:

- Manual approach: Using web page and its source code, computer programmer identifies patterns and designs program to extract target data. But this approach is not scalable to a large number of websites.
- Wrapper induction: This is a semiautomatic supervised learning approach. In this approach, a set of extraction rules are learned from a collection of manually labeled pages or data records. Furthermore, rules are employed to extract target data from other similarly formatted pages.
- Automatic extraction: This approach is the unsupervised one. It finds patterns automatically from a single or multiple pages. Naturally, it can scale up data extraction to a large number of sites and web pages.

Because the Web consists primarily of text, IE is central to any effort that would use the Web as a resource for knowledge discovery. An IE system can be thought of as an attempt to convert information from different text documents into database entries. Hence, successful IE from World Wide Web can turn the Web into a database. IE is a relatively new field, which has developed over the last decade, and which have met new challenges in the problem of extracting information from web pages. This chapter gives an introduction to the field of IE and then looks at the development of the field of WG for web sources. Furthermore, we present an overview of systems developed for IE from websites and look at different applications of the technology.

7.1.1 Structured data

It is standard for database researchers to refer to data as structured, semistructured, or unstructured. Unfortunately, this usage is often imprecise. Generally, structured data refer to data expressed using the relational model; semistructured data mean extensible markup language (XML) data; and unstructured data refer to documents such as text, web pages, spreadsheets, and presentations. Confusingly, semistructured data are sometimes described as being contained in XML documents; we will reserve the word "document" to describe a piece of unstructured data.

These terms are unsatisfactory for a number of reasons. First, one might think that semistructured XML data are somehow less formally defined than structured relational data, but this is false. Indeed, it is also easy to give a formal definition for an unstructured document (e.g., a text document is just a linear array of tokens drawn from the set of valid words and punctuation symbols). Second, an unsuspecting reader may think that unstructured data lack a formally defined query language. But web search queries are essentially Boolean selection queries that could be expressed in structured query language (SQL). It is possible (though arguably unwise) to implement a search engine using a relational database. Finally, it is tempting to believe that these terms refer to whether the data are intended for machine use (structured) or human consumption (unstructured) or somewhere in-between (semistructured). This usage is probably accurate to some extent—"unstructured" documents are often meant for human consumption. But a row in a structured relational database can be very easy for a person to read, and unstructured spreadsheets often contain abstruse statistical data.

There is one interpretation that appears to match general usage and is very relevant to this discussion. We suggest that the terms structured, semistructured, and unstructured roughly describe the extent to which a dataset supports queries with domain-specific operations. (In this thesis, we will use the word domain in its nonmathematical sense, i.e., as a synonym for topic.) For example, a very simple (structured) relational database about employees might support the following SQL query:

SELECT employeeName, yearsOfEducation, yearsOfService WHERE
yearsOfEducation > 20 AND yearsOfService < 12

Writing such a query entails contributions from at least three different parties:

- The authors of the SQL language standard
- The authors of the employee database schema, which includes concepts of employeeName, yearsOfEducation, and yearsOfService
- The author of the query, who has supplied the overall logical structure and the constants 20 and 12

A traditional document-centric search engine is not sufficient to support the aforementioned query. We could index this database with a search engine by converting the data into an unstructured format: we simply write out all the contents to a series of text files, with one tuple per file. We then use the search engine to index the resulting files. However, there would be no way to express the aforementioned query—a search user could issue the query 20 and 12, but this would simply return all documents (tuples) that contain those terms, without regard to comparisons or the correct data attribute, that is, yearsOfEducation vs. yearsOfService.

The query language does not support comparison operators nor do domain-specific notions like the data attribute names. Search engine query languages support multiple topic-insensitive operators (e.g., testing term presence, testing phrase presence, testing the site's domain, possibly testing whether two terms are NEAR each other, etc.) and multiple "fields" of the data (such as the uniform resource locator [URL] and the domain name system [DNS] domain mentioned earlier). But such systems do not support fields relevant to each document's actual subject.

Of course, it is possible to design a relational schema that hardly appears domain-specific at all. Instead of a table with columns for employeeName, yearsOfEducation, and yearsOfService, one could populate a three-column table with columns tupleID, attrName, and value, spreading a single tuple's data across many rows. With such a design, it would still possible to pose questions against domain-specific elements by rewriting the user's query; topic-specific knowledge would be embedded in the query-rewriting system rather than the relational schema itself.

If structured data allow operations on domain-specific data elements, and unstructured data do not, then one might imagine that just a fraction of semistructured data elements are domain specific. Indeed, this is stereotypically the case for such canonical XML datasets as health records, which have a mix of relational style and textual components.

7.1.2 Information extraction

IE is originally the task of locating specific information from a natural language document and is a particular useful subarea of natural language processing (NLP). IE systems have been developed both for structured text with tabular information and for free text such as news stories. A key element of IE systems is a set of text extraction rules or extraction patterns that identify relevant information to be extracted (Soderland 1999).

The dramatic growth in the number and size of online textual information sources has led to an increasing research interest in the IE problem. IE is different from the technology of information retrieval (IR). Rather than to extract information, the objective of IR is to select a relevant subset of documents from a larger collection based on a user query. The user must then browse the returned documents to get the desired information. The contrast between the aims of IE and IR systems can be stated as follows: IR retrieves relevant documents from collections, while IE extracts relevant information from documents. Hence, the two techniques are complementary and used in combination they can provide powerful tools for text processing (Gaizauskas and Wilks 1998). The difference is illustrated in Figure 7.1.

IE and IR differ not only in aims, but they also differ in the techniques usually deployed. These differences are due partly to their different aims and partly to the history of the fields. Most work in IE has emerged from research on rule-based systems in

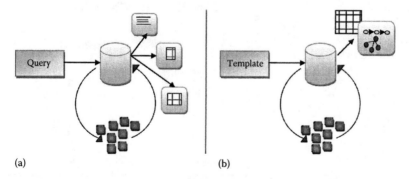

(a)   (b)

Figure 7.1 (a) Information retrieval vs. (b) information extraction.

computational linguistics and NLP, while information theory, probability theory, and statistics have influenced IR.

While the science of automatic IR is a mature field, which has basically been around as long as databases of documents have existed, the field of automatic IE has only been driven forward in the last decade. Two factors have been important for the development of the field, the exponential growth in the amount of both online and offline textual data, and the focus on the field through the message understanding conferences (MUCs) during the last few years. Development of IE is shown in Figure 7.2.

A precursor of IE was and is the field of text understanding. AI researchers have been building various systems where the goal is to get an accurate representation of the contents of an entire text. These systems typically operate in very small domains only, and they are usually not very portable to new domains.

Since the late 1980s, the U.S. government has been sponsoring MUC to evaluate and advance the state-of-the art in IE. The MUCs involve a set of participants from different sites, usually a mix of academic and industrial research labs. Each participating site builds an IE system for a predetermined domain. The IE systems are all evaluated on the same domain and text collection, and the results are scored using an official scoring program.

The objective of the conferences has been to get a quantitative evaluation of IE systems, which prior to these conferences had been performed only sporadically and often on the same data on which they had been trained. The conferences provided the first large-scale effort to evaluate NLP systems. How to evaluate the systems has been a nontrivial issue, and through the conferences standard scoring criteria have been developed. The focus of the various MUCs has been tasks like Latin American terrorism, joint ventures, microelectronics, and company management changes.

IE research has been rather successful in the past 5 or 6 years, and name recognition components of the leading systems have achieved near-human performance in English

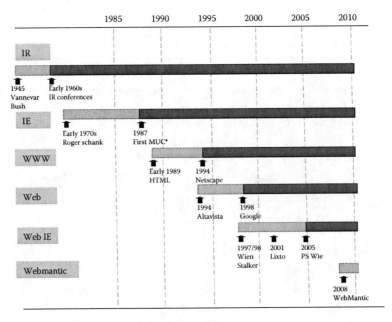

Figure 7.2 Web information extraction developments.

and Japanese. Through the MUCs, it has been demonstrated that fully automatic IE systems can be built with state-of-the-art technology, and that, for some selected tasks, their performance is as good as the performance of a human expert. However, in several of the subtasks, the scores in the top group in every MUC evaluation since 1993 have been roughly the same (bearing in mind however that the MUC tasks have become more complex). The primary advance has been that more and more sites are able to perform at this level, because the techniques used have converged. Moreover, building systems that perform at this level currently requires a great investment in time and expertise. In addition, the vast bulk of the research so far has been done only on written text and only in English and a few other major languages.

7.1.3   Evaluation metrics

The necessity for evaluation metrics for the IE problem came with the MUCs. The starting points for the development of these metrics were the standard IR metrics of recall and precision. However, the definitions of these measures have been altered from those used in IR, although the names have been retained. The alterations allow for reporting possible overgeneration in IE where, unlike IR, data not present in the input can be erroneously produced.

In the IE task, recall may be crudely interpreted as a measure of the fraction of the information that has been correctly extracted and precision as a measure of the fraction of the extracted information that is correct. Recall then refers to how much of the information that was correctly extracted, while precision refers to the reliability of the information extracted. Precision and recall are defined as follows:

$$\text{Precision} = \frac{\text{No. of correct answers}}{\text{No. of answers produced}}$$

$$\text{Recall} = \frac{\text{No. of correct answers}}{\text{No. of total possible corrects}}$$

Both recall and precision are always on the interval $[0, 1]$, their optimum being at 1.0. They are, however, inversely related to each other, meaning that by allowing for a lower recall you can achieve a higher precision and vice versa.

When comparing the performance of different systems, both precision and recall must be considered. However, as it is not straightforward to compare the two parameters at the same time, various combination methods have been proposed. One such measure is the *F*-measure, which combines precision, *P*, and recall, *R*, in a single measurement as follows:

$$F = \frac{(\beta^2 + 1)PR}{\beta^2 P + R}$$

The parameter β determines how much to favor recall over precision. Researchers in IE frequently report the *F*1 score of a system where $\beta = 1$, weighing precision and recall equally. Using the *F*-measure, the relative performance of systems reporting different values for recall and precision can be easily compared.

7.1.4   Approaches to information extraction

There are two main approaches to the design of IE systems, which can be called the knowledge engineering approach and the automatic training approach (Ashish and Knoblock 1997).

In the knowledge engineering approach, grammars expressing rules for the system are constructed by hand using knowledge of the application domain. The skill of the knowledge engineer plays a large role in the level of performance of the system, but the best-performing systems are often handcrafted. However, the development process can be very laborious, and sometimes, the required expertise may not be available.

For the automatic training approach, there is not the same need for system expertise when customizing the system for a new domain. Instead, someone with sufficient knowledge of the domain and the task at hand annotates a set of training documents. Once a training corpus has been annotated, a training algorithm is run, training the system for analyzing novel texts. This approach is faster than the knowledge engineering approach, but requires that a sufficient volume of training data is available.

7.1.5   Free, structured, and semistructured text

Originally, the aim of IE was to develop practical systems, which could take short natural language texts and extract a limited range of key pieces of information from them. For example, the texts might be news articles about terrorist attacks, and the key information might be the perpetrators, their affiliation, the location, the victims, etc. Or the texts might be pharmaceutical research abstracts and the key information might be new products, their manufacturers, patent information, etc.

IE systems for free text have generally used natural language techniques, and the extraction rules are typically based on patterns involving syntactic relations between words or semantic classes of words. Several steps are required including syntactic analysis, semantic tagging, recognizers for domain objects such as person and company names, and extraction rules. The rules or patterns can be hand-coded or generated from training examples annotated with the right label by a human expert.

The state-of-the-art IE from free text is not comparable with human capability but still provides useful results. This is true whether the rules are hand-coded or automatically learned. Unrestricted natural language understanding is a long way from being solved. However, IE methods can work because they depend on strong a priori restrictions on the kinds of patterns they need to search for.

Structured text is defined as textual information in a database or file following a predefined and strict format. Such information can easily be correctly extracted using the format description. Usually, quite simple techniques are sufficient for extracting information from text provided that the format is known; otherwise, the format must be learned.

Semistructured data are an intermediate point between unstructured collections of textual documents and fully structured tuples of typed data. Such texts fall between structured and free text and have previously been almost inaccessible to IE systems.

Semistructured text is ungrammatical and often telegraphic in style and does not follow any rigid format. NLP techniques are deployed to design rules for extraction of information from free text. However, these methods that are appropriate for grammatical text will usually not work for semistructured text, which seldom contains full sentences. Hence, for semistructured texts, the traditional techniques of IE cannot be used, and at the same time, simple rules used for rigidly structured text will not be sufficient.

Some form of structuring is, however, present in semistructured text, and extraction patterns are often based on tokens and delimiters like hypertext markup language (HTML) tags. Syntactic and semantic information can only be utilized to a limited extent.

7.1.6   Web documents

The World Wide Web provides a vast source of information. This information is often semistructured, although you may also find both structured and free text. The information is also dynamic, it contains hyperlinks and can be represented in different forms and is globally shared over multiple sites and platforms. Hence, the Web provides a special challenge and has been the driving force behind research on IE from structured and semistructured text.

Some define all web pages as semistructured as they all contain some structuring information concerning display styles. However, Hsu and Dung (1998) gave a better categorization of types of web pages: a web page that provides itemized information is structured if each attribute in a tuple can be correctly extracted based on some uniform syntactic clues, such as delimiters or the orders of attributes. Semistructured web pages, however, may contain tuples with missing attributes, attributes with multiple values, variant attribute permutations, and exceptions. A web page is unstructured if linguistic knowledge is required to extract the attributes correctly.

In the following, we will talk about web pages both as structured, semistructured, and unstructured depending on how the contents are organized. However, the structuredness of a web page will always depend on the attributes the users want to extract. Usually, machine-generated web pages are very structured, while hand-generated web pages are less structured, but there are plenty of exceptions.

When it comes to extracting information from web pages, the same applies to web documents as to other semistructured documents: The traditional NLP techniques are not well suited, as the sources often do not exhibit the rich grammatical structure such techniques are designed to exploit. In addition, NLP techniques tend to be slow, and this can be a problem as the volume of document collections on the Web can be large and the extraction is often expected to be performed on the *y*.

Large portions of the data on the Web are rendered regularly as itemized lists of attributes, such as many searchable web indexes. For these semistructured web pages, the regularity of their appearance can be exploited for extracting data instead of using linguistic knowledge.

The organization and the hyperlinking of documents are important aspects when extracting information from web pages that is not present in text documents for the traditional IE task. For instance, it may be necessary to follow hyperlinks to obtain all the information you are looking for. The extraction rules will be dependent on the overall organization of the web page, and some rules will have limitations that prohibit them from being used on some types of pages.

Web pages that appear as results from queries to online databases often result in a set of hyperlinked pages. Such semistructured web pages are classified by Chidlovskii et al. (1997) as either

1. One-level one page result, where one page contains all items related to the original query
2. One-level multipage result, where more links must be followed to get the full listing of answers
3. Two-level pages, where for each item in the first level a link must be followed in order to navigate to a page containing all information related to the items

7.2   Wrapper induction

The Internet presents a large and growing number of information sources, which can be found either by manual browsing or by using a search engine. These information sources live isolated, with no real connections with one another, and each service exists independently. This has created a need for IE from the Web, which can extract and collect information from independent sources.

The publication of structured and semistructured data on the Web is a trend that is likely to increase, and there is also a growth of the so-called hidden web. This refers to web pages generated on the *y* from some database, based on user requests. About 80% of the Web is already in the hidden web. These pages are not available to web crawlers for indexing and cannot be reached through search engines. This means that there will be a special need for tools that can extract information from such pages. IE from websites is often performed using wrappers.

7.2.1   Wrappers

A wrapper can be seen as a procedure that is designed for extracting content of a particular information source and delivering the content of interest in a self-describing representation. In the database community, a wrapper is a software component that converts data and queries from one model to another. In the Web environment, its purpose should be to convert information implicitly stored as an HTML document into information explicitly stored as a data structure for further processing.

A wrapper for a web source accepts queries about information in the pages of that source, fetches relevant pages from the source, extracts the requested information, and returns the result. It consists of a set of extraction rules and the code required to apply these rules and is specific to one source. To extract information from several independent sources, a library of wrappers are needed. Wrappers should execute quickly, because they are usually used online to satisfy users' queries. Ideally, the wrapper should also be able to cope with the changing and unstable nature of the Web, like network failures, ill-formed documents, change in the layout, etc.

There are two primary advantages to building wrappers around web sources: The ability to obtain the relevant information from an individual source is enhanced, and all the sources for which a wrapper is built can be queried using a common query language. It is then possible to get an integrated access to several sources, and the Web sources may be queried in a database-like fashion using a common query language.

7.2.2   From information extraction to wrapper generation

The need for tools that could extract and integrate data from multiple web sources led to the development of the WG field. This field appeared independently of the traditional IE community, and a typical WG application extracts data from web pages that are generated online, based on user queries, using predefined HTML templates. In the WG community, such a collection of documents is called a semistructured source. In order to combine data coming from these sources, the relevant data must be extracted from the HTML templates. Hence, the wrappers are merely an IE application for this particular information source.

Traditional IE systems use extraction patterns based on a combination of syntactic and semantic constraints. However, as previously mentioned, for semistructured documents like those of a WG application, linguistic extraction patterns are usually not applicable. In order to deal with the new types of application domains, researchers introduced new sets of extraction patterns, and a typical WG system generates delimiter-based extraction patterns that do not use linguistic constraints. For this type of web pages, which are generated on the Web, all documents are generated by filling in the same template. After seeing a couple of sample documents, one can therefore usually identify the fragments of the template that represent the delimiters of each individual field. Although the web pages, which are the target of WG applications, follow syntactic regularities, the IE from these sources is not trivial. Scalability is for instance an important challenge, as there is both a large number of sites and a large variation in formatting styles. Flexibility is another challenge, as the format of sources may change.

7.2.3   Wrapper generation

The construction of a wrapper can be done manually, or by using a semiautomatic or automatic approach. The manual generation of a wrapper often involves the writing of ad hoc code. The creator has to spend quite some time understanding the structure of the document and translating it into program code. Though it is simpler to program the IE by hand for semistructured web pages than for free text, the task is not trivial, and hand-coding can be tedious and error-prone. Structure of contemporary IE systems is shown in Figure 7.3.

Tools for helping the manual construction of wrappers have been developed. Some approaches make use of expressive grammars in which the structure of a web page may be described, and provide tools for generating code for the extraction based on the specified grammar. However, even specifying the grammars is tedious and time-consuming, and it requires a high level of expertise.

Although many wrappers to date are hand-written, manually constructed IE systems cannot adapt to domain changes and must be modified for each new problem domain. This means that manually created wrappers require high maintenance costs. For web sources, this is a problem as the number of sources of interest is often very large, and the content and structure of different information sources may vary significantly. In addition,

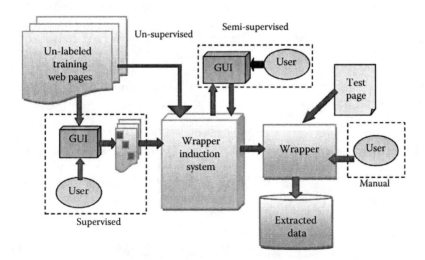

Figure 7.3 Information extraction systems.

new sources appear frequently and the format of existing sources may change. Therefore, mechanisms and technology to aid the construction of wrappers are essential for automatic extraction of web information.

Semiautomatic WG benefits from support tools to help design the wrapper. Some approaches offer a demonstration-oriented interface where the user shows the system what information to extract. Using a graphical interface, one may then perform programming by demonstration, showing the application what fields to extract. This approach means that expert knowledge in wrapper coding is not required at this stage, and it is also less error-prone than coding. However, it must be demonstrated for each new site and for each changed site how the data should be extracted as these systems cannot themselves induce the structure of a site.

Automatic WG uses machine learning techniques, and the wrapper research community has developed learning algorithms for a spectrum of wrappers—from the very simple to the relatively complex. Even automatic generation systems do however require a minimum of intervention of human experts. The systems must usually go through a training phase, where it is fed with training examples, and in many cases, this learning has to be supervised.

Wrapper induction is a technique for automatically constructing wrappers, where inductive learning methods are used to generate the extraction rules. The user labels the relevant data on a set of pages, and the system learns extraction rules based on these examples. The accuracy of these rules will depend on both the number and the quality of the examples. The examples are of good quality if they are representative of the pages to be processed.

Once a wrapper is generated, it is applied to other web pages that contain similar data and formatted in a similar fashion as the training examples. This gives rise to two issues:

- Suppose the website changes, whether the wrapper knows this change or not. This is known as wrapper verification problem.
- Suppose the change is detected, then how to automatically repair the wrapper? This is known as the wrapper repair problem.

One approach to tackle these two issues is to learn the characteristic patterns of the target items. These items further used to monitor the extraction to check whether the extracted items are correct. If they are not correct, then the same patterns can be used to locate the correct items assuming that the page changes are minor changes. This is a *relabeling*. Once relabeling is done, relearning is performed to produce a new wrapper. These two tasks are very difficult because contextual and semantic information is often needed to detect changes and to find the new locations of the target items.

7.2.3.1 *Semiautomated wrapper generation*

7.2.3.1.1 *Xwrap.* First generation of WG was semiautomated, that is, the system could find structure and data with the help of user guidance. A famous work in this area was the Xwrap-system (Liu 2000), which was presented in 2000. This system was developed not only to extract data, but also to generate general wrappers in executable code (Java). The Xwrap architecture is composed of four components as shown in Figure 7.4:

- Syntactical structure normalization: Fetches the web page from the desired URL
- Cleans up bad HTML tags and generates the parse tree

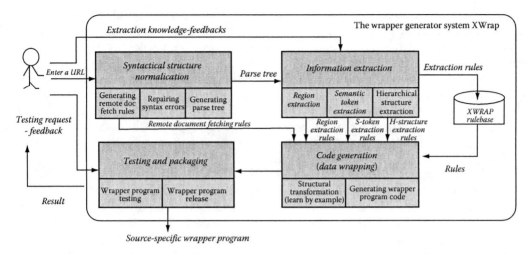

Figure 7.4 Xwrap system architecture for data wrapping.

- IE: Identifies interesting regions and semantic tokens in the parse tree and finds hierarchical structures in order to generate the extraction rules
- Code generation: Uses the extraction rules derived in earlier step and generates the executable code
- Testing and packing: The user may now test the code with similar URLs from the same web source, and this step is used for wrapper program debugging and to make sure that the wrapper is somewhat generalized toward the Web source

The Xwrap-system uses a graphical user interface (GUI) that guides the user through the whole process. The user is presented with a parse tree, and he/she can then click to define which regions are interesting. When the user has defined the semantically meaning of nodes in the tree, the system generates the extraction rules with a feedback-driven interaction with the user. The system prompts with heuristic-based guesses in an iterative process with an attempt to describe the syntactic structure of the document in a context-free grammar. The extraction rules are specified in a well-formed XML template that is passed onto the code generator, which generates the wrapper code. The code and the extraction rules can then be tested with other pages to see which rules need to be altered in order to make the wrapper code effective.

The system's easy-to-use interface makes the process fairly easy, but the weakness of the system is still the need of human supervision. Later research has been made in order to make the human interaction process obsolete.

7.2.3.1.2   Information extraction based on pattern discovery.   This system was designed to use pattern discovery techniques in order to extract the data. Information extraction based on pattern discovery (IEPAD; Chang and Lui 2001) makes use of PAT trees to find repetitive patterns in an effective way. According to Chang and Lui (2001), a PAT tree is a "Patricia tree (Practical Algorithm for Retrieve Information Coded in Alphanumeric) constructed over all the possible suffix strings" (Gonnet et al. 1992; Morrison 1968).

It is in essence a binary tree where the edges are labeled with a repetitive substring. All internal nodes are labeled with a number designating a bit position in the given string, and all external nodes (leafs) are labeled with a number that indicates the starting position of that particular substring in the encoded string. These properties give the ability to retrieve possible substrings by traversing from the root node to a leaf node. This structure also gives the ability to retrieve repetitive patterns in a quick fashion by examining the internal and external node labels.

The system includes three components that are necessary to the extraction process, namely, extraction rule (pattern) generator, pattern viewer, and extractor module given in Figure 7.5. The first component is called the extraction rule generator, which takes a web page as input and generates the extraction rules for the wrapper. This component can be subdivided into four other components, namely, the token translator, PAT tree constructor, validator, and the rule composer, as shown in Figure 7.6.

The token translator converts the HTML code into tokens of two kinds, either an HTML tag token or a text token. These tokens are encoded as binary strings for use in the PAT tree, which encodes the entire document into a suffix tree structure. The validator is used to sort out undesired information since a lot of patterns derived are not interesting for the user. The validator uses three criteria that can be configured by the user, namely, regularity, compactness, and coverage, which consists of threshold values that can be individually set or ignored. Regularities specify the standard deviation of the spacing between adjacent pattern occurrences, compactness is a measure of the density of the occurrences (i.e., if the patterns are scattered or not) and coverage is specified by the amount of the entire document that the patterns cover. For example, consider the following string element set for generalization:

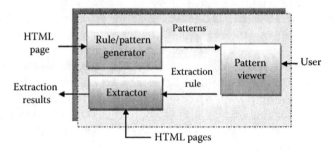

Figure 7.5 IEPASD architecture.

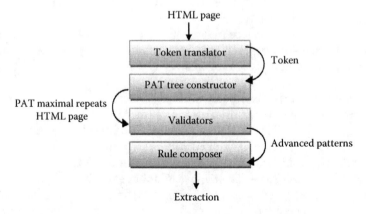

Figure 7.6 IEPASD pattern generator.

$$
\begin{array}{ccccccc}
a & b & c & d & f & e \\
a & b & c & e & f & - \\
a & b & c & e & f & e \\
\end{array}
$$

These strings can be generalized into $abc[d|e]f[e| -]$. The rule composer uses a technique of multiple string alignment to generalize strings that are approximate matches. The idea is that several extracted patterns are quite similar and this component tries to merge those strings into general strings. When the patterns are extracted and the rules have been generated, the user is prompted with the pattern viewer, which is the second component of the IEPAD system. The pattern viewer is a GUI that allows the user to select from several target patterns that contain the desired information. When the user has selected which patterns are to be used, they are forwarded to the final component, which is called the extractor module. This component uses the patterns on other input web pages to execute the pattern matching and IE. The system takes no regard to the semantics of the extracted data, and the patterns to be (in contrast to RoadRunner, which is discussed later) are dependent on user input.

7.2.3.2   Automated wrapper generation

Several projects have been conducted to find ways to generate these wrappers automatically without the need of human supervision, and some of them are discussed in this section.

7.2.3.2.1   RoadRunner.

In an attempt to implement an extraction system that fully automated the WG, the RoadRunner (Crescenzi et al. 2001) was developed. The system performs a number of queries on the underlying database provided by the target site and examines two different documents from the same source at the same time. The similarities and differences are compared to generate a general union-free regular expression that matches both documents.

The idea is to take a document as an initial wrapper page, and compare it tag by tag with a second page (called the sample page) and progressively refine it by solving mismatches until a general wrapper page is generated. The mismatches are divided in string mismatches and tag mismatches, where the tag mismatches are used to identify either optionals or iterators. The basic assumption of this method is that data originated from the database should be different from different search queries, whereas the data (text, tag structure) generated by the HTML template script should be identical.

When two strings differ from the documents, it is assumed that these strings represent some form of element in a data record. When this happens, the wrapper page (initially the first page) is modified and the string is replaced with #PCDATA, which is a token that the system identifies as a data field element.

Different tag structures often indicate some optional field or some repeated pattern. This happens, for example, when two different data tables are compared, which contains different numbers of rows. To solve this mismatch, the system first tries to see if the tag mismatch could be rounded up in a repeated pattern. The system finds the initial and terminal tag for the mismatched block and defines it as a square. This square is then matched against an upward portion of the sample to see whether it indicates a repeated pattern or not, for instance, if it represents a row in a table. If a repeated pattern is found, the wrapper page is modified with an iterator token, which in manners of regular expression would be to enclose the body within a statement like (...)+. If the system fails to identify

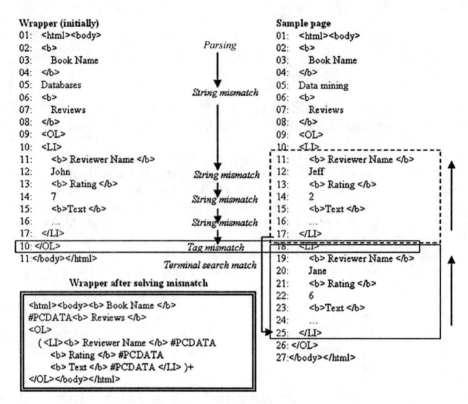

Figure 7.7 A sample execution of the RoadRunner algorithm, similar to that illustrated in Crescenzi et al. (2001) on analyzing tree structure. The system consists of three phases that performs the extraction process.

an iterator, it does a cross-search in the wrapper and the sample page to see whether this mismatched tag could be skipped. If the system is available to resume parsing (continue identifying similarities) after the mismatched block, it is marked as an optional block, which would be specified by a statement like (...)?. A sample execution of the algorithm is illustrated in Figure 7.7, where an iterator is detected and written into the final wrapper expression.

The method of finding patterns is recursively defined since the process of identifying iterators could lead to more iterators or optionals. New mismatches could be found during the upward search, which generates internal mismatches, which is dealt with in the same manner as other mismatches with the exception that the two squares within the document are compared instead of two different documents.

The RoadRunner system examines several web documents from the target site in order to produce a wrapper expression that is as general as possible. The result is generated as an HTML document with the same internal tag structure, but the fields are specified with labels {A,B,C, ...}. The result is promising but there are a few remarks worthy of mentioning.

The system succeeds in identifying data fields within the document, but this method requires the target site to provide several pages of query results. As stated earlier, this is not always the case, and a problem arises when the set of tuples generated by the queries contains a field with a homogenous content. As an example of this, consider a search query on a bookstore that only (for this or that particular time being) has books from one designated publisher. The field that represents the publisher would be interpreted as a common text label and not a field originated from the underlying database. The system also lacks the ability to automatically define the semantic meaning of the extracted data. The goal of the project was only to find ways to extract data from sites without any prior knowledge, not to extract specific data or to define the meaning of the content. Since the labels are specified {A,B,C, …}, it requires a human hand to define the semantics.

7.2.3.2.2 *Omini.* Another attempt to fully automate the extraction process was conducted in 2001 and called Omini (Buttler et al. 2001). The aim was similar to that of RoadRunner, to make the extraction fully independent of human intervention, but the approach was more concentrated.

The web page is fetched from a user-specified URL and is transformed into a well-formed document using syntactic normalization algorithms. After the document has been cleaned, a tag tree representation is constructed based on the nested structure of start and end HTML tags.

Next phase tries to locate the data-rich regions of the page using two consecutive steps. The first step is called object-rich subtree discovery, and the goal of this task is to locate the minimal subtree of the document, which contains all the objects of interests. This is done by combining three heuristic evaluations of the subtrees, which includes the number of children in each node (the fanout of the branch), the size of data in bytes in each node, and the count of subtrees. The next step is called object separator extraction, which is responsible for deriving which tags (or nodes) are semantically defined as separators of the data records. Five different heuristic functions are used that independently rank each candidate tag, and a statistical probability function is used to combine these measures. The functions include the standard deviation heuristic, which calculates the distance (in characters) between two consecutive occurrences of a candidate tag. The repeating pattern heuristic counts the number of occurrences of all pairs of candidate tags that have no text between them. The intuition behind this is that tags that have a closely repeated pattern often are used to designate some form of data field layout. Identifiable path separator tag heuristic ranks the tags by examining the specific tags that are normally used as separators. An example of this is that <tr> or <td> tags are often used as separators within the <table> tag. Sibling tag heuristic counts pairs of tags that are immediate siblings in the minimal subtree, and the candidate tag is ranked by counting the occurrences of these pairs. The final function partial path heuristic counts the number of paths that exist from each candidate tag to any other node reachable within that subtree (refer Buttler et al. 2001 for more details).

The final phase is responsible for extracting the data using the separators defined in previous step. After the object separators are chosen, the desired objects must be extracted with the regard that sometimes the separators are between the data object, and sometimes, they reside in a subtree under the separator.

7.2.3.2.3 *Data extraction and label assignment.* The data extraction and label assignment (DeLa; Wang and Lochovsky 2003) system consists of four components whose structure is quite similar to earlier approaches with some new features and add-ons. A crawler performs queries to a web page to generate the documents, a wrapper generator finds a common regular expression, a data aligner derives nested data, and the label assigner tries to define the semantic meaning of the extracted data.

A form crawler called HiWe is used to perform all necessary search queries. The resulting web pages are fed into the wrapper generator, which is greatly inspired by the IEPAD system (Chang and Lui 2001). First, they employ the data-rich section extraction (DSE) algorithm to sort out noninteresting data from the documents, which works by comparing two different documents from the same source to identify similarities. When the data-rich sections have been identified, they build a token suffix tree of the tokens in order to locate continuous repeated (C-repeated) patterns. The suffix tree is iterated and a pattern tree is generated to expose which patterns are dependent on each other to be found, as some patterns cannot be extracted until some others have been defined. The pattern tree starts as an empty root node, and each discovered pattern is inserted as child to that root node.

After a pattern from the suffix tree is identified, the patterns discovered right after that are inserted as children to that node of the pattern tree. The pattern with the highest nested level in the tree is chosen as the general pattern for that web page. As the C-repeated patterns are interpreted as kleene star in regular grammar, this method, however, is not sufficient to identify optionals or disjunctions in the structure. To identify, the system downloads several web pages and merges the derived expressions using a string alignment algorithm similar to that of IEPAD.

The innovation of this system lies in the data alignment and label assignment components. To extract nested data into a table similar to that of a relational database management system (DBMS), they employ a data tree for the regular expression generated by the wrapper (Figure 7.8).

The tree is generated by examining the nested structure of the expression, and each nested expression is defined as a child to the enclosing expression as the tree is generated recursively. Each node represents a partial table, and these tables are merged by constructing unions and Cartesian products of the subtables.

Before the data are inserted, an attribute separation is performed. The HTML tags are stripped and the system tries to find what the actual data are in each cell. The assumption here is that some cells contain comma-separated strings or other noisy information that is not interesting for the extraction.

The label assignment component uses heuristics to define the semantic meaning of each column in the table. The form element labels in the Web query page are examined to retrieve some clues, as most search engines often provide some sort of label to identify the text box for the user. Labels are also searched within the parsed document, and some cells can be identified by their formats. For instance, a date usually follows a significant format ("dd/mm/yy") and email addresses contain the symbol "@".

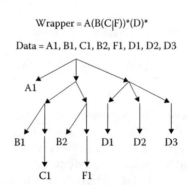

Wrapper = $A(B(C|F))^*(D)^*$

Data = A1, B1, C1, B2, F1, D1, D2, D3

Figure 7.8 A tree representing nested levels of a regular expression.

7.2.3.2.4   EXALG.   The EXALG algorithm (Arasu and Garcia-Molina 2003) uses a rather different approach from earlier works. The system works in two stages: the first is called equivalence class generation module (ECGM) and the second is called Analysis Module. The main objectives of the first stage is to find and derive equivalence classes, which is defined as the maximal set of tokens having the same number of occurrences in each input page. A token in this system is defined as a word or an HTML tag, and the module counts the occurrences of each token to find what words or tags are commonly used in the set of input web pages. The assumption is that the repeated occurrences of these tokens often are generated by the page template. EXALG also differentiates the meaning of these tokens by examining the relation between their occurrences, which can be observed by comparing different paths from the root in the HTML parse tree. The sets of these equivalence classes are refined in an iterative process within this module (the reader is referred to Arasu and Garcia-Molina 2003 for more details about this process), and the output in these sets and the web pages represented as a set of strings of these tokens. This is used by the analysis module to generate the templates.

7.2.3.2.5   Mining data records.   The algorithm proposed by Mining Data Records (MDRs) in web pages (Liu et al. 2003) compares nodes in the HTML tag structure to generate a wrapper. The algorithm automatically mines all data records formed by table- and form-related tags, that is, <TABLE>, <FORM>, <TR>, <TD>, etc., assuming that a large and majority of web data records are formed by them. The algorithm is based on two observations.

1. A group of data records are always presented in a contiguous region of the web page and are formatted using similar HTML tags. Such region is called a data region.
2. The nested structure of the HTML tags in a web page usually forms a tag tree and a set of similar data records are formed by some child subtrees of the same parent node.

The algorithm works in three steps:

Step 1. Building the HTML tag tree by following the nested blocks of the HTML tags in the web page.

Step 2. Identifying the data regions by finding the existence of multiple similar generalized nodes of a tag node. A generalized node (or a node combination) is a collection of child nodes of a tag node, with the following two properties:

1. All the nodes have the same parent.
2. The nodes are adjacent.

Then, each generalized node is checked to decide whether it contains multiple records or only one record. This is done by string comparison of all possible combinations of component nodes using normalized edit distance method. A data region is a collection of two or more generalized nodes with the following properties:

1. The generalized nodes all have the same parent.
2. The generalized nodes all have the same length.
3. The generalized nodes are all adjacent.
4. The normalized edit distance (string comparison) between adjacent generalized nodes is less than a fixed threshold.

Step 3. Identifying the data records involves finding the data records from each generalized node in a data region.

As shown in the aforementioned algorithm, the three steps to complete this task are performed by first building a tag tree representation of the web page, mine it for data regions by comparing strings and subtree, and then identify data records within each region. The method to accomplish this is to generate generalized nodes that are defined as similar sibling nodes with the properties that they are adjacent and have the same parent. The function is a recursive depth-first comparison where all combinations of each child node are compared in order to find which nodes that could be grouped together. During the first iteration of each node, the comparison is done consecutively, the second iteration compares them two by two, and so on. For example, given a set of nodes {A,B,C,D,E,F}, the first iteration compares (A − B), (B − C), (C − D), (D − E), (E − F), followed by (A,B − C,D), (C,D − E,F), and (A,B,C − D,E,F). Each node is furthermore examined recursively to discover nested tag structures. The data records in the tree nodes are identified by comparing string edit distance between different nodes.

The second approach, data extraction based on partial tree alignment (DEPTA), also known as MDR-2, is similar to MDR in its data region identification mechanism. DEPTA uses visual information to build the HTML tag tree, to eliminate the problems caused by HTML tag structure irregularities. DEPTA uses tree edit distance for identifying similar data records. A single data record may be composed of multiple subtrees due to noisy information. MDR may find wrong combinations of subtrees. DEPTA (Zhai and Liu 2005) makes use of the visual gaps between data records to deal with the aforementioned problem.

However, as in Liu et al. (2003) and Zhai and Liu (2005), it also requires content analysis to identify the main data region from the set of data regions obtained. Furthermore, it also relies on TABLE tags for identifying data regions. This technique proposes a two-step strategy.

Step 1. Identifying individual data records in a page.
Step 2. Aligning and extracting data items from the identified data records.

Specifically, this method also uses visual cues to find data records. Since DEPTA is tag dependent, it requires considerable time in building tag tree, traversing whole tag tree and string comparison. These automatic methods are tag dependant, incorporate time-consuming tag tree construction, and make many assumptions, which do not always hold good for all web pages.

7.2.3.2.6 Web data extractor. A new way of using tree edit distance to extract data was presented in 2007 called the Web data extractor (WDE). In similarity with MDR, they compute clusters of similar tree nodes using tree edit distance, but in contrast they use an algorithm that approximates the cost due to the performance cost of finding the actual edit distance. They also assign different weights to nodes depending on their height and internal depth. All possible candidate records are enumerated and compared using tree edit distance, and the records are clustered into sets based on their similarities. These clusters are used to generate data extraction patterns, which according to their own evaluation are superior to MDR with respect to loosely structured records (in contrast to strictly structured documents, like big tables, etc.).

7.2.3.2.7 Visual content. Although most research has been conducted in examining the structure of web pages, some attempts have been made to extract structure based on visual layout of documents. According to Rosenfeld et al. (2002), text lines, paragraphs, and columns can be identified by grouping objects (characters, words, and images) according to their structural layout relationships. Their system was designed to examine portable document format (PDF) documents and is based on a machine learning approach to examine different documents within a training set. Although the principle is interesting to consider when extracting product information, the idea would probably not be applicable as a standalone extraction system.

7.2.4   Inductive learning of wrappers

Various machine learning techniques like symbolic learning, ILP, wrapper induction, statistical methods, and grammar induction have been applied for the problem of IE. In wrapper induction, the problem of wrapper construction is posed as one of inductive learning.

At the highest level, inductive learning is the task of computing from a set of examples of some unknown target concept, a generalization that explains the observations. The idea is that a generalization is good if it explains the observed examples and makes accurate predictions when previously unseen examples are encountered. Inductive learning has proven useful for classification problems, knowledge acquisition, knowledge discovery from large databases, and program construction from partial specifications.

Inductive learning is accomplished through inductive inference, the process of reasoning from a part to a whole, from particular instances to generalization, or from individual to universal. A teacher provides examples for the learner, and the learner generalizes the given examples to induce the general rules. Because human learning is mostly based on experimental observation (empirical learning), it is easier for us to produce good examples than to generate explicit and complete general rules. In general, inductive methods can be characterized as search methods over a hypothesis space.

Inductive learning methods for supervised learning can be classified as zero order or first order. The principal difference between zero-order and first-order supervised learning systems are the form of training data and the way that a learned theory is expressed. Data for the zero-order learning programs such as classification and regression tree (CART) and C4.5 comprise preclassified cases; each described by its values for a fixed collection of attributes. These systems develop theories in the form of decision trees or production rules that relate a case's class to its attribute values. Unfortunately, decision tree learners lack expressiveness because they are based on propositional logic. They cannot learn concepts including relations between objects such as family relationship. From the database point of view, they can deal only with one relation consisting of attribute–value pairs.

The relational first-order learning methods allow induction over structured examples that can include first-order logical predicates and functions and unbounded structures such as lists or trees. In particular, ILP studies the induction of rules in first-order logic and the learning of logic programs and other relational knowledge from examples.

ILP research stands at the intersection of the traditional fields of machine learning and logic programming. Most other machine learning algorithms are restricted to finite feature-based representations of examples and concepts and cannot learn complex relational and recursive knowledge. However, due to the expressiveness of first-order logic, ILP methods can learn relational and recursive concepts that cannot be represented in the attribute–value representations assumed by most machine learning algorithms. ILP allows learning with much richer representations and can learn much more complex concepts than decision tree learners. Hence, ILP techniques have been applied to the problem of learning to extract information from documents with more complex structures and relations.

ILP algorithms use two different approaches to induction: bottom-up (generalization) or top-down (specialization). The bottom-up approach is data-driven, and starts with selecting one or more examples and formulates a hypothesis to cover those examples and then generalizes the hypothesis to cover the rest of the examples. The top-down approach starts with the most general hypothesis available, making it more specific through the introduction of negative examples. In general, top-down algorithms can induce a large class of logic programs, but need a relatively large number of samples. On the other hand, bottom-up algorithms work with a very small number of examples but induce only a small class of programs.

Several experimental ILP systems have been developed, where first order learning system (FOIL) (Quinlan and Cameron-Jones 1993) and GOLEM (Muggleton and Feng 1990) are the best known. FOIL was developed by Quinlan in 1989 and is a top-down ILP algorithm. Based on a training set of positive and negative facts, a clause that covers some positive and no negative facts is found, and all the facts covered by this clause from the training set is removed until there are no positive facts in the training set. GOLEM (Muggleton and Feng 1990) uses a greedy covering algorithm. The clause construction is bottom-up, based on the construction of least general generalizations of more specific clauses. Generalization is performed until all positive examples are covered, and none of the negative examples are implied.

7.3   Locating data-rich pages

In order to extract the structure from the document, the nondata regions of the document have to be excluded. It is possible to omit this step in the process and derive the information anyway, but as we shall see this could lead to immense complexity increase and aggravate the heuristic functions that are used in most methods.

7.3.1   Finding tables

Yalin Wang and Jianying Hu did a research on how a machine-based learning approach could be applicable to detect data-rich tables on a web page. They defined tables as genuine or nongenuine depending on their data content and structure, and they examine the <TABLE> tags to find features including layout, content type, and word groups in order to classify each table. With statistical and heuristic functions, they compare among other things the table layout, relation between rows and columns, the length of data in each cell and contents (images, links, and texts) within each cell in the target page with a ground trusted data collection. The problem with this approach is that you need an entire data collection of ground trusted data in order for it to work. Even though the system seems to find data-rich tables, there is no guarantee that they find the correct data-rich tables. If you are looking for product information, you just as might find company information, addresses, etc., and most product pages (like those containing books, computers, and hardware) contain lots of images and links that would aggravate their heuristic functions used for classification. Product pages will have fundamental differences in layout, and even if you use very varying input, the result is totally dependent on the ground trusted data.

7.3.2   Identifying similarities

Another approach is to examine similarities between different pages within the same product website. They employ an algorithm called DSE, which compares the tree structure from two different pages and sorts out the identical subtrees. The concept is that if you do some search queries within the site, the resulting pages will be identical (they are generated with the same script) except for the tables that contain information from the underlying relational database. The idea is solid and the method is effective, but it still requires the database to have enough information that it would require several result pages. This is true in most common sites (big bookstores, etc.), but some product pages do not have that many products. Many product pages do not even have a search form in order to do the query, as the main page is just a single page containing the company-specific products.

7.3.3   Heuristics on product properties

Some systems that have a clear view of what their product properties are can use heuristics to find the tables that contain correct data. Some properties like dates, international standard book number (ISBN), or specific product serial numbers could easily be recognized by regular expressions and could therefore be used to identify which tables contain the desired information. Features among text strings like length, paragraph size, and word occurrences can be used as heuristics to identify news information. This approach is also applicable to labeling columns and identifying data semantics.

7.3.4   Human intrusion

The most basic and easy way is of course to use humans to identify the sections. As discussed earlier, this is error-prone, costly, and not very scalable, but in some cases it is actually the last resort. Even though a system could identify the right data 95% of the time, it is sometimes required that a human monitors the process in order to guarantee the correctness of the lasting 5%.

7.4   Systems for wrapper generation

The early approaches to structuring and wrapping websites were essentially based on manual techniques. Here, it is assumed that a human programmer examines a site and manually codes wrappers that abstract the logical features of HTML pages and store them in a database. One of the first approaches to a framework for manual building of web wrappers is the Stanford-IBM manager of multiple Information Sources (TSIMMIS) system in 1995. The goal of TSIMMIS is to provide tools for accessing, in an integrated fashion, multiple information sources, and to ensure that the information obtained is consistent. The focus is on the development of languages and tools to support this wrapping process.

For websites where the volume is large and the content and structure change dynamically, there is however a need for a more effective construction of wrappers. Generally, the database communities have focused on how the heterogeneous information can be integrated, while wrappers are designed manually. On the other hand, the AI communities have focused on how machine learning can be used to automate the learning of websites. We will discuss systems that use machine learning techniques for semiautomatic and automatic generation of wrappers.

The complexity of a wrapper and the WG will depend on the level of structure in the websites. In Section 7.4.1, systems based on techniques that are tailored for relatively well-structured web pages will be described. These systems typically arise from the

WG community. Then systems based on techniques intended for web pages with a less rigorous structure are presented. The latter systems are more influenced by the traditional IE field.

7.4.1　Structured and semistructured web pages

In this section, the systems ShopBot, wrapper induction environment (WIEN), SoftMealy, WebMantic, and STALKER are described. These systems belong to the field of WG, where the typical application is to extract data from web pages that are generated online based on queries to a database. These systems use delimiter-based extraction patterns and do not use syntactic or semantic constraints, and they are limited to work on fairly structured data.

7.4.1.1　ShopBot

ShopBot (Doorenbos et al. 1996, 1997) is a comparison-shopping agent, specialized to extract information from web vendors. As such ShopBot is more restricted than most of the other systems that will be described. The algorithm focuses on vendor sites with form-based search pages returning lists of products with a tabular format. Information is extracted from the resulting pages using a combination of heuristic search, pattern matching, and inductive learning techniques.

The ShopBot operates in two phases: the learning phase, which is performed offline, and the online comparison-shopping phase. During the learning phase, the vendor sites are analyzed to learn a symbolic description of each site. In the comparison-shopping phase, the learned vendor descriptions are used to extract information from the sites and find the best price for the product specified by the user.

In the learning phase, some simple heuristics are used to determine the correct search form, and how to pose a query to this form. Then the learner must determine the format of the result page. The result pages for a query are assumed to consist of a header, a body, and a tail, where the header and tail are consistent across different pages and the body contains all the desired product information. The format of the result page is determined in three steps. First, the failure template, appearing for nonexisting products, is learned by analyzing the result pages of dummy queries for nonwords (e.g., \xldccxx-no-product). Then by performing several queries for potential products, the head and tail of the result pages are identified, assuming matching prefixes and suffixes over pages.

Finally, the format of the body containing the product description is determined. Initially, a number of possible abstract formats of product descriptions are defined and represented as sequences of HTML tags and text strings. The body is broken into logical lines representing vertical-space-delimited text, and the learning algorithm compares the different abstract formats with the logical lines to find the best match. In this way, the algorithm is able to induce the format of the descriptions of the products, but it does not induce the labels of the information slots. The price, which is the most important information in comparison shopping, is extracted using special hand-coded techniques.

7.4.1.2　Wrapper induction environment

The WIEN (Kushmerick 1997; Kushmerick et al. 1997) is a tool for assisting with wrapper construction. The wrapper induction is designed for automatic learning of web pages and is strongly influenced by ShopBot. However, Kushmerick is the first to introduce the term wrapper induction. The method is not designed for a specific area. It works on structured text containing tabular information, and it is demonstrated for, but not restricted to, HTML documents.

The approach can handle web pages that have what they call a head-left-right-tail (HLRT) organization, where there is a head delimiter, a set of right and left delimiters for each fact to be extracted, and a tail delimiter at the end. It looks for uniform delimiters that identify the beginning and end of each slot and for delimiters that separate the tabular information from surrounding text. Pages that conform to this regularity are nearly always automatically formatted responses to a search index or a listing of an underlying database.

Kushmerick seeks to automate wrapper construction as much as possible, and thereby avoiding the task of hand-labeling a set of example documents. Hence, a set of techniques for automatically labeling example documents has been developed. The labeling algorithm takes as input domain-specific heuristics for recognizing instances of the attributes to be extracted. The system requires that these heuristics are provided as input, but is not concerned with how they are obtained. They may have been defined manually; however, this is still a smaller job than hand-labeling each example site. Inductive learning is used to perform the wrapper induction, generalizing from example query responses. The induction algorithm takes as input a set of labeled pages. It then searches the space of wrappers defined by the HLRT wrapper model and iterates over all possible choices of delimiters until a HLRT wrapper, which is consistent with the labeled pages, is found. A model based on computational learning theory is used to predict how many examples the learning algorithm must observe to ensure that the probability of failure for the resulting wrapper is below a specified limit.

Example 7.1: A sample WIEN rule for extracting the restaurant name and area code from a document.

```
D1: 1.Joe's: (313)323-5545 2. Li's: (406)545-2020
D2: 1.KFC: 818-224-4000 2. Rome: (656)987-1212
WIEN rule: ' '.' (*) ':' * '(' (*) ')'
Output: Restaurant {Name @1} {AreaCode @2}
```

The rule has the following meaning: ignore all characters until you find the first occurrence of '.' and extract the restaurant name as the string that ends at the first ':'. Then, again, ignore all characters until you find '(' and extract the string that ends at ')'. In order to extract the information about the other restaurants within the same page, the whole pattern is applied repeatedly until it fails to match. It is easy to see that the WIEN rule can be successfully applied to document D1, but it fails on D2 because of the different phone number formatting. The WIEN rule is an instance of left-right (LR) class, which the simplest type of WIEN rules. The classes HLRT, open-close-left-right (OCLR), and head-opening-closing-left-right-tail (HOCLRT) are extensions of LR that use document *head* and *tail* delimiters, tuple delimiters, and both of them, respectively. WIEN defines two other classes, N-LR and N-HLRT, but their induction turned out to be impractical.

WIEN uses only delimiters that immediately precede and follow the data to be extracted (Muslea 1999) and cannot wrap sources in which some items are missing or sources where the items may appear in a varying order. Multislot rules are used for the extraction. This means that the extraction rules are able to link together related information, as opposed to single-slot rules that can only extract isolated data (e.g., in a document that contains several names and addresses, single-slot rules cannot specify which is the address of a particular person).

7.4.1.3 *SoftMealy*

SoftMealy (Hsu 1998; Hsu and Dung 1998) is a system that learns to extract data from semi-structured web pages by learning wrappers specified as nondeterministic finite automata.

This representation and learning algorithm is, as opposed to Kushmerick's system, said to handle missing values, slots with multiple values, and variable permutations. An inductive generalization algorithm is used to induce contextual rules from training examples. A training example provides an ordered list of the facts to be extracted together with the separators between these facts. The wrapper induction takes as input the set of labeled tuples, providing information on the positions of the separators and the permutations of the facts to be extracted. The algorithm takes these positions as training examples and generalizes their context into contextual rules, which are the output. The induced wrapper is a nondeterministic finite automaton where states represent the facts to be extracted and state transitions represent contextual rules defining the separators between them. State transitions are determined by matching contextual rules that characterize the context delimiting two adjacent facts. To extract the facts, the wrapper recognizes the separators surrounding it. The general rules of SoftMealy allow for wildcards and handle both missing items and items appearing in various orders. However, in order to deal with items of various orders, SoftMealy has to see training examples that include each possible ordering of the items. The extraction patterns of SoftMealy are more expressive than the ones defined for WIEN (Muslea 1999).

> **Example 7.2: A SoftMealy extraction rule that can deal with the different formatting of the area code.**
>
> ```
> D1: 1.Joe's: (313)323-5545 2. Li's: (406)545-2020
> D2: 1.KFC: 818-224-4000 2. Rome: (656)987-1212
> SoftMealy rule: ˙ '.' (*) EITHER ':' (Nmb) '-'
> OR ':' ˙ '(' (Nmb) ')'
> Output: Restaurant {Name @1} {AreaCode @2}
> ```
>
> The SoftMealy rule reads along these lines: ignore all tokens until you find a '.'; then extract the restaurant name, which is the string that ends before the first ':'. If ':' is immediately followed by a number, extract it as the area code; otherwise, ignore all characters until you find a '(' immediately followed by a number, which represents the area code. SoftMealy's extraction patterns are obviously more expressive than the WIEN ones; their main limitation consists of their inability to use delimiters that do not immediately precede and follow the relevant items.

7.4.1.4 *Supervised learning algorithm for inducing extraction rules*

STALKER (Muslea et al. 1998a,b, 1999) is a supervised learning algorithm for inducing extraction rules. Training examples are supplied by the user who has to select a few sample pages and mark up the relevant data (the leaves of a so-called EC tree (ECT)). When the page has been marked, the sequences of tokens that represent the content of the page, together with the index of the token that represents the start of an item, are generated. The sequences of tokens (words, HTML tags) and wildcards can then be used as landmarks to locate an item to be extracted on a page, and the wrapper induction algorithm generates extraction rules that are expressed as simple landmark grammars. The extraction process handles text, but no link information.

Web documents are described by the so-called embedded catalog (EC) formalism. An EC description of a page is a tree structure in which an internal node is either a homogeneous list of items or a heterogeneous tuple of items. The content of the root node in the EC tree is the whole sequence of tokens (the entire document), while the content of an arbitrary node represents a subsequence of the content of its parent. The end nodes are the items of interest to the user (i.e., the data to be extracted). The tree is shown in the following Figure 7.9.

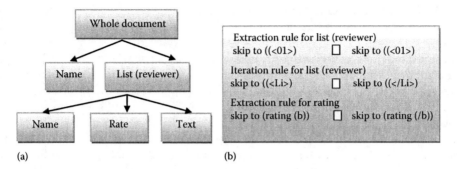

Figure 7.9 (a) STALKER embedded category tree; (b) extraction rules.

STALKER uses a sequential covering algorithm, meaning that it starts by generating linear landmark automata, which can generate as many as possible of the positive training examples. The linear landmark automaton is a nondeterministic finite automaton where a transition between states takes place only if the input string is accepted for the transition between the current and the next state. Then it tries to generate new automata for the remaining examples, and so on. When all the positive examples are covered, STALKER returns the solution, a simple landmark grammars (SLG) where each branch corresponds to a learned landmark automaton.

> **Example 7.3: Let us consider a sample document that refers to a restaurant chain that has restaurants located in several cities. In each city, the restaurant may have several addresses, and at each address, it may have several phone numbers. It is easy to see that the multislot output schema is not appropriate for extraction tasks that are performed on such documents with multiple levels of embedded data.**

```
Name: Taco Bell <br> <p><br>
- LA: 400 Pico; (213)323-5545,(800) 222-1111.
211 Flower; (213) 424-7645.<p>
- Venice: 20 Vernon; (310) 888-1010.<p><hr>
Embedded Catalog Tree:
Document ::= Restaurant LIST(City)
City ::= CityName LIST(Location)
Location ::= Number Street LIST(Phone)
Phone ::= AreaCode PhoneNumber
Restaurant extraction rule: ' 'Name :' (') '<br>'
LIST(City) extraction rule: ' '<br>' ' '<br>' (') '<hr>'
LIST(City) iteration rule: ' '-' (') '<p>'
CityName extraction rule: ' (') ':'
```

In order to cope with this problem, STALKER introduces the ECT formalism to describe the hierarchical organization of the documents. The ECT specifies the output schema for the extraction task, and it is also used to guide the hierarchical IE process. For a given ECT, STALKER generates one extraction rule for each node in the tree, together with an additional iteration rule for each LIST node. The extraction process is performed in a hierarchical manner. For instance, in order to extract all CityNames in a document, STALKER begins by applying to the whole document the extraction rule for the LIST(City), which skips to the second <br> in the page and extracts everything until it encounters a <hr>; then in order to extract each individual city, it applies the LIST(City) iteration rule to the *content of the list*. Finally, STALKER applies to the content of each extracted city the CityName extraction rule.

STALKER is able to wrap information sources that have an arbitrary number of levels. Each node is extracted independently of its siblings; hence, the ordering of the items in the document need not be fixed, and it is possible to extract information from documents with missing items or documents with items appearing in various orders. This makes STALKER more flexible than WIEN, which is only able to handle sources with a fixed ordering of items. As opposed to SoftMealy, which has the same ability to handle missing items and items appearing in varying order, STALKER does not need to see training examples that include each possible ordering of the items.

STALKER rules are, unlike WIEN, single slot. However, this does not represent a limitation, because STALKER uses the ECT to group together the individual items extracted from multislot templates.

7.4.1.5   WebMantic

In general, three main functions need to be implemented in a wrapper: First, they must be able to download HTML pages from a website. Second, they must search for, recognize, and extract the specified data. Third, they have to save this data in a suitably structured format to enable further manipulation. We know that XML is very interesting to structure information, as it is, de-facto, the standard data format in web specifications such as extensible hypertext markup language (XHTML) or simple object access protocol (SOAP). WebMantic (Camacho et al. 2008) is an assistant generator wrapper that allows us to create wrappers that obtain XML documents from HTML pages. A filtering and preprocessing technique allows us to translate some pieces of information, which contain the desired information, into a more understandable and semantic representation. The system translates required portions of the page. Limitation of this system is only structured information, such as data stored in lists or tables, will be considered. WebMantic algorithm allows us to generate some predefined rules that can be used to represent complex and nested structures in the web page.

WebMantic architecture is shown in Figure 7.10. WebMantic modules are HTML parser, Tree generation module, HTML$_2$XML rule generator module, subsumption module, and XML parser module. The WebMantic application follows the next steps to obtain the set of rules called S_g, and finally generates the XML document from a particular HTML page:

1. An HTML page to be translated is provided (by the user) to WebMantic. A preliminary preprocessing of the HTML document is done by the *Tidy* parser, so a well-formed HTML page is obtained.
2. Tables and lists are sequentially located inside the page. The HTML document is sequentially processed and an HTML tree is built where every node represents an HTML tag. For each tag inside the structure, the related XML tag is requested from the user (the user must interact with the application). If no XML tag is provided, a predefined value is used. If the user does not need a particular list or table, it will be marked as "void". This value is used to remove this structure in the transformation process. Once the HTML document is completely processed, a tree structure is generated that represents all the possible structures that can be gathered from this HTML document (or other documents following the same structure).
3. From the HTML tree, a set of HTML$_2$XML rules are generated using the previous interaction with the user. Therefore, if a particular piece of information is not desired by the user, this rule will be marked as "void".

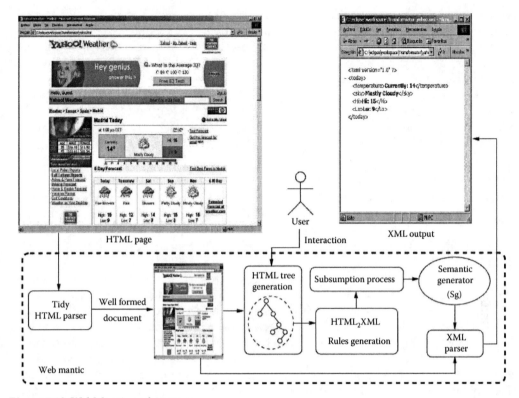

Figure 7.10 WebMantic architecture.

4. For these rules, a subsumption (generalization) process is carried out. This process allows minimizing the number of rules needed to translate the target structures. The new semantic generator S'_g verifies that $S'_g \subset S_g$. The algorithm used to minimize the number of semantic generators can be summarized as follows:

  4.1 For each rule that represents a target structure (table or list) in the S_g. It looks for all the rules with the same header until a different header is found.

  4.2 Those rules that have the same header and body are removed.

  4.3 This process is repeated for all rules until no more rules can be removed.

After all this processing, a minimum set of HTML$_2$XML rules are obtained. In other words, the semantic generator S_g for this page is built. Using this S_g, WebMantic filters the HTML page (that previously has been preprocessed by Tidy) parsing the marked (desired) information by the user into an XML document. The other structures in the page that have been marked as void will be ignored in the parsing process. This S_g can be used for other pages with the same structure (typically, many web servers provide information in different pages, but identically structured). Complete details of the WebMantic and experimental results can be found in Camacho et al. (2008).

7.4.2   *Semistructured and unstructured web pages*

In this section, the systems robust automated production of information extraction rules (RAPIER), sequence rules with validation (SRV), and WHISK are described. These systems belong to a more sophisticated class of wrapper generators than those pre-sented in the previous section, and they can handle a wider range of texts. Although they work on multiple types of text, they do not rely on the use of semantic and syntactic information, but can make use of it when it is available and are able to employ hybrid extraction patterns.

These systems are closer to the traditional IE approach and can be said to lie between the field of IE and WG as their focus is to develop machine learning methods for the IE problem. The methods are based on ILP or relational learning and are related to induction algorithms like FOIL (SRV, WHISK) and GOLEM (RAPIER).

7.4.2.1 Robust automated production of IE rules

The RAPIER (Califf 1998; Califf and Mooney 1997) learns rules for the complete IE task and works on semistructured text. It takes pairs of documents and filled templates indicating the information to be extracted and learns pattern-matching rules to extract fillers for the slots in the template. The human interaction of the system consists of providing texts with filled templates.

The learning algorithm incorporates techniques from several ILP systems and learns unbounded patterns that include constraints on the words and part-of-speech tags sur-rounding the filler. The learning algorithm consists of a specific to general search (bottom-up), beginning with the most specific rule that matches a target slot in the training. Pairs of rules are chosen at random and a beam search is conducted to find the best generalization of the two rules, taking a least general generalization, then adding constraints until no progress is made in several successive iterations. The extraction patterns of RAPIER are based both on delimiters and content description, using rules represented by patterns that exploit the syntactic and semantic information. A part-of-speech tagger is used to obtain the syntactic information, while a lexicon of semantic classes is used to obtain the seman-tic information. The tagger takes sentences as input and labels each word as noun, verb, adjective, etc. A part-of-speech tagger is faster and more robust than a full parser, but does not give as much information. The rules, for the IE, are indexed by a template name and a slot name and consist of three parts:

- A prefiller: a pattern that should match the text preceding the target text
- A filler: a pattern that should match the target text
- A postfiller: a pattern that should match the text immediately following the target text

Each pattern is a sequence of pattern items, matching exactly one word, or pattern lists, matching N words. The text must fulfill the requirements of the patterns to give a match. Possible requirements are that the text must be

1. A list of words, where one word must match the document text
2. A list of syntactic tags, where one tag must match the tag of the document text
3. A list of semantic classes, where the document text must belong to one of these classes

The approach with extraction of fields centered on the target phrase means that the system can only perform single-slot extraction. However, it might be possible to perform multislot extraction by dividing the text into more than three fields (Soderland 1999).

Example 7.4: We take typical RAPIER extraction task: a sample document, the information to be extracted, and the extraction rule for the area slot.

```
ORIGINAL DOCUMENT:              EXTRACTED DATA:
AI. C Programmer. 38-44K.       computer-science-job
Leading AI firm in need of      title: C Programmer
an energetic individual to      salary: 38-44K
fill the following position:    area: AI

AREA extraction pattern:
Pre-filler pattern: word: leading
Filler pattern: list: len: 2
tags: [nn, nns]
Post-filler pattern: word: [firm, company]
```

Here, every "filler pattern" consists of a (possibly empty) list of *pattern items* or *pattern lists*. The former matches exactly one word/symbol from the document, while the latter specifies a maximum length N and matches 0 to N words/symbols from the document. The constraints imposed by the pattern items/lists consist of exact match words, parts of speech, and semantic classes. For instance, in the earlier example, the pre- and postfiller patterns specify that information to be extracted is immediately preceded by the word "leading" and is immediately followed either by "firm" or by "company". The "filler pattern" imposes constraints on the structure of the information to be extracted: it consists of *at most* two words that were labeled "nn" or "nns" by the part-of-speech (POS) tagger. That means one or two singular or plural common nouns.

7.4.2.2   Sequence rules with validation

The SRV is a top-down relational algorithm for IE (Freitag 1998a–c). Input to SRV is a set of pages, labeled to identify instances of the fields to extract, and a set of features defined over tokens. The output is a set of extraction rules. In SRV, the IE problem is viewed as a classification problem where all possible phrases from the text (up to a maximum length) are considered as instances. Every candidate instance in a document is presented to the classifier, and the system assigns to each of these phrases a metric indicating confidence that the phrase is correct filler for the target slot. The original version of SRV uses a classifier that is a relational rule learner that does a top-down induction similar to FOIL. Two additional classifiers, a "\rote" learner and a naive Bayes classifier, are compared to the original SRV by Freitag (1998c).

Example 7.5: The following pattern extracts the names of the companies that were the target of the acquisition process.

```
DOCUMENT-1: … to purchase 4.5 mln Trilogy shares at …
DOCUMENT-2: … acquire another 2.4 mln Roach shares …
Acquisition:- length(<2 ),
some(?A [] capitalized true),
some(?A [next-token] all-lower-case true),
some(?A [right-AN] wn-word 'stock').
```

The extraction rule says that the company name consists of a single, capitalized word (first two predicates) and is followed by a lowercase word (third predicate). Last predicate imposes the constraints. The "right AN" construct refers to the *"right AN link"* in a link grammar, which connects a noun modifier with the noun it modifies. In our example, the information to be extracted (i.e., "?A") is connected by "[right-AN]" to the word that follows it, which, in turn, is one of the WordNet syntax associated with stock.

The features used in SRV come in two varieties: simple features and relational features. Given a token drawn from a document, a number of obvious features may be used, such as length, character type, orthography, part of speech, or lexical meaning, and also relational features that encode token adjacency. The relational features are what give SRV its relational character. SRV's example space consists of all text fragments from the training document collection as long (in number of tokens) as the smallest field instance in the training corpus but no longer than the largest. The extraction process involves examining every possible text fragment of appropriate size to see whether it matches any of the rules.

SRV starts (as FOIL) with the entire set of examples, positive and negative, where a negative example is any fragment that is not tagged as a field instance. Induction proceeds by matching all examples not covered by previously learned rules. When a rule is good enough, that is, it either covers only positive examples or a further specialization is judged to be unproductive, all positive examples matching it are removed from the training set, and the process is repeated. SRV's rule representation is expressive and able to incorporate orthographic features and other evidence such as part of speech or semantic classes when available. No prior syntactic analysis is required. SRV is similar to STALKER and RAPIER, in that it is able to extract particular items independently of other relevant items. The relational learner is also as RAPIER only designed to extract single slots. This is different from, for instance WIEN, which learns rules to extract multiple slots.

7.4.2.3   WHISK

The WHISK system (Soderland 1999) is a learning system that generates extraction rules for a wide variety of documents ranging from rigidly formatted to free text. That means, it is designed to handle all types of extraction problems, from very structured text to the semistructured text common to web documents, and is used in conjunction with a syntactic analyzer and semantic tagging, it also handles extraction from free text such as news stories. When applied to structured or semistructured text, WHISK does not require prior syntactic analysis, but for free text WHISK works best with input annotated by a syntactic analyzer and semantic tagger.

WHISK is a supervised learning algorithm and requires a set of hand-tagged training instances. The tagging process is interleaved with the learning. In each iteration, WHISK presents the user with a batch of instances to tag, and then WHISK induces a set of rules from the expanded training set. It starts with a set of untagged instances and an empty training set of tagged instances, where an instance is a smaller unit of a document, like a sentence. In each iteration, a set of untagged instances are selected and presented to the user to annotate. The user adds a tag for each case frame to be extracted from the instance. What constitutes an instance depends on the domain. For structured or semistructured text, a text is broken into multiple instances based on the HTML tags or other regular expressions. For free text, a sentence analyzer segments the text into instances where each instance is a sentence or a sentence fragment. The tags of the training instances are used to guide the creation of rules and to test the performance of proposed rules. If a rule is applied successfully to an instance, the instance is considered to be covered by the rule. If the extracted phrases exactly match a tag associated with the instance, it is considered correct.

Example 7.6: Let us take a sample WHISK extraction task from online texts. The sample document is taken from an apartment rental domain that consists of ungrammatical constructs, which, without being rigidly formatted, obey some structuring rules that make them human understandable.

```
DOCUMENT:                     EXTRACTED DATA:
Capitol Hill- 1 br twnhme.    <Bedrooms: 1
D/W W/D. Pkg incl $675.       Price: 675>
3BR upper flr no gar. $995.   <Bedrooms: 3
(206) 999-9999 <br>           Price: 995>

Extraction rule: ' (<Digit>) 'BR' ' '$' (<Nmb>)
Output: Rental {Bedrooms @1} {Price @2g}
```

This pattern says that ignore all the characters in the text until you find a digit followed by the "br" string, extract that digit, and fill the first extraction slot with it (i.e., "Bedrooms"). Then ignore again all the remaining characters until you reach a dollar sign *immediately* followed by a number. Extract the number and fill the "Price" slot with it. A more sophisticated version of the pattern could replace the "br" string by the semantic class "Bedroom", which is defined as

```
Bedroom ::= ( br || brs || bdrm || bedrooms || bedroom ).
```

So, the semantic class "Bedroom" is a placeholder for any of the aforementioned abbreviations.

WHISK belongs to the family of machine learning algorithms known as covering algorithms and is related to algorithms that learn classification rules by top-down induction. First, the most general rule that covers the seed is found, and then terms are added to a rule one at a time until the errors are reduced to zero or a pre-pruning criterion has been satisfied. The metric used to select a new term is the Laplacian expected error of the rule, $(e + 1/n + 1)$, where n is the number of extractions made on the training set and e is the number of errors among those extractions. The learning process is repeated until a set of rules has been generated that covers all positive extractions from the training. Post-pruning is then performed to remove rules that may be overfitting the data.

WHISK shares SRV and RAPIER's ability to handle either structured or semistructured text, but does not have their limitation of single-slot extraction. Like WIEN, WHISK associates related information into multislot case frames. WHISK also differs from SRV and RAPIER in that rather than operating on documents WHISK operates on instances, which are typically sentences or similarly sized units.

7.5   *Applications and commercial systems*

The World Wide Web makes enormous amounts of information available to users regardless of location. Agents that can perform IE are useful for automatically gathering and analyzing this information on a user's behalf, and the number of applications for this technology is large.

In this section, the first section gives examples of different application areas for which IE has been tested, and the first commercial systems that have appeared on the scene are presented.

7.5.1   *Examples of applications*

The Internet presents numerous sources of useful information like telephone directories, product catalogs, stock quotes, weather forecasts, etc. The data in the web pages may originate from different sources. Often the original source is a database, and the web page presented to the user is a result of forming a query to the database and using a cgi-script to automatically generate the result page.

In many cases, it can be useful to combine information from several such sources to obtain the complete picture. However, the Web's browsing paradigm does not readily support retrieving and integrating data from multiple sites. Tools for IE can therefore be useful for a number of applications where the objective is to extract and collect specific information from a set of different web pages. The systems presented in this chapter have been tested for a number of different types of web information, and some of these are reviewed in the following:

- Product descriptions: ShopBot is specially designed for this type of application (Doorenbos et al. 1996, 1997) and compiles an overview of product offers by extracting product information from several web vendors and summarizing the result for the user. For comparison shopping, the extracted product descriptions are sorted by price.
- Restaurant guides: Information on restaurants can be spread out over different websites. In experiments with STALKER, information is extracted from a set of web pages where each HTML page contains exactly one restaurant review. The information extracted consists of items like the name of the restaurant, the type of food, cost, cuisine, address, phone number, and the review (Muslea et al. 1998a,b).
- Seminar announcements: Here the task can be to extract information like speaker, location, and time from a collection of web pages with seminar announcements. This is one of the experiments performed with SRV (Freitag 1998b).
- Job advertisements: Such advertisements can be found several places on the net, for instance as newsgroup postings. This application is among others tested for RAPIER and WHISK, which extracts information like title, salary, location, etc. (Califf and Mooney 1997).
- Executive succession: This represents a task for the more traditional IE field, as it includes IE from free text. In an experiment with WHISK, a collection of Wall Street Journal articles was analyzed searching for management succession events. The target was to extract the name of the corporation, the position, the name of the person moving into that position, and the name of the person moving out of the position.

This is just a selection of applications for which the technology can be useful, and there are obviously many more. Some additional examples are rental ads, geographic information, holiday and travel information, weather reports, bibliographic information, etc. In general, agents that perform IE and collection can be used for any list-type of data where information is spread out over a set of web pages.

7.5.2   *Commercial systems*

Of the applications mentioned in the previous section, comparison shopping is mainly where this technology has been used in commercial systems. One reason for the commercial focus on this application is the general focus on electronic commerce and the general growth in applications on the Internet connected to this.

Another reason is that such sites are well suited for the task because they are designed for users to find things quickly and they have a uniform look and feel. The online vendors have found it useful to obey certain regularities to facilitate sales to human users. This also facilitates the operation of systems for comparison shopping and the possibility of automating the process. As different vendors often sell the same products, a service that can collect and compare information from several vendors is useful for web shoppers. Often, the information that these vendors provide is fetched from a database and is generated on the y based on user queries. This makes the information part of the hidden web, which cannot be indexed by search engines. Agents for comparison shopping are therefore the only alternative to manual collection of product information.

In the following paragraphs, three commercial comparison shoppers will be presented: Junglee, Jango, and mySimon. These systems use a somewhat different approach to the problem of product IE. Jango and mySimon use a real-time approach, gathering product information whenever a shopper makes a request, while Junglee takes a different approach, collecting a database of product information locally and updating it when necessary. Each shopping agent takes user inputs and returns a list of matching products, where the user can compare the offers on this list and decide from which merchant to make the purchase of the product. In the following, a brief description of each system will be given.

7.5.2.1 Junglee

Junglee was founded in June 1996 by graduates from Stanford University and bought by Amazon in August 1998. Their comparison shopper uses a so-called virtual database (VDB) technology and exploits a mix of HTML and XML to present data from multiple sources (Quinlan and Cameron-Jones 1993; Rajaraman 1998). The VDB gathers structures and integrates the data from disparate data sources and provides the application programmer with the appearance of a single unified database system. Wrappers interface with the data sources, transforming them into a database. The VDB has two main components, the data integration system and the data publishing system. Data are extracted from different sources by the integration system and kept in a database. The updating of this database is scheduled by the publishing system. The data integration system has three elements: a set of wrappers, a mapper, and an extractor. The wrappers give a common interface to the different websites and are created using descriptive programming in a language specifically designed to capture the structure of websites and the relation between hyperlinked sites. The mapper transforms the extracted data to a common format using defined mapping rules. The extractor extracts structure from unstructured textual data using dictionaries and linguistic rules to describe how to extract the required features from the text. In both cases, specifically designed languages are used to formulate the rules. There will be one wrapper for each website while an extractor is typically created for an entire collection of websites with similar information.

7.5.2.2 Jango

Jango was previously known as ShopBot and is a product of NETBot. It is based on research by Oren Etzioni and DanWeld from the University of Washington (Doorenbos et al. 1996, 1997). Excite bought NetBot for $35 million in October 1997 and integrated Jango into its shopping channel. Jango consists of four components:

- A natural language front-end that transforms a request to logical product descriptions
- A query router that determines product category and associates it with a set of websites

- An aggregation engine that queries the selected sites in parallel, and finally
- The filter that extracts the information from the websites using a ShopBot-like analysis

From the URL of a store's home page and from knowledge about product domains, Jango learns how to shop at the stores during a learning phase. In this phase, it learns the format of the product descriptions of each vendor and learns to extract product attributes like price. During the shopping phase, the learned descriptions are used to extract information on products specified by the user. This information is extracted in parallel from each online vendor, and the results are sorted by ascending order of price and presented to the user.

7.5.2.3   MySimon

mySimon was cofounded by Michael Yang and Yeogirl Yun in April 1998. A so-called virtual learning agent (VLA) technology, which was developed by Yeogirl Yun, is used to learn websites. The VLA technology operates by creating a number of intelligent agents that are able to mimic human shopping behavior and can be trained to extract specific information from any merchant site on the Web. The agents are manually trained by the use of a GUI environment to teach them how to shop at a merchant site. The people performing the manual training need not be programmers and are called Simon Product Intelligence (SPI). The SPI surfs the Internet for the merchants' product sites. At the product site, the GUI environment is used to copy information from the site to an online form. Based on the SPI's behavior and the copied information, the code that makes the shopping agent work is generated automatically.

7.6   Summary

IE can be performed on structured, semistructured, and free text. For free text, techniques from NLP are often used. For structured and semistructured text, which seldom contains full grammatical sentences, delimiter-based techniques that exploit the structure of the documents are used. Web pages have been the main target for the research on IE from structured and semistructured documents. Wrappers are developed to extract information from a specific website, and through a library of wrappers for different web pages, a uniform presentation of the data and their relations can be obtained.

The construction of wrappers is often tedious and requires expert knowledge, and as web pages are very dynamic, the costs of maintaining wrappers can be high. Hence, automatic construction of wrappers for websites has become a focused problem, and machine learning techniques based on inductive learning have been applied for this task. Several (academic) systems for semiautomatic and automatic generation of wrappers have appeared. These systems use machine learning algorithms to generate extraction patterns for online information sources. ShopBot, WIEN, SoftMealy, and STALKER generate wrappers for well-structured websites using delimiter-based extraction patterns. RAPIER, WHISK, and SRV are able to handle sources that are less structured. These methods are closely related to the field of traditional IE and use relational learning. There are a series of application areas where IE and WG for websites can be useful. Currently, only one of these areas has become the arena of commercial systems, namely, the area of comparison shopping. Here, the objective is to extract product information from different online vendors, presenting a unified list to the user. The most prominent and successful systems in this area have been Jango, Junglee, and mySimon.

The search engines of today are not powerful enough for all tasks. They return a collection of documents, but they cannot extract the relevant information from these documents. There is also an increase in the so-called hidden web, which search engines are unable to access. Hence, there is a need for tools that can facilitate the task of extracting and gathering relevant information from web pages.

The use of machine learning techniques for the problem will still be highly relevant, due to the need to automate the process as much as possible to be able to cope with the large amount of dynamic data found on the Web. A combination of different types of approaches, obtaining adaptive systems, is a proper direction for the development of the technology. Also, a combination of methods, using a hybrid of both linguistic and syntactic features, is another practical way.

Finally, we see key advantages and disadvantages of wrapper induction and automatic data extraction. Wrapper induction extracts only the data that the user is interested in. Due to manual labeling, there is no integration issue for data extracted from multiple sites as the problem is solved by the user. Wrapper induction is not scalable to a large number of sites due to considerable manual efforts. Also finding the pages to label is nontrivial. Automatic extraction is scalable to a huge number of sites due to the automatic process, and there is little maintenance cost. Demerits of this technique are that it may extract a large amount of unwanted data because the system does not know what is interesting to the user. Domain heuristics or manual filtering may be needed to remove unwanted data. Extracted data from multiple sites need integration, that is, their schemas need to be matched.

Exercises

7.1   What are the different approaches for web data extraction?
7.2   Explain two types of data-rich pages.
7.3   What is wrapper induction? How wrapper induction system works?
7.4   Identify different shortcomings of WG using supervised learning.
7.5   Write a note on tree matching.
7.6   Discuss web DEPTA.

References

Arasu, A. and Garcia-Molina, H. 2003. Extracting structured data from web pages. Paper presented at the *ACM SIGMOD International Conference on Management of Data*, pp. 337–348, New York.

Ashish, N. and Knoblock, C. A. 1997. Semi-automatic wrapper generation for internet information sources. Paper presented at the *Second IFCIS Conference on Cooperative Information Systems (CoopIS)*, pp. 160–169, Kiawah Island, SC.

Buttler, D., Liu, L., and Pu, C. 2001. Omini: A fully automated object extraction system for the world-wide-web. Paper presented at the *21st International Conference on Distributed Computing Systems*, p. 361, Washington, DC.

Califf, M. E. 1998. Relational learning techniques for natural language information extraction. PhD dissertation, The University of Texas at Austin, Austin, TX.

Califf, M. E. and Mooney, R. J. 1997. Relational learning of pattern-match rules for information extraction. Paper presented at the *ACL Workshop on Natural Language Learning*, pp. 9–15, Madrid, Spain.

Camacho, D., R-Moreno, M. D., Barrero, D. F., and Akerkar, R. 2008. Semantic wrappers for semi-structured data extraction. *Computing Letters (CoLe)* 4(1–4):21–34.

Chang, C. H. and Lui, S. C. 2001. IEPAD: Information extraction based on pattern discovery. Paper presented at the *10th International Conference on World Wide Web*, pp. 681–688, New York.

Chidlovskii, B., Borghoff, U. M., and Chevalier, P. Y. 1997. Towards sophisticated wrapping of web-based information repositories. Paper presented at the *Fifth International RIAO Conference*, Montreal, Quebec, Canada.

Crescenzi, V., Mecca, G., and Merialdo, P. 2001. Roadrunner: Towards automatic data extraction from large web sites. Paper presented at the *27th International Conference on Very Large Databases*, pp. 109–118, Lyon, France.

Doorenbos, R. B., Etzioni, O., and Weld, D. S. 1996. A scalable comparison-shopping agent for the world wide web. Technical report UW-CSE-96-01-03, University of Washington, Seattle, WA.

Doorenbos, R. B., Etzioni, O., and Weld, D. S. 1997. A scalable comparison-shopping agent for the world-wide-web. Paper presented at the *First International Conference on Autonomous Agents*, pp. 39–41, Marina Del Rey, CA.

Freitag, D. 1998a. Information extraction from HTML: Application of a general machine learning approach. Paper presented at the *15th National Conference on Artificial Intelligence*, Madison, WI.

Freitag, D. 1998b. Machine learning for information extraction in informal domains. PhD dissertation, Carnegie Mellon University, Pittsburgh, PA.

Freitag, D. 1998c. Multistrategy learning for information extraction. Paper presented at the *15th International Conference on Machine Learning (ICML-1998)*, pp.66–73, Madison, WI.

Gaizauskas, R. and Wilks, Y. 1998. Information extraction: Beyond document retrieval. *Computational Linguistics and Chinese Language Processing* 3(2):17–60.

Gonnet, G. H., Baeza-Yates, R. A., and Snider, T. 1992. New indices for text-PAT trees and PAT arrays. In *Information Retrieval—Data Structures and Algorithms*, eds. W. B. Frakes and R. Baeza-Yates. Upper Saddle River, NJ: Prentice Hall, pp. 66–82.

Hsu, C. H. 1998. Initial results on wrapping semistructured web pages with finite-state transducers and contextual rules. Paper presented at the *Workshop on AI and Information Integration, in Conjunction with the 15th National Conference on Artificial Intelligence (AAAI-98)*, pp. 66–73, Madison, WI.

Hsu, C. H. and Dung, M. T. 1998. Generating finite-sate transducers for semi-structured data extraction from the web. *Information Systems* 23(8):521–538.

Kushmerick, N. 1997. Wrapper induction for information extraction. PhD dissertation, University of Washington, Seattle, WA.

Kushmerick, N., Weld, D. S., and Doorenbos, R. 1997. Wrapper induction for information extraction. Paper presented at the *15th International Joint Conference on Artificial Intelligence (IJCAI-97)*, pp. 729–735, Nagoya, Japan.

Liu, B., Grossman, R., and Zhai, Y. 2003. Mining data records in web pages. Paper presented at the *Ninth ACM SIGKDD International Conference on Knowledge Discovery and Data Mining*, pp. 601–606, New York.

Liu, L. 2000. Xwrap: An xml-enabled wrapper construction system for web information sources. Paper presented at the *16th International Conference on Data Engineering*, pp. 611–621, Washington, DC.

Morrison, D. R. 1968. Patricia-practical algorithm to retrieve information coded in alphanumeric. *Journal of the ACM* 15(4):514–534.

Muggleton, S. and Feng, C. 1990. Efficient induction of logic programs. Paper presented at the *First Conference on Algorithmic Learning Theory*, pp. 368–381, New York.

Muslea, I. 1999. Extraction patterns for information extraction tasks: A survey. Paper presented at the *Workshop on Machine Learning for Information Extraction*, Orlando, FL.

Muslea, I., Minton, S., and Knoblock, C. 1998a. STALKER: Learning extraction rules for semistructured, web-based information sources. Paper presented at the *Workshop on AI and Information Integration, in Conjunction with the 15th National Conference on Artificial Intelligence (AAAI-1998)*, Madison, WI.

Muslea, I., Minton, S., and Knoblock, C. 1998b. Wrapper induction for semistructured web-based information sources. Paper presented at the *Conference on Automatic Learning and Discovery*, Pittsburgh, PA.

Muslea, I., Minton, S., and Knoblock, C. 1999. A hierarchical approach to wrapper induction. Paper presented at the *Third International Conference on Autonomous Agents*, Seattle, WA.

Quinlan, J. R. and Cameron-Jones, R. M. 1993. FOIL: A midterm report. Paper presented at the *European Conference on Machine Learning*, pp. 3–20, Vienna, Austria.

Rajaraman, A. 1998. Transforming the internet into a database. Paper presented at the *Workshop on Reuse of Web Information, in conjunction with WWW7*, pp. 55–58, Brisbane, Queensland, Australia.

Rosenfeld, B., Feldman, R., and Aumann, Y. 2002. Structural extraction from visual layout of documents. Paper presented at the *International Conference on Information and Knowledge Management*, pp. 203–210, McLean, VA.

Soderland, S. 1999. Learning information extraction rules for semistructured and free text. *Machine Learning* 34(1–3):233–272.

Wang, J. and Lochovsky, F. H. 2003. Data extraction and label assignment for web databases. Paper presented at the *12th International Conference on World Wide Web*, pp. 187–196, New York.

Zhai, Y. and Liu, B. 2005. Web data extraction based on partial tree alignment, Paper presented at the *14th International World Wide Web Conference*, pp. 76–85, Chiba, Japan.

Semantic web and web knowledge management

chapter eight

Semantic web

8.1 Introduction to semantic web

The advent of the World Wide Web (WWW) gave mankind an enormous source of available information. To guarantee interoperability at various levels, the Web is based on a set of established standards and protocols, for example, the transmission control protocol/Internet protocol (TCP/IP) provides a basis for transportation of bits, and hypertext transfer protocol (HTTP) and hypertext markup language (HTML) provide a standard way of retrieving and presenting hyperlinked text documents. Through suitable application interfaces, users can easily make use of this basic infrastructure for problem solving, decision support, and advisory. The current web is made up of a huge number of web documents/pages. Though machines hold the content, they are unaware of the content they hold. Every document is treated in a similar fashion by a machine regardless of the material it presents. Software like server operating system, indexing/crawling mechanisms, and search algorithms, which are developed to manage and explore the content on the Web, also do not "know" the items they need to manage. The existing utilities for web exploration are rather mainly syntactic, not semantic. The huge pool of the content on the Web and insufficient representation of knowledge contained within the content make searching the "right" content challenging for human beings. Most of the content representation schemes (such as HTML) are well suitable for human consumption, but not for machine processability. The main reason for this is both the machine and the software really do not understand the content, and hence, there is less chance to provide effective and relevant material to the users. The concept of semantic web tries to improve the situation by adding "meaning"/"knowledge" to the content that helps the Web in content management and exploration process in order to impart qualitative factors such as relevance and applicability. Semantic web is considered as an extension of the current web with meaning of the content it possess, which is useful for both people and machines.

The idea of semantic web is influenced by earlier work dating back to Vannevar Bush's idea of the "memex" machine in the 1940s based on a universal library, completed with a searchable catalog (Bush 1945). After then, Berners-Lee et al. (2001) provided the concept of the semantic web where machines were able to access and locate information and services instead of people to carry out routine transactions and decision making. This can be done by providing sufficient information/context about resources on the Web and also providing the mechanisms to use the context so that machines find appropriate information. According to them,

> The Semantic Web will bring structure to the meaningful content of
> Web pages, creating an environment where software agents roaming
> from page to page can readily carry out sophisticated tasks for users.

The semantic web enables intelligent services for machine-processable web such as information brokers, search agents, and information filters, which offers greater functionality and interoperability than current stand-alone services (Decker et al. 2000).

In 1994, 5 years after inventing the WWW, Tim Berners-Lee founded the WWW Consortium (W3C)* at the Massachusetts Institute of Technology (MIT).[†] The mission of W3C is "to lead the WWW to its full potential by developing protocols and guidelines that ensure long-term growth for the Web." Two major working groups of the W3C, the resource description framework (RDF) Core Working Group and the Web Ontology Working Group, have produced major sets of recommendations. The W3C concentrates on exploratory and advanced activities within W3C in the area of semantic web. The work is accelerated within two groups, namely, (i) the Semantic Web Best Practices and Deployment Working Group and (ii) the RDF Data Access Working Group. The best practices group aims to support and extend the practical application of the semantic web in various fields by providing sample tools and general descriptive vocabularies in key areas. The RDF Group contributes in the development of tools and languages for querying and processing semantic annotations across the Web.

This chapter introduces semantic web and techniques of embedding "semantics" along with the content presented on the Web in its Section 8.1. Section 8.2 extends the discussion by presenting need of metadata and discusses metadata considering objective, scope, standards, and examples of metadata.

Original architecture of the semantic web presented by Berners-Lee (1998) is discussed in Section 8.3 with standard components such as uniform resource identifier (URI), extensible markup language (XML), RDF, schema, logic, trust, and proof. This architecture is further refined in Section 8.4.

To demonstrate the implementation of a semantic web, tools and techniques like XML, RDF, web ontology language (OWL), ontology interchange language (OIL), SPARQL protocol and RDF query language (SPARQL), etc., are discussed thoroughly with examples in Section 8.5. This section includes topics like sample XML documents, supporting [document type definition (DTD) and style sheet] documents, advantages of XML, simple example for RDF, OWL flavors, and OIL.

Section 8.6 presents an abstract on meta-ontology and ontology tools that help in defining metadata. Ontology tools, editors, and annotation tools are discussed thoroughly with examples in Sections 8.7 and 8.8. Section 8.9 represents a brief introduction on inference engine to infer knowledge from the Web content.

Semantic web provides a larger platform to store, share, and use content without experiencing any barriers like time and location. A few (selective) semantic web applications, which have greater impact on world's business, are described in Section 8.10. Semantic web shares vast amount of content represented in various ontology and representation schemes. Interoperability between the ontology is must to handle the content in a systematic way. Such interoperability is desirable at syntactic as well as semantic level. Section 8.11 introduces interoperability and mining issues on the semantic web.

The chapter concludes by presenting social communities on the Web, intelligent search, and research issues in the area of semantic web in Sections 8.12 through 8.14, respectively.

8.2   Metadata

Adding meaning/knowledge to the standard content is possible by adding some more data about the content—called metadata within the content itself. Originally, the term "meta" comes from a Greek word that denotes "alongside, with, after, next." Metadata, then, can be thought of as data about other data. A metadata record consists of a set of attributes, or

---

* http://www.w3.org/
[†] http://mit.edu/

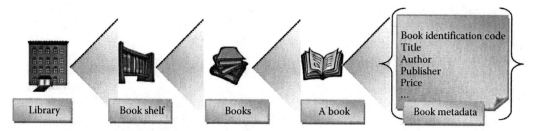

Figure 8.1 Library book metadata.

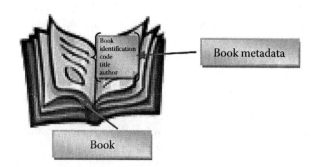

Figure 8.2 Library book metadata embedded.

elements, necessary to describe the given resource. For example, a library catalog contains a set of metadata records with elements that describe a book or other library item: author, title, date of creation or publication, subject coverage, and the identification number that specifies location of the item on the shelf.

Figure 8.1 demonstrates library book metadata as described.

Similarly, the resource description for web document may include title of the document, type of the document, name of the author, and date of creation/modification.

Metadata provide a systematic and generic way to describe resources, thereby improving the accessibility and application of the resource. The metadata can be linked with the Web document in two different ways. The first one is that the metadata describing the resource can be stored separately and retrieved on need. Another way is to store metadata along with the resource itself and retrieved simultaneously while retrieving the resource. The library book metadata can be described along with book description as denoted in Figure 8.2.

These metadata can only be automatically processed if the metadata have followed some common and unique representation criterion, called metadata standard. A metadata standard defines a fixed number and type of items to be included/supported with every document accepted commonly. According to Weibel and Lagoze (1997), "the association of standardized descriptive metadata with networked objects has the potential for substantially improving resource discovery capabilities by enabling field-based (e.g., author and title) searches, permitting indexing of nontextual objects, and allowing access to the surrogate content that is distinct from access to the content of the resource itself."

The Dublin Core Metadata Initiative (DCMI)* defines interoperable metadata standards that support a broad range of purposes and business models. There are implementa-

---

* http://dublincore.org/

tions where Dublin Core metadata are used to describe resources held, owned, or produced by companies, governments, and international organizations to supporting portal services or internal knowledge management. Furthermore, such standard can be used as a common exchange format supporting the aggregation of collections of metadata, such as the case of the Open Archives Initiative (OAI) to improve content retrieval for specific applications/user communities.

Besides the Dublin Core metadata, other well-known formats are MAchine-Readable Cataloging (MARC), ONline Information eXchange (ONIX), and publishing requirements for industry standard metadata (PRISM). MARC,* developed by the Library of Congress presents an XML representation for metadata representation. ONIX[†] is developed for Books Product Information Message, which is the international standard for representing and communicating book industry product information in electronic form XML representation. PRISM[‡] establishes for PRISM specification that defines an XML metadata vocabulary for magazine, news, catalog, book, and journal content.

8.2.1   Dublin core metadata standard

The Dublin Core metadata standard offers a set of elements for describing a wide range of networked resources by categorizing them into two levels. The first level known as *simple Dublin Core* comprises 15 elements (Hillmann 2007) as shown in Table 8.1.

The second level called *qualified Dublin Core* includes three additional elements, namely, audience, provenance, and RightsHolder, along with qualifiers to refine the semantics of the elements. Each element in both the category is optional and may be repeated. Most elements may use qualifiers, adjectives, or refinements that clarify the meaning of the element. These elements are shown in Table 8.2.

Each metadata defined by Dublin Core emphasizes on unique identification of entity. This principle is known as *one-to-one principle*. Furthermore, the qualification of Dublin Core properties is guided by a rule known as the *dumb-down principle*. This deals with the fact that though qualifier is present and defined by the metadata, user may not use it. In this situation, the entity is treated as unqualified entity, provided it is useful and can be tracked through discovery. For this purpose, generally qualifiers are the adjectives adding values to the base/correct meaning of the entity. Here, qualifier can be used as refining adjective to the entity. The third principle states the appropriateness of the qualifiers. One thing one must keep in mind is that not only machines, but humans also use and interpret the metadata. Hence, the qualifier of an entity must be of appropriate values and exhibits correct and same values to machines as well as to human beings.

8.2.2   Metadata objectives

Metadata should be applied to all kinds of resources. The major objectives of such element set are as follows:

8.2.2.1   Simplicity of creation and maintenance

The element set should be kept simple and avoid any extra fields. This leads to ease of creation and maintenance. Also, it should be understandable by noncomputer professionals and cover all aspects of different types of documents using minimum number of fields.

---

* http://www.loc.gov/standards/marcxml/
† http://www.editeur.org/onix.html
‡ http://www.prismstandard.org/about/

Table 8.1 Simple Dublin Core Elements

Elements	Description
Contributor	An entity responsible for contributing resource such as person, organization, or service
Coverage	Scope and applicability of the resource, or the jurisdiction under which the resource is relevant
	Examples:
	Coverage="1994–2011"
	Coverage="India"
	Coverage="21st Century"
Creator	An entity primarily responsible for making the resource, typically author
	Examples:
	Creator="John "
	Creator="Anonymous"
	Creator="P-Learning Pvt. Ltd."
Date	A point or period of time associated with an event in the lifecycle of the resource
	Examples:
	Date="2010-08-06"
	Date="2010-08"
	Date="2010"
Description	Description may include but is not limited to an abstract, a table of contents, a graphical representation, or a free-text account of the resource to present an account of the resource
	Examples:
	Description="Illustrated guide to the knowledge-based systems consisting of theory principles, research trends, and practical project in the area of knowledge-based systems using artificial intelligence techniques. The major chapters included in this books are …"
	Description="This is a science fiction novel describing an accidental invention of new computerized time machine utilizing neuro-science and computer science advancement by an old scientist, two research students and a young superkid. The story turns out to be a suspense thriller when the superkid is found Alien"
Format	The file format, physical medium, or dimensions of the resource including size and duration
	Example:
	Title="Dublin Core Icon"
	Identifier="http://pssprod/images/myicon"
	Type="Image"
	Format="image/tif"
	Subject="Cherry"
Identifier	An unambiguous reference to the resource within a given context
	Examples:
	Identifier=http://pssprod/images/myicon
	Identifier="ISBN:0-7637-7647-5 (pbk)"

(continued)

Table 8.1 (continued) Simple Dublin Core Elements

Elements	Description
Language	A language of the resource
	Examples:
	Language="English"
	Language="Spanish"
	Language="Primarily US English, partly Spanish"
Publisher	An entity responsible for making the resource available
	Examples:
	Publisher="Sardar Patel University"
	Publisher="Trendy Hosting, Inc."
	Publisher="Miracle Press"
Relation	A related resource, if any
	Examples:
	Title="Alien"
	Relation="One of the famous Alien Triology Books"
	Subject="Knowledge-Based Systems"
	Relation="Expert Systems " [a kind of the knowledge based system]
Rights	Information about rights held in and over the resource. This may refer to the intellectual property rights
	Examples:
	Rights="For registered members only"
	Rights="http://pss-products/Terms&quote;"
Source	A related resource from which the described resource is derived. "part-of," "version-of," "has-format," "has-reference," "is-based-on," etc. keywords may be used
	Examples:
	Source=reference number of the document is "AI386.A48R912 2010"
	Source="Image from page 4 of the 2010 edition of Systems Science"
Subject	The topic of the resource
	Examples:
	Subject="Knowledge-Based Systems"
	Subject="Alien"
	Subject="Science Fiction"
Title	A name given to resource, by which the resource is formally known
	Examples:
	Title="An Advisory to Course Selection"
	Title="When I met an Alien"
	Title="More art and Less Science"
Type	The nature or genre of the resource
	Examples:
	Type="Image"
	Type="Sound"
	Type="Text"
	Type="Animated movie"

Table 8.2 Qualified Dublin Core Elements

Elements	Description
Audience	A class of entity for whom the resource is intended or useful. This is determined by the creator or the publisher or by a third party
	Examples:
	Audience="Primary School Teachers"
	Audience="Deaf Adults"
Provenance	A statement of any significant in ownership and custody of the resource useful for its authenticity, integrity, and interpretation
	Examples:
	Provenance="This copy once owned by Miracle Corporation"
	Provenance="The National Museum"
RightsHolder	A person or organization owning or managing rights over the resource. This may be a URI or name of the rights holder to indicate the entity
	Examples:
	RightsHolder="John"
	RightsHolder="Miracle Corporation"

8.2.2.2   Commonly understood semantics

The description utilized in describing entity should be understood by various types of users including machines. All the fields must describe the entity in unique way to avoid misconceptions and wrong interpretation from time to time.

8.2.2.3   International scope

Multilingual support and support from aliases of the adjectives used to describe entity should be considered. The use of equivalent descriptive word (from the same or other languages) increases the scope of the content use.

8.2.2.4   Extensibility

The data element set describing an entity must be extensible to facilitate additional definition of the entity. One major objective of doing so is to support administration and resource discovery.

8.2.2.5   Interoperability

The metadata description should follow a standard to set platform for the interoperability to allow different communities to use the elements. Semantic web initiation took place by W3C after introduction of the semantic web road map by Berners-Lee (1998).

After that, the RDF model and syntax specification,[*] and the RDF schema specification[†] highly influenced the semantic web development. This leads to the identification of technologies, tools, and standards, which form the basic building blocks of the semantic web.

Interoperability is achieved by ensuring that the information is consistently encoded (syntax) and uses symbols that have a formally defined meaning such that they can be consistently interpreted (semantics). An effective semantic web will ensure interoperability

[*] http://www.w3.org/TR/REC-rdf-syntax/
[†] http://www.w3.org/TR/rdf-schema/

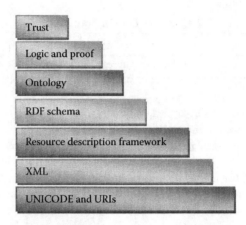

Figure 8.3 Original semantic web layered.

between cyberinfrastructure components including capacity to capture knowledge, infrastructure to publish and share information, and efficient middleware for question answering and knowledge discovery.

8.3   Layered architecture of semantic web

Tim Berners-Lee initially proposed a layered architecture as shown in Figure 8.3.
The architecture presented in Figure 8.3 encompasses the following components.

8.3.1   Unicode and uniform resource identifier

Unicode, the standard for computer consistent representation of character developed in conjunction with the universal character set with more than 100,000 characters covering almost 90 scripts by the Unicode Consortium.* The Unicode Consortium is a nonprofit organization founded to develop, extend, and promote the use of the Unicode Standard. URI, as its name denotes, is the standard for identifying and locating resources on the Web. The Unicode and URI provide a platform for representing characters used in most of the languages in the world, and for identifying resources.

8.3.2   Extensible markup language

XML is designed to describe the user data by specifying the application-specific tags. Along with an XML document with the user-defined tags, XML requires DTD for understanding and validating tags and CSS for customized presentation. The XML along with standards like namespaces and schemas forms a common means for structuring data on the Web. Further details about the XML are presented in Section 8.5.1.

8.3.3   Resource description framework

RDF is designed as a metadata model and used as a general description for the information on the Web. This is the first layer of the semantic web where metadata can be

* http://unicode.org/

incorporated. RDF is a simple metadata representation framework, using URIs to identify web-based resources along with description of relationships between resources. Several syntactic representations are available, including a standard XML format.

8.3.4 RDF schema

RDF schema describes classes of resources and properties between them in the basic RDF model. It provides a simple reasoning framework for inferring types of resources.

8.3.5 Ontology

The semantic web provides the languages for modeling and representing data about real-world objects, in formats suitable for computers. Modeling data with well-defined structure provide machine understandable meaning or *semantics* to the data (Akerkar 2009). A specification called an *ontology* is usually created in a particular domain (area of interest) to model the semantic web data. Ontology is a formal representation of the knowledge by a set of concepts within an application domain and the relationships between those concepts. It is used to reason about the properties of that domain and may be used to describe the domain. Ontology provides a shared understanding of a domain of interest to support communication among human and computer agents represented through a machine-processable representation language. Hence, ontology is seen as key enablers for the semantic web.

8.3.6 Logic and proof

This is a reasoning system provided on top of the ontology structure in order to infer to make deductions to identify and use the Web resources.

8.3.7 Trust

The last layer of the architecture addresses issues of trust and reliability that the semantic web should support. According to Matthews (2005), this component has not progressed far beyond a vision of allowing people to ask questions of the trustworthiness of the information on the Web, in order to provide an assurance of its quality.

8.4 Refined architecture of semantic web

The architecture presented in the Figure 8.3 is further refined by its founders as shown in Figure 8.4.

Degree of semantics increases from the lower levels toward the top of the stack as shown in Figure 8.4. Resources, identified by the appropriate URI defined through Unicode, forms the base of the stack. The next semantic layer is the semantically rich domain-specific XML along with its namespaces. Here, the namespace indicates a simple mechanism for creating and accessing globally unique names for the entities used in the markup language. On top of XML is the RDF, which describes whole resources/full documents. RDF schema is a language following object-oriented principles that enable the creation of RDF vocabularies based on an object-oriented approach. Ontology is constructed from structured vocabularies with appropriate semantics.

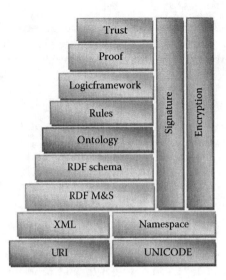

Figure 8.4 Modified semantic web layered architecture.

In particular, ontology makes knowledge reusable by featuring classes (general things), instances (particular things), relationships between those things, properties for those things (with their values), functions involving those things, and constraints on and rules involving those things.

8.5 Ontology and ontology constructs

In philosophy, ontology studies the nature of being and existence. The term "ontology" is derived from the Greek words "onto," which means *being*, and "logia," which means *written or spoken discourse*. Ontology (or Ontologies) plays an important role in enabling semantic representation, processing, sharing, and reuse of web content. As stated earlier, ontology is defined as shared formal conceptualizations of particular domains to provide a common understanding of topics that can be communicated between people and application systems. The artificial intelligence literature contains many definitions of ontology. One of such definition is as follows:

> Ontology is a formal explicit description of concepts in a domain of discourse consisting of class/concepts, slots (roles or properties), and constraints on slots (facets or restrictions). Ontology along with a set of related instances (member entities) of the classes defined in it, form a knowledge base. The ontologies that define the structure and organization of knowledge base are called meta knowledge. That is why it is said that there is a fine line between ontology and knowledge base.

Ontology typically contains a hierarchy of concepts within a domain and describes each concept's crucial properties through an attribute–value mechanism (Decker et al. 2000). The relations between the specified concepts are described through additional logical sentences. Constant values (such as "1st January 2011") may be assigned to one or more concepts (such as "Date of Creation").

Explicit ontology helps in increased reuse of content encoded into software systems. Hence, appropriate ontology languages are needed to realize explicit ontology with respect to three important aspects such as conceptualization, vocabulary, and axiomatization.

Conceptualization refers to the ability to fit the concepts by choosing an appropriate reference model, such as entity-relationship model and object-oriented model, and provides corresponding ontology constructs to represent factual knowledge, such as definitions of entities and relationship between them.

Vocabulary plays an important role in covering the syntax such as symbol assignment (i.e., assigning symbols to concepts) and grammars (i.e., serializing the conceptualism into explicit representation).

In addition to factual knowledge, rule and constraints are needed to capture the semantics for inference for better understanding, computing, new rule generation, and validation. Ability to infer required content from the available content on the Web helps in this procedure. In addition to these, the ontology should be extensible and visible.

With the ontology, the following basic advantages can be achieved:

- It is possible to share common understanding and perception about the domain entities.
- The ontology once defined, the domain assumptions are explicit, unique, clear, and homogeneously structured within domain.
- It is possible to reuse the ontology by separating domain knowledge from the operational knowledge.
- To analyze and apply domain knowledge in easy and friendly way.

For ever increasing semantic web, it is necessary to develop ontology in such a way that it must be extensible. This can be achieved by incremental development of popular abstract concepts. For example, "student" and "teacher" concepts can be extended from the "people" concept.

The semantic web content is equally accessed by human users and machines. In order to make knowledge visible on the Web, additional common ontological ground on syntax and semantics is required between content publishers and consumers; without this, machines cannot understand the content.

The semantic web inherits the power of representation from existing conceptualisms, such as *semantic networks* (Sowa 1991), and enhances interoperability at both syntactic and semantic levels. It can function as a distributed database or a collaborative knowledge base according to application requirements. In particular, *extensibility* is offered not only by the underlying URI-based vocabulary but also by the simple graph data model of RDF (Klyne and Carroll 2004).

Ontologies have their own spectrum, where ontologies are arranged according to increasing degree of semantics, as described in Figure 8.5.

Items like glossary, vocabularies, controlled vocabularies, taxonomies, data dictionaries, etc., need to be defined first and present lower degree of semantics as denoted in Figure 8.5. Hence, these terms form base of the ontology spectrum as shown in Figure 8.5. It includes simple list of terms, definitions, naming conventions, basic validations, and data dictionaries.

Second layer of the ontology spectrum includes modified and extended version of vocabulary and data dictionaries by providing advanced control checks on the terms and fields, arrangement and/or methods of the terms used, etc.

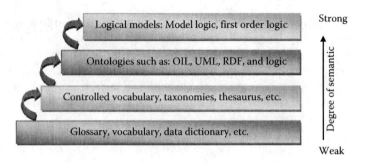

Figure 8.5 Ontology spectrum.

The third layer consists of ontology presented using OIL, OWL, schemas, and models. Forth layer consists of entities that exhibit higher degree of semantics, for example, first-order logic and models.

Technologies like XML and RDF have their merits as a foundation for the semantic web. The following section describes ontology constructs like XML, RDF, and OWL.

8.5.1   Extensible markup language

XML is designed for markup in documents of arbitrary structure using domain-specific tags to support the extensibility. Unlike rigid HTML, where only predefined fix tags can be used, in XML, a tree of nested sets of open and close user-defined tags can be used. As there is no fixed tag vocabulary or predefined allowable combinations, it is necessary to provide definitions of the domain-specific user-defined tags. For this purpose, a DTD is used. A DTD defines grammar to specify allowable combinations and nesting of tag names and attribute names.

XML is a tool to develop, store, and share structured content data. If same grammar/ tag set is used to describe a certain kind of information, an XML application can assist users in communicating their information in a more robust and efficient manner. XML is a right tool to exchange information between cooperating entities. XML documents with the same elements can "pass" content/data to each other, and multiple users/applications can form a platform to store, update, and display information from multiple sites and addresses.

Unfortunately, XML does not share/describe page layout or formatting functionality. Hence, it must be accompanied with style sheet. An XML document can be presented/ viewed in different fashion by using various style sheets.

Currently, major browsers such as Microsoft Internet Explorer,[*] Firefox,[†] and Netscape[‡] support XML. The real beauty of XML lies in the fact that the features of XML can be extended or "added to," that is, the user can specify new features and add them to a document.

XML is used to serve a range of purposes:

- To represent content using domain-specific tags
- For serialization syntax for other markup languages like artificial intelligence markup language (AIML)[§] and synchronized multimedia integration language (SMIL)[¶]

[*] http://www.microsoft.com/
[†] http://www.mozilla.com/
[‡] http://browser.netscape.com/
[§] http://www.alicebot.org/aiml.html
[¶] http://www.w3.org/AudioVideo/#SMIL

- For semantic markup of web pages. An XML can be used in a web page with a style sheet to render different elements appropriately
- For uniform data exchange format. An XML can also be transferred as a data object between two applications

Table 8.3 presents an example of an XML file describing employee information along with necessary DTD in Table 8.4 and style sheet documents in Table 8.5.

The output of the previous sample employee XML block is as shown in Figure 8.6.

As the content on the Web is to be accessible by anybody, there is no fix format of the content. Hence, it is necessary that the representation strategy must support all possible formats to satisfy different users' need. XML fulfills such universal expressive power requirement. With the help of domain-specific tags/grammar, many applications can be encoded in XML. An XML parser can parse any XML data and is usually a reusable component, and supports syntactic interoperability requirement. However, semantic

Table 8.3 XML Example Showing Employee Information

```
<?xml version="1.0" ?>
<!DOCTYPE Employee SYSTEM "Employee.dtd">
<?xml-stylesheet type="text/xsl" href="Employee.xsl"?>
<Emp>
  <Employee>
    <Emp_Id> 0981 </Emp_Id>
    <Emp_Name> James </Emp_Name>
    <Emp_Jdate> 01-08-2006 </Emp_Jdate>
    <Emp_Desig> Manager </Emp_Desig>
    <Emp_Mobileno> 9999999999 </Emp_Mobileno>
    <Emp_E-mail> james@email.com </Emp_E-mail>
  </Employee>
  <Employee>
    <Emp_Id> 1001 </Emp_Id>
    <Emp_Name> John </Emp_Name>
    <Emp_Jdate> 16-07-2011 </Emp_Jdate>
    <Emp_Desig> Supervisor </Emp_Desig>
    <Emp_Mobileno> 9999999998 </Emp_Mobileno>
    <Emp_E-mail> john@email.com </Emp_E-mail>
  </Employee>
</Emp>
```

Table 8.4 Document Type Definitions Example for Employee Information XML

```
<!ELEMENT Emp (Employee)>
<!ELEMENT Employee (Emp_Id, Emp_Name, Emp_Jdate, Emp_Desig,
 Emp_Mobileno, Emp_E-mail)>
<!ELEMENT Emp_Id (#PCDATA)>
<!ELEMENT Emp_Name (#PCDATA)>
<!ELEMENT Emp_Jdate (#PCDATA)>
<!ELEMENT Emp_Desig (#PCDATA)>
<!ELEMENT Emp_Mobileno (#PCDATA)>
<!ELEMENT Emp_E-mail (#PCDATA)>
```

Table 8.5 Stylesheet Example for Showing Employee Information XML

```
<?xml version="1.0" encoding="ISO-8859-1" ?>
<xsl:stylesheet version="1.0"
xmlns:xsl="http://www.w3.org/1999/XSL/Transform">
<xsl:template match="/">
<html>
<body>
  <h2>Employee Information</h2>
  <table border="1">
  <tr bgcolor="#9acd32">
    <th>Id</th>
    <th>Name</th>
    <th>Joining Date</th>
    <th>Designation</th>
    <th>Mobile No</th>
    <th>Email Id</th>
  </tr>
<xsl:for-each select="Emp/Employee">
  <tr>
    <td> <xsl:value-of select="Emp_Id" /> </td>
    <td> <xsl:value-of select="Emp_Name" /> </td>
    <td> <xsl:value-of select="Emp_Jdate" /> </td>
    <td> <xsl:value-of select="Emp_Desig" /> </td>
    <td> <xsl:value-of select="Emp_Mobileno" /> </td>
    <td> <xsl:value-of select="Emp_E-mail" /> </td>
  </tr>
</xsl:for-each>
</table>
</body>
</html>
</xsl:template>
</xsl:stylesheet>
```

Employee information					
Id	Name	Joining date	Designation	Mobile No	Email Id
0981	James	01-08-2006	Manager	9999999999	james@email.com
1001	John	16-07-2011	Supervisor	9999999998	john@email.com

Figure 8.6 Output of employee information.

interoperability needs understandable content. In this aspect, the XML has disadvantages. XML just describes grammars. There is no way to recognize a semantic unit from a particular domain because XML aims at document structure and does not provide any mechanism to interpret meaning embedded within the document. XML is useful for data/content interchange between applications that both know what the content is, but not for situations where new communication partners are decided/added dynamically, which is frequent on the Web.

8.5.2 Resource description framework

The RDF is a framework written in XML for describing resources on the Web that facilitates automatic content understanding. Like XML, RDF is also well suited to represent content on the Web. The RDF is a W3C recommendation used for definition of metadata—descriptions of web-based resources. RDF is a graphical language used for representing content/data about resources on the Web. The basic building block in RDF is an object, attribute, and value triple, commonly written as *A(O,V)*. That is, an object *O* has an attribute *A possesses* with value *V*. An alternate form to model this relationship is as a labeled edge between two nodes: [*O*]: *A* → [*V*]. The graph in Figure 8.7 expresses the following three relationships in *A(O, V)* format:

```
hasName
  ('http://www.w3.org/employee/id0981', "James")
authorOf
  ('http://www.w3.org/employee/id0981', http://www.books.org/
  ISBN076XXX64XX)
hasPrice
  ('http://www.books.org/ISBN076XXX64XX', "$74").
```

According to Klyne and Carroll (2004), the design of RDF is intended to meet the following goals:

- Having a simple data model
- Having formal semantics and provable inference
- Using an extensible URI-based vocabulary
- Using an XML-based syntax
- Supporting the use of XML schema data types
- Allowing anyone to make statements about any resource

To meet these objectives, RDF uses the key concepts like graph data model, URI-based vocabulary, data types, literals, XML serialization syntax, expression of simple facts, and entailment. In the RDF recommendation, targets of the graph can be pieces of text, called literals, instead of resources. Though writing direct text is syntactically correct in RDF documents, there is a better and cleaner way of doing the same by using a fragment identifier. By doing so, the literal node could be replaced by a standard URI node in the RDF graph.

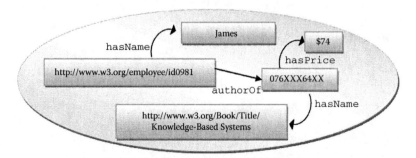

Figure 8.7 RDF showing relationship between an employee, book, and price.

There are three kinds of concepts in RDF: fundamental concepts, schema definition concepts (useful for defining new vocabularies), and utility concepts (concepts that are not absolutely necessary, but likely to be useful in any application domain) (Champin 2001). The fundamental concepts define resources, properties, and statements using syntax such as rdf:Resource, rdf:Property, and rdf:Statement, respectively. The schema definition concepts define rdfs:subPropertyOf, rdfs:Class, rdf:type, rdfs:subClassOf, rdfs:domain, rdfs:range, and rdfs:Literal. Utility concepts define rdfs:Container, rdfs:ConstraintResource, rdfs:ConstraintProperty, rdfs:seeAlso, rdfs:isDefinedBy, rdfs:label, and rdfs:comment.

As with XML, the RDF data model provides no mechanism for declaring property names that are to be used (Decker et al. 2000). The RDF, as stated earlier, is designed to provide a basic object–attribute–value data model for metadata. It does not make data modeling commitments. It does not support any reserved terms for further data modeling.

RDF schema "semantically extends" RDF enabling interaction with classes of resources and the class properties. For this purpose, the RDF schema lets developers define a specific vocabulary (set of URI references) for RDF data (such as authorOf) and specify the types of object to which these attributes can be applied (Brickley and Guha 2000). This type of system uses some predefined terms, such as Class, subPropertyOf, and subClassOf, for application-specific schema. These terms can be further used in RDF expressions. RDF objects can be defined as instances of one or more classes using the type property. The subClassOf property is used to specify the hierarchical organization of classes. The sub-PropertyOf is used to specify the hierarchical organization of properties. Domain and range constructs on properties are utilized to set constraints.

Some more examples on RDF and resource description framework schema are given in Chapter 9.

8.5.3   Web ontology language

OWL is considered as an extension of RDF schema as it uses the RDF meaning of classes and properties (rdfs:Class, rdfs:subClassOf, etc.). Purpose of OWL is to define ontologies that include classes, properties, and their relationships for a specific application domain. When you want to describe any resource, these terms can be used in the published RDF documents; therefore, everything we say, we have a reason to say it. And moreover, a given application can implement reasoning process to discover implicit or unknown facts with the help of the ontologies.

RDF schema has some very powerful modeling primitives, such as the rdfs:Class (the class of all classes) and rdf:Property (the class of all properties). However, compared to RDF schema, OWL provides us with the capability to express much more complex and richer relationships. Therefore, we can construct applications with a much stronger reasoning ability. Thus, we often want to use OWL for the purpose of ontology development.

In short, we can define OWL as follows:

OWL = RDF Schema + new constructs for better expressiveness

Example: Let us see a definition of *class* beer.

```
<owl:Class rdf:ID="Beer">
<rdfs:subClassOf rdf:resource="&food;PotableLiquid" />
<rdfs:subClassOf>
```

```
<owl:Restriction>
<owl:onProperty rdf:resource="#hasMaker" />
<owl:cardinality rdf:datatype=
"&xsd;nonNegativeInteger">1</owl:cardinality>
</owl:Restriction>
</rdfs:subClassOf>
<rdfs:subClassOf>
<owl:Restriction>
<owl:onProperty rdf:resource="#hasMaker" />
<owl:allValuesFrom rdf:resource="# brewery" />
</owl:Restriction>
</rdfs:subClassOf>
<rdfs:subClassOf>
<owl:Restriction>
<owl:onProperty rdf:resource="#madeFromMalt" />
<owl:minCardinality rdf:datatype=
"&xsd;nonNegativeInteger">1</owl:minCardinality>
</owl:Restriction>
</rdfs:subClassOf>
<rdfs:subClassOf>
<owl:Restriction>
<owl:onProperty rdf:resource="#hasAlcohol" />
<owl:cardinality rdf:datatype=
"&xsd;nonNegativeInteger">1</owl:cardinality>
</owl:Restriction>
</rdfs:subClassOf>
<rdfs:subClassOf>
<owl:Restriction>
<owl:onProperty rdf:resource="#hasFlavor" />
<owl:cardinality rdf:datatype=
"&xsd;nonNegativeInteger">1</owl:cardinality>
</owl:Restriction>
</rdfs:subClassOf>
<rdfs:subClassOf>
<owl:Restriction>
<owl:onProperty rdf:resource="#hasBody" />
<owl:cardinality rdf:datatype=
"&xsd;nonNegativeInteger">1</owl:cardinality>
</owl:Restriction>
</rdfs:subClassOf>
<rdfs:subClassOf>
<owl:Restriction>
<owl:onProperty rdf:resource="#hasColor" />
<owl:cardinality rdf:datatype=
"&xsd;nonNegativeInteger">1</owl:cardinality>
</owl:Restriction>
</rdfs:subClassOf>
<rdfs:subClassOf>
<owl:Restriction>
<owl:onProperty rdf:resource="#locatedIn"/>
<owl:someValuesFrom rdf:resource="&vin;Region"/>
</owl:Restriction>
</rdfs:subClassOf>
<rdfs:label xml:lang="en">beer</rdfs:label>
<rdfs:label xml:lang="fr"> bière</rdfs:label>
</owl:Class>
```

The W3C's Web Ontology Working Group has defined the OWL as three different sublanguages as follows.

8.5.3.1 *OWL full*

The entire language is called OWL Full and uses all the OWL language primitives. It also allows combining these primitives in arbitrary ways with RDF and RDF schema. This includes the possibility to change the meaning of the predefined primitives, by applying the language primitives to each other. For example, in OWL Full, one can restrict the number of classes that can be described in ontology by defining a cardinality constraint. The OWL Full is that it is fully upward compatible with RDF, both syntactically and semantically. That is, a valid RDF document is also a valid OWL Full document, and so is true for the RDF schema.

8.5.3.2 *OWL DL*

OWL DL is based on description logics based on set theory. It is a sublanguage of OWL Full, which restricts the way in which the constructors from OWL and RDF can be used. OWL DL focuses on common formal semantics and inference decidability. Description logics offer additional ontology constructs like union, intersection, and negation along with inference mechanisms. OWL DL uses all OWL ontology constructs with some restrictions.

8.5.3.3 *OWL lite*

OWL Lite is a subset of OWL DL, the simplest and easiest to implement of the three species. OWL Lite does not use all vocabularies of OWL. To offer simplicity, some OWL terms used in the OWL Lite are restricted. OWL Lite may exclude enumerated classes, disjoint statements, and arbitrary cardinality.

According to Antoniou and van Harmelen (2009)

- Every legal OWL Lite ontology is a legal OWL DL ontology
- Every legal OWL DL ontology is a legal OWL Full ontology
- Every valid OWL Lite conclusion is a valid OWL DL conclusion
- Every valid OWL DL conclusion is a valid OWL Full conclusion
- OWL still uses RDF and RDF schema to a large extent
- Instances are declared as in RDF, using RDF descriptions and typing information
- OWL constructors like owl:Class, owl:DatatypeProperty, and owl:ObjectProperty are all specializations of their RDF counterparts

Figure 8.8 shows the subclass relationships between some modeling primitives of OWL and RDF/RDFS.

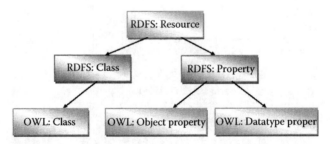

Figure 8.8 Modeling primitives of OWL and RDF.

The original hope in the design of OWL was that there would be a downward compatibility with corresponding reuse of software across the various layers. However, the advantage of full downward compatibility for OWL (that any OWL aware processor will also provide correct interpretations of any RDF schema document) is only achieved for OWL Full, at the cost of computational intractability.

8.5.4 Ontology interchange language

OIL is an ontology representation and inference language. The OIL ontology encompasses of slot definitions (slot-def) and class definitions (class-def). A slot-def describes a binary relation between two entities (Table 8.6). A class-def associates a class name with a class description and consists of the following optional components:

Table 8.7 presents an example of an ontology defining African wildlife (Decker et al. 2000).

The OIL and OWL extend RDFS emphasize support for richer logical inference. Besides inheriting advantages from Frame Systems, these ontology languages provide a rich set of constructs based on model theoretic semantics (Hayes 2004; Patel et al. 2004).

8.5.5 OWL2 profile

OWL2 is the latest version of OWL that efficiently addresses the trade-off between logical expressivity and scalability that is inherent to formal knowledge representation by specifying extra lightweight language profiles.

On October 27, 2009, OWL 2 has become a W3C standard, which has the following core specifications:

- OWL 2 Web Ontology Language Structural Specification and Functional-Style Syntax
- OWL 2 Web Ontology Language Mapping to RDF Graphs
- OWL 2 Web Ontology Language Direct Semantics

Table 8.6 OIL Components

Component	Description
Definition type	"defined" or "primitive"
	Complete class definition (defined) or primitive (with conditions)
Slot constraint	Possible value of slot for an instance of the class
	Main components of a slot constraints are as follows:
	• Name: a string that delineates the slot being constrained
	• Value-type: a list of one or more class expressions for which the value of the class must be an instance of each class expression in the list if an instance of the defined class has the current slot (e.g., a class "Employee" could have a slot "Boss" with the slot-constraint value-type "Employee," which means if an employee has a "Boss," the "Boss" must also be an "Employee")
	• Has-value: a list of one or more class expressions. If class "Employee" has a slot "Friend" with the slot constraint *has-value* "Colleague," then every "Colleague" is the "Friend" of other "Employee"
Subclass	Relates the defined class to a list of one or more class expressions such as class names, class slots, constraints, etc.

Table 8.7 Example Ontology Defining African Wildlife

Slot component	Description
class-def animal	Animals are a class
class-def plant	Plants are a class
subclass-of NOT animal	That is disjoint from animals
class-def tree	
subclass-of plant	Trees are a type of plants
class-def branch	
slot-constraint is-part-of	Branches are parts of trees
has-value tree	
class-def leaf	
Slot-constraint is-part-of	Leafs are parts of branches
has-value branch	
class-def defined carnivore	Carnivores are animals
subclass-of animal	
Slot-constraint eats	That eat only other animals
value-type animal	
class-def defined herbivore	Herbivores are animals
subclass-of animal	
Slot-constraint eats	That eat only plants or parts of plants
value-type plant	
OR (slot-constraint is-part-of **has-value** plant)	
class-def giraffe	Giraffes are herbivores
subclass-of herbivore	
Slot-constraint eats	And they eat leaves
value-type leaf	
class-def lion	
subclass-of animal	Lions are also animals
Slot-constraint eats	But they eat herbivores
value-type herbivore	
class-def tasty-plant	Tasty plants are plants that are eaten by
subclass-of plant	Both herbivores and carnivores
Slot-constraint eaten-by	
Has-value herbivore, carnivore	

- OWL 2 Web Ontology Language RDF-Based Semantics
- OWL 2 Web Ontology Language Conformance
- OWL 2 Web Ontology Language Profiles

OWL 2 provides three profiles, namely, OWL 2 EL, OWL 2 QL, and OWL 2 RL. Each of these profiles targets different application scenarios. The OWL 2 profiles are defined by placing restrictions on the functional style syntax of OWL 2. An ontology written in any of these profiles is a valid OWL 2 ontology. Each profile is designed to trade some expressive power for efficiency of reasoning. For example, the OWL 2 EL profile trades expressivity for the benefit of polynomial time subsumption testing. Similarly, reasoning for the OWL 2 RL profile can be implemented using a rule engine.

The important modeling features of OWL 2 EL profile are class conjunction and SomeValuesFrom restrictions. The use of negation, disjunction, AllValuesFrom restrictions, and cardinality restrictions are not allowed to achieve tractability. In order to preserve its good computational properties, the data types supported by OWL 2 EL have been selected to ensure that their intersection is either empty or infinite. Many large-scale ontologies can be captured using this profile.

OWL 2 QL is basically designed for data-driven applications and provides a suitable means for vendors of RDF stores to include some kind of OWL support without excluding the advantages of a database type implementation. OWL 2 QL is based on the DL–Lite family of description logics. The speciality of this profile is that it has many features required for capturing conceptual models. This profile is suitable in cases where a limited extension of RDF schema is desired.

OWL 2 RL has been designed to allow the smooth adoption of OWL by vendors of rule-based inference tools. Naturally, it offers better interoperability with knowledge representation languages based on rules. This profile allows for most constructs of OWL 2; however, to permit rule-based implementations of reasoning, the way these constructs can be used in axioms has been restricted.

OWL ontologies and traditional classification systems share a great deal of common characteristics, especially in terms of presenting various kinds of classes and relationships of classes. Classes in OWL can be understood as sets of individuals. OWL 2 has added a new syntactic subset in a profile to accommodate ontologies needing to represent rather complex entities. OWL ontologies exhibit a huge number of classes and have a heavy use of classification to manage their terminology.

In OWL 2, classes and property expressions are used to construct class expressions and complex concepts. The most useful characteristics used in dealing with the issues of classification are summarized in the following:

1. OWL 2 supports various ways of describing classes: class identification, the intersection and union of two or more class descriptions, the complement of a class description, property restrictions, and the enumeration of individuals that form class instances.
   - Complex ClassExpressions include

     ```
     ObjectIntersectionOf | ObjectUnionOf | ObjectComplementOf |
     ObjectOneOf |
     ObjectSomeValuesFrom | ObjectAllValuesFrom | ObjectHasValue |
     ObjectHasSelf | ObjectMinCardinality | ObjectMaxCardinality |
     ObjectExactCardinality |
     ```

   - All standard Boolean connectives AND, OR, and NOT are supported. The **ObjectIntersectionOf, ObjectUnionOf**, and **ObjectComplementOf** provide for the standard set-theoretic operations on class expressions. The **ObjectOneOf** class expression contains exactly the specified individuals.
   - Class expressions in OWL 2 can be formed by placing restrictions on *object property* expressions. For example, the **ObjectSomeValuesFrom** allows for existential quantification over an object property expression, and it contains those individuals that are connected through an object property expression to at least one instance of a given class expression.
   - Class expressions in OWL 2 can be formed by placing restrictions on the *cardinality* of object property expressions. Cardinality restrictions can be qualified or

unqualified. The class expressions **ObjectMinCardinality**, **ObjectMaxCardinality**, and **ObjectExactCardinality** contain those individuals that are connected by an object property expression to at least, at most, and exactly a given number of instances of a specified class expression.

All of these are particularly useful when representing various types of classes, regardless if these classes are already established in a classification scheme or instructed to synthesize in the classifying process. Various class expressions can be used to precisely express the situations where, for example, values from one or more auxiliary tables are allowed to be used; or, in certain cases, if some values from a class can be added to another class.

2. OWL 2 provides axioms (statements that say what is true in the domain) that allow relationships to be established between class expressions, including the following:
   - **SubClassOf** axiom: Allows one to state that each instance of one class expression is also an instance of another class expression, and thus to construct a *hierarchy* of classes.
   - **EquivalentClasses** axiom: Allows one to state that several class expressions are *equivalent* to each other.
   - **DisjointClasses** axiom: Allows one to state that several class expressions are *pairwise disjoint*—that is, they have no instances in common.
   - **DisjointUnion** class expression: Allows one to define a class as a *disjoint union* of several class expressions and thus to express *covering* constraints. Such axioms are sometimes referred to as covering axioms.

Subclass axioms are a fundamental type of axioms in OWL 2 and can be used to construct a class hierarchy. This would be most widely used in a classification scheme. Other axioms can solve special problems, for example, the "alternative class position" issue.

3. OWL 2 supports two kinds of object property expressions. Object properties are the simplest form of object property expressions, and **inverse** object properties allow for bidirectional navigation in class expressions and axioms. The inverse object properties would be especially useful for the expressions of a class and its related index entries. Object property expressions can be employed to represent various kinds of rules for building classification numbers.

8.5.6   SPARQL

SPARQL is the standardized query language for RDF, the same way structured query language (SQL) is the standardized query language for relational databases. You will see some similarities between these two query languages because SPARQL shares several keywords such as SELECT, WHERE, etc. It also has new keywords that you have never seen if you come from a SQL world such as OPTIONAL, FILTER, and much more.

Recall that RDF is a triple comprised of a subject, predicate, and object. A SPARQL query consists of a set of triples where the subject, predicate, and/or object can consist of variables. The idea is to match the triples in the SPARQL query with the existing RDF triples and find solutions to the variables. A SPARQL query is executed on an RDF dataset, which can be a native RDF database, or on a relational database to RDF (RDB2RDF) system, such as Ultrawrap. These databases have SPARQL endpoints that accept queries and return results via HTTP.

Example: Assume we have the following RDF triples in our database

```
:id1 foaf:name "John Park"
:id1 foaf: based_near :Oslo
:id2 foaf:name "Jo"
:id2 foaf:based_near : Bergen
```

And we want to find the names of all the people in our database. This SPARQL query would look like

```
SELECT ?name
WHERE {
?x foaf:name ?name
}
```

We shall break down this query from the beginning. The query starts with the keyword SELECT followed by the variable names that we would like to project, which in this case is ?name. Note that all variable names have a question mark in the beginning. Afterward, we find the WHERE keyword, which is followed by a triple between curly braces. The triple in the query must also consist of a subject, predicate, and an object but in this case, either one can be a variable. In this case, the subject and the object are variables while the predicate is a constant value. This triple in the query is evaluated against all the RDF triples in your database. Constant values in the query triples are matched with constant values of the RDF triples in your database. For example, in our query triple, the only constant value is in the predicate, which is foaf:name. Out of our four RDF triples, two of them have foaf:name as a constant in the predicate; therefore, these two RDF triples match our query triples. Therefore, we have two solutions:

```
1.?x=id1, ?name="John Park"
2.?x=id2, ?name="Jo"
```

Because our query is only selecting the values assigned to the variable ?name, the final answer is John Park and Jo.

Example: Now let us consider a little complicated example. Assume we want to find the names of people who are based near Oslo. The SPARQL query would be

```
SELECT ?name
WHERE {
?x foaf:name ?name.
?x foaf:based_near :Oslo.
}
```

In this query, we have two triples. The first one is the same as our previous example and we already know the solution to it. Now let us look at the second query triple. In this case, the predicate has a constant value of foaf:based _ near and the object has a constant value of:Oslo, which can only match to one of our RDF triples. The solution is

```
3.?x=id1
```

Now each of the triples of our queries has its own solution. As you can see, both of these triple queries share a variable: ?x. This means that both this solutions can be joined. Therefore, the final solution is only

```
?x=id1, ?name="John Park"
```

SPARQL 1.0 is the first version of SPARQL, which was standardized in January 2008. It only allows you to query an RDF database, and it does not allow you to insert or update the database. Some interesting features are described in the following.

8.5.6.1   Result syntaxes

The results of SPARQL queries can be expressed in different formats. There is a standard SPARQL Query Result XML format, or in JSON. The result of a CONSTRUCT query is always an RDF graph, which can be serialized in all the corresponding RDF syntaxes (RDF/XML, N-triples, etc).

8.5.6.2   Query for relationships

If you have a triple pattern in a query where the predicate is a variable, then you can explore the database to find relationships. For example, the query

```
SELECT ?p
WHERE {
:John ?p :Mary
}
```

returns the type of link between:John and:Mary. That is not possible in SQL.

8.5.6.3   Transform data with CONSTRUCT

Through the CONSTRUCT operator, which is an alternative to SELECT, SPARQL allows you to transform data. The result is an RDF graph, instead of a table of results. Imagine you have RDF data that have been automatically generated and you would like to transform it to use well-known vocabularies. For example,

```
PREFIX foaf: <a href="https://docs.google.com/document/pub?id=1fiCI6B9R35
KrPesxNVyutsST0YlO_0djVhhApI-sdwg"><http://xmlns.com/foaf/0.1/>
</a>PREFIX ex: <http://myexample.com/>
CONSTRUCT {
?x foaf:name ?name
}
WHERE {
?x ex:nombre ?name .
}
```

8.5.6.4   OPTIONAL

An interesting operator in SPARQL is OPTIONAL. If you are coming from the SQL world, this operator is equivalent to the LEFT OUTER JOIN. The question is, why do we need this? Consider the following RDF triples:

```
:id1 foaf:name "John Park"
:id1 foaf: based_near :Oslo
:id2 foaf:name "Jo"
```

and the following query:

```
SELECT ?name ?loc
WHERE {
?x foaf:name ?name .
?x foaf:based_near ?loc .
}
```

If you have the SQL experience, you would expect two results: {?name = "John Park", ?loc = :Oslo} and {?name = "Jo", ?loc = null}. However, there is no triple with subject :id2 and predicate foaf:based_near; therefore, there is nothing to join on. Additionally, there are no nulls in RDF so you cannot explicitly say that Jo has a location, which is null. Therefore, this solution is not possible. The actual answer is just {?name = "John Park", ?loc = :Oslo}. So how do we get the previous results? This is where OPTIONAL comes in. The query would have to be

```
SELECT ?name ?loc
WHERE {
?x foaf:name ?name .
OPTIONAL {?x foaf:based_near ?loc .}
}
```

This query can be read as "find all the names, and oh by the way, if there is a foaf:based_ near attached, return that too, otherwise, don't worry about it". The actual solution would be {?name = "John Park", ?loc = :Oslo} and {?name = "Jo"}.

8.5.6.5 *Negation*

Negation in SPARQL 1.0 is based on negation as failure and it is implemented using OPTIONAL, the bound filter, and the logical NOT operator. The OPTIONAL operator binds variables to the triples that we want to exclude, and the filter removes those cases. For example, find people who do not have a location. Following our previous example dataset, the query would be

```
SELECT ?name
WHERE {
?x foaf:name ?name .
OPTIONAL {?x foaf:based_near ?loc .}
FILTER(!bound(?loc))
}
```

and the result is

{?x = "Jo"}

There are several features that are missing in SPARQL 1.0, and this is where SPARQL 1.1 comes in, which was chartered in 2009. Some of the key features that are missing are aggregates, subqueries, and a natural negation operator. Key features of SPARQL 1.1 are

- Aggregates: ability to group results and calculate aggregate values (e.g., count, min, max, avg, and sum)
- Subqueries: allows a query to be embedded within another
- Negation: includes two negation operators: NOT EXIST and MINUS
- Property paths: query arbitrary length paths of a graph via a regular-expression-like syntax
- Update: an update language for RDF
- Service description: a vocabulary and discovery mechanism that describes the capabilities of a SPARQL endpoint
- Entailment regimes: defines conditions under which SPARQL queries can be used for inference under RDF, RDF schema, OWL, or rule interchange format (RTF) entailment

- Query federation: ability to split a single query and send parts of it to different SPARQL endpoints and then combining the results from each one
- Projected expressions: ability for query results to contain values derived from constants, function calls, or other expressions in the SELECT list

8.6   Meta-ontology

The ontology languages like RDF, RDFS, and OWL are in fact meta-ontologies themselves; and their instances are semantic web ontology. Such meta-ontologies offer a small vocabulary and corresponding axioms as the building blocks for any conceptualisms, and they are backed by inference engines with built-in support for their ontology constructs and axioms (Ding et al. 2006). For example, an RDFS inference engine can understand the semantics of *rdf:subClassOf* and infer RDF triples by propagating *rdf:type* statement through subclass relations. Such ontology only provides necessary components for the reference model without considering any domain concepts. Other examples of such meta-ontology are semantic web rule language (SWRL) (Horrocks et al. 2003) (a combination of OWL and RuleML) and Rei declarative policy language (Kagal et al. 2003). In addition to the object-oriented constructs provided in RDF(S) and OWL, ontology constructs for concept organization like thesaurus (e.g., concept, narrower-concept, and related-concept) have been modeled in simple knowledge organization system (SKOS).

8.7   Ontology tools and editors

Ontology editors allow for creation and editing ontology generally by providing visual/graphical interface. These tools allow to create a hierarchy of concepts (such as "Employee is a subconcept of person") and to model relationships between those concepts (such as "An employee works in an institute"). OntoEdit* is the most prominent commercial ontology editor. The specialty of this editor is that it encompasses with a strong inference backbone. Different extensions and plug-ins like OntoBroker allow different tasks such as the modeling, database mapping, and the use of powerful rules for applications.

Protégé[†] is the most well-known academic ontology editor, which provides a flexible plug-in framework like OntoEdit, for example, PROMPT plug-in, which allows for merging of two given ontologies into a single one.

KAON[‡] is an ontology editor and simultaneously provides open-source ontology management infrastructure targeted at the use of traditional ontologies for business applications.

Ontobroker (initially developed at the Institute AIFB/University of Karlsruhe and now commercialized by the company Ontoprise) and SHOE (University of Maryland) were two ontology-based systems, which are pioneers in this field. Both systems relied on additional semantic markup, which was put into regular web pages known as annotations. These systems could successfully demonstrate the process of adding semantics to make the content machine processable. The work heavily influenced the current semantic web standards of the W3C.

TopBraid[§] is a commercial visual modeling environment for developing and managing domain models and ontologies in semantic web standards RDF schema and OWL. TopBraid has a commercially available triple store to build a multiuser web accessible system that

---

* http://www.ontoprise.com
[†] http://protege.stanford.edu/
[‡] http://kaon.semanticweb.org
[§] http://www.topquadrant.com/products/TB_Composer.html

supports working practices of collaborative authoring. TopBraid composer is founded on the Eclipse platform and uses Jena as its underlying application programming interface (API). This supports the rapid development of semantic applications in a single platform. Composer can be used to edit RDFS/OWL files in various formats, and also provides scalable database backends (Jena, AllegroGraph, Oracle 10g, and Sesame) as well as multiuser support. It is a very flexible platform that enables Java programmers to add customized extensions or to develop stand-alone semantic web applications. Some more tools are given in Chapter 9.

8.8 Annotation tools

Annotations are elements of contributed text that anyone may add to a web page. Annotation tools* allow for adding semantic markup to the resource documents in order to automate the challenging task of annotation for large-scale resources.

OntoMat-Annotizer[†] is an example of prominent annotation tool based on a full-fledged annotation framework called CREAM. CREAM is extended to support semi-automatic annotations of documents and databases.

Annotea[‡] is a W3C project to demonstrate the use of RDF for annotating web pages. Annotea defines a protocol for accessing the annotations from an annotation server, and an RDF format for storing the annotation text with the help of an annotation-aware experimental browser Amaya. Annotations may be specific to a region of a page, which may be defined by an XML-based pointer called Xpointer. Once an annotation has been defined, other annotation users can reply to it, similar to a threaded email discussion.

Altova's SemanticWorks[§] software is a commercially available application that provides good performance and flexibility for ontology editing/creation. Altova's built-in semantic reasoner allows the user to find any flaws in their coding or logic and correct any issues within the ontology. SemanticWorks supports all three OWL dialects in addition to full support for RDF and RDFS. It allows user to create complex ontologies visually, using intelligent entry helpers, a fairly intuitive icon system, and shortcuts. SemanticWorks also autogenerates the RDF/XML or N-triples code that corresponds to user's design.

8.9 Inference engines

Inference engines allow reference and processing of existing knowledge available on the Web. The process of inference might generate/deduce new knowledge from given content using either general logic-based inference engines or specialized problem solving algorithms. Using the first approach, one can distinguish between different kinds of representation languages such as higher order logic, first-order logic, description logic, and logic programming.[¶] Project Halo[**] provides examples and interesting results on inference engine. Inference engines are very flexible and adaptable to different usage scenarios such as information integration or intelligent advisors. *Ontobroker*[††] is the most prominent and capable commercial inference engine. It is based on frame logic, tightly integrated with the ontology engineering environment OntoEdit and provides connectors to typical

---

* http://annotation.semanticweb.org/
† http://annotation.semanticweb.org/ontomat
‡ http://www.w3.org/2001/Annotea/
§ http://www.altova.com/semanticworks.html
¶ http://semanticweb.org/inference.html
** http://www.projecthalo.com/
†† http://www.ontoprise.com

databases. It was already used in numerous industrial and academic projects. *FaCT** is one of the most prominent description logics based inference engines.

8.10   Semantic web applications

8.10.1   Search engine

As the volume of content on the Web grows, software agents will need their own search engines to help them find the relevant and trustworthy knowledge required to carry out their tasks.

Semantic web browsers extend the concept of the web browser into the semantic web by allowing the RDF annotations of resources to be read and presented in a structured manner, for example, Haystack[†] web browser from MIT. According to claims made by the product, it aggregates RDF from multiple arbitrary locations and presents it to the user in a human-readable fashion, with point and click semantics that let the user navigate from one piece of semantic web data to other, related pieces.

Swoogle[‡] is another example of a search engine for the semantic web on the Web. Swoogle crawls the WWW for a special class of web documents called *semantic web documents*, which are written in RDF. Swoogle is a research project being carried out by the eBiquity Research Group in the Computer Science and Electrical Engineering Department at the University of Maryland, Baltimore County (UMBC). Currently, Swoogle provides the following services:

- Search semantic web ontology
- Search semantic web instance data
- Search semantic web terms, that is, URIs that have been defined as classes and properties
- Provide metadata of semantic web documents and support browsing the semantic web (Ding et al. 2005)
- Archive different versions of semantic web documents

Other prominent semantic web search and browsers are Ontaria[§] and ontoSearch[¶] that may be considered here. DAML Crawler,[**] RDF Crawler,[††] OCRA (Ontology CRAwler),[‡‡] and Scutter[§§] are examples of crawler on semantic web.

There are some ontology repositories available online and maintained manually. These include schemaweb,[¶¶] DAML ontology library,[***] SemWebCentral,[†††] protege's OWL ontology library,[‡‡‡] rdfdata.org,[§§§] and SIMILE[¶¶¶] project at MIT.

---

* http://www.cs.man.ac.uk/~horrocks/FaCT/
† http://haystack.lcs.mit.edu/
‡ http://swoogle.umbc.edu/
§ http://www.w3.org/2004/ontaria/
¶ http://www.ontosearch.org/
** http://www.daml.org/crawler/
†† http://ontobroker.semanticweb.org/rdfcrawl/
‡‡ http://www.mindswap.org/~golbeck/downloads/ocra.shtml
§§ http://wiki.foaf-project.org/w/Scutter
¶¶ http://www.schemaweb.info/
*** http://www.daml.org/ontologies/
††† http://www.semwebcentral.org/
‡‡‡ http://protege.stanford.edu/plugins/owl/owl-library/
§§§ http://www.rdfdata.org/
¶¶¶ http://simile.mit.edu/

8.10.2 Semantic web portals

Semantic web portals use the organization provided by annotating web pages using ontology, to structure and display the information. Examples of the semantic web portals are SEAL (Maedche et al. 2003), Ontoweaver* and SWED,[†] which have been used to deliver websites such as knowledge web.[‡]

8.10.3 Catalog management and thesaurus

Catalog management, thesaurus, and classification schemes are effectively managed through semantic web techniques. For example, classification of products into standard catalogs like United Nations Standard Products and Services Code (UNSPSC), North American Industry Classification Systems (NAICS) Codes, and eClass are required for some e-commerce systems, for example, Commerce One.[§] This problem is related to thesauri for digital libraries and thesauri of controlled terms for government document repositories. The semantic web techniques can be utilized to ensure efficient processing of large vocabularies, automated mapping, and classification between vocabulary versions and development of concept ontologies for use as stable intermediaries.

In addition to this, the semantic web techniques might provide a means for integrating and capturing partial mappings between catalogs. Ontology mapping discovery, integration of partial ontology mappings, and adaptation of ontology mappings to track ontology evolution are the key benefits achieved through semantic web techniques.

8.10.4 Call center

Call centers are the platform for companies to communicate with their customers and the market. It can be considered as one of the major support tools that help in improving customer relationships for growth of the business. If incoming requests to call center are handled effectively, it might offer great rewards in terms of better customer service, lower overheads, lower operational costs, and increased profitability.

Semantic technologies are also being used for the exchange of interpersonal meaning in call center conversations as denoted by Wan (2008).

8.10.5 e-Learning

The semantic web can be effectively utilized for various forms of learning such as classroom-based learning, distance learning, e-learning, personalized learning, and mobile learning. The concept of a "learning object" as an independent reusable unit of educational material, which can be integrated with other learning objects has been a central feature of electronics-based learning systems (Sajja 2009). Learning objects can be organized into repositories and shared across peer-to-peer (P2P) networks. The Edutella[¶] project is seeking to provide an RDF-based P2P network for sharing learning objects. Rich semantic annotation languages for learning objects are also upcoming. Examples for the same

---

* http://kmi.open.ac.uk/projects/akt/ontoweaver/
† http://www.swed.org.uk/swed/index.html
‡ http://knowledgeweb.semanticweb.org/index.html
§ http://www.commerceonefinancial.com/
¶ http://edutella.jxta.org/

are educational modeling language (EML),* IMS global learning consortium's proposed set of integrated standards for e-Learning subjects along with a metadata specification,† and the learning object metadata (LOM), a standard defined by the Learning Technology Standardization Committee (LTSC)‡ of IEEE. All these are currently defined in XML but are adaptable into RDF for use in the semantic web. This will allow a richer interaction with the learning material, with ontology-based brokers for negotiating the requirements of learners to the available learning materials.

Beyond the search and discovery of learning objects, the development of learning plans and courses can be controlled via workflow languages and knowledge charts as defined by Stutt and Motta (2004).

8.10.6   Tourism

There are many important data exchange standards and semantic initiatives in the tourism sector. The tourism sector has a very heterogeneous information landscape consisting of a detailed patchwork of websites in all sizes, from the tiniest personal web pages to enterprise portals. This poses big challenges to integration and information exchange. Several initiatives have been launched to try to make some order in the seemingly chaotic information domain.

"Standards" will often be the answer to the challenges of information exchange. A standard is an established form or requirement that needs to be followed in order to allow components of different nature and origin to fit and work together. A standard is usually expressed in a formal document. The ISO/IEC Guide 2 defines a standard "a document established by consensus and approved by a recognized body that provides for common and repeated use, rules, guidelines, or characteristics for activities or their results, aimed at the achievement of the optimum degree of order in a given context."

Standards are intended to be a summary of good and best practices rather than general practice. Everyone seems to agree that standards are good and what we should strive for. But is it so that standards always are the answer and that the more standards, the better? Standards involve costs and can also in some cases hamper innovation.

Open Travel Association (OTA) is a nonprofit trade association established in 1999 by travel companies. Their primary activity is to develop and maintain a library of XML schemas for use by the travel industry. These schemes constitute the OpenTravel XML specification.

World Tourism Organisation (WTO) thesaurus on tourism and leisure provides an authoritative terminology for its domain. The thesaurus is a guide to tourism terminology for the standardization and normalization of a common indexation and research language, at an international level. This thesaurus is multilingual in English, French, and Spanish. Terms of the tourism domain have been defined in great detail so that individuals unfamiliar with this vocabulary can also use the thesaurus. At the moment, the thesaurus covers approximately 1800 concepts.

Semantic technologies have been utilized to manage novel methods of facilitating effective integration of (tourism) information originating from various sources on top of ontology. Ding et al. (2008) report some work done in the OnTourism project (funded by Austria Government) in order to improve information creation, maintenance, and delivery in the tourism industry by introducing semantic technologies to this domain. The

---

* http://eml.ou.nl/eml-ou-nl.htm
† http://www.imsglobal.org/
‡ http://ltsc.ieee.org/wg12/

main component of this OnTourism architecture is the document repository built upon the existing document repository of Austria Call Center. The system aims to create a semantic content management solution based on the existing Microsoft SharePoint employed by the Austrian Tourism Call Center in order to make full usage of both semantic and social metadata.

There are many ontology project initiatives in this domain. We will discuss some of them in the following paragraphs.

The Harmonise project was funded by the European Commission. Technically, the project run from July 2001 to December 2002, but the work has continued in for instance the Tourism Harmonisation Trans-European Network, Harmo-TEN. Moreover, the aim of the project was to build a technological infrastructure based on a shared ontology and to enhance the cooperation of European SMEs in the tourism sector. According to Dell'Erba et al. (2005), the following three components were developed in the Harmonise project:

- *Networks of cooperating actors* in the tourism domain working together to achieve information interoperability and to define a common view of the tourist domain: the "tourist harmonization ontology."
- *Tourism ontology* to model and maintain the basic concepts used in the tourism domain: the "interoperability minimum ontology (IMHO)."
- *Mediating platform* is a mediator tool for a conceptual level alignment of local data models and subsequent information translation utilizing semantic mapping and reconciliation techniques: the Harmo Suite System.

The European Tourism Portal is developed using the Harmonise platform, which can be considered as a suitable example for the Mediating platform.

Semantically-Interlinked Online Communities (SIOC) Project[*] is a semantic web technology. SIOC provides methods for interconnecting discussion methods such as blogs, forums, and mailing lists to each other. It consists of the SIOC ontology, an open-standard machine readable format for expressing the information contained both explicitly and implicitly in Internet discussion methods, of SIOC metadata producers for a number of popular blogging platforms and content management systems, and of storage and browsing/searching systems for leveraging this SIOC data.

The OnTour Ontology[†] is an ontology created especially for the tourism domain using OWL and was developed by Digital Enterprise Research Institute (DERI). In addition to normal tourism concepts (location, accommodation, etc.), it also includes concepts that describe leisure activities and geographic data. This ontology was based on an international standard: the *Thesaurus on Tourism & Leisure Activities* of the World Tourism Organization. This thesaurus is a very extensive collection of terms related to the area of tourism. A documentation of the ontology is available at http://e-tourism.deri.at/ont/index.html

Mondeca[‡] tourism ontology includes important concepts of the tourism domain, which are defined in the WTO thesaurus managed by the World Tourism Organization (WTO).[§] The WTO thesaurus includes information and definitions of the topic tourism and leisure activities. The dimensions that are defined within the Mondeca Ontology are tourism object profiling, tourism and cultural objects, tourism packages, and tourism

[*] http://sioc-project.org/
[†] http://ontour.deri.org/ontology/ontour-02.owl
[‡] http://www.mondeca.com
[§] http://www.world-tourism.org

multimedia content. The used ontology language is OWL, and the ontology itself contains about 1000 concepts.

Another comprehensive and precise reference ontology is known as comprehensive ontology for the travel industry (COTRIN). The objective of the COTRIN ontology is the implementation of the semantic XML-based OTA specifications. Major airlines, hoteliers, car rental companies, leisure suppliers, travel agencies, and others will use COTRIN to bring together autonomous and heterogeneous tourism web services, web processes, applications, data, and components residing in distributed environments.

One of the important initiatives on applications of semantic web technologies in tourism domain is SeSam4 project.* The main aim of SeSam4 is to allow smaller, specialized groups, and organizations to enter the semantic world by providing easy conversion, low-cost solutions, and understandable processes. SeSam4 contributes to bridge the gap between unstructured, informal indexes generated by current text mining methods, and structured semantic information needed for interoperability between multiple content management systems. The SeSam4 project has established methods and standards for a simplified, structured, step-by-step process to establish a semantic, maneuverable knowledge model for particular business sectors of industries.

8.10.7   Publishing

SemNews is a semantic news service that monitors different really simple syndication (RSS) news feeds and provides structured representations of the meaning of news. As new content appears, SemNews extracts the summary from the RSS description and processes a sophisticated text understanding system OntoSem (Java et al. 2006).

8.10.8   Community and social projects

Community portals provide central platforms where virtual communities can communicate and share information, find contacts, and discuss. Semantic web technology is being used to construct such portals to provide a richer approach to organizing and searching community portals. Community archives, community formation, community book marking, specially designed portals for a community, etc., can be benefited by the semantic web techniques. Scholnet,[†] SeLeNe,[‡] planetonto,[§] AKTiveSpace,[¶] etc., are examples to name a few.

An application based on semantic web technology is designed to support intranet-based virtual communities for the British Telecom Call Centre. British Telecom (United Kingdom) is a leading company on the telecom market, and its subdivision BTExact Technologies focuses on the development and application of new technologies. The system named "Ontoshare" developed here allows storage of best practice information in ontology and the automatic dissemination of new best practice information to relevant call center agents. In addition, call center agents can browse or search the ontology to find the information of most relevance to the problem they are dealing with at any given time. The system provides a sharable structure for the knowledge base and a common language for communication between call center agents.

---

[*] http://sesam4.net/
[†] http://www.ercim.eu/activity/projects/scholnet.html
[‡] http://www.dcs.bbk.ac.uk/~ap/projects/selene/homepage.html
[§] http://projects.kmi.open.ac.uk/planetonto/
[¶] http://triplestore.aktors.org/demo/AKTiveSpace/

8.10.9   e-Commerce

Personal agents to support or automate purchases, to provide assistance in finding product location, price comparison, access to ratings and opinions, etc., can be developed using semantic web techniques. Examples are Botspot,* Epinions,† and Amazon‡ customer reviews. M-commerce (mobile commerce) and K-commerce (knowledge commerce— related to packaging and marking knowledge) are two areas related to the e-commerce can also be benefited using the platform of web and semantic web.

8.10.10   Health care

The Semantic Web Health Care and Life Sciences Interest Group, part of the semantic web activity, is to develop, advocate for, and support the use of semantic web technologies for biological science, translational medicine, and health care. These domains stand to gain tremendous benefit by adoption of semantic web technologies, as they depend on the interoperability of information from many domains and processes for efficient decision support.

Initially driven by the need to query gene and gene product annotation across a number of model organisms, the gene ontology (GO) has emerged as an increasingly comprehensive controlled vocabulary of biological processes, molecular functions, and cellular components.§ Since its inception, GO strives to more accurately describe their 20,000+ terms principally organized via an "is a" axis, but also augmented with other relations (e.g., parthood). Following the GO model, there are now over 150 open biomedical ontologies (OBO) that are listed at the National Center for Bio-Ontology (NCBO) BioPortal, which now spans molecular, anatomical, physiological, organismal, health, and experimental information. Hoping to consolidate efforts, the OBO Foundry (Smith et al. 2007) is promoting a set of orthogonal reference ontologies, by mounting these against the restricted types defined by the philosophically inspired basic formal ontology (BFO) in combination with a limited set of basic relations defined in the relational ontology (RO).

Web services define APIs by structuring messages and content with the Web services description language (WSDL). A new semantic web services framework project, SADI, uses OWL ontologies to formally describe services, in which the semantic health and research environment (SHARE) query system undertakes service matchmaking and invocation through a SPARQL query (Vandervalk et al. 2009). This has been put to use in CardioSHARE, a system that integrates patient data with analytical services so as to identify *bona fide* cardiovascular health indicators.

There are many challenges for building efficient semantic web for health care. To name a few, consistent knowledge representation, scalable semantic web technologies, and axiomatic description of ontologies. Significantly, more research in human–computer interface is required to identify better ways to work with hyper-dimensional data from multiple (and possibly untrustworthy) sources.

8.10.11   Digital heritage

Digital preservation has been a very real concern of heritage institutions. Public funding of the major digital heritage research initiatives started around the turn of the millennium,

---

* http://www.botspot.com/
† http://www.epinions.com/
‡ http://www.amazon.com/
§ GO Consortium (2008). The Gene Ontology project in 2008. *Nucleic Acids Research*, 36(Database issue), D440–4.

notably the National Digital Information Infrastructure and Preservation Program (NDIIPP) established in 2000 by the U.S. congress and comparable European research initiatives. That shows that the mainstream of digital preservation research is about as old as the semantic web. However, both strands of research have only interacted in rather limited ways so far.

The digital preservation initiatives usually explored two types of approaches for the problem of semantic aging: migration and emulation—as well as combinations of both. *Migration* is especially useful for document-centered workflows, including those used in the humanities and in cultural–historic research. The ideal target format for migration is published under an open-source license, comes with an explicit account of its semantics, and possesses a large community of users.

Emulation constitutes the best solution for archives of highly interactive media, for example, interactive art or video games. Emulation strives for authenticity, for a reenactment of a user experience from the past. However, being able to run the software, which created the data does not make it interoperable with present day technology. Migration, on the other hand, aims at the integration of past content into future knowledge-based workflows. Because of the focus on data and interoperability, migration seems to blend more easily with the different flavors of the semantic web, definitely with the idea of a web of semantically interoperable knowledge bases but to a certain extent also with the more recent idea of a web of linked data.

8.10.12   Open archives

A knowledge-based society is characterized by the exchange of scientific knowledge through publication. Earlier this was done by the distribution of preprints and reprints and by the consultation of scientific journals. This situation has, however, completely changed with the advent of PCs and the WWW that made publication, storage, and distribution considerably cheaper and the knowledge published potentially more accessible. The advent of new technologies provided alternative and innovative solutions to disseminate low-cost scientific literature and provided noncompetitive and complementary strategies to assure open access (OA) to the results of public-funded research. This prompted the creation of OA journal and archives such that now "about 15–20% of non-OA journal articles annually are being self-archived by their authors (green OA) today and about 10–15% of the 20–25,000 peer-reviewed journals are open access journals (gold OA), as indexed by the Directory of Open Access Journals. Of the more than 10,000 non-OA peer-reviewed journals indexed in the Romeo directory of publisher policies (which includes most of the journals indexed by Thomson Reuters/ISI, over 90% endorse some form of author self-archiving (green or "pale-green" OA): 62% endorse self-archiving the author's final peer-reviewed draft or postprint ("green journals"); 29% the pre-refereeing preprint ("pale-green journals")*."

In addition to the papers referred to by the preceding statistics, there are results and raw data that are only stored in the internal information system of the research institutions. In order to make these results accessible to external users, there are ongoing activities related to the development of a network of current research information system (CRIS), some managed as national systems, others by universities and research institutes. The European Union has been supporting this activity by adopting a strategy to stimulate development of the national CRIS based on Common European Research Information

---

* http://en.wikipedia.org/wiki/Open_access_(publishing)

Format (CERIF) data model, which represents the data on published research results. At this point, we would like to stress the importance of making raw data available to others to run their own analysis. There is a need for openness and public accountability of available raw data.

The multitude of repositories makes it difficult to find all relevant information, a situation that will worsen because of the rapid growth of information. One of the encouraging applications of semantic web technologies is devoted to the connection of the scientific knowledge in a sole universal network where documents can be made machine readable by annotating them with Dublin Core metadata expressed as RDF. Due to the metadata harvesting protocol of the OAI-Protocol for Metadata Harvesting (OAI-PMH), the goal of obtaining a unique universal OA network has become possible. However, despite these developments, which considerably modify the nature of scientific publishing as well as the existing system of quality assurance, the application of web semantic technology is still limited to archiving and cataloging, and the main issue of semantic web, selection by quality criteria, is lacking in application.

8.11   *Semantic web interoperability and web mining*

Interoperability refers to a property to handle diverse content representations and organizations in such as way that they can "talk" (inter-operate) with each other just like content in homogeneous environments. Syntactic interoperability allows communication and exchange of data and understands only predefined syntax. Semantic interoperability enables systems to understand the meaning of the content represented in other systems. It is beyond the ability to just understand predefined words and syntax in order to communicate and exchange of content. Such systems automatically interpret the information exchanged meaningfully and accurately in order to produce useful results as defined by the end users of both systems. The operations on semantic web require interoperability at syntactic and semantic level. Web mining is one such standard and frequently performed operation. On semantic web, mining can be done syntactically at lower level and semantically considering the interoperability between the ontologies such as RDF, OWL, and XML. Semantic mining is actually a hybridization of web mining concepts into the semantic web. Specific crawlers can be designed that consider semantic web ontologies. That is, instead of a web crawler that considers HTML pages, it may consider RDF or other semantic web ontology.

A majority of the semantic web mining techniques employ phases such as ontology finding, ontology mapping, and ontology merging/integration. The process of ontology merging takes as input of more than one source ontologies and returns a merged ontology. Manual ontology merging using conventional tools is difficult, labor-intensive, and error-prone. However, no program can replace human intelligence fully, semi-automatic, or, human guided process can be developed to do so. Ontology mapping is the process of relating concepts of an ontology and their instances to the concepts of other ontology.

8.12   *Semantic web and social communities*

As we have studied in earlier sections, semantic web aims to bridge computers and human beings by enabling the computers to understand the meaning (semantics) of information and services on the Web. In essence, two core tasks to realize semantic web are defining semantics and satisfying users' requests based on the semantic information. In the past years, many research activities have been conducted to this end. However, a prevalent method is to ask the user to create the semantics on the Web, and then domain experts define reasoning rules to help locate the information to satisfy users' requests. This method has been criticized recently due to its high infeasibility. The Web is evolving rapidly. A rule may be correct at a specific time, but may quickly become out-of-date.

On the other hand, with the emergence and rapid proliferation of social applications and media, such as instant messaging (e.g., IRC, AIM, MSN, Jabber, Skype), sharing sites (e.g., Flickr, Picassa, YouTube, Plaxo), blogs (e.g., Blogger, WordPress, LiveJournal), wikis (e.g., Wikipedia, PBWiki), microblogs (e.g., Twitter, Jaiku), social networks (e.g., MySpace, Facebook, Ning), collaboration networks (e.g., digital bibliography and library project [DBLP]), to mention a few, there is little doubt that social network is becoming a popular research topic, attracting tremendous interest from mathematics, biology, physics, computer science, and sociology. The social web provides an opportunity to obtain users' generated data, for example, users on Twitter now send out more than 60 million tweets per day; at the same time, it also poses several unique challenges. Most existing researches have focused on finding the macrolevel mechanisms of the social influence such as degree distributions, diameter, clustering coefficient, communities, and small world effect. However, these methods provide us limited insight into the microlevel dynamics of the social network such as how an individual user changes his behaviors (actions) and how a user's action influences his friends.

In general, the social web and the semantic web can complement each other to address the challenges both worlds are facing. The semantic web can provide well-defined structure to the data on the social web so that they can be processed by machines. The semantic web can provide the standards needed for interoperability among online applications of the social web. On the other hand, the social web provides platforms that can be easily understood and used by ordinary people. By facilitating interaction and collaboration among people on the social web, consensus can be achieved and standards can emerge. We will discuss such issues of semantic web in the social web era in Chapter 10.

8.13   Semantic web and intelligent search

Many search engines search for keywords to answer the queries from users. The search engines basically search web pages for the required information. However, they filter the pages from searching unnecessary pages by using advanced algorithms. These search engines can answer topic wise queries efficiently and effectively by developing state-of-art algorithms. Nevertheless, they are weak in answering intelligent queries from the user due to the dependence of their results on information available in web pages. The focus of these search engines is solving these queries with close to accurate results in small time using much researched algorithms. However, it shows that such search engines are weak in answering intelligent queries using this approach.

The semantic web supports more efficient discovery, automation, integration, and reuse of data and provides support for interoperability problem, which cannot be resolved with current web technologies. At present, research on semantic web search engines is in the premature stage, as the established search engines such as Google, Yahoo, and Bing (MSN) and so forth still dominate the present markets of search engines. Intelligent semantic technology gives the closer to desired results by search engines to the user.

Nowadays, many of semantic search engines are developed and implemented in different working environments, and these mechanisms can be put into use to realize present search engines. A semantic search engine stores semantic information about web resources and is able to solve complex queries, considering as well the context where the

Web resource is targeted, and how a semantic search engine may be employed in order to permit clients obtain information about commercial products and services, as well as about sellers and service providers, which can be hierarchically organized. Semantic search engines may contribute to the growth of e-business applications since it is based on strong theory and broadly accepted standards.

Bhagwat and Polyzotis propose a semantic-based file system search engine—Eureka, which uses an inference model to build the links between files and a File Rank metric to rank the files according to their semantic importance (Bhagwat and Polyzotis 2005). Eureka has two main parts, namely, crawler that extracts file from file system and generates two kinds of indices: keywords' indices that record the keywords from crawled files and rank index that records the File Rank metrics of the files; and when search terms are entered, the query engine will match the search terms with keywords' indices and determine the matched file sets and their ranking order by an information retrieval-based metrics and File Rank metrics.

Kandogan et al. (2006) develop a semantic search engine—Avatar, which combines the traditional text search engine with the use of ontology annotations. Avatar has two main functions:

1. Extraction and representation—by means of unstructured information management architecture (UIMA) framework, which is a workflow consisting of a chain of annotators extracted from documents and stored in the annotation store
2. Interpretation—a process of automatically transforming a keyword search to several precise searches

Avatar consists of two central elements: semantic optimizer and user interaction engine. When a query is entered into the former, it will output a list of ranked interpretations for the query; then, the top ranked interpretations are passed to the latter, which will display the interpretations and the retrieved documents from the interpretations.

Maedche et al. (2003) designed an integrated technique for ontology searching, reuse, and update. In its architecture, an ontology registry is designed to store the metadata about ontologies, and ontology server stores the ontologies. The ontologies in distributed ontology servers can be created, replicated, and evolved. Ontology metadata in ontology registry can be queried and registered when a new ontology is created. Ontology search in ontology registry is executed under two conditions—query-by-example is to restrict search fields and search terms, and query-by-term is to restrict the hyponyms of terms for search.

There are some important issues in the existing semantic search engines and methods are concluded as follows:

1. Low precision and high recall: Some intelligent semantic search engines cannot show their significant performance in improving precision and lowering recall.
2. Identity intention of the user: User intention identification plays an important role in the intelligent semantic search engine.
3. Specific user patterns can be extrapolated to global users: In early search engine that offered disambiguation to search terms. A user could enter in a search term that was ambiguous (e.g., Java) and the search engine would return a list of alternatives (coffee, programming language, island in the South Seas).
4. Inaccurate queries: Users do not include all potential synonyms and variations in the query; in fact users have a problem but are not sure how to phrase.

8.14   Semantic web research issues

A significant and enthusiastic effort is being given to the development of the semantic web to convert Tim Berners-Lee's vision into a reality. The following is the list of some research issues that need to be explored.

1. Development of shared vocabulary, ontology, and digital libraries
2. Ontology mapping, merging, and integration tools such as ontology management systems along with ontology editors and other facilities
3. Development of metadata standards
4. Virtual communities on the Web
5. Semantic search engine
6. Semantic querying to the distributed databases
7. Semantic inference and editing tools
8. Semantic grid framework
9. Semantic web services
10. Trust, logic, and proof algorithms
11. Security standards and quality metrics
12. Knowledge/wisdom web
13. Application of artificial intelligent techniques for semantic web development such as knowledge representation and knowledge management
14. Building portal, communities, and collaborations
15. e-Learning
16. e-Government packages
17. e-Commerce framework and agents
18. Domain-specific application such as development of vocabularies, metadata, and communities in domain such as
    a.   Training and education
    b.   Health care
    c.   Tourism applications and travel guide systems
    d.   Call center systems
    e.   Publishing and advertising, etc.

Exercises

8.1   What is the intention of semantic web layered model?

8.2   What are the basic components of ontologies?

8.3   Draw a diagram representing the statement: "John believes that the creator of the resource http://www.stsu.net is Joe", in RDF data model.

8.4   Define RDF description of your course website and some of the documents available on the website. Include a description of the exercises as a sequence in your RDF description.

8.5   Model an ontology of tour planning. Here, you have to create primitive and defined classes and appropriate relations between them.

8.6   Determine in general which features of OWL are necessary.

8.7   Express the following knowledge in OWL DL. (You should define classes, individuals, and properties as necessary. You may omit the preamble such as namespaces.):
Breakbone Fever is a disease with the following symptoms: headache, joint, and muscle pain.

8.8   (Project) The goal of this project is to give you hands-on experience in using semantic web technologies. The tools you will use in your lab are *Protege*, an ontology modeling tool, *Jena*, a Java framework for RDF and OWL. Design an ontology for music. Make sure to create an "RDF files" project in Protege. The output consists of all the files generated by Protege. Furthermore, use *Jena* to query your ontology. Find a simple introduction into using *Jena* to query SPARQL. You can use the *ARQ* command line utilities to execute SPARQL queries. You may have to download the *ARQ distribution* separately to obtain the command line utilities. Otherwise, you can create a Java program for executing the queries. Create at least FOUR queries for your ontology.

References

Akerkar, R. 2009. *Foundations of the Semantic Web: XML, RDF and Ontology*. New Delhi: Narosa Publishing House.

Antoniou, G. and van Harmelen, F. 2009. Web ontology language: OWL. In *Handbook on Ontology*, eds. S. Staab and R. Studer., New York: Springer Berlin Heidelberg, pp. 91–110.

Berners-Lee, T. 1998. Semantic web road map. http://www.w3.org/DesignIssues/Semantic.html (accessed September 13, 2011).

Berners-Lee, T., Hendler, J., and Lassila, O. 2001. The semantic web. *Scientific American* 284(5):34–43.

Bhagwat, D. and N. Polyzotis. 2005. Searching a file system using inferred semantic links. Paper presented at the *16th ACM Conference on Hypertext and Hypermedia*, pp. 85–87, Salzburg, Austria.

Brickley, D. and Guha, R. 2000. Resource description framework (RDF) schema specification 1.0. W3C Candidate Recommendation, 2000. http://www.w3.org/TR/2000/CR-rdf-schema-20000327/ (accessed September 13, 2011).

Bush, V. 1945. As we may think. *The Atlantic Monthly* 176(1):101–108.

Champin, P. 2001. RDF tutorial. http://www710.univ-lyon1.fr/~champin/rdf-tutorial/rdf-tutorial.pdf (accessed September 13, 2011).

Decker, S., Melnik, S., Harmelen, F., Fensel, D., Klein, M., Broekstra, J., Erdmann, M., and Horrocks, I. 2000. The semantic web: The roles of XML and RDF. *IEEE Internet Computing* 15(3):63–74.

Dell'Erba, M., Fodor, O., Hopken, W., and Werthner, H. 2005. Exploiting semantic web technologies for harmonizing e-markets. *Information Technology & Tourism* 7(3–4):201–219.

Ding, L., Kolari, P., Ding, Z., Avancha, S., Finin, T., and Joshi, A. 2006. Using ontologies in the semantic web: A survey. *Ontologies* 14:79–113.

Ding, L., Pan, R., Finin, T., Joshi, A., Peng, Y., and Kolari, P. 2005. Finding and ranking knowledge on the semantic web. *Lecture Notes in Computer Science* 3729:156–170.

Ding, Y., Herzog, C., Luger, M., Prantner, K., and Yan, Z. 2008. ONTOURISM: Semantic etourism portal. Paper presented at the *Second International Scientific Conference of the e-Business Forum—E-Business in Travel, Tourism and Hospitality*, Athens, Greece.

Hayes, P. 2004. RDF semantics. W3C Recommendation. http://www.w3.org/TR/2004/REC-rdf-mt-20040210/ (accessed September 13, 2011).

Hillmann, D. 2007. Using Dublin Core—The elements. DCMI Recommended Resource, 2007. http://dublincore.org/documents/usageguide/elements.shtml (accessed September 13, 2011).

Horrocks, I., Patel, P., Boley, H., Tabet, S., Grosof, B., and Dean, M. 2003. SWRL: A semantic web rule language combining OWL and RuleML. http://www.daml.org/2003/11/swrl/ (accessed September 13, 2011).

Java, A., Finin, T., and Nirenburg, S. 2006. SemNews: A semantic news framework. Paper presented at the *21st National Conference on Artificial Intelligence*, pp. 1939–1940, Boston, MA.

Kagal, L., Finin, T., and Joshi, A. 2003. A policy based approach to security for the semantic web. Paper presented at the *Second International Semantic Web Conference*, Florida, FL.

Kandogan, E., Krishnamurthy, R., Raghavan, S., Vaithyanathan, S., and Zhu, H. 2006. Avatar semantic search: a database approach to information retrieval. Paper presented at the *International Conference on Management of Data*, pp. 790–792, Chicago, USA.

Klyne, G. and Carroll, J. 2004. Resource description framework (RDF): Concepts and abstract syntax. W3C Recommendation. http://www.w3.org/TR/rdf-concepts/ (accessed September 13, 2011).

Maedche, A., Motik, B., Stojanovic, L., Studer, R., and Volz, R. 2003a. An infrastructure for searching, reusing and evolving distributed ontologies. Paper presented at the *World Wide Web Conference*, pp. 439–448, Budapest, Hungary.

Maedche, A., Staab, S., Stojanovic, N., Studer, R., and Sure, Y. 2003b. SEmantic PortAL—The SEAL approach. In *Spinning the Semantic Web*, eds. D. Fensel, J. Hendler, H. Lieberman and W. Wahlster. Cambridge: MIT Press, pp. 317–359.

Matthews, B. 2005. Semantic web technologies. JISC Technology and Standards Watch. http://www.jisc.ac.uk/uploaded_documents/jisctsw_05_02bpdf.pdf (accessed September 13, 2011).

Patel, P., Hayes, P., and Horrocks, I. 2004. OWL web ontology language semantics and abstract syntax. W3C Recommendation. http://www.w3.org/TR/2004/REC-owl-semantics-20040210/ (accessed September 13, 2011).

Sajja, P. S. 2009. Multi-tier knowledge-based system accessing learning object repository using fuzzy XML. In *Handbook of Research on Practices and Outcomes in E-Learning: Issues and Trends*, eds. H. Yang and S. Yuen. Hershey, PA: IGI Global Book Publishing, pp. 471–492.

Smith, B., Ashburner, M., Rosse, C., Bard, J., Bug, W., and Ceust-ers, W. 2007. The OBO Foundry: Coordinated evolution of ontologies to support biomedical data integration. *Nature Biotechnology* 25(11):1251–1255.

Sowa, J. 1991. *Principles of Semantic Networks: Explorations in the Representation of Knowledge*. San Mateo, CA: Morgan Kaufmann Publishers.

Stutt, A. and Motta, E. 2004. Semantic webs for learning: A vision and its realization. Paper presented at the *14th International Conference on Engineering Knowledge in the Age of the Semantic Web*, pp. 132–143, Whittlebury Hall, U.K.

Vandervalk, B. P., McCarthy, E. L., and Wilkinson, M. D. 2009. Moby and Moby 2: Creatures of the deep (web). *Briefings in Bioinformatics* 10(2):114–128.

Wan, Y. N. 2008. The exchange of interpersonal meaning in call centre conversations. In *Systemic Functional Linguistics in Use*, ed. N. Nørgaard, Odense Working Papers in Language and Communication, Vol. 29, pp. 825–829.

Weibel, S. L. and Lagoze, C. 1997. An element set to support resource discovery: The state of the Dublin Core. *International Journal on Digital Libraries* 1(2):176–186.

chapter nine

Web knowledge management

9.1 About knowledge

It is said that knowledge is power. The power of knowledge can be utilized for setting foundations for successful business. An organization achieves success if it can meet users' continuous and ever-changing needs in value-added way through its products, processes, and people. Knowledge is a kind of intellectual capital, which can be utilized to get the strategic and competitive advantages and resided mainly within the mind of people and procedures of the business. It is obvious that from a lot of environmental and business data processing, one could generate meaningful information. Knowledge is generated by employing procedures like analyzing, comparing, and synthesizing the available information. By applying morals, values, and principles, the knowledge becomes wisdom. Generation of wisdom is abstract and time taking procedure. Obviously, the final destination of such processing should be intelligence. This process is shown in Figure 9.1.

Knowledge can be factual, procedural, or embedded within the formal procedures and minds of experts. Knowledge that is directly available is generally factual knowledge. The factual knowledge is of low level, data centric, and less powerful to solve a problem. Factual knowledge is explicit and easy to codify. It is used in many situations as it forms an independent reusable unit at lower level in a flexible way. On the other hand, the embedded procedural knowledge, also called tacit knowledge, is high-level knowledge that helps a lot in specific problem solving and decision making. In spite of its high degree of usability, tacit knowledge utilization is costly, as most of the tacit knowledge is less flexible and lies in the subconscious minds of experts. Moreover, it is not easily represented electronically. This situation is shown in Figure 9.2.

Though knowledge is hard to characterize, continuously changing, and does not increase with time, it can play an important role in every business. Especially in unstable and global economy, knowledge of various components like target audience, products, and procedures and policies has become critical for survival. It is advised to manage such important resources in an effective way to make intelligent decision, future training, and impart quality in business. The formal process of knowledge management and typical process architecture of a knowledge management system is discussed in the next section.

9.2 Knowledge management fundamentals

Knowledge management is a discipline that deals with an integrated approach to identifying, managing, and sharing different types of knowledge assets within various components of the business. According to Skyrme (2002), the knowledge management can be defined as "the explicit and systematic management of vital knowledge and its associated processes of creating, gathering, organizing, diffusing, use, and exploitation, in pursuit of organizational objectives." With the help of such knowledge management, the organization gets better understanding, sharing, and utilization of existing knowledge. Knowledge repository is generated as a result of an efficient knowledge management process. This

Figure 9.1 Evolution of knowledge.

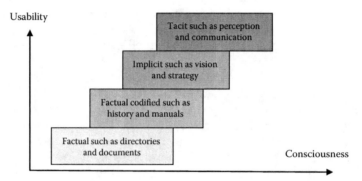

Figure 9.2 Types of knowledge.

repository contains knowledge assets like business processes, customer, key people of the business, organizational memory, and knowledge in relationships. The repository can be used to get competitive advantages and offers new platform and opportunity to create new innovative knowledge to satisfy customers. Typical drivers that initiate the require-ment of knowledge management can be given as follows:

- Size and span of an organization
- Business transaction nature, volume, and complexity
- Reducing risk and uncertainty
- Need to increase market value and improve an organization's brand and quality
- Need to improve quality and efficiency of decisions
- Need to improve customer relationships
- Need for technology-centered support
- Requirement of intellectual asset management
- Safekeeping and documentation of knowledge
- Future use of knowledge in decision making and training
- Shorter product cycles
- Restricted access and added security

9.2.1 Architecture of the knowledge management process

Knowledge management process encompasses four main phases. These phases are (i) knowledge discovery, (ii) knowledge use and test, (iii) knowledge documentation, and (iv) sharing of knowledge. Various knowledge sources including media, printed material from books and journals, and knowledge from expert minds are collected, tested, codified, and shared by variety of tools. The developer known as knowledge engineer acquires, compiles, tests, and shares knowledge into/through a centralized knowledge repository/ knowledge base. It is clear that the repository reflects learning of the knowledge engineer. That is, knowledge engineer's knowledge reflects within the knowledge base. The drivers mentioned in the previous section work as catalysts for the knowledge management process. The knowledge collected and stored within the repository should meet some ethical, technological, and business standards. The process architecture of knowledge management is shown in Figure 9.3.

The knowledge management process generally begins with knowledge discovery. Knowledge discovery is the phase of collection and compilation of knowledge existing within the organization. This phase is also known as knowledge acquisition. The explicit and factual knowledge can be available from dictionary, documents, and data collected from the domain of the business. This type of content is easily codified and stored electronically. Low-level procedures like simple searching and formatting are required to manipulate such content. The summary reports, history, and manuals for carrying out procedures for the business transaction are kind of partially implicit knowledge, to discover knowledge from which little more effort is required. The implicit and tacit tasks involving vision, strategy, and perception and negotiation with important element of the business require intelligence and hence difficult to codify. This type of knowledge embedded within the experts' minds and deep in procedures. In order to discover knowledge from tacit and implicit tasks, high-level preprocessing and inference are required. Presentations, interactive dialogs, meetings, information audits, profiling, and conceptual mapping are tools that help in knowledge discovery. However, knowledge discovery is more art and less science. Fully automatic knowledge discovery falls under the mundane tasks of artificial intelligence. Such tasks are simple for human being like balancing, walking, perceiving, etc., but difficult to automate. Intelligent agent partially fulfills this requirement. Besides discovering knowledge from people, policies, and procedures, such intelligent agent may learn new knowledge from the existing knowledge on need. Such knowledge innovation is also possible with intelligent agents. Figure 9.4 shows the tools used in knowledge management process.

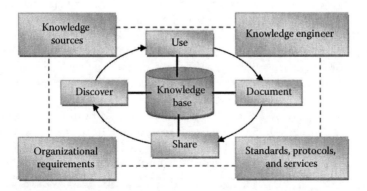

Figure 9.3 Knowledge management process.

Figure 9.4 Knowledge management tools.

The phase of knowledge documentation and representation deals with proper representation of the discovered knowledge. The discovered knowledge is processed, compiled, and categorized according to its application and nature by the knowledge engineer. Appropriate metaknowledge (knowledge about the compiled knowledge into the repository) chunks are also generated to facilitate efficient use of the knowledge. The power and usefulness of the stored knowledge often depends on the representation schemes utilized. Enough care should be taken at this time to store the smaller units of knowledge in impendent fashion. This increases modularity and reusability of the knowledge. The techniques of efficient retrieval and storage are also developed during this phase. There should be some empty space within the repository/knowledge base to accommodate self-learned knowledge. The tools like programming language that allows metatags for semantic embedding, algorithms, thesaurus, knowledge tree, and metadata tools (key words, index, etc.) are helpful in organizing and representing the collected knowledge.

To share the collected knowledge, the knowledge engineer has to ensure the availability of the knowledge repository. For better accessibility, such repository is kept on centralized place or web platform. Portals, groups and social networking platform, customized (application specific) content management sites, etc., can be developed to facilitate the use of the repository.

9.2.2 Benefits of knowledge management

Benefits of knowledge management can be divided into three main aspects. The first aspect is benefits offered by knowledge. The compiled and well-documented knowledge is available in machine-readable form for future use. The centralized repository increases high level of availability and accessibility. The repository also ensures prevention, safekeeping, and redundancy of knowledge. Second aspect is organizational benefits of the knowledge management. The organization need not be dependent on experts as knowledge is always available on demand. This reduces dependencies on experts who are rare and costly commodities of their fields. This leads to better service and product quality with productivity. Customer relationship, improved brand image of the organization, and good quality product are the main advantages of the knowledge management to the organizations. Such knowledge management system provides ease of control and administration and supports best practices as well as research. Third aspect is about individual benefits. The employees and customers may have individual benefits such as high-quality decision support, better and timely services, and recognition.

9.2.3   Challenges of knowledge management

The first difficulty with any knowledge management system is the nature of knowledge. The knowledge within the repository (which is a key component of a knowledge management system) keeps on changing and demands continuous update. There is little support available from the field of artificial intelligence and software engineering methodology to develop such systems. To consider cultural, ethical, and social issues while problem solving is another challenge for such systems. The marketplace is gradually becoming more competitive, and the rate of innovation is growing, so knowledge must evolve and be incorporated within the system from time to time.

Knowledge management for modern business is really a challenge due to technological advancements. The inventions and facilities offered by information and communication technology (ICT) such as Internet, web, and other software systems have increased span of business. Management of content (knowledge) becomes a challenge considering the complexity size of the Web.

9.3   Ontology revisited

To incorporate knowledge into web content representations, artificial intelligent (AI) techniques can be used. Ontology is one of the AI techniques that help in imparting knowledge by explicit formal representation of domain entities in more effective way. Ontology has become obvious for the modern web. Chapter 8 defines and discusses various ontologies and related concepts. This section presents extended ontology fundamentals suitable for web.

9.3.1   Ontology examples

Classes constitute an important part of ontology as they describe concepts and allow instantiation based on the class definitions. The focus of most ontologies is the notion of classes and members generated through the class definition. Classes describe basic concepts and functionalities related to a group of entities in the domain. For example, a class of *chocolates* represents all chocolates along with their major characteristics. Specific chocolates are members or instances of the *chocolate* class. The specific chocolate, say *fruit and nuts*, is an instance of the class of *chocolates*. A class can have subclasses that represent concepts that form special groups and are within the scope of the main class. That is, class of chocolates can be divided into drinking chocolates, white chocolates, dark chocolates, and milk chocolates. There is a chocolate company, say *chocomak* that produces chocolates. This situation is demonstrated in Figure 9.5. Similarly, Table 9.1 illustrates a resource description framework (RDF) for the same environment.

RDF provides a way to specify resource and property types. A property can be associated with a resource. However, the type of property cannot be specified with it. An RDF schema does this. RDF schema develops classes for both resources and properties. An example of RDF schema is presented in Table 9.2.

In general ontology, development includes identification and definition of classes, relationship between the classes, definition of slots, their values, and constraints. Any general ontology model represents only a consensual agreement on the concepts and relations that characterize the way knowledge in the domain is expressed. Higher level ontology shares model common knowledge instead of specific data. Important notions in connection with web-related ontology are a vocabulary of basic terms and a precise specification of what

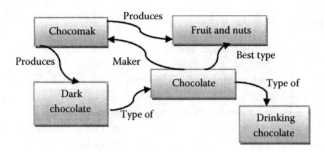

Figure 9.5 Chocolate ontology.

Table 9.1 RDF Example with Output

```
<?xml version="1.0"?>

<rdf:RDF
xmlns:rdf="http://www.w3.org/1999/02/22-rdf-syntax-ns#"
xmlns:chocolate="http://www.myshop.fake/chocolate#">

<rdf:Description
rdf:about="http://www.myshop.fake/chocolate/Nut Treasure">
<chocolate:Manufacturer>Miracle</chocolate:Manufacturer>
<chocolate:Type>Milk</chocolate:Type>
<chocolate:Weight>20</chocolate:Weight>
<chocolate:Price>20.00</chocolate:Price>
<chocolate:Batch>Aug10</chocolate:Batch>
</rdf:Description>

<rdf:Description
rdf:about="http://www.myshop.fake/chocolate/Black Silk">
<chocolate:Manufacturer>Miracle</chocolate:Manufacturer>
<chocolate:Type>Dark</chocolate:Type>
<chocolate:Weight>40</chocolate:Weight>
<chocolate:Price>25.00</chocolate:Price>
<chocolate:Batch>Sep10</chocolate:Batch>
</rdf:Description>
.
..
</rdf : RDF>
```

The output generated through the aforementioned RDF segment with the help of appropriate style sheet is shown as follows:

Name	Manufacturer	Type	Weight (g)	Price ($)	Batch
Nut Treasure	Miracle	Milk	20	20.00	August 10
Black Silk	Miracle	Dark	40	25.00	September 10

Table 9.2 Resource Description Framework Schema (RDFS) Example

```
<?xml version="1.0"?>

<rdf:RDF
xmlns:rdf="http://www.w3.org/1999/02/22-rdf-syntax-ns#"
xmlns:rdfs="http://www.w3.org/2000/01/rdf-schema#"
xml:base="http://www.myshop.fake/chocolates#">

<rdf:Description rdf:ID="chocolate">
<rdf:type rdf:resource="http://www.w3.org/2000/01/rdf-schema#Class"/>
</rdf:Description>

<rdf:Description rdf:ID="Milk">
<rdf:type rdf:resource="http://www.w3.org/2000/01/rdf-schema#Class"/>
<rdfs:subClassOf rdf:resource="#chocolate"/>
</rdf:Description>
<rdf:Description rdf:ID="Dark">
<rdf:type rdf:resource="http://www.w3.org/2000/01/rdf-schema#Class"/>
<rdfs:subClassOf rdf:resource="#chocolate"/>
</rdf:Description>
    .
    .
    .
</rdf:RDF>
```

those terms mean. The consensus standard vocabularies can be handled by defining reusable vocabularies, and customizing and extending them.

Some well-known ontologies from linguistics and knowledge engineering areas are as follows:

- *WordNet*: It is top-down ontology (in upper layer) in linguistic domain containing structured vocabulary of English language with lexical categories and semantic relations.
- *Cyc*: It is a common ontology consisting of knowledge captured from different domains.
- *SENSUS*: It is a linguistic domain ontology built by extracting and merging information from existing electronic resources for the purpose of machine translation.

9.3.2   Ontology classification

The ontology can be classified by type of the knowledge conveyed by the ontology:

- A generic ontology, also known as top ontology, specifies general concepts defined independently of a domain of application and which can be used in different application domains. Ontologies defined for general principle of time, mathematics, etc., are examples of the generic ontology.
- A domain ontology is dedicated to a particular domain, which remains generic for this domain and which can be used and reused for particular tasks in the domain. Blood disease, trigonometry, enterprise modeling, etc., are examples of domain ontology.

- An application ontology gathers knowledge dedicated to a particular task including more specialized knowledge of the experts for the application. In general, it is not reusable. The example can be theorem proving and drug analysis and design.
- A metaontology or representation ontology specifies the knowledge representation principles used to define concepts of domain and generic ontology, for example, what is a class, a relation, and a function.

Ontology can also be classified as heavy weight and lightweight ontology according to their expressiveness of the content. The parameters for such expressiveness are introduced by McGuinness (2003) and summarized in Table 9.3.

A systematic evaluation of ontology and related technologies might lead to a consistent level of quality and thus acceptance by industry. For the future, this effort might also lead to standardized benchmarks and certifications.

9.3.3   Parameters to build ontology

Because of the complexity of the task and the many demands on ontology in terms of usability and reusability, many ontology engineering methodologies have been developed. The ontology should be clear in the sense that meaning of each entity within the defined ontology is clear and does not have many interpretations. The ontology must be consistent, logical, and formal enough to represent real application entities. There should be scope to add some new slots, subclasses, and restriction on the inherited classes on need. Existing ontology can also be combined with new ontology. This quality refers to the extendibility of the ontology. As stated earlier, obviously the ontology is meant for frequent use and reuse. The ontology should be independent from application tools, formatting schemes, and operational logic. Existing ontology can be combined in order to create new ontology. This makes the ontology independent, reusable, and sharable within different applications.

Table 9.3 Parameters of Expressiveness of Ontology

Controlled vocabulary	A list of terms with controls and checks
Thesaurus	Relations between terms, such as synonyms, are provided
Informal taxonomy	There is an explicit hierarchy (generalization and specialization are supported), but there is no strict inheritance; an instance of a subclass is not necessarily also an instance of the super class
Formal taxonomy	There is strict inheritance
Frames	A frame (or class) contains a number of properties, and these properties are inherited by subclasses and instances
Value restrictions	Values of properties are restricted (e.g., by a data type)
General logic constraints	Values may be constraint by logical or mathematical formulas using values from other properties
First-order logic constraints	Very expressive ontology languages allow first-order logic constraints between terms and more detailed relationships such as disjoint classes, disjoint coverings, inverse relationships, part-whole relationships, etc.

A classical "skeletal model" given by Uschold and King (1995) presents a framework for the design and evaluation of ontology. The steps are given as follows:

1. Identifying purpose and scope
2. Building the ontology
   a. Ontology capture
   b. Ontology coding
   c. Integrating existing ontology
3. Evaluation
4. Documentation

In general, the ontology should be evaluated against the parameters like declarative specification and correctness, reusability, adequacy, modifiability, and extensibility.

9.3.4 Standards and interoperability for ontology

Content and system on the Web need to share/exchange/reuse data and utilities with their intended meanings. This is called *semantic interoperability*. Achieving semantic interoperability among different information systems is very laborious, tedious, and error-prone in a distributed and heterogeneous environment like the World Wide Web (WWW). Information heterogeneity occurs at three levels, that is, syntax, structure, and semantics (Stuckenschmidt and Harmelen 2005). The machine-readable aspects of data representation including formatting and organizing information are considered for the syntactic interoperability. Representational heterogeneity that involves data modeling constructs, which are relevant to structural interoperability, can be considered as structured level interoperability. The schematic heterogeneity related to structured database is also an aspect of structural heterogeneity. Semantic interoperability requires the system to automatically understand the semantics of the content as well as users' requirements to satisfy in a better fashion. Among these, the syntactic heterogeneity is the simplest heterogeneity problem caused by the usage of different data formats. To solve the syntactic heterogeneity, standardized formats such as extensible markup language (XML) (Bray et al. 2004), RDF/RDFS (Manola and Miller 2004), and web ontology language (OWL) (McGuinness and Harmelen 2003) have been widely used to describe data in a uniform way that makes automatic processing of shared information easier.

9.3.5 Ontology on the Web

This section describes some ontology language and tools that enable knowledge representation on the Web. Ontologies on the Web help in achieving advantages like sharing of common understanding of the concepts, reusability, and structuredness by keeping (and treating) operation ontologies and domain ontologies in separate fashion. The popular ontologies include taxonomy, thesaurus, XML, RDF, RDF Schema, proof, logic, and trust. These ontologies are arranged in the architecture of web proposed by Berners-Lee (2005). By incorporating ontologies and representing knowledge through the ontologies, we are moving toward semantic web. See Chapter 8 for further details on semantic web.

Various ontologies have been proposed to facilitate content representation on the Web. RDF, OWL, Protégé, OiLEd, Apollo, RDFedt, OntoLingua, K-Infinity, etc., are some popular ontology languages and tools. Some of these tools are described in the following.

Protégé is developed by Stanford Medical Informatics as an extensible plug-in architecture. The Protégé supports graph view, consistency check, web accessibility, and ontology merging. This efficient tool, however, does not support addition of new basic types and offers limited multiuser support.

OiLEd developed by Information Management Group, CS Department, University of Manchester, U.K., is very simple. It supports consistency check and web compatibility. However, it does not support graph view and cannot be extensible. Hence, it is not considered as a full ontology development environment.

Apollo, developed by Knowledge Media Institute of Open University, U.K., supports consistency checks and hierarchical view of ontology. Its modeling is based on basic primitives like classes, instances, functions, and relations. This tool also does not support graph view, web accessibility, and multiuser functionality.

RDFedt developed by Jan Winkler, Germany, is basically a textual language editor and works for Windows. It is not platform independent. It supports limited consistency check and web accessibility. This tool also does not support graph view and multiuser functionality.

OntoLingua developed by Knowledge Systems Lab, Stanford University, provides a distributed collaborative environment and supports consistency check, provides web access, and offers multiuser functionality. This tool does not allow creation of extensible ontologies and also does not support graph view.

While discussing the knowledge management for the Web, one must consider a prominent tool called K-Infinity, which was developed by Intelligent Views, Germany, especially for knowledge network. This tool provides two different workspaces: one for graph editor and another for concept editor. It supports graph view and automatic management of references. However, this tool does not support web accessibility and extensibility.

There are many tools and packages available commercially as well as open source. Denny (2002) summarized the available tools. It is observed that most of the tools are moving toward good graphical user interface (GUI), knowledge abstraction, platform independence, interoperability, reasoning and inference, and data resource integration.

9.4   Utilization of knowledge management methodologies on semantic web

As discussed in the previous section of the chapter, the knowledge management offers individual, organizational, and knowledge-oriented benefits. The platform of web and ontology language and tools help in facilitating the accessibility and availability to the stored knowledge as well as procedures developed for the knowledge management system. In other words, the Web and knowledge management technology contribute each other and mutually beneficial. The Web provides platform for accessibility and availability for the organization-wide knowledge and serves an efficient online repository. The knowledge management technology offers management of knowledge stored in the repository. In order to encash maximum advantages of the knowledge orientation and semantics embedding on the Web, the knowledge management procedures need to undergo paradigm change. That is, the current approach of knowledge management in any organization is document centric. Lots of documents are generated containing meaningful information during span of the business, which can offer a big amount of knowledge. However, nature of these documents diminishes the reuse of the documents. The benefit of such documents can only be taken if there is a systematic and structured way of document generation. That is, the documents related to the business should be generated in such a way that it can be reused and facilitate automatic knowledge discovery through a well-defined procedure in future. This document centric approach has the following limitations:

- Lack of efficient searching
- Extraction of information and knowledge discovery
- Restricted use of the content due to unorganized collection
- Availability, accessibility, and sharing of the content or knowledge extracted
- Safekeeping and utilization of knowledge for future use
- Security and backup with proper validation

Many organizations prefer documents repository on global platform like the Web to get an advantage of anywhere availability and unique centralized location. Why should not the concepts of semantic web, technology, and tools be utilized to effectively discover, store, utilize, and share the organizational knowledge? Additionally, the semantic technologies on the Web can be further enriched by advances of intelligent techniques. By this way, an organization gets the multifold advantages of the Web, knowledge management, and artificial intelligence field.

9.4.1   Literature review

Brewster et al. (2002) discuss user-centered learning and automatic creation of ontology. In this tool, user-centered ontology is automatically created and validated by users themselves. According to them, the retrieved example ontologies are validated by the user and used by an adaptive information extraction (IE) system to generate patterns that discover other lexicalizations of the same objects in the ontology, possibly identifying new concepts or relations. New instances are added to the existing ontology or used to tune it. This process is repeated until a satisfactory ontology is obtained. The methodology largely automates the ontology construction process, and generated ontology can be used to create further ontology modifications.

To model user ontologies, a tool is developed by Razmerita et al. (2003). In this work, authors addressed aspects of ontology-based user modeling and presented a generic architecture for modeling users based on ontologies. The main contributions of the work are (1) identifying aspects of user modeling relevant to KMSs and (2) integrating them in a generic framework based on ontologies.

Aldea et al. (2003) have proposed a multiagent framework for the knowledge management on the Web. The work describes the development of a knowledge management platform for web-enabled environments featuring intelligence and insight capabilities.

Mohame et al. (2004) have introduced a model named K Asset to support backend activities of knowledge management. This tool supports organizational learning activities in a typical software organization.

Yang et al. (2004) have proposed a model for ontology-enabled annotation and knowledge management for collaborative learning in virtual learning community. This model provides semantic web services from three perspectives, namely, personalized annotation, real-time discussion, and semantic content retrieval.

Ontology-based collaborative interorganizational knowledge management network is proposed by Leung and Kang (2009). According to the authors, the organization-based knowledge management (KM) approaches have caused collaboration problem in which an organization is not capable of reusing interorganizational knowledge, even though the required knowledge is available in other organizations and their proposed network models solve this problem.

The EU IST-1999-10132 project *On-To-Knowledge*1 develops methods and tools to employ the full power of the ontological approach for facilitating knowledge management.

Many other tools and packages are also developed for knowledge management and ontology development, which are discussed in Section 9.3.5. From the conclusion derived after reviewing these tools, it is clear that there is a need of efficient knowledge management for web content that supports reusability, flexibility, adaptivity, interoperability, and intelligent support. Above this, there is a need to modify the typical knowledge management procedure so as to fit (on) the semantic web structure. Such knowledge management innovation should be generic and domain independent. To meet this objective, a design of a generic architecture of knowledge management through ontology is illustrated in the following section.

9.4.2   General architecture for web knowledge management

The architecture proposed here consists of three main layers, namely, (i) knowledge discovery from the Web, experts, and other resources; (ii) knowledge processing and storage; and (iii) knowledge presentation and use. The knowledge discovery layer contains the Web and content exploration mechanisms such as crawler and inference. The quality standards and third party services are also included here on need. The crawler crawls and searches information from the Web and other specified resources. The inference mechanism is enriched with the utilities like chaining mechanism to infer knowledge from the knowledge bases. The generated knowledge is stored within knowledge repository acting in the knowledge-processing layer. The knowledge-processing layer also contains metadata to ensure effective utilization of knowledge base by providing whereabouts of the knowledge base content. Besides metadata and knowledge, domain ontology is also required. The application-dependent terminology of domain entities and their relation contributes a lot in addition to the metadata. The local documents, user profiles, temporary results, and editing facility are available at the knowledge presentation layer. To facilitate native interaction in user's native language, a natural language processing (NLP) component may be also added (refer Chapter 5 for NLP components). This architecture is generic and application independent. Figure 9.6 illustrates the architecture.

The knowledge repository contains knowledge about the domain application. Any ontology representation language like RDF, OWL, or ontology tool can be utilized to represent

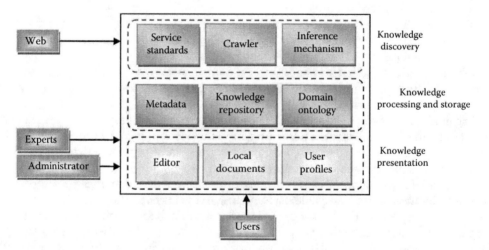

Figure 9.6 KM architecture on the Web.

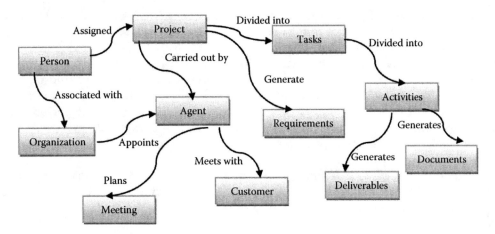

Figure 9.7 Organizational ontology.

Documents
Document unique id
Document title id
Document author
Document type
Document content
Document date of creation
Document detail
Document previous version
Document next version
...
...

Figure 9.8 Components of organizational documents.

the concepts. The typical organization knowledge incorporates entities like project, activity, agent, customer, documents, deliverables, meeting, person, tasks, etc. The generic organization ontology consisting of these entities can be presented as shown in Figure 9.7.

The benefit of such well-organized ontology is its well-structured organization. The components playing key role in an organization have low coupling to offer high degree of independence. Such modularity increases reusability. Furthermore, each document is divided into blocks with fields like content type, content, author, date of creation, and additional details as denoted in Figure 9.8. The block may contain previous and next links to other person or blocks for version management. Here, the block is considered as subclass of documents. The knowledge base (repository) of the system can be enriched with such multiple ontologies according to the concerned application and nature of the business transactions.

9.4.3   Semantically enhanced knowledge management

The vision of the semantic web as a KM environment introduces a new set of challenges. While some metadata extraction is achieved manually, its capability of being automated and processed by tools and applications is a major issue that determines the potential of the Web as a KM platform to enable efficient data sharing. There are several information access and delivery processes enabled by the semantic web that are very distinctive and suitable for the KM.

The semantic web helps users to visualize and understand relationships between the search results against an ontology. The benefit for knowledge workers is that they do not have to read all contents to get representative view of all the search results. Searching against a semantically driven ontology helps to remove the ambiguity around text-based searches. So, user can expand and enrich their web searches to include related information. Semantic tools that provide reasoning algorithms can help knowledge workers to make deductions about their relationships to better understand the linkages of content, authors, and sources. This further boosts a defined search strategy with metadata extracted from the documents that the knowledge worker finds most relevant to his/her task.

One important aspect of semantics web is that knowledge workers easily discover what content coworkers with similar interests and tasks have found valuable in a collaborative environment. In semantic web, the content (i.e., uniform resource locator [URL] of the content) is saved to a collaborative workplace, and its associated metadata will detect a prospective readership.

9.4.3.1   Semantic wiki

A *semantic wiki* extends a wiki by semantic technologies like RDF, OWL, Topic Map, or Conceptual Graphs. The basic idea is to make the inherent structure of a wiki, given by the strong linking between pages, accessible to machines (agents and services) beyond simple navigation. This is commonly done by annotating existing navigational links with symbols that describe their meaning. For example, a link from Mahatma Gandhi to India could be annotated with *"born in"*. Such annotations are useful for many purposes, for example, enhanced presentation by displaying contextual information, enhanced navigation by giving easy access to relevant related information, and enhanced semantic search that respects the context in addition to the content. Practically, most of the semantic wikis allow annotating links by giving them certain types. The idea behind this is that a link created by a user almost always carries meaning beyond mere navigation. Many semantic wikis can change the way content is presented based on semantic annotations. This can include enriching pages by displaying of semantically related pages in a separate link box, displaying of information that can be derived from the underlying knowledge base (e.g., a box with a graphical tree presentation for content belonging to a hierarchy, or license information), or even rendering the content of a page in a different manner that is more appropriate for the context. Most semantic wikis allow a "semantic search" on the underlying knowledge base. Usually, queries are expressed in the language SPARQL, a query language proposed as W3C recommendation for RDF querying. Using "semantic search," users can ask queries like "retrieve all speeches by Mahatma Gandhi." The semantic wikis have reasoning support. Reasoning means deriving additional, implicit knowledge from the facts entered into the system using predefined or user-defined rules in the knowledge base. For example, from the fact that "Mahatma Gandhi" wrote "The Story of My Experiments with Truth," a system capable of reasoning could deduce that "Mahatma Gandhi" is a "writer." Although reasoning is an important feature, it is only supported by a small number of wikis. The reasons for this might be that it is time-consuming, memory intensive, and can yield results that are not expected and/or traceable by the user.

Annotated links provide more information for navigation. Whereas a traditional wiki only allows following a link, a semantic wiki offers additional information about the relation the link describes. Such information can be used to offer additional or more sophisticated navigation. For instance, links are more independent from the textual context they appear in and can be displayed, for example, in a separate "related information" box. The page describing Mahatma Gandhi could, for example, offer a separate box with references categorized by "born in," "wrote," etc. Semantic wikis offer advanced searching and navigation capabilities as described earlier. They are therefore very well suited for knowledge management.

9.4.3.2 Semantic annotation tools

In this section, we will overview specific tools, which can produce semantic annotations, that is, annotations that refer an ontology.

The *Mangrove* system is example of manual but user-friendly annotation (McDowell et al. 2003). The purpose of this system was to persuade users into marking up their hypertext markup language (HTML) using the data created in a number of semantic services such as a departmental who's who and a calendar of events. The annotation tool itself is a straightforward GUI that allows users to associate a selection of tags to text that they highlight. Mangrove has recently been integrated with a semantic e-mail service, which supports the initiation of semantic e-mail processes, such as meeting scheduling, via text forms.

Vannotea (Schroeter et al. 2003) has been developed by the University of Brisbane for adding metadata to MPEG-2 (video), JPEG2000 (image), and Direct 3D (mesh) files, with the mesh being used to define regions of images. It is of particular interest from the viewpoint of distributed knowledge management because it has been designed to allow input from distributed users. This has, for example, allowed it to be deployed to annotate cultural artifacts in a collaborative annotation exercise involving both museum curators and indigenous groups.

SHOE Knowledge Annotator (Heflin and Hendler 2001) was an early system, which allowed users to mark up HTML pages in SHOE guided by ontologies available locally or via a URL. Users were assisted by being prompted for inputs. The SHOE Knowledge Annotator did not have a browser to display web pages, which could only be viewed as source code. *Running SHOE* (Heflin and Hendler 2001) took a step toward automated markup by assisting users to build wrappers for web pages that specify how to extract entities from lists and other pages with regular formats.

Lixto is a web IE system, which allows wrappers to be defined for converting unstructured resources into structured ones. The tool allows users to create wrappers interactively and visually by selecting relevant pieces of information (Baumgartner et al. 2001). It was first developed at the Technical University of Vienna by Gottlob and colleagues and is now distributed by the spin-off *Lixto Software GmbH* (http://www.lixto.com).

Melita (Ciravegna et al. 2002) is a user-driven automated semantic annotation tool that makes two main strategies available to the user. It provides an underlying adaptive IE system (Amilcare) that learns how to annotate the documents by generalizing on the user annotations. Annotation is therefore a process that starts by requiring full user annotation at early stages, but ends in having the user merely verify the correctness of suggestions made by the system. It also offers facilities for rule writing (based on regular expressions) to allow sophisticated users to define their own rules. In Melita, documents are not selected randomly for annotation, but rather selected automatically based on the expected usefulness, to the IE system, of annotating the document. The Amilcare IE system has been incorporated in "K@", a legal KM system with RDF-based semantic capabilities produced by Quinary.

KIM (Popov et al. 2004) uses IE techniques to build a large knowledge base of annotations. The annotations in KIM are metadata in the form of named entities (individuals, places, etc.), which are defined in the Knowledge and Information Management Ontology (KIMO) ontology and identified mainly from reference to exceptionally large gazetteers.

This is a major research challenge to extend the KIM methodology to domain-specific ontologies. However, named entities are a class of metadata with broad usage. For example, in the *Rich News*, application KIM has been used to help annotate television and radio news by exploiting the fact that web news stories on the same topics are often published in parallel (Dowman et al. 2005). The KIM platform is well designed to showcase the kinds of retrieval and data analysis services that can be provided over large knowledge bases of annotations. For instance, the KIM server is able to use a variety of plug-in front ends, including one for Microsoft's Internet Explorer, a web user interface that provides different semantic search services, and a graph viewer for exploring the connections between entities.

9.4.4   Issues and challenges

The ontology-oriented knowledge management earns advantages of the Web and knowledge incorporation for an organization. However, the ontology developed for the organization cannot be fully generic. Working with totally generic ontology helps in integrating the concern application with other applications or external ontologies developed by other organizations. However, it does not support the customized solution and detail knowledge of an organization. Every business and applications/procedures within it are unique. There should be a nice balance between the integratability and specificness of the ontologies used in the organization.

   Another issue is the nature of knowledge. The knowledge is actually hard to characterize. It is continuously changing, and a large amount of knowledge is needed to solve even simple tasks. An organization has to continuously maintain its knowledge-based system.

   In spite of all these, there is a need to envision future use of knowledge and business expansion opportunities for the organization where knowledge management system is to be developed and used. Employee psychology and awareness are also some other issues that must be considered and handled while planning for an organization-wide knowledge management system.

   Some technical issues incorporate availability of knowledge models, tools, and standards. W3C consortium has contributed some standards for web ontologies. Some KM standards are also available. Still there is a need of more standards, which can be applied specifically on the hybridization of knowledge management and web ontologies. The size, complexity, and heterogeneous structure of ever-expanding web are other major challenges that the knowledge engineer should consider before implementing the system.

9.5   Exchanging knowledge in virtual entities

9.5.1   Virtual world

Virtual world facilitates an imaginary environment where individual can experiment real-like situations. This environment is often computer based, in which users can interact with the system as well as other users. It may be 2D or 3D. Virtual worlds are also called "digital worlds," "simulated worlds," and massively multiplayer online game (MMOG). Such environments are used for gaming, learning, training, social networking, and e-commerce. Therefore, they raise need/opportunity for new methods of knowledge management. Obviously, the virtual world is characterized with multiuser capability as the objective is to create whole world (or at least a complete scenario). Besides this, there are a few more characteristics (Mueller et al. 2011) that can be thought for a typical virtual world as shown in Table 9.4.

Table 9.4 Characteristics of Virtual World

Multiuser	Facilitating the interaction of multiple, geographically dispersed users
Interface and media richness	Virtual world provides very good graphical 2D or 3D virtual environment to provide feeling of real-like environment. It offers a variety of communication channels including 3D visuals, voice, text, and body language
Immediacy and synchronous	Enabling users to interact with each other in real time
Interactivity	The world allows users to alter, develop, build, or submit customized content
Embodied	Representing the user by digital proxies called "avatar"
Persistence	The program continues to run whether the users are logged in or not. It remembers the location of people and things as well as the ownership of objects
Socialization and community support	It allows and encourages the formation of in-world social groups like teams, groups, clubs, neighborhoods, etc.

Virtual world has its applications in the field of education, military training, debate and political expression, gaming, and socialization. Virtual world also facilitates knowledge acquisition, knowledge use and sharing, and other activities of knowledge management between geographically dispersed institutes and individuals. Trouble shooting, monitoring, and training can be made easy and accessible through the virtual world. In this case, the virtual world becomes platform for the knowledge management activities for the selected organizations.

Adobe Systems Incorporated announced Adobe® Atmosphere™ software, a new professional web tool for authoring, viewing, and interacting with immersive and virtual 3D worlds. The product allows designers to create graphically rich, true-to-life 3D worlds, enabling end-users to virtually "walk the Web" and communicate in real time for a richer, more realistic web experience.

9.5.2   Virtual organizations

Many times, organizations need to work with deliverables and procedures that are across different locations, at differing work cycles, and across cultures within a span of the selected organization. Such organizations are often known as virtual organizations. It may be thought as a subset of a virtual world concerns with the given business. Knowledge management and other web intelligence technique also contribute here in order to effectively manage and operate the business functions. Area-specific virtual world techniques are more generic in nature and can be applied to all the businesses, organizations, and environments of the category. Whereas techniques for the virtual organization are specific and customized according to the organization needs.

Virtual organizations knowledge base is obviously distributed in nature in order to take advantages of geographical distance location, remote customers, distributors, and suppliers, and remotely distributed resources. This makes knowledge management and business transactions, which are the most important procedures in the virtual organizations, more complex, risky, effort taking, and hence challenging.

Henderson et al. (1996) and Burn and Ash (2000) have identified three dimensions of virtual organizing as

- Virtual encounters
- Virtual sourcing
- Virtual work

Virtual encounters refer to the extent to which you virtually interact with the market defined at three levels of greater virtual progression:

- Remote product/service experience
- Product/service customization
- Shaping customer solutions

Virtual sourcing refers to competency leveraging from

- Efficient sourcing of standard components
- Efficient asset leverage in the business network
- Creating new competencies through alliances

Virtual work refers to

- Maximizing individual experience
- Harnessing organizational expertise
- Leveraging of community expertise

9.5.3 Knowledge management and intelligent techniques within virtual entities

It is possible to design and use dedicated knowledge management as well as other web intelligence techniques at given geographical area for a virtual organization. All the local level techniques contribute to form a global (here virtual) consortium of techniques. The abstract view of the scenario is presented in the form of Figure 9.9. The figure demonstrates different knowledge management techniques such as knowledge discovery, knowledge organization, knowledge sharing, and knowledge use. Once knowledge is efficiently

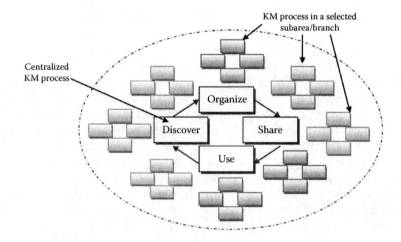

Figure 9.9 Overall KM process in virtual organization (abstract view).

managed at local level, this can be used at other locations using information and communication methodology for any procedure such as discovery, use, etc.

In similar fashion, the idea of virtual office works. A virtual office is a combination of off-site live communication and address services that allow users to reduce traditional physical office costs while maintaining business professionalism. Servcorp Virtual Office* is an example of such virtual office that provides services to run a business professionally without the costs of a full-time physical office suite.

The intelligent techniques that may be used to manage the virtual world or any virtual scenario are as follows:

Autonomous agents

- Intelligent agents, mobile agents, and interface agents for various tasks
- Human like Avatar and chatbots for effective interactions
- Intelligent searching from multimedia knowledge base

Knowledge management models

- Models for distributed virtual world
- Models for knowledge discovery
- Models of knowledge transfer
- Managing virtual teams

Knowledge representation techniques and ontology

- Knowledge reorientation in remote as well as distributed sources
- Ontology extraction, conversion, and integration
- Ontology-based knowledge management system

Interface- and graphics-related jobs

- Ontology-based information retrieval and presentation according to user profile
- Image and simulation generation and transmission to support transaction, discussion, and learning

Other tools

For security, backup, and archive management

Furthermore, the AI techniques developed for managing virtual world may be benefited by the real-world scenario in terms of learning. The techniques as well as the virtual world are complementing each other. Techniques help in managing the virtual world, and virtual world provides cases, feedbacks, and other environmental inputs to the techniques.

Virtual worlds and community are becoming more and more ubiquitous in modern edge. The advances of ICT and AI techniques help in accelerating the use of the concept of virtual world. The cost of scarce infrastructure, avoiding unnecessary commutation and transportation of people and other resources, availability of expertise, saving of time, etc., can be the major advantages of the virtual world. Virtual world can be used not only for experimenting and studying the existing world scenario, such as sciences, business,

---

* http://www.virtualoffice.com/

games, education, training, and simulation, but also for synthesizing new universes and philosophies into the real world.

9.5.4   Virtual communities and semantic web

A virtual community can be a virtual enterprise, a virtual team, or a social virtual community. A virtual enterprise is usually defined as a temporary or permanent alliance of organizations for the accomplishment of a task by way of ICT, a virtual team is a group of people that rely primarily or exclusively on electronic forms of communication to work together in accomplishing goals, and a social virtual community is a community of interest on the Internet. Rheingold (1993) deals with the emergence of social virtual communities. He describes virtual communities as "social aggregations that emerge from the Net when enough people carry on those public discussions long enough, with sufficient human feeling, to form webs of personal relationships in cyberspace."

Hagel and Armstrong (1997) look at virtual communities as "virtual enterprises." Many social communities on the Internet are opposed to the idea of commercialization but the authors argue that once these communities realize their full market potential they will be willing to engage in purchasing transactions.

Following Schubert (1999), we define virtual communities by

> Virtual Communities describe the union between individuals or organizations who share common values and interests using electronic media to communicate within a shared semantical space on a regular basis.

Akerkar and Aaberge (2011) have proposed a framework for semantically interlinked virtual communities (SIVC) that aims to interconnect virtual communities. SIVC will thus provide a way to overcome the limitations of current sites in making related pieces of information more accessible to users; by searching on one forum, the ontology and interface will allow users to find similar information on other sites that use an SIVC-based system architecture. A possible SIVC-based search is illustrated by the following use case. A person is searching for information in view of the installation of a home automation system in his house. There is a post A discussing local system vendors on site 1, a forum dedicated to home automation, which references both a Usenet post B comparing various functions of a system controlling the physical environment and a mailing list post C explaining how to install home automation system. Presently, the user will have to traverse at least three sites in order to find the relevant information. However, by making use of the SIVC ontology and remote RDF querying, he/she will access the necessary information through one search for the system installation on the home automation forum that also will yield the relevant text from the interlinked Usenet and mailing list posts B and C. There are some challenges for SIVC. The main challenge is adoption by community sites, that is, how can the users be enticed to make use of the SIVC ontology. By using concepts that can be easily understood by site administrators and by providing properties that are automatically created by an end-user, the SIVC ontology can be adopted in a useful way. A second challenge is how best to use SIVC with existing ontologies. This can be partially solved by mappings and interfaces to commonly used ontologies. Another challenge is how SIVC will scale. We will keep the scaling challenge in mind when creating a future architecture for an interconnected system of community sites. Making community semantics more explicit would enable new community members to make use of it without having to acquire it gradually.

This could make their interactions with the community more meaningful and less wasteful. Moreover, explicit semantics would lend itself to machine processing. Making user's semantics accessible to machines allows them to process the community archive, mine it, and present information to the community in an intelligent and context-suitable way than is presently taking place.

The level of expressiveness and functionality realized in the semantic web development surpasses previous attempts to model computer-based knowledge management systems. It is the idea of an open community, essential to the notion of the Web, which attracts so many people to the field and generates so many results. Anyone can use open standards to develop personal systems, use open source software to express his/her knowledge, or can engage in the development of standards. This openness of the development process has resulted in the remarkable range and richness of topics covered by the semantic web. Moreover, the organic development that grows from the interests and energy of the supporting community persuades an increasing number of researchers to adopt both web standards and the open development principle as the foundations for development in their professional domains.

9.6 Case study

The science collaboration framework (SCF; Das et al. 2008) is reusable, open source software toolkit to establish structured virtual organizations for researchers in biomedicine that leverages existing biomedical ontologies and RDF resources on the semantic web. To create interoperable communities, the SCF community knowledge is structured in a machine interpretable format as well as reuse existing, available knowledge bases. SCF supports structured virtual community discourse among biomedical researchers that is centered on a variety of interlinked heterogeneous data resources such as research articles, news items, interviews, and other viewpoint. The SCF GPL software consists of the Drupal core content management system and customized modules. Drupal is a very flexible and modular system and allows the implementation of custom content and functionality by developing a new module, in hypertext processor (PHP) code, that implements Drupal interfaces. Any community that wants to use SCF and has an existing Drupal site can install a SCF module easily through a forms-based administrative interface. A community administrator has the option of installing selections of these modules if there is an existing Drupal site or of installing the entire framework, with configuration being performed through the normal Drupal administrative control panel. At the other end of the spectrum, a developer can extend SCF functionality and create new custom content. Another advantage of choosing Drupal is that we can leverage a large active community of over 2000 developers.

The SCF framework provides the ability to publish articles, interviews, and news; annotate these with biological resources such as genes, animal models, and antibodies; and create informal discourse of community members around these resources as well as the current scientific articles. The information of a content type (e.g., gene and article) is contained in a unit called "node" in Drupal; a site can create instances of gene nodes, article nodes, etc., using these modules. Bioinformatics data tend to be heterogeneous; hence, there was a need to instantiate nodes from heterogeneous data sources such as XML and RDF. The knowledge representation of biological resources is based on the Semantic Web Applications in Neuromedicine (SWAN) ontology. Gene information is imparted into the Drupal system from a remote existing RDF repository using the RDF query language (SPARQL) interface. SCF use "foaf:Person" class to represent the member and "foaf:topic interest" to capture his or her research interest. The architecture makes it possible to define common schemas in OWL for a set of web communities and to enable interoperability across biological resources, SWAN research statements, or other objects of interest defined in the shared schemas. It is planned to make these graphs available via RDFa embedded within the HTML, and this work is being carried out in parallel with efforts to integrate RDFa into Drupal core.

9.7 Building the World Wide Why

The problem with trying to keep up with enormous amount of data is that business at the "speed of thought" hits a bottleneck, predominantly as our technological evolution has been all about data and very little about enhancing the thought process in a way that helps us make better sense of the data. While the medium has changed, the basic elements for describing our world also remain the same, consisting of the *who, what, when, where, how,* and *why* of the topic being discussed. "WWW" today actually stands for the World Wide *What.* We need to begin transforming it into the World Wide *Why.* This transformation will lead us to a great opportunity to partial access to the reasoning behind the data. Instead of finding the answers and then digging for the hidden rationale, we need to flip the approach. Imagine the ability to quickly see an entire thought process, and then click to the embedded data that drove the decisions. Obviously, transparency will be measured not by the number of documents we place online for others to read, but by the clarity with which our options and choices are presented. It will be transformation from *accessibility of data* to *accessibility of reason.*

9.8 Conclusion and applications

Dual advantages of the Web ontologies and knowledge management can be achieved by employing knowledge management through ontologies. Advantages of modularity, reusability, knowledge orientation, and learning are earned through such integration. The paradigm shift from document centric organization to knowledge centric organization brings significant amount of opportunities and advantages to the organization. There are many future-oriented changes that such hybridization may think for. The primary among them is user-friendly user interface. By adding good interface acceptability, scope of such system can be increased to satisfy need on global business. Additionally, NLP unit to talk in user's native language earns some extra benefits besides the intended ones. An independent ontology editor can be designed, which can be used in conjunction with such system. Such editor may be designed as a generic commercial product. This ontology editor gives a representation and editing platform for selected ontology. Another scope is in the area of searching the content from the Web. Searching and crawling can be distributed, filtered through application-specific heuristic, and ranked according to relevance. This type of search can contribute for knowledge discovery. Special purpose ontologies can be developed. Reasoning, inference, and knowledge generation techniques can be considered as a new area of research. Similarly, knowledge groups, networks, portal, and platforms can be designed as tools for knowledge use and share. Security, backup, services, and standards are some additional aspects where *R & D* can be thought for. These areas are short-listed as follows:

- User interface and NLP for interface
- Visual editor and What You See Is What You Get (WYSIWYG) support for ontology creation and management

- Ontology mapping, merging, and integrating
- New ontology development and hybridization
- Learning and reasoning from ontology
- Automatic self-learning and inference
- Searching, crawling, ranking, and filtering functions and algorithms
- Knowledge discovery techniques and automatic knowledge acquisition
- Knowledge groups, portals, and trust-based networks
- Test case generation for testing the ontologies
- Other services, standards, security, backup, etc.

Exercises

9.1 Describe the various stages of knowledge model construction and typical activities to be carried out during each stage.

9.2 Explain the knowledge management cycle with specific example.

9.3 What do you mean by virtual community and how knowledge management is useful for virtual community?

9.4 Explore various challenges in web knowledge management.

9.5 Discuss with examples advantages of using semantic annotations for KM.

9.6 (Project) Knowledge automation goes ahead of the boundaries of traditional knowledge management since it streamlines and automates the authoring and workflow process, helping to make service and support organizations more efficient. By means of knowledge automation, technology is applied to these critical processes to adapt to the way that people actually work. There is a need for such human expertise automated to help in-house staff as well as customers. Examples of such systems are given as follows. You can select one of them and explore how the technology based on intelligent (reasoning) system will convert tactic human expertise into explicit knowledge.

    a. Online college admission

    b. Recommender system

References

Akerkar, R. and Aaberge, T. 2011. Semantically linking virtual communities. In *Virtual Community Building and the Information Society: Current and Future Directions*, eds. C. El Morr and P. Maret. Hershey, PA: IGI Global Publishers, pp. 192–207.

Aldea, A., Banares-Alcantara, R., Bocio, J., Gramajo, J., Isern, D., Kokossis, A., Jimenez, L., Moreno, A., and Riano, D. 2003. An ontology-based knowledge management platform. Paper presented at the *Workshop on Information Integration on the Web at the 18th International Joint Conference on Artificial Intelligence*, Acapulco, Mexico.

Baumgartner, R., Flesca, R., and Gottlob, G. 2001. Visual web information extraction with Lixto. Paper presented at the *International Conference on Very Large Data Bases*, pp. 119–128, Roma, Italy.

Berners-Lee, T. 2005. Web for real people. Keynote speech at the *14th International Conference on World Wide Web*, Chiba, Japan.

Bray, T., Paoli, J., Sperberg-McQueen, C. M., Maler, E., and Yergeau, F. 2004. Extensible markup language (XML) 1.0. W3C Recommendation. http://www.w3.org/TR/2004/REC-xml-20040204/ (accessed September 14, 2011).

Brewster, C., Ciravegna, F., and Wilks, Y. 2002. User-centred ontology learning for knowledge management. Paper presented at the *Seventh International Conference on Applications of Natural Language to Information Systems*, Stockholm, Sweden.

Burn, J. M. and Ash, C. 2000. Knowledge management strategies for virtual organizations. *Information Resource Management Journal* 13(1):15–23.

Ciravegna, F., Dingli, A., Petrelli, D., and Wilks, Y. 2002. User-system cooperation in document annotation based on information. Paper presented at the *13th International Conference on Knowledge Engineering and KM*, Sigüenza, Spain.

Das, S., Girard, T., Weitzman, L., Lewis-Bowen, A., and Clark, T. 2008. Building bio-medical web communities using a semantically aware content management system. *Briefings in Bioinformatics* 10(2):129–138.

Denny, M. 2002. Ontology building: A survey of editing tools. http://www.xml.com/pub/a/2002/11/06/ontologies.html (accessed September 14, 2011).

Dowman, M., Tablan, V., Cunningham, H., and Popov, B. 2005. Web-assisted annotation, semantic indexing and search of television and radio news. Paper presented at the *14th International World Wide Web Conference*, pp. 225–234, Chiba, Japan.

Hagel, J., and Armstrong, A. 1997. *Net Gain: Expanding Markets through Virtual Communities*. Boston, MA: Harvard Business School Press.

Heflin, J. and Hendler, J. 2001. A portrait of the semantic web in action. *IEEE Intelligent Systems* 16(2):54–59.

Henderson, J. C., Venkatraman, N., and Oldach, S. 1996. Aligning business and IT strategies. In *Competing in the Information Age: Strategic Alignment in Practice*, ed. J. F. Luftman. New York: Oxford University Press, pp. 21–42.

Leung, N. K. and Kang, S. H. 2009. Ontology-based collaborative inter-organizational knowledge management network. *Interdisciplinary Journal of Information, Knowledge, and Management* 4:37–50.

Manola, F. and Miller, E. 2004. RDF primer. W3C Recommendation. http://www.w3.org/TR/2004/REC-rdf-primer-20040210/ (accessed September 14, 2011).

McDowell, L., Etzioni, O., Gribble, S., Halevy, A., Levy, H., Pentney, W., Verma, D., and Vlasseva, S. 2003. Enticing ordinary people onto the semantic web via instant gratification. Paper presented at the *Second International Semantic Web Conference*, pp. 754–770, Sanibel Island, FL.

McGuinness, D. L. 2003. Ontologies come of age. In *Spinning the Semantic Web: Bringing the World Wide Web to Its Full Potential*, eds. D. Fensel, J. Hendler, H. Lieberman, and W. Wahlster. Cambridge, MA: MIT Press, pp. 171–194.

McGuinness, D. L. and Harmelen, F. 2003. OWL web ontology language. W3C Recommendation. http://www.w3.org/TR/2003/CR-owl-features-20030818 (accessed September 14, 2011).

Mohame, A. H., Lee, S. P., and Salim, S. S. 2004. An ontology-based knowledge model for software experience management. *Journal of Knowledge Management Practice* 5(3):265–272.

Mueller, J., Hutter, K., Fueller, J., and Matzler, K. 2011. Virtual worlds as knowledge management platform—A practice-perspective. *Information Systems Journal* 21(6):479–501.

Popov, B., Kirayakov, A., Ognyanoff, D., Manov, D., and Kirilov, A. 2004. KIM—A semantic platform for information extraction and retrieval. *Natural Language Engineering* 10(3/4):375–392.

Razmerita, L., Angehrn, A., and Maedche, A. 2003. Ontology-based user modeling for knowledge management systems. *Lecture Notes in Computer Science* 2702:213–217.

Rheingold, H. 1993. *The Virtual Community: Homesteading on the Electronic Frontier*. Reading, MA: Addison-Wesley Publishing Company.

Schroeter, R., Hunter, J., and Kosovic, D. 2003. Vannotea—A collaborative video indexing, annotation and discussion system for broadband networks. Paper presented at the *Workshop on Knowledge Markup and Semantic Annotation*, pp. 1–8, Florida.

Schubert, P. 1999. Aufbau und Management Virtueller Geschäftsgemeinschaften in Electronic Commerce Umgebungen. Dissertation, University of St. Gallen, St. Gallen.

Skyrme, D. J. 2002. Knowledge management: Approaches and policies. http://www.providersedge.com/docs/km_articles/KM_-_Approaches_and_Policies.pdf (accessed September 14, 2011).

Stuckenschmidt, H. and Harmelen, F. 2005. Information sharing on the semantic web series. *Advanced Information and Knowledge Processing* 276.

Uschold, M. and King, M. 1995. Towards a methodology for building ontologies. Paper presented at the *Workshop on Basic Ontological Issues in Knowledge Sharing*, Montreal, Quebec, Canada.

Yang, S. J. H., Chen, I. Y. L., and Shao, N. W. Y. 2004. Ontology enabled annotation and knowledge management for collaborative learning in virtual learning community. *Educational Technology & Society* 7(4):70–81.

chapter ten

Social network intelligence

10.1 Introduction to social networking

In recent years, online social networking has moved from niche phenomenon to mass adoption. Although the concept dates back to the 1960s, vital growth and commercial interest only arose well after the advent of the Internet. One of the first networking sites, SixDegrees.com, was launched in 1997 but shut down in 2000 after struggling to find a purpose for its concept.

The rapid increase in participation in very recent years has been accompanied by a progressive diversification and sophistication of purposes and usage patterns across a multitude of different sites. The Social Software Weblog (http://www.socialsoftware. weblogsinc.com/) groups hundreds of social networking sites in nine categories, including business, common interests, dating, face-to-face facilitation, friends, pets, and photos.

Social networking, also referred to as social media, encompasses many Internet-based tools that make it easier for people to listen, interact, engage, and collaborate with each other. Social networking platforms such as Facebook (FB), MySpace, YouTube, LinkedIn, Twitter, blogs, message boards, Wikipedia, and countless others are becoming popular day by day. People use social networking to share recipes, photos, and ideas and to keep friends updated on our lives.

In this chapter, we shall begin with an overview of online social networks and discuss how open and distributed semantic social network can be created through definitions such as Friend-Of-A-Friend (FOAF), XHTML Friends Network (XFN), enabling interoperability between different social network systems.

Unlike the Web, which is largely organized around content, online social networks are organized around users. Participating users join a network, publish their profile and (optionally) any content, and create links to any other users with whom they associate. The resulting social network provides a basis for maintaining social relationships, for finding users with similar interests, and for locating content and knowledge that has been contributed or endorsed by other users.

In general, a web-based social network (WBSN) must meet the following criteria:

1. It is accessible over the Web with a web browser. This excludes networks where users would need to download special software in order to participate and social networks based on other technologies, such as mobile devices.
2. Users must explicitly state their relationship with other people by stating a relationship. Although social networks can be built from many different interactions, a WBSN is more than just a potential source of social network data; it is a website or framework that has the development of an explicit social network as a goal. These criteria rule out building social networks from auction transactions, copostings, or similar events that link people when a connection is created as a side effect of another process.
3. The system must have explicit built-in support for users making these connections. The system should be specifically designed to support social network connections.

This means that a group of friends who each maintain a simple hypertext markup language (HTML) page with a list of his or her friends would not qualify as a WBSN because HTML itself does not have explicit built-in support for making social connections. There must be some greater over-arching and unifying structure that connects the data and regulates how it is presented and formatted.

4. Relationships must be visible and browsable. The data do not necessarily have to be public (i.e., visible by anyone on the Web) but should be accessible to at least the registered users of a system. Websites where users maintain completely closed lists of contacts are not interesting for their social networking properties—neither to users nor to people performing a network analysis—and are thus ignored for these purposes. For example, some websites allow users to bookmark the profiles of other users, and others allow users to maintain address books. Even when these lists are explicit expressions of social connections, they would not qualify a system as a WBSN if they cannot be seen and browsed by other users. One important note here is that the system itself does not need built-in browsing support. Rather, each user's data must be made accessible with unambiguous pointers to each social connection.

These criteria qualify most of the major social networking sites. Today's most popular social networking websites are as follows:

- Google+ a social network operated by Google, Inc., launched on June 28, 2011, with integrations across a number of Google products, including Buzz and Profiles. One key element of Google+ is a focus on targeted sharing within subsets of your social group, which are what Google calls Circles. Circles are simply small groups of people that you can share to, each with names like friends, family, classmates, and co-workers. Another feature that is widely discussed is "Hangouts," Google's new group chat feature. Instead of directly asking a friend to join a group chat, users instead click "start a hangout" and they are instantly in a video chatroom alone.

- Blogs are sites that people set up to provide information and opinions about events, ideas, or anything else they want to discuss. Blogs can include links to other related sites, photos, videos, and sound as well as text. The number of bloggers is growing exponentially; eMarketer estimates that in 2009 there were almost 30 million U.S. bloggers and more than 98 million blog readers.

- Twitter is a microblogging site. Twitter members post text messages called "tweets" of 140 characters or less, using either a computer or a cell phone. Other Twitter users can "follow" your posts, but you can decide if you want to let them follow you or not. Compete.com, a web traffic analysis service, says that Twitter had 8 million unique visits in February 2010.

- FB is a social networking site where you can set up a profile, join different communities, and connect with friends. More than 175 million people are using FB in August 2011—and the fastest growing demographic is people over the age of 35 years.

- LinkedIn is a social networking site with about 38 million members. While it shares a lot of the same features and capabilities you will find on FB, LinkedIn focuses specifically on helping people build career and business communities.

- Wikipedia is a free encyclopedia that anyone can edit. Articles provide links to related information. In 2008, Wikipedia had 684 million visitors and 75,000 contributors working on more than 10 million articles.

- YouTube is a site to share and watch videos. Anyone can record a video and then upload and share it via the YouTube site. Everyone can watch the videos on YouTube. In January, The U.S. Congress and YouTube announced the launch of official Congressional YouTube channels, which gives each member of the House and Senate the opportunity to create his or her own YouTube channel.

Social Networking sites provide new opportunities for users to express their own opinions, find others with similar interests and experiences, and share and learn in a virtual environment. Artists can debut albums, film-makers showcase their creations, anybody can sell whatever they wish, advertise local events, things to do, and places to go, share vital videos. Young people want to express themselves, are socially highly interactive, and mobilize around issues very quickly, for example, environmental issues such as the Tsunami.

As with any form of online communication, there are risks. Primarily, because these are public spaces used by anyone, young people and adults alike and published content can be seen by a worldwide audience. There are risks of bullying, online predators, identity theft and the promotion of violent and inappropriate content. It is important to underline those children, and young people may not only fall victim to such harmful behavior but may also be involved in initiating, maintaining, or perpetrating it against others.

In addition to member relationship in online communities, social network analysis (SNA) has been applied to many other types of social networks. For example, Xu and Chen (2003) created, analyzed, and visualized a network of known criminals and their relationships. Their analysis identifies various groups and subgroups, key individuals, and links between groups. Centrality can be detected using graph properties including degree (the number of direct links), betweenness (geodesics passing through), and closeness (sum of geodesics). Each of these indices is evidence for different individual roles: a high degree suggests leadership and high betweenness indicates a "gatekeeper."

This increased understanding enables law enforcement officers to target specific criminals, to disrupt criminal organizations, and to achieve higher rates of conviction. Chen (1999) describes the development and application of visualization techniques allowing users to access and explore information in a digital library effectively and intuitively based on cocitation relationships. Salient semantic structures and citation patterns are extracted from several document collections using latent semantic indexing and pathfinder network scaling. Author cocitation patterns are visualized through a number of author cocitation maps highlighting important research areas in the field. This approach provides a means of transcending the boundaries of collections of documents and visualizing more profound patterns in terms of semantic structures and cocitation networks.

An in-depth understanding of the graph structure of online social networks is necessary to evaluate current systems, to design future online social network-based systems, and to understand the impact of online social networks on the Internet. For example, understanding the structure of online social networks might lead to algorithms that can detect trusted or influential users, much like the study of the Web graph led to the discovery of algorithms for finding authoritative sources in the Web.

Link structure analyses and graph theory have been applied to crawling the Web for virtual communities. The FOAF project takes the social networking aspect of the Web still further (Dumbill 2002a,b), allowing the information collected to be aggregated, integrated, and fused.

10.1.1 Web patterns and social ecosystem

There were simpler forms of social organizations on the Web (or web communities) before the eruption of social networks. A web community can be simply seen as a collection of web pages that deal with a common topic, presumably created by people with common interests. There is a natural ontology that sociological scientists use to understand and contextualize all those forms of social patterns: social ecosystems. They can be referred as the agglutination and interaction of different web communities (such as social networks or blogs). It is broadly accepted that current and prevailing social ecosystems are mainly shaped and populated by the social networks, or more concretely, by a synergy between classical blogs with social networks.

Social ecosystems are dynamic, open, and inclusive of both public and private organizations, and remain independent of geography and language. In this context, we can make a classification of the different flavors of web communities that may form a social ecosystem attending to the following patterns:

- Horizontal social patterns: they typically represent public places where participants have an equal status (i.e., friendship).
- Vertical social patterns: they are commonly focused on common interests (i.e., common hobbies).

10.1.2 Types of social networks

In order to understand what types of social networks exist on the Web, it is important to look at all facets of how people interact online with each other. The term "social networking" is generally related to the largest and most popular "general use" social networks present on the Web today. We can break down the existing social networks into the following major categories:

1. General purpose or friend-based: General social networks do not focus on a particular topic
2. Informational: The objective of these networks is to offer answers to daily challenges
3. Professional: Professional social networks are used to find new opportunities within your career or industry
4. Educational: Educational networks are platforms to enhance the student's experience
5. Hobbies: These networks are a meeting point to people with the same likes
6. Academic: Social networks are an obvious benefit for academic researchers offering an update source of knowledge
7. News: Another popular type of social network is the one related to the publishing of "community content"

In other words, a social network consists of a finite set or sets of actors and the relation or relations defined on them. In case of human social networks, actors refer to individual persons while relations could be interpreted in a variety of ways. Depending on the source of data, relations in a social network could come from a verbal or written communication, scientific collaboration, kinship, physical or virtual proximity, and so on. Based on whether the links are explicitly described, we classify social networks into two types: salient and latent social networks. In latent social networks, social links are formed through shared resources or context such as comembership and conversation relationship. As a result, two persons who are directly linked in a latent social network do not necessarily know each other. In contrast, in a salient social network, links are explicitly articulated in social networks such as FOAF, and such links generally reflect actual social relations. On the semantic web, social network relations are represented with semantic information. FOAF defines a set of terms for letting users describe personal profiles including whom they know. Especially, `foaf:knows` relations can form ties in social networks on the semantic web by directly linking two `foaf:person`. FOAF has been recognized as means of sharing social network data between social networking websites, and the ease of producing semantic web data is promoting this evolution.

10.2   Friend-of-a-friend

At the basic technical level, FOAF is just a resource description framework (RDF) vocabulary, originated by Dan Brickley and Libby Miller in 2002. The FOAF Vocabulary (Brickley and Miller 2007) contains terms for describing personal information, membership in groups, and social connections.

The most important component of a FOAF document is the FOAF vocabulary, which is identified by the namespace uniform resource identifier (URI) http://xmlns.com/foaf/0.1/. The FOAF vocabulary defines both classes (e.g., `foaf:Agent`, `foaf:Person`, and `foaf:Document`) and properties (e.g., `foaf:name`, `foaf:knows`, `foaf:interests`, and `foaf:mbox`) grounded in RDF semantics. In contrast to a fixed standard, the FOAF vocabulary is managed in an open source manner, that is, it is not stable and is open for extension. Therefore, inconsistent FOAF vocabulary usage is expected across different FOAF documents.

FOAF terms, by class (categories or types) and by property, are given as follows:

Classes: | Agent | Document | Group | Image | OnlineAccount | OnlineChatAccount | OnlineEcommerceAccount | OnlineGamingAccount | Organization | Person | Personal ProfileDocument | Project |

Properties: | accountName | accountServiceHomepage | aimChatID | based_near | birthday | currentProject | depiction | depicts | dnaChecksum | family_name | firstName | fundedBy | geekcode | gender | givenname | holdsAccount | homepage | icqChatID | img | interest | isPrimaryTopicOf | jabberID | knows | logo | made | maker | mbox | mbox_sha1sum | member | membershipClass | msnChatID | myersBriggs | name | nick | page | pastProject | phone | plan | primaryTopic | publications | schoolHomepage | sha1 | surname | theme | thumbnail | tipjar | title | topic | topic_interest | weblog | workInfoHomepage | workplaceHomepage | yahooChatID |

Table 10.1 lists the concepts and properties of the FOAF vocabulary. The property "knows" is used to create social links between people (i.e., one person knows another person). This property is somewhat vague as it is not specified what is actually meant by "knowing" a person. However, according to the FOAF specification, it is purposefully vague. While there are proposed extensions to change this behavior, more accurate relationship definition in basic FOAF is left up to the search engines and other "postprocessors" of the information. It is envisioned that these automatic tools could be used to find assumed relationships; for example, two persons who work for the same company are likely to be colleagues. Similarly, if a document exists that lists two people as their creators, they are likely to be collaborators on some level. Obviously, finding accurate information about interpersonal relationships through such data mining techniques is slow and unreliable at best.

The FOAF vocabulary is represented as semantic web ontology. The semantic web is an extension to the current web and is designed to encode information in a way that is

Table 10.1 FOAF Vocabulary Summary

FOAF basic	Personal info	Online accounts/IM
Agent	Weblog	OnlineAccount
Person	Knows	OnlineChatAccount
name	Interest	OnlineEcommerceAccount
nick	currentProject	OnlineGamingAccount
title	pastProject	holdsAccount
homepage	Plan	accountServiceHomepage
mbox	based_near	accountName
mbox_sha1sum	workplaceHomepage	icqChatID
img	workInfoHomepage	msnChatID
depiction (depicts)	schoolHomepage	aimChatID
surname	topic_interest	jabberID
family_name	publications	yahooChatID
givenname	geekcode	
firstName	myersBriggs	
	dnaChecksum	
Project & Groups	Document & Images	
Project	Document	
Organization	Image	
Group	PersonalProfileDocument	
member	topic (page)	
membershipClass	primaryTopic	
fundedBy	Tipjar	
Theme	sha1	
	made (maker)	
	thumbnail	
	Logo	

More detail about each term and its use can be found at http://xmlns.com/foaf/0.1

machine readable. Like the current web of hypertext documents, semantic web information is maintained in documents stored on servers. Instead of using HTML, the semantic web uses a hierarchy of languages, including the RDF and web ontology language (OWL). These languages are used to create ontologies, comprising classes (general categories of things) and their properties. The concepts from those ontologies are then used to describe data. There are several forms that data modeled with RDF, and OWL can take. N3 is one of them. The examples presented here are shown in the N3 language. This shows the subject listed with each of its properties and their values.

In Table 10.1, terms with initial capital letters are classes, and terms in all lowercase are properties. A FOAF file will generally contain a semantic web-based description of at least one person with some personal information and who that person knows. The following code example contains a simple FOAF description of a person:

```
:John a foaf:Person;
foaf:depiction <http://example.com/me.jpg>;
```

```
foaf:firstname "James";
foaf:lastname "Bond";
foaf:knows :David,
:R,
:Q.
```

From this snippet, a program that understands OWL and RDF will be able to process the information. Using the FOAF vocabulary, it can recognize that there is a person named "James Bond" with a picture online who knows David, R, and Q. The semantic web acts much like a large distributed database. There may be information about a person stored in many places. Using the basic features of RDF and OWL, it is easy to indicate that information about a person is contained in several documents on the Web and provide links to those documents. Any tool that understands these languages will be able to take information from these distributed sources and create a single model of that person, merging the properties from the disparate sites.

Example of FOAF: A very basic document describing a person

```
<!DOCTYPE rdf:RDF>
<rdf:RDF xmlns:rdf="http://www.w3.org/1999/02/22-rdf-syntax-ns#"
xmlns:rdfs="http://www.w3.org/2000/01/rdf-schema#" xmlns:foaf="http://
xmlns.com/foaf/0.1/" xmlns:owl="http://www.w3.org/2002/07/owl#"
xml:base="http://www.tmrfindia.org/foaf.rdf">
<foaf:PersonalProfileDocument rdf:about="">
<foaf:maker rdf:resource="#me"/>
<foaf:primaryTopic rdf:resource="#me"/>
<owl:sameAs rdf:resource="http://tmrfindia.org/foaf.rdf"/>
<owl:sameAs rdf:resource="http://www.tmrfindia.org/foaf.rdf"/>
</foaf:PersonalProfileDocument>
<foaf:Person rdf:ID="me">
<owl:sameAs rdf:resource="http://www.vestforsk.no/tilsette/rajendra-
akerkar"/>
<owl:sameAs rdf:resource="http://www.tmrfindia.org/ra.html"/>
<owl:sameAs rdf:resource="http://dblp.l3s.de/d2r/resource/authors/
Rajendra_Akerkar"/>
<owl:sameAs rdf:resource="http://www.tmrfindia.org/foaf.rdf#me"/>
<owl:sameAs rdf:resource="http://semanticweb.org/id/Rajendra_Akerkar"/>
<owl:sameAs rdf:resource="http://twitter2foaf.appspot.com/id/raa"/>
<rdfs:seeAlso rdf:resource="https://profiles.google.com/akerkar8#akerkar/
about"/>
<foaf:holdsAccount>
<foaf:OnlineAccount rdf:about="http://www.facebook.com/RAkerkar">
<foaf:accountServiceHomepage rdf:resource="http://www.facebook.com/"/>
<foaf:acountName>
RAkerkar
</foaf:acountName>
</foaf:OnlineAccount>
</foaf:holdsAccount>
<foaf:holdsAccount>
<foaf:OnlineAccount rdf:about="http://twitter.com/raa">
<rdfs:seeAlso rdf:resource="http://twitter2foaf.appspot.com/user/raa"/>
<foaf:accountServiceHomepage rdf:resource="http://twitter.com/"/>
<foaf:acountName>
```

```
raa8
</foaf:acountName>
</foaf:OnlineAccount>
</foaf:holdsAccount>
<foaf:holdsAccount>
<foaf:OnlineAccount rdf:about="http://www.linkedin.com/pub/rajendra_
akerkar/5/245/723">
<foaf:accountServiceHomepage rdf:resource="http://www.linkedin.com/"/>
<foaf:acountName>
Rajendra Akerkar
</foaf:acountName>
</foaf:OnlineAccount>
</foaf:holdsAccount>
<foaf:interest rdf:resource="http://dbpedia.org/resource/Natural_
Language_Interfaces"/>
<foaf:interest rdf:resource="http://dbpedia.org/resource/Semantic_Web_
Technologies"/>
<foaf:interest rdf:resource="http://dbpedia.org/resource/Knowledge_
engineering"/>
<foaf:interest rdf:resource="http://dbpedia.org/resource/Resource_
Description_Framework"/>
<foaf:interest rdf:resource="http://dbpedia.org/resource/SPARQL"/>
<foaf:interest rdf:resource="http://dbpedia.org/resource/Music"/>
<foaf:interest rdf:resource="http://dbpedia.org/resource/India"/>
<foaf:interest rdf:resource="http://dbpedia.org/resource/Norway"/>
<foaf:name>
Rajendra Akerkar
</foaf:name>
<foaf:title>
Professor
</foaf:title>
<foaf:givenname>
Rajendra
</foaf:givenname>
<foaf:surname>
Akerkar
</foaf:surname>
<foaf:firstName>
Rajendra
</foaf:firstName>
<foaf:family_name>
Akerkar
</foaf:family_name>
<foaf:familyName>
Akerkar
</foaf:familyName>
<foaf:lastName>
Akerkar
</foaf:lastName>
<foaf:birthday>
05-07
</foaf:birthday>
<foaf:nick>
Raj
```

```
</foaf:nick>
<foaf:openid rdf:resource="http://www.tmrfindia.org/"/>
<foaf:mbox_sha1sum>
35a8d4858ba240996a6f77636d93fbfdcd2b4843
</foaf:mbox_sha1sum>
<foaf:homepage>
<foaf:Document rdf:about="http://www.tmrfindia.org/">
<rdfs:seeAlso rdf:resource="http://www.tmrfindia.org/metadata.rdf"/>
</foaf:Document>
</foaf:homepage>
<foaf:depiction rdf:resource="http://www.tmrfindia.org/images/raa.jpg"/>
<foaf:phone rdf:resource="tel:+4790983895723"/>
<foaf:phone rdf:resource="fax:+4740332259"/>
<foaf:phone rdf:type="http://skype.com/" rdf:resource="callto://raa"/>
<foaf:workplaceHomepage rdf:resource="http://www.tmrfindia.org/"/>
<foaf:workplaceHomepage rdf:resource="http://www.westforsk.no/"/>
<foaf:currentProject>
<foaf:Project>
<foaf:homepage rdf:resource="http://www.sesam-4.no/"/>
</foaf:Project>
</foaf:currentProject>
<foaf:knows>
<foaf:Person rdf:about="http://harmann.org/alan/foaf#ah">
<rdfs:seeAlso rdf:resource="http://www.harmann.org/alan/foaf.rdf"/>
<foaf:name>
Alan Harmann
</foaf:name>
<foaf:homepage rdf:resource="http://www.harmann.org/alan/"/>
</foaf:Person>
</foaf:knows>
<foaf:knows>
<foaf:Person>
<foaf:name>
C. Bo
</foaf:name>
<rdfs:seeAlso rdf:resource="http://www.real-programmer.com/foaf/chris.foaf"/>
<foaf:homepage rdf:resource="http://www.real-programmer.com/"/>
</foaf:Person>
</foaf:knows>
<foaf:knows>
<foaf:Person>
<foaf:name>
```

In order to make a profile public, the FOAF description is saved to a file and stored on the web server. The de facto standard for the name of this file has become "foaf.rdf." However, the discovery aspect of the FOAF specification is still a subject that is somewhat open and actively discussed in the FOAF community. One suggested method to enable search engines to find the information is to use the HTML link tag to point to the FOAF descriptions. This would then allow any search engine indexing the page to also find the FOAF description at the specified file. For example, the following could be placed in the HEAD section of a website's index.html:

```
<link rel="meta"
  type="application/rdf+xml"
  title="FOAF"
  href="foaf.rdf" />
```

FOAF supports users by

1. Allowing provenance tracking and accountability (Dumbill 2003). On the Web, the source of information is just as important as the information itself in judging its credibility. Provenance tracking RDF tools can tell where and when a piece of information is obtained. A practice common to the FOAF community is to attach the source URI to each RDF statement.
2. Providing assistance to new entrants in a community. For example, people unfamiliar with a community can learn the structure and authority of a research area from the community's FOAF files.
3. Locating people with common interests. Users tend to have interests and values similar to those they desire in others (Adamic et al. 2003). Peer-to-peer relationships are an essential ingredient to collaboration, which is the driving force of online communities.

To aid the creation of a FOAF description, some automated tools have been introduced. One example is a FOAF-a-Matic (available at http://www.ldodds.com/foaf/foaf-a-matic), which generates a FOAF description from a web-form filled out by a user with personal information. This can be saved in a file and linked to as described earlier.

A tool for exploring the FOAF links and information is FOAFNaut, which presents the information in an intuitive scalable vector graphics (SVGs) format. In addition to applications utilizing FOAF, several FOAF extensions and modifications have been developed. For example, a substantially simpler "version" of FOAF called really simple syndication (RSS)–FOAF has been specified for use in RSS feed.

10.3   *Semantically interlinked online communities*

The Semantically Interlinked Online Communities (SIOC) initiative is aimed at interlinking related online community content from platforms such as blogs, message boards, and other social websites (Breslin and Decker 2007; Breslin et al. 2005). In combination with the FOAF vocabulary for describing people and their friends, and the Simple Knowledge Organisation Systems (SKOS) model for organizing knowledge, SIOC lets developers link discussion posts and content items to other related discussions and items, people (via their associated user accounts), and topics (using specific "tags" or hierarchical categories). As discussions begin to move beyond simple text-based conversations to include audio and video content, SIOC is evolving to describe not only conventional discussion platforms, but also new web-based communication and content-sharing mechanisms.

Since disconnected social websites require ontologies for interoperation, and due to the fact that there is a lot of social data with inherent semantics contained in these sites, there is potential for high impact through the successful deployment of SIOC. Many online communities still use mailing lists and message boards as their main communication mechanisms, and the SIOC initiative has created a number of data producers for such systems in order to lift these communities to the semantic web. As well as having applications to social websites, there is a parallel track of integration between social software and other systems in enterprise intranets. So far, SIOC has been adopted in a framework of 50 applications or modules deployed on over 400 sites.

A sample fragment of SIOC RDF is given in the following, representing a blog post, its metadata, and associated follow-up comments.

```
<sioc:Post
rdf:about="http://rakerkar.in/blog/2009/05/04/introduction-to-sioc/">
    <dc:title>Introduction to SIOC</dc:title>
    <dcterms:created>2009-05-04T02:43:20Z</dcterms:created>
    <sioc:has_container
rdf:resource="http://rakerkar.in/blog/index.php?sioc_type=site#weblo
g"/>
    <sioc:has_creator>
        <sioc:User rdf:about="http://rakerkar.in/blog/author/oc/"
rdfs:label="OC">
        <rdfs:seeAlso
rdf:resource="http://rakerkar.in/blog/index.php?sioc_type=user&sioc_
id=1"/>
        </sioc:User>
    </sioc:has_creator>
    <sioc:content>The SIOC project was started in 2004 by John Breslin and
    Uldis Bojars at DERI, NUI Galway. In 2007, SIOC became a W3C Member
    Submission. </sioc:content>
    <sioc:topic rdfs:label="Semantic Web"
rdf:resource="http://rakerkar.in/blog/category/semantic-web/"/>
    <sioc:topic rdfs:label="Blogs"
rdf:resource="http://rakerkar.in/blog/category/blogs/"/>
    <sioc:has_reply>
    <sioc:Post
rdf:about="http://rakerkar.in/blog/2009/05/04/introduction-to-
sioc/#comment-145758">
        <rdfs:seeAlso
rdf:resource="http://rakerkar.in/blog/index.php?sioc_type=comment&si
oc_id=145768"/>
    </sioc:Post>
    </sioc:has_reply>
</sioc:Post>
```

So far, work on SIOC has focused on producing social semantic data, but the augmentation of this data with rules to aid with reasoning is the next step [e.g., as discussed by the ExpertFinder initiative (http://expertfinder.info/)]. By combining information from one's explicitly defined social network and from implicit connections that may be derived through common activities (e.g., commenting on each other's content, participating in the same community areas), the suggestion of experts can be enhanced.

10.4   *Social network analysis*

SNA is the mapping and measuring of relationships between individuals, groups, organizations, computers, uniform resource locators (URLs), and other connected information (and/or knowledge) entities. The nodes in the network are the people and groups while the links show relationships or flows between the nodes. SNA provides both a visual and a mathematical analysis of human relationships.

To understand networks and their participants, we evaluate the location of actors in the network. Measuring the network location is finding the centrality of a node. These measures give us insight into the various roles and groupings in a network, such as

- Who are the connectors, leaders, bridges, and isolators?
- Where are the clusters and who is in them?
- Who is in the core of the network?
- Who is on the periphery?

Social network researchers measure network activity for a node by using the concept of degrees, that is, the number of direct connections a node has. In the network shown in Figure 10.1, D has the majority direct connections in the network, making D the most active node in the network. It is a "connector" or "hub" in this network. Common understanding in personal networks is "the more connections, the better." This is not forever true. What really matters is where those connections lead to and how they connect the otherwise unconnected. Here, D has connections only to others in its immediate cluster (clique). It connects only those who are already connected to each other.

While D has many direct ties, H has few direct connections, lesser than the average in the network. Yet, in several ways, it has one of the best locations in the network, that is, H is between two important constituencies. It plays a "broker" role in the network. H plays a dominant role in the network, at the same time it is a single point of failure. Without H, I and J would be cut off from information and knowledge in D's cluster. A node with great *betweenness* has influence over what flows in the network. H may control the outcomes in a network.

F and G have fewer connections than D, yet the pattern of their direct and indirect ties allows them to access all the nodes in the network more rapidly than anyone else. They have the shortest paths to all others, and they are near to everyone else. They are in an exceptional location to monitor the information flow in the network. Therefore, they have the best visibility into what is happening in the network. Individual network centralities provide insight into the individual's location in the network. The relationship between the centralities of all nodes can uncover a lot about the overall network structure.

A very centralized network is dominated by one or a few very central nodes. If these nodes are removed or damaged, the network quickly fragments into unconnected

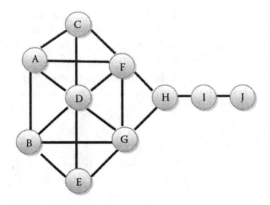

Figure 10.1 A network.

subnetworks. A highly central node can become a single point of failure. A network centralized around a well-connected hub can fail sharply if that hub is disabled or detached. Hubs are nodes with high degree and betweenness centrality. A less centralized network has no single point of failure.

More and more research shows that the shorter paths in the network are more important. The "small world" in which we live is not one of "six degrees of separation" but of direct and indirect connections more than three steps away. Therefore, it is vital to know: who is in your network neighborhood? Who are you aware of, and who can you reach?

Nodes that connect their group to others usually end up with high network metrics. Boundary spanners such as F, G, and H are more central in the overall network than their immediate neighbors whose connections are only local, within their immediate cluster. You can be a boundary spanner via your bridging connections to other clusters or via your concurrent membership in overlapping groups.

Boundary spanners are well-positioned to be innovators, since they have access to ideas and information flowing in other clusters. They are in a position to combine different ideas and knowledge, found in various places, into new products and services.

10.5   Social network data

There are several conventional methods of collecting social network information namely, administering questionnaires, conducting interviews, performing observational studies, and studying archival records. Extracting data from the Web puts forward a set of challenges but also offers some advantages over conventional methods.

Analyzing web-based social network data is of great importance and perhaps even more useful than extracting structured data because of the sheer volume of valuable information of nearly every possible type contained in them. Web-based data collection certainly enables longitudinal studies, allowing the dynamics of networks to be investigated, as opposed to surveying, where repeated data collection would be time-consuming and maybe impossible if the subjects are reluctant or unable to repeat the survey.

Semantic web technologies can significantly help the process of harvesting social networks. It is possible to do reasoning on the data and infer relations from certain properties. Furthermore, it is viable to extract a network of typed nodes and links.

Extracting a social network from the Web is to investigate explicitly stated connections. Social networking sites and other types of social software allow users to express lists of friends. For instance, blogging platforms may allow users to add a blogroll, which is a list of preferred blogs. Depending on the platform, these connections may denote a directed or undirected link between users.

Example: A query for extracting the social network formed by explicit foaf:knows relationships follows using the SPARQL protocol and RDF query language (SPARQL) query language.

```
PREFIX rdf: <http://www.w3.org/1999/02/22-rdf-syntax-ns#>
PREFIX foaf: <http://xmlns.com/foaf/0.1/>
SELECT ?s ?o
WHERE {
    ?s rdf:type foaf:Person.
    ?o rdf:type foaf:Person.
    ?s foaf:knows ?o.
}
```

Links between people may be inferred due to links to some common objects, for example, appearing in the same pictures, tagging the same documents, and replying to each other's blog posts.

10.6 *hCard and XFN*

hCard is an HTML adaptation of the vCard format. It is a microformat used to describe people, their contact details, and affiliations. It was created by Tantek Celik and Brian Suda based on the vCard IETF format (www.ietf.org/rfc/rfc2426.txt). Regardless of how your address book or email contact software displays the contact information, the underlying makeup of the vCard is based on the standard, and if you were to export one of your contacts, save it as a.vcf format, and then open it in a text editor, you would see something like this:

```
BEGIN:VCARD
VERSION:2.1
N:Wick;Helmut;;;
FN:Infosystem International
ORG:Inforsystem International;
TITLE:Vice Precident
EMAIL;INTERNET;HOME:hwick@infosystem.com
TEL;WORK:0091 22 23885277
ADR;WORK:;;1 Gulmohar Complex;Warli;Mumbai;400002;
END:VCARD
```

If you wanted to specify contact details for this person on a website, you could not use simple HTML/XHTML to do so. Though you can use hCard to mark up your HTML, reusing the naming conventions is set out in the vCard format. The address details given earlier could be expressed as follows:

```
<div class="vcard">
  <span class="fn"><span class="given-name">Helmut</span>
  <span class="family-name">Wick</span></span>,
  <span class="title">Vice Precident</span>,
  <div class="org">Infosystem International</div>
  <div class="adr">
    <div class="street-address">1 Gulmohar Complex</div>
    <span class="locality">Warli</span>,
    <span class="region">Mumbai</span>
    <span class="postal-code">400002</span>
  </div>
  <div>Tel: <span class="tel">0091 22 23885277</span></div>
  <div>Email:
  <span class="email"> hwick@infosystem.com </span></div>
</div>
```

Note that there is nothing here that would cause the HTML to be invalid—it is purely a set of div and span elements with class attributes, the values of which tally with the vCard naming conventions. You could use other kinds of HTML as you see fit, perhaps using a table, or a list, depending on the usage.

XFN is another social network-based microformat. XFN was created by the Global Multimedia Protocols Group (GMPG), with the first draft written in May 2003. XFN allows one to define relationships between individuals by defining a small set of values that describe personal relationships. In HTML and XHTML documents, these are given as values for the *rel* attribute on a hyperlink. XFN allows authors to indicate, which of the weblogs they read belong to friends, whom they have physically met, and other personal relationships. Using XFN values, which can be listed in any order, people can humanize their blogrolls and link pages, both of which have become a common feature of weblogs.

Example: Jack and Jill have met each other through social contact and had some exciting discussion at social gatherings where they found they had several interests in common. They have linked to each other as follows:

```
<a href="http://jack.net/" rel="met friend">Jack</a>
<a href="http://jill.org/" rel="social contact">Jill</a>.
```

The XFN profile specifies the allowed attributes for describing relationships. They are categorized under friendship, physical, professional, geographical, family, romantic, and identity categories. Table 10.2 presents differences between FOAF and XFN.

As with FOAF, the structure of XFN also presents a number of issues, only different kinds. Firstly, in XFN, there is no way to enforce that only valid set of values are entered for any links. Indeed, any combination of valid or invalid values could be written to the *rel* attribute but it is assumed that people participating in the creation of the social network do not misbehave in this way.

Forging relationships is, in theory, easy with XFN. For example, person A might claim that a person B is his or her close friend. If the other party reciprocates the friendship linkage (i.e., by linking back to person A as his/her friend), the situation is clear. However, in the absence of a reciprocating link, there is no reliable method of knowing if the alleged relationship is true. It might be that the other party simply does not yet support XFN. The other possibilities are that the claimed friendship is indeed false or that the friendship is considered unilateral—the other person may only consider the other party as an acquaintance instead of a friend.

Table 10.2 Differences between FOAF and XFN

	FOAF	XFN
Underlying technology	RDF/XML vocabulary	XHTML metadata profile, uses *rel* attribute
Described information	Wide variety of personal information and relationships	Only social relationships
Manual profile creation possible?	Yes, but format complicated	Yes; Relationships defined purely text-based
Vulnerability to fraudulent information	Yes; there is no way to "mod" or rate given pieces of FOAF information	Not serious; alleged relationships remain one-way
Identity model	Personal information defined in the FOAF description: additional pages can be linked from the description. No assumed relationship to website hosting the description	The originating page is assumed to contain all necessary information about the person Links to "me" can also be provided

10.7 Advantages and disadvantages of social networking

In this section, we can list some merits and demerits of social networking. Social networks work best when they are optimized with correct set of tags and keywords. They are search engine friendly and indexing can occur within minutes once you submit a story. In order to get finest results, ensure that your content is precious and if possible unique.

10.7.1 Advantages of social networking

- Users can save their favorite pages online and revisit them anytime.
- A tag- or category-based classification makes it easier for people to assign and search the content when needed.
- Sharing the bookmarks with friends and family increases its reach.
- A social media network can help increase the page rank and traffic for a website.
- One can rank his/her bookmarks.
- A social bookmarking account acts like a one stop shop containing all your online bookmarks. Hence, it results in easy management and tracking.

On the other hand, there are some of the apparent disadvantages associated with social networks, such as the following:

- As no standard set of keywords are associated with a type of content, searching for quality content and stories becomes an issue.
- A few people can end up submitting duplicate stories and content on different social bookmarking sites. Hence, the overall user experience can become negative.

10.8 Social graph application programming interface

The usage of social networks (SNs) like Xing, Twitter, LinkedIn, or FB has increased massively, and their APIs have become very powerful and standardized [apart from FB almost all SNs provide Google's OpenSocial (OS) application programming interface (API)].

In May 2007, FB opened the website for third-party apps (applications) by launching the so called—FB Platform. Apps are displayed in a container inside an FB page and can include FB widgets (e.g., the like button) and access users' profile data. The app can be implemented as usual JavaScript-enhanced HTML page (iframe) or in the FB markup language (FBML) and FB JavaScript (FBJS). To interact with FB's backend, a representational state transfer (REST) API is provided and user data can be accessed via the FB Query Language (FQL) (Graham 2008). In December 2008, FB Connect became available, allowing developers to include FB's widgets into independent websites not running as apps inside FB.

In 2010, the REST API was replaced by the more modern Graph API, giving developers three possibilities for interaction with the Social Networks (SN):

1. FB for websites allows the usage of social plug-ins and comfortable solutions like a single sign-on procedure on any website
2. Apps on Facebook.com allows to run web apps in a dedicated iframe on FB, place widgets on users' profile pages, and update a user's FB stream
3. Mobile Apps is a collection of services for web apps running on mobile devices.

In contrast to the proprietary Social Graph API, which is limited to FB, Google released version 0.7 of its counterpart OS API in late 2007 under an Apache 2.0 and Creative Commons license. Most SNs have implemented the OS API so far. So Google's aim to provide an API for cross-platform apps seems to be achieved, although different versions of the API are implemented in the SNs (version 1.1 was released in November 2010, but version 0.8 is still very wide-spread). OS can be seen as a container for apps written in HTML, JavaScript, and cascade style sheet (CSS), which can be placed on web pages inside SNs, providing a standardized Asynchronous JavaScript (AJAX) request mechanism to contact the app developer's web server and also standardized access to user data in the SN. For security and data protection reasons, SN users can define access rules for apps in general or individually when they add an app to their profile page.

As Xing is the most popular business network in Germany, it supports three OS views, home view (HV), canvas view (CV), and profile view (PV). The HV is an app container to be included in the user's personal page with a fixed size of 315 × 180 pixels. It is only available for users who added the app to their accounts. HV can access user data if permitted by the user. CV can be larger than HV and therefore display more content. Like HV, it is only accessible for the user himself and can access the same data as HV. PV can be as large as CV and is displayed inside the user's profile page, which is available to other users depending on the user's permissions. Apart from the owner's data, PV can also access data of the user viewing the app on another user's profile page.

10.9   Social search and artificial intelligence

Google has long understood the importance of developing systems capable of understanding human behavior but has always been prevented from developing such systems by the abstract nature of much of the data available on the Web. Concepts such as funniness escape traditional search engine algorithms as they are built to analyze only the elements the engineers have programmed into them. With the birth of the social internet in the second half of the last decade, things began to change. Sites that facilitated the sharing of content, such as Digg, Reddit, del.icio.us, and others provided search engines with an insight into human behavior they had not previously had, and the search engines deployed a different type of spider to carefully monitor the kind of behavior observed on social bookmarking sites.

The key to developing an intelligent search engine is to gain an understanding of how humans viewed a website. We can use "funniness" as the example, as this represents one of the major challenges for search engines. Social bookmarking sites allowed user to share a link, and then attribute tags to that shared link to aid the categorization of the content for others to find. Human examination of the tags provided by users to their shared links was found to be extremely accurate in regard to the content on the destination URL. Rarely was funny content tagged as relating to content the humans investigating found to be outside of the realm of what can be considered funny. With the tagging passing a human test, Google deployed bots to index the shared content on social networking sites to build profiles of websites based on the tagged categorization provided by the social bookmarking users. This enabled Google to query their bot and ask questions such as "what is funny?"—the bot would be able to provide results based not on the traditional algorithmic method of looking for link popularity and contextual presence of the queried term in text but rather by measuring what humans consider funny through the sharing of content. The bot was capable of measuring volumes of shares—as well as frequency of shares to build a real-time picture of what is considered funny today rather than a historical record of what was considered funny in the past. This evolution of search engine technology was a key step forward in combating one of the major downfalls of search engine algorithms—their lack of understanding of humans and how they think.

Since the earliest developments of building into a search engine the first primitive learning and understanding capabilities as described earlier, the social nature of the Internet has accelerated and gone beyond the socialized sharing of content on largely anonymous social bookmarking networks. The key to advancing machine learning was to place these attributes applied to content within some framework. What is funny to a 19 year old person in Oslo may be very different from what a 45 year old woman in Bonn finds funny. Additional dimensions had to be built into machine's understanding for it to frame content, so that valid search results could be built.

Since that early investment in FB, Bing has begun work on its enhanced social search engine utilizing its aggregated data from shared content on social bookmarking sites, access to personal data stored inside FB, and sharing habits inside FB as well. Bing has a distinct advantage as it is privy to the sharing habits and traffic for all FB users, regardless of whether they have profile privacy enacted or not. The big advantage for Bing here is the access they have to the billions of "likes" that occur within the FB on any given day. These likes are essential in building an accurate and real-time social search engine. The aggregation of the "likes" data allows Bing to build a profile for search results highly relevant to any particular demographic and geographic profile.

Bing has an archive of indexed URLs from social bookmarking sites, and Bing knows what content is considered by actual anonymous humans as funny. An FB user who is 19 years old and from Oslo shares some content on FB. Bing can then compare the shared content against its vast record of tagged URLs and come to the conclusion that this individual user is sharing funny content. (The vast majority of content shared from a particular domain is tagged as funny in social bookmarking sites; therefore, that domain's content is funny). If another 100,000 19 year old FB users from across the globe also share content from the same domain as our user from Oslo, Bing will be able to conclude that 19 year old users think that domain is also funny. In terms of building social search result, a 19 year old searching for "funny" via a search platform integrated in to FB would not be presented with the dictionary entry or the Wikipedia page for that query, but rather sites that individuals within the same social profile actually think are funny.

Early development of a social search engine is the introduction of semantic analysis for shared content on FB. Understanding what humans are saying is one of the most difficult things for a computer to deal with. Two individuals could share the same content: one could add the following comment with the content "this is horrible!" and the other could add this comment "this is dizzy!" From the machine's perspective, it will struggle with understanding whether the second user is saying the content is good or bad? Until this hurdle can be overcome, a large part of the social search engine solution is missing from sites such as FB.

The main benefits for the development of social search technology are twofold. First, compiling search results based on human preferences, as opposed to the mechanical measurement of link popularity and other traditional measurements of authority, will build results more engaging and relevant. Second, the search engines will be able to exclude manufactured authority from the search results.

We can expect the acceleration to continue over the coming years toward the deployment of the first social search engine. Both Google and Bing are well placed to roll out the first incarnations of their learning machines, and we can also expect the deployment to be incremental and usage to be voluntary. The key to being the best will be dependent on the level of artificial intelligence (AI) built into the machines, and their capability to understand humans, which, even for humans, is no easy task.

10.9.1   Intelligent social networks

The competition between different platforms such as FB, Twitter, Tuenti, etc., requires a big effort to guarantee efficiency, security, and innovative ways to improve the social connections. The social network platforms are systems as integrated in the society as mobile phones or email, and it is not wrong to start to assume they can become the main communication channel in a few years. Then, the next is, what aspects are key to determine the success or failed of one of these platforms? First, we think a system is successful when it increases the number of users in its first years. When the growing number of people is established, the platform should provide services that allow the users to find help for solving common problems they can encounter. There are many metrics to set the success of the network solution. One of them is the *MetCalfe law*. It says that the value of a telecommunications network is proportional to the square of the number of connected users in the system so the social networks must progress to make the user's life easier with the aim of becoming more essential in their day to day routine. The integration of AI techniques to solve current problems is a help to achieve intelligent environments offering adaptive behaviors depending on the user's intentions. In order to identify the required steps to contribute to the evolution of these systems, we list the current challenges that we propose to face using AI techniques:

- To customize and provide commercial solutions based on behavioral targeting
- To create a custom user interface to improve the user experience
- To improve and design new systems to avoid identity fraud actions and extortions, especially among nonadult members

10.10   Research future

There is an ever-growing amount of multimedia of different formats becoming available on the Internet. Current techniques to retrieve, integrate, and present these media to users are incomplete and would benefit from improvement. Semantic technologies make it possible to give good descriptions to media, facilitating the process of locating and combining diverse media from various sources. Making use of online communities can give additional benefits. Two main areas in which social networks and semantic technologies can support multimedia management are annotation and recommendation.

One of the important challenges to working with a large, integrated social (FOAF) network is scalability. Running a single breadth first search to compute a shortest path between two people in a network with several million nodes will exceed the memory capacity of most desktop computers and small servers. Aside from memory requirements, the complexity of many analysis algorithms makes handling tens of millions of nodes exceptionally difficult.

Some challenges must also be overcome regarding the online identity aspect and authentication or privacy for users of social websites. An attractive facet of social networking and media sharing websites is that the majority people use different websites because they want to fragment their online identity, that is, uploading pictures of family on FB, forming business contacts on LinkedIn, etc. While the semantic web and in particular reasoning principles allow us to merge this data and provide vocabularies, methods, and tools for data portability among social websites, this identity fragmentation must be taken into account. Thus, there is a need for further research to authenticate queries or carry out inferencing, by delivering data in different manners depending on which social subgraph the person requesting the data belongs to.

Exercises

10.1 How are relationships between persons expressed in FOAF?

10.2 In RDF, resources (e.g., persons) are identified using URIs. In FOAF, it is also possible to use URIs to identify persons; another way of identification is actually the preferred in FOAF. How are persons identified in FOAF?

10.3 List out four limitations of social networks.

10.4 Describe data portability with FOAF and SIOC.

10.5 What is the purpose of SIOC?

10.6 Search on the Web for tools providing advance tagging features using semantic web technologies and describe some of them.

10.7 Explore the following terms and discuss the characteristics of each of them.
   a. Blog
   b. Structured blog
   c. Semantic blog
   d. Microblog
   e. Semantic microblog

10.8 (Project) This is a "hands-on" study related to one or more web applications. The exact project description should be determined by instructor or students themselves. The project should have an adequately challenging component, and it should be relevant to the content of this book. For example,
   a. You can write a new (or modify an existing open source) application that is related to the book topics.
   b. You can measure or experiment with existing applications, evaluating their performance or other characteristics.
   c. You can study the social network of an online community application.

References

Adamic, L. A., Buyukkokten, O., and Adar, E. 2003. A social network caught in the web. *First Monday* 8(6). http://firstmonday.org/article/view/1057/977.

Breslin, J. G. and Decker, S. 2007. The future of social networks on the internet: The need for semantics. *IEEE Internet Computing* 11:86–90.

Breslin, J. G., Harth, A., Bojārs, U., and Decker, S. 2005. Towards semantically interlinked online communities. In *ESWC 2005*, eds. A. Gómez-Pérez and J. Euzenat, LNCS, 3532. Springer, Heidelberg, Germany, pp. 500–514.

Brickley, D. and Miller, L. 2007. FOAF vocabulary specification 0.9. Namespace Document. http://xmlns.com/foaf/0.1/ (accessed August 22, 2011).

Chen, C. 1999. Visualising semantic spaces and author co-citation networks in digital libraries. *Information Processing and Management* 35(3):401–420.

Dumbill, E. 2002a. XML watch: Finding friends with XML and RDF. IBM's XML Watch. http://www.ibm.com/developerworks/xml/library/x-foaf/index.html (accessed August 22, 2011).

Dumbill, E. 2002b. XML watch: Support online communities with FOAF. IBM's XML Watch. http://www.ibm.com/developerworks/xml/library/x-foaf2/index.html (accessed August 22, 2011).

Dumbill, E. 2003. Tracking provenance of RDF data. IBM's XML Watch. http://www.ibm.com/
    developerworks/xml/library/x-rdfprov/index.html (accessed August 22, 2011).
Graham, W. 2008. *Facebook API Developers Guide*. New York: Apress.
Xu, J. and Chen, H. 2003. Untangling criminal networks: A case study. Paper presented at the *1st
    NSF/NIJ Conference on Intelligence and Security Informatics*, pp. 232–248, Tucson, AZ.

part four

Agent-based web, security issues, and human–computer interaction

chapter eleven

Agent-based web

11.1 Introduction

The World Wide Web (WWW) is a vast pool of information and techniques that allow people to use and contribute its content from remote locations. It has become popular for its reach and availability to common people to spectacular domain experts. It is a platform that enables sharing of ideas and aspects of a variety of fields such as typical commercial transactions, education, entertainment, service-oriented business, and even social networking. Basically, the Web is a service that runs on the Internet platform and is a collection of interconnected documents and services. Being a consortium of a variety of services and documents, the structure of the Web is not homogeneous. In addition to this, there is no single institute of author that publishes on the Web. According to worldwidewebsize. com presently, the indexed web contains at least 19.42 billion pages.

During its first phase, the Web remained to be a collection of documents and services as conceived by Tim Berners-Lee in 1989. However, that was not the dream of the developers. Soon the need arose that the machine should understand the content and present more meaningful content to the users. Hence, Tim Berners-Lee proposed an idea of semantic web. With this, it was possible for machines to understand the meaning of the Web content and to satisfy users' requests in a better way. Tim Berners-Lee in 1999 expressed his vision as follows:

> I have a dream for the Web, in which computer becomes capable of analyzing all the data on the Web –the content, links, and transactions between people and computers. A 'semantic web', which should make it possible, has yet to immerge, but when it does the day to day mechanisms of trade, bureaucracy and our daily lives will be handled by machines talking to other machines. The 'intelligent agents' people have touted for ages will finally materialize.

The idea presented by Tim Berners-Lee as stated earlier initiated the second phase of the Web development. In his idea, Tim Berners-Lee mentioned about intelligent agents. These are independent utilities that perform intended tasks with intelligence on behalf of users. This chapter introduces agent theory in brief and presents the idea of agent-based web (ABW) for both web and semantic web. As stated earlier, the Web as well as the semantic web is a consortium of heterogeneous and unstructured pool of content contributed by people. Varieties of independent tasks/facilitates are required to contribute, use, and manage the Web. This chapter highlights the typical tasks for the Web and conceives the Web as a consortium of different agents, in which each agent is doing specified tasks. Furthermore, all these typical agents are fit within a framework of a multiagent system (MAS). This generic structure serves on the standard web and can be applied to any business/domain. An example case of personalized learning and content representation system through a hybrid agent is also discussed here. The chapter also presents list of other possible agents and research ideas.

11.2   Agents

An agent is a computational entity that acts on behalf of its user to perform intended tasks. Functionality of an agent is achieved through software and/or hardware, which is capable to accomplish tasks as its user. An agent generally looks for complete automation of complex processes through artificial intelligence (AI) techniques acting on behalf of its users. For such a problem solving assistance, agents are supposed to have knowledge of target users, environment, and tasks to be carried out. It is observed that the level of knowledge required is directly related to the complexity of the tasks intended for the agents. An agent has characteristics like autonomy, proactivity, and cooperation to carry out its tasks. These characteristics are discussed in Section 11.2.1.

11.2.1   Characteristics and advantages

As agents are required to work on behalf of its users, they must be blessed with the autonomy. For this purpose, they are supposed to possess necessary techniques and enriched with required resources directly or indirectly. Besides user, an agent also has to interact with the environment and other agents. That is, an agent needs to work in cooperation with users and other entities (including other agents) in order to learn and complete their tasks. Such learning and cooperation are driven by a set of techniques, which may be decided from list of objectives or functionalities expected by agents. The agents may have predefined list of goals/tasks. It is also possible for an agent to determine the tasks dynamically if the agent is provided the broad task outlines. Another important characteristic that agents may have is the mobility. Agent may travel in different networks or domains to perform the tasks as data collection, housekeeping, installing some programs, inspection of software and hardware, and perform necessary checks, etc. Furthermore, an agent can be proactive or reactive. Agents that act in response to their environment when they are provoked (triggered) by prespecified events are called reactive agents. Agents that can exhibit goal-oriented behavior by taking initiative are proactive agents. Figure 11.1 represents the architecture and characteristics of agents with brief explanation.

Agents are autonomous, which means that they are independent and make their own decisions. The property of autonomy indicates that agents can operate on their own, because they have internal states and goals. Agents have free will and this influences their behavior.

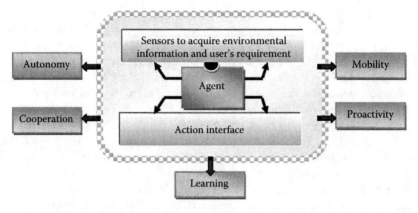

Figure 11.1 Architecture and characteristics of an agent.

They decide on what they do, and with whom they want to cooperate. An autonomous agent interacts with the environment like a human with a specified goal. To clarify the concept of this property, an example considering a cab driver is given here. The cab driver is the agent, with free will and capability to make decisions. Objects are used to give physical descriptions of things in the environment, from which the goal of the agent is to drive to a specified address. To actually get there, the agent has to interact with the environment. Since the cab driver agent is autonomous, it decides by itself how it will achieve the goal.

According to the definition, an agent is situated in an environment. This characteristic can be considered for almost all kinds of software. To distinguish between agents and objects, one possibility is to take a look at the types of environments they are able to handle well. Agents tend to be used when the environment is dynamic, unpredictable, and unreliable. This type of complex environment can change rapidly, and it can be difficult to predict the system's behavior on a case-by-case basis. To illustrate how important the environment is for the performance of an agent, the following definition is suitable (Padgham and Winikoff 2004):

> An autonomous agent is a system situated within and a part of an environment that senses that environment and acts on it, over time, in pursuit of its own agenda and so as to effect what it senses in the future.

This definition illustrates that agents use the environment actively to pursuit their own agenda and to affect their own future. In the example of the cab driver agent, the environment will change each time the agent decides to change direction or stop the cab. The cab driver agent's decisions are based on what it experiences through interaction with the environment.

Since agents can be situated in environments that can change fast and without forewarning, they need to be reactive. Reactivity means that when the agent perceives changes in its environment, it will respond in a timely fashion to these changes. Events represent changes, which the agent must take into consideration when deciding upon a plan of action. The reaction will be in accordance with the current goal of the agent. The taxi driver agent will, for example, change direction if the road is blocked by an obstacle.

An agent is able to pursue persistent goals; it has a goal-directed behavior and is therefore proactive. When an agent senses changes in the environment and handles events, goals are used to reason rationally about what actions to take to achieve a desired system state. Consequently, an agent can make several steps in a sequence of actions to reach different goals. Even if the environment changes or the procedure of reaching one goal fails, the agent will try to find a different way to reach the goal. As already mentioned, the goal of the cab driver is to drive to a specified address. The goal says nothing about where the agent has to drive to get there. The decision is completely made by the agent. The agent will change direction, which means plan for achieving the goal, if unexpected events happen.

Agents have flexible behavior because they can achieve goals in several ways. Agents have different plans they can choose. To reach a goal, an agent chooses a plan to be followed. If the plan fails for some reason, the agent can choose between numbers of other possibilities to get the desired result. In our example, the agent can choose between different directions to get to the address.

To handle complex environments, the agent needs to be robust. Robustness can be described as the ability to persistently pursue goals even if a failure occurs. Robustness is closely related to flexibility because this property helps the agent to recover from failure by giving it the opportunity to pick another plan. The agent will try all other suitable plans until the goal has been achieved or all options are exhausted. In the case of the taxi driver, the agent will find another way if one of the plans fails. Another aspect of robustness is that an agent is able to behave effectively when the environment changes dramatically.

Agents have goal-driven behavior, and to accomplish goals, they sometimes need to collaborate and negotiate with each other. This interaction is described in terms of human interaction types and illustrates what agents are able to do in collaboration with each other. The most common interaction types are teamwork, negotiation, and coordination. Agents can, as an example, perform teamwork if several agents have the same goal. Sometimes, it is also necessary for an agent to negotiate with others to get the right conditions in the environment. Reasoning about goals and conditions, and the ability to contact other agents to achieve a goal, makes agents social. Imagine there are several cab driver agents. To avoid accidents in the traffic, they have to communicate with each other. The cab drivers can also cooperate to serve their customers as fast as possible. When the drivers receive a new address to pick up a customer, the closest agent communicates that he is most suitable for the task.

Different properties and characteristics of agents have now been presented. We will now distinguish between agents and objects, in Section 11.2.2.

11.2.2   Agents and objects

The agents are independent and autonomous in nature. Furthermore, the agents have a generic functionality. These characteristics make agent a reusable entity and increase the scope of its usage. An agent, once attached with a given system, provides necessary functionality on demand. That is, an agent is an independent and reusable object. Obviously, all the objects are not reusable and independent; hence, they are not agents. Furthermore, like agents, objects are not proactive and cannot determine the methods to be executed independently. Agents can learn from environment and can be proactive to execute method, which leads to the specified goal. However, according to the paradigm of object orientation, agents are real-life entities and hence can be thought as objects. That is, all the agents are objects but reverse is not true. Same is true for the expert system. Expert system is an intelligent system that replaces expert in a narrow domain. Expert systems do not use sensory interfaces like agents. Instead, expert systems interact directly with users. Agents can interact with users as well as use sensory interfaces. Similarly, expert systems do not deal with other expert system without human interference. On the other hand, agent can interact with other agents and exhibits sociality. Section 11.3.5 discusses these characteristics in detail. The differences and similarities between agents and objects are given in Table 11.1.

11.2.3   Agents and web services

A web service is defined as software system enabling interoperable interactions between two machines in a network. It has an interface described in a machine-executable format such as web services description language (WSDL). A web service may interact with other system using simple object access protocol (SOAP) messages. According to W3C, there are two major classes of web services, representational state transfer (REST)-compliant web services, in which the primary purpose of the service is to manipulate extensible markup language (XML) representations of web resources using a uniform set of "stateless" operations; and arbitrary web services, in which the service may expose an arbitrary set of operations. Web services are self-contained application components on distributed

Table 11.1 Differences and Similarities between Objects and Agents

Characteristics	Objects	Agents
Differences		
Autonomy	Method invocation	Society interaction
Learning	Programmed	Inference
Cooperation	Restricted thru access modifiers	More cooperative and social
Mobility	No	Yes
Reactivity	Reactive and static	Proactive
Organization	Central	Distributed
Creativity	Liberally created and destroyed	Created in predefined environment and can control their own behavior
Control	With system/program in which they are created	With agents themselves
Execution	Synchronous	Asynchronous and parallel
Similarities		
Both agent technology and object technology use modular programming		
Both have their own internal parameters		
Both can interact with their surrounding elements		
Both uses encapsulation and information hiding		

environment that serves some purpose. Web services can communicate using open protocols such as hypertext transfer protocol (HTTP) with XML-based tools and can be discovered using universal description, discovery, and integration (UDDI). XML provides a language, which can be used between different platforms and programming languages, and still expresses complex messages and functions.

The agents have some similarities with the Web services. To name a few characteristics, we may state that both have their internal parameters. They both offer predefined functionalities, mobility, and reusability. However, there are some major differences between them. Table 11.2 describes important differences between the agents and web services.

Agents are used to solve problems where the resources and knowledge to solve the problem are distributed in nature. Agents solve large and complex problem, allow for the interconnection and interoperation of multiple existing legacy functionalities, and provide features such as modularity, flexibility, and reusability in problem solving. Agents can also solve problems that are beyond the scope of a single methodology or programming paradigms by interacting with other agents.

11.3   Typology of agents

There are different types of agents. Agents are classified according to their reactivity, nature, and role. The popular types are discussed in the following.

11.3.1   Collaborative agent

Agent dedicated for large domain requires multiple functionalities that need to collaborate with each other. Such collaborating entities are developed and used in parallel for better control, faster development, and ease of use. A collaborative agent collaborates with

Table 11.2 Agents and Web Services

Characteristics	Agent	Web service
Cooperation	Agents are cooperative and aware of other agents. Because of this feature, they can provide higher level of services	Web service only knows about itself
Proactive	Agents are proactive and take initiative in order to fulfill the intended goal	Web service can complete the indeed tasks
Customization	Agent customizes itself according to requirement. Agents are more flexible	Web service does not customize itself. Only through programming flexibility can be achieved
Ontology management	Agents can use and reconcile ontologies	Web services, unlike agents, are not designed to use and reconcile ontologies
Communication and social ability	Agents are inherently communicative and social	Web services are not inherently communicative and social
Autonomy	Agents are autonomous	Web services are not autonomous; rather they need to be called
Alerts and updates	Agents can provide alerts and updates	Web services need to be called and execute manually for alerts and updates

different functionalities in order to get acquire with problems, resources, and expertise from distributed platform. This enhances the structuredness and modularity of the system. The collaborative agent also collaborates with other agents in the environment to meet the intended goals. In the case of a collaborative agent, more emphasis is given to autonomy and cooperation of the agent. For example, an agent can be developed for an education society/trust, which takes care of admission, suggests career by examining candidate's aptitude, manages resources of the trust, and facilitates teaching aids such as time table generation, online quiz and interaction, etc. Collaboration with other agents requires explicit means such as agent's communication tools. Examples of such tools are agents communication language (ACL) and knowledge query and manipulation language (KQML). Figure 11.2 presents this scenario as an example of a collaborative agent. In Figure 11.2, a centralized data dictionary is used, which provides handy reference to different functionalities such as query manager, resource manager, communication such as mail and chat, reporting, and interface mechanism.

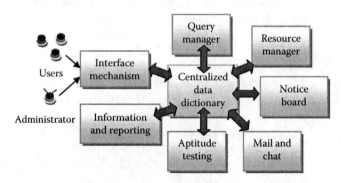

Figure 11.2 Example of a collaborative agent.

11.3.2   Interface agent

Interface agents provide user-friendly environment to work with a highly technical application. It can be considered as a kind of personal assistance that is provided through such agent in helping users to interact with the system. Such agents can enhance their work and become more effective by "knowing" users through user profile and other information provided by users. Unlike collaborative agents, agents of this type do not require specific collaborative means to communicate with other agents. Figure 11.3 illustrates an interface agent. Such interface agents typically consist of local databases, documents, user's data, history, and log files, as well as temporary results.

Interface agent needs to be in thorough contact with users to identify user's goal, need, and requirements. This can be done by constantly observing users, getting feedback and instructions from users, and collaborating with other agents. Personal organizers, interface to the operating system like flavors of the UNIX and Linux, and natural language-based editors can fit in the category of interface agent.

11.3.3   Mobile agent

Mobile agents are also known as traveling agents as these agents shuttle themselves or their code and state to other applications in the network environment such as WWW. The agents may possess strong or weak mobility. Mobile agent is provided list of locations/machines that has to be traversed. This list can be generated dynamically. After loading a machine, a mobile agent performs the indented task, prepares a report, and goes to another destination in the list. Many times such mobile agent travels in a given domain for collecting information and performing repetitive tasks on set of locations. Often the mobile agents used to return back with necessary report and acknowledgement. Mobile agents can be used for tasks such as data collection and monitoring a segment or domain of computer network. Figure 11.4 represents working of a mobile agent. The fact that the agent is mobile reduces the workload on the owner's network. It is possible for the agent to perform the task even if the owner is not connected, and this makes asynchronous computing possible. Since the agents are proactive, they can take the initiative to share information with other agents, which brings up new ways of distributing data.

11.3.4   Information agent

As we know, vast amount of information is available for people due to advances of information and communication technologies. However, the information available has to be checked for its reliability and usability. Furthermore, the information is contributed in a cooperative fashion by common people as well as domain experts, institutes, and

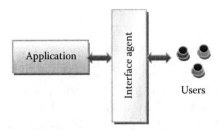

Figure 11.3 An interface agent.

Figure 11.4 Working of a mobile agent.

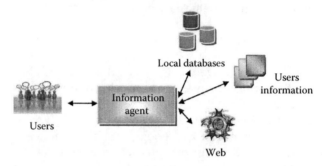

Figure 11.5 Information agent.

authorities such as the government. Such pool of information is not in homogeneous and structured form. There may be multiple different formats representing similar information simultaneously. The bulk of content and method of representation makes the information retrieval and presentation little bit difficult. The information agent helps in finding, retrieving, and presenting information to the users from one or more information resources from distributed environment. Optionally, the information retrieval may support ranking of information, filtering of information, and natural language processing (NLP) utilities. Figure 11.5 presents view of an information agent.

Agents have also been associated with the semantic web. It has been suggested that they can be used to outsource knowledge and make independent decisions about which kind of information is appropriate for the user. These agents require reasoning and learning abilities to efficiently access the needed information. Making it possible for agents to understand semantics of documents is a main task in the development of the semantic web.

11.3.5   Intelligent agent

Agents are expected to act in a cooperative but mutually independent manner and possess intelligent characteristics such as learning. Agents are supposed to "know" objectives of the tasks assigned to them, users, environment as well as other agents. Artificial intelligent techniques help agents in achieving these characteristics. Since intelligent agents are blessed with intelligent techniques, they are able to behave in intelligent fashion. Such

intelligent agent learns multiple objectives, creates a plan for acting, processes the information received, and performs reasoning (e.g., inference, synthesis, and analysis) through AI
techniques. The major components of an intelligent agent are knowledge base, inference
engine, interface to users, and a task manager. The prime source of intelligence is knowledge. The know-how about solving tasks, knowledge tasks, knowledge about users and
environments, knowledge about other agents, etc., are required to carry out the intended
tasks in intelligent way. The knowledge base consists of the knowledge in a variety of different knowledge structures such as semantic net, rules, frames, and scripts. The inference
engine manages the execution, learning, and managing knowledge base. It is considered
as a control program for the knowledge base. The user interface manages input/output
and facilitates interaction with the users of the system. The task manager manages objectives, goal list, and status of the tasks in execution. Since users tend to set the goal and
objectives to the agents dynamically, there is separate component possessing matching
ontology. With the time, an agent may learn to solve new tasks; hence, there is a dynamic
tasks list containing executable tasks list. The controller controls overall framework with
the stored prototype architectural behavior. An intelligent agent also contains a controller
to enable overall control on the performance of the agent. Generic architecture of an intelligent agent is shown in Figure 11.6.

Intelligent agents, also called rational agents, can independently make good decisions
about actions to perform. Progressively, agents become more and more intelligent and
their communication skills become better. Intelligent agents are able to handle knowledge
management, supply chains, and real-world problems.

The advantages offered by AI such as intelligent behavior, explanation and reasoning,
learning, dealing with uncertainty, etc., can also be enchased by agents. That is, an intelligent agent offers dual advantages of intelligence as well as agent technology.

However, agents cannot be compared with the expert system, which is a popular
AI-based tool. An expert system is a tool that works in a given narrow domain in order to
replace an expert's functionalities. An expert system is an independent system that uses
knowledge base, inference engine, self-learning, explanation, and reasoning utilities. They
can be used as colleague, assistance, or cross-verification tool when invoked. They are not
social, autonomous, and cooperative like agents. The key differences between the agents
and experts systems are shown in Table 11.3.

One of the first intelligent agents, Maxim, is an intelligent e-mail agent that operates
on top of the Eudora e-mail system (Maes 1994). This agent relies on a form of learning
known as case-based reasoning. Maxim constantly monitors what the user does and stores
this information as examples. The situations are described in terms of fields and keywords

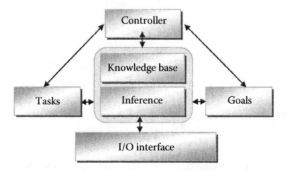

Figure 11.6 An intelligent agent.

Table 11.3 Differences and Similarities between Expert Systems and Agents

Characteristics	Expert systems	Agents
Differences		
Execution environment	No specific platform required	Require agent's execution platform
Behavior	Generally not proactive	Proactive
Interaction	Obtain data through middle man	Obtain data through sensors as well as users
Sociality	Not social	Social
Cooperation	Not cooperative. They do not cooperate with other expert systems	Agents can cooperate with other agents
Mobility	Not mobile and do not survive in other environment	Survive in other environment
Similarities		
Both expert system and agents are able to learn from environment and cases		
Both expert system and agent are cable to exhibit intelligent behavior		

in the message (i.e., the "From," "To," and "Cc" lists and the keywords in the "Subject" field), and the actions are those performed by the user with respect to the message (e.g., the order in which the user reads it, whether the user deleted or stored it, and so on). When a new situation occurs, the agent analyzes its features based on its stored cases and suggests an action to the user (such as read, delete, forward, or archive). The agent measures the confidence, or fit, of a suggested action to a situation. Two levels of confidence are used to determine what the agent actually does with its suggestion. If the confidence is above the "do-it" threshold, the agent automatically executes the suggestion. If the confidence is above the "tell-me" threshold, the agent will offer a suggestion and wait for input from the user.

11.3.6   Hybrid agent

Hybrid agent refers to the agent topology in which two or more agents' philosophies are combined. For example, an agent facilitating effective information searching from large databases by traveling to different locations and providing information as well as acknowledgement in well-designed format is a hybrid agent encompassing methodology of an information agent as well as a mobile agent. Such hybrid agents can be placed at upper level of hierarchy of the agents and hence become application specific.

11.4   Multiagent systems

An MAS is a consortium of multiple agents working together toward a predefined goal. It is a loosely coupled network of problem solver functionalities that work together to find answers of the problems that are beyond the capacity of any individual problem solving entity. If a problem domain is particularly complex, large, or unpredictable, then the only way it can reasonably be addressed is to develop a number of functionally specific and (nearly) modular components (agents) that are specialized at solving a particular problem aspect. The agents in an MAS may not follow homogeneous methodology. However, the agents strictly require common communication means and execution platform. MAS development and usage are easy to carry out in parallel fashion. Hence, development control is better in case of the MAS. The agents in an MAS have low coupling. That is, degree of relationship between the agents is minimum. This increases the opportunity to isolate an agent from the framework of an MAS and test it thoroughly.

11.4.1 Multiagent system framework

The generic framework of an MAS with at least one control agent can be given as shown in Figure 11.7.

The architecture illustrated in Figure 11.7 consists of three layers, namely,

1. Repository layer
2. Domain agent layer
3. Control layer

The repository layer contains databases and links to the Web for managing online resources and information. This layer works as repository of the domain knowledge and other related information. To make the model more generic and reusable, this layer is kept independent of the procedures of domain.

The domain-specific procedures are handled by the immediate layer called domain agent layer. All the tasks supported by the system may not be accessible to all the users. It is required to hide unnecessary details and functionalities from users for transparent and friendly working of the system. Furthermore, locking of the selected functionalities can be easily done, if they are developed as separate agents. Many readymade or external agents can be reused in this system as well as many agents of this system can be reused elsewhere if applicable.

As its name denotes, the control layer controls the overall functionalities of the systems. Since the system has to complete its task autonomously, it needs at least one intelligent (or knowledge-based) agent in it. The control agent in the control layer interacts with other agents of the system as well as repository layer of knowledge base and databases. The control agent plays a key role in managing knowledge base (and optionally databases if needed) as well as facilitates different agent actions and communications. On requirement, middle-agent services and external agents can be included in this layer. The control layer also serves as the meeting place of the agents facilitating communication between agents with the added workspace. For example, if there is a need of interacting with users in their native language, an interface agent with NLP capability may be included in this

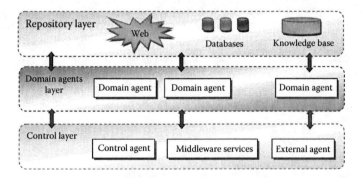

Figure 11.7 Generic framework of a multiagent system.

layer. This layer can be used to manage temporary local documents, registered users' pro-files, and history for effective presentation.

11.4.2   Communication between agents

Agents are cooperative and social. Agents need to interact with environment, users, and other agents to exhibit these characteristics. To talk with other agents, there are several communication means available. Agent communication language (ACL), proposed by the foundation for intelligent physical agents (FIPAs),* is a proposed standard language for agent communications. KQML is another proposed standard. FIPA was originally formed as a Swiss-based organization in 1996 to produce software standard specifications for heterogeneous and interacting agents and agent-based systems. As mentioned, the most popular ACLs are

- ACL by FIPA
- KQML

Both rely on speech act theory developed by Searle[†] in 1960 and enhanced by Winograd[‡] and others in the 1970s. They define a set of performatives (actions) and their meaning (e.g., send). The content of the performative is not standardized, but varies from system to system.

KQML considers each agent with its under-laying virtual knowledge base. The virtual knowledge base can be written in content languages like Knowledge Interchange Format (KIF), resource description framework (RDF), and Semantic Language (SL). The objective of the virtual knowledge base is to provide knowledge transfer from one agent to another agent. With every agent having a virtual knowledge base, agent can query and manipulate the content of each other knowledge bases. KQML basically follows a white box approach in interacting with agents through a collection of messages or performatives such as send, ask, receive, register, etc. These messages/performatives are also extendable for specific application.

11.5   Agent-based web

Though the Web is client–server oriented and MAS is peer-to-peer-oriented approaches, there are some similarities between them. As mentioned earlier, the Web is a world of heterogeneous and loosely coupled consortium of a variety of content and services. Any single methodology alone may not fulfill different tasks of web usage and management. Here, the agent technology serves a lot. For each independent work, an agent may be developed, reposited, and used on demand. Most of the agents are web-enabled entities and survive on the Web. Some examples of such agents are internet agent, web interface agent, and mobile agent. The nature of web communication is also similar to agent col-laboration and execution process. The Web is a distributed platform on which agent can be created, used, and stored. Furthermore, the Web can be explored and used in parallel way such as agents in MAS. Table 11.4 illustrates the similarities between working of the Web and MAS.

* http://www.fipa.org/
† http://ist-socrates.berkeley.edu/~jsearle/
‡ http://hci.stanford.edu/~winograd/

Table 11.4 Similarities between the Web and Agents in MAS

Distributed nature: Both the Web and agents in MAS or other environment are distributed in nature

Reusability of the component: Components available on the Web or agent can be developed once and used many times

Parallel execution of different tasks: Multiple web components (and services) as well as agents can be used in parallel

Loosely coupled network of functionality (web) and tasks (agents): Web components and agents are as independent as possible. This is advisable for parallel working of agents

Requires means and platform to communicate: Web requires Internet and agents require ACE-agent communication environment

Besides this, the Web and agents are beneficial to each other. The Web provides a platform to the agents where they can be created, recited, and accessed. The Web is a medium through which the agents can communicate.

Furthermore, the advanced web concepts such as semantic web require the support of some specific methods such as support from artificial intelligent techniques. Here, a special type of agent known as intelligent agent is useful. The tasks like analysis, learning and understanding, explanation and justification, etc., can be facilitated by such intelligent agents. Considering the similarities between the Web and MAS, a generic architecture of Agent Based Web (ABW) is proposed in Section 11.5.1.

11.5.1   Generic architecture of agent-based web

The Web is built with contribution by people utilizing on technologies that provide platform (such as Internet) for the pool of contributed content and facilities to upload, share, and use the content globally. Besides these, there are standards, protocols, and generic facilitates such as search engine and browsers help in smoothing the task of the Web. This has been discussed in Chapter 1. Also, semantic web, as discussed in Chapter 2, has different components and facility such as ontology, signature, encryption, unicode/uniform resource identifier (URI) management, and namespace. Figure 11.8 shows the Web and semantic web components as discussed in Chapter 2.

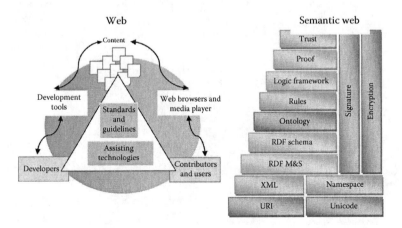

Figure 11.8 Web and semantic web components.

Both the ordinary web and semantic web have reusable and independent components and functionalities. For example, URI and address management are available with the Web and the semantic web. Similarly, protocols, standards, and development tools are required for both the Web. Some generic user-oriented functionalities such as search engine, browser, and tools to edit, share, and upload contributions from common person to experts, etc., are required to work with both the Web. The Web (as well as the semantic web) can be conceived as consortium of multiple agents that work in parallel to carry out routine activities on the Web. That is, to facilitate parallel development of different components of web and their better management, various reusable agents can be designed. Agents provide lot of benefits to the Web at different levels as discussed earlier. Some of the advantages of utilizing agent technology for web (either ordinary or semantic) are summarized as follows:

- The development of the Web components can be done in parallel fashion.
- Access rights of some models are provided to selected users only and hence to hide unnecessary models from user to create simple and transparent working. Also security of the system will be enhanced.
- Any agent can be isolated from the Web, tested, and repaired if necessary without having much impact of working of the Web. This increases the reliability of the Web.
- Agents developed for the Web are reusable on similar distributed environment. This increases the cost benefit ratio, etc.

The general architecture of ABW is illustrated in Figure 11.9. The architecture consists of Internet and the Web as its enabling components. It also consists of a layer of core services such as ontology tools, one or more search engines, and query tools. These tools and facilities are ubiquitous and regardless of any application they are used everywhere. Furthermore, the application-specific agents are placed at advanced layer called

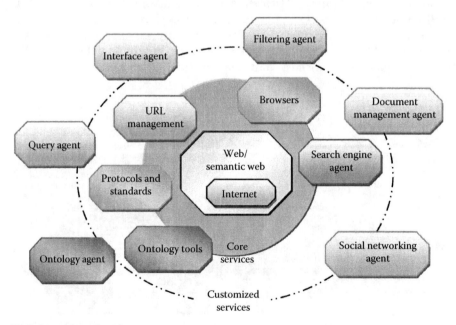

Figure 11.9 Agent-based web.

customized services. The examples can be an interface in a given native language for a target audience, information filtering and reporting agent, document management systems, and social networking agents.

11.5.2 Example agents

Some example agents shown in Figure 11.9 are discussed in this section. These agents are generic and described in very abstract fashion so as to customize on need and fit into a variety of applications based on the Web.

11.5.2.1 Agent for query and information retrieval

Many times information is to be fetched from network environment including intranet and Internet. Though it is simple, it is difficult for noncomputer professionals to write formal query and code for the same. Users may enjoy the utility of an agent that generates query for the selected fields and prints the report for view, print, or sent to a remote location. The agent may have support from predefined query templates or readymade sample queries. Besides the typical information retrieval, information extraction and even information analysis can be done with the help of dedicated intelligent agents. Figure 11.10 represents a generic structure of an information retrieval agent. According to Figure 11.10, client approaches the agent through browser. The agent consists of query manager, search mechanism, visualization for query results and reports, etc. Through these functionalities, knowledge base, domain databases, and other documents are accessed. These resources may be available on distributed resources.

11.5.2.2 Filtering agent

This agent provides a facility similar to the information retrieval. Required information can be found, filtered from the huge source such as Internet, and presented to the users in attractive and meaningful format. This can be applied to all multimedia information. Besides text, images, videos, sounds, and animation/movie files are retrieved by such agent. Once the necessary content is retrieved, it undergoes filtering process in order to

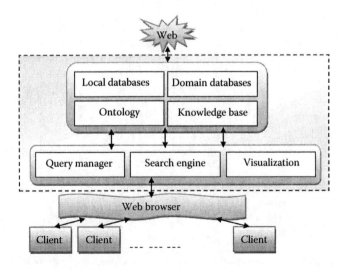

Figure 11.10 Information retrieval agent.

remove noise, errors, and viruses if any. Required information is filtered from the cleaned cluster of the content. Filtering process can be advanced with the help of an intelligent agent that uses users' profiles. The users' profiles contain users' basic information, type of job, purpose/usage of required information, etc., in their own fashion and might be helpful to identify the information in which they are interested. A detailed discussion on a hybrid agent is given in Section 11.6, which uses user profiles for decision making.

11.5.2.3   *Interface agent*

The work of information retrieval, extraction, filtering, and analysis can be further strengthened by putting suitable interface to increase ease of use and user friendliness of an agent. As many information and communication technology (ICT) utilities are meant for noncomputer professionals, adding facilities of interacting in their native style (or native language) can enhance effectiveness of the system. An interface agent may use fuzzy logic to take advantages of linguistic parameters in vague form and reasoning capability. Furthermore, an interface agent may use the existing databases and files generated through the automations of the transaction in the business. These logs are mined using an interface agent for some meaningful objectives.

11.5.2.4   *Personal assistance agent*

The personal assistance agent helps user to carry out tasks such as acquisition, reporting and information presentation, managing resources, maintaining, approving, and related documentation. The personal assistance agent is needed to be customized according to the user's environment. This is done through user profile that stores information such as basic personal information such as name, address, birth date, job profile, and duties assigned to the user. With the help of user's profile, services and information will be provided so that the user may not be troubled with unnecessary services and information. To automatically carry out such user-specific filtering, the content and services are marked with predefined user categories. At the time of creation of user profiles, the user category information can be added. Such a category may be simple such as the following: "*Student*," "*Teacher*," "*Employee*," "*Bank*," "*EB001*" (entrepreneur of business type 1), etc. Figure 11.11 shows the typical architecture of Agent Based System showing personal

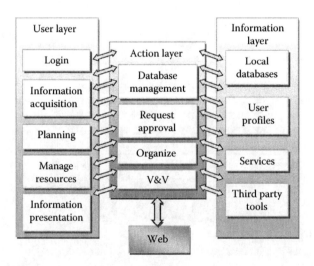

Figure 11.11 Agent based system for personal assistance.

assistance agent with other functionalities. The architecture consists of three layers, namely, (i) user layer, (ii) action layer, and (iii) information layer. The user interacts with the system through the user layer. A log-in functionality allows users to log in the system and assigns appropriate rights. The basic information from the user-id acquired through information acquisition module and necessary results are presented to the user through information presentation module. Occasionally, the planning and resource management alternatives are presented to the user, and preferences are collected from the user. Action layer manages the databases, user profiles, and call for services and approves requests according to the plan. The cross-verification of planes and meeting is also done here. The information layer works as repository of the information with copy of third party tools and services, if required.

11.5.2.5 e-Commerce agent

The field of e-Commerce deals with buying and selling of products or services over electronic systems such as the Internet and other computer networks. To carry out this task, there is a need of market information, buyers' information, sellers' information, and products' information. Users' information and choices are also needed to guide presenting items for shopping, guiding shopping process, and enabling the money matters and other transactions such as compare prices. To facilitate this, an e-commerce agent that provides these functionalities can be developed. Figure 11.12 shows general architecture of an e-commerce agent.

11.5.2.6 e-Communities and agents

e-Communities are virtual locations on the Internet, where people with common interests gather to share knowledge and experiences. The communities can store a large amount of information and data, and members of the community have the possibility to collaborate and interact through questions. Systems that support virtual communities have functionality that facilitates communication and discussion between people all around the world. Agent-based systems have been developed to support communities because they can handle huge amounts of resources. They can also maintain the virtual environment to meet the requirements of the community members.

A division of British Telecommunications, BTexact, has developed an MAS called Intelligent Distributed Information Management System (IDIoMS) to support e-communities (Simon et al. 2001). The motivation for the development was the need for intelligent information services. BTexact wanted to develop e-communities that

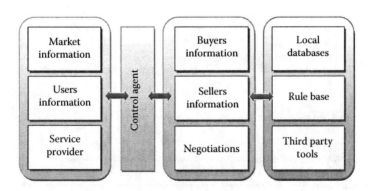

Figure 11.12 Agent based system for e-commerce business.

maximized the information benefits to the members. They wanted the members to have access to all the information they desired without feeling overloaded. BTexact also wanted the system to promote member interaction and maintain community involvement. To create a community feeling, the system should support functionality to connect members with same interests. IDIoMS consists of collaborating agents with different roles. The agents provide data sharing, personalized services, and knowledge dissemination. In addition, the agents maintain user privacy and promote interaction between the members of the community.

11.5.2.7 Ontology management

Content on the Web cannot be analyzed and understood by machine unless it is written in an ontology that machine understands. Ontology is a tool that enables semantic analysis of the content on the Web and helps in the evolution of the semantic web. The Web or semantic web contains a lot of information in a variety of ontologies. The tasks involved in the management of ontology include defining ontology, analyzing ontology, mapping one ontology into another in order to automatically convert content written in one ontology to another, and extending and/or integrating ontologies. For each task, a separate subagent/ functionality is provided. Figure 11.13 illustrates the design of such multiagent functionalities for ontology management.

Agent-based technology has wide scope and high degree of applicability in various domains. Some other example agents can be given as follows:

- Agent for semantic analysis
- Verification and validation (V&V) agent
- Finding suitable web services agent
- Crawler agent
- Explanation and reasoning agent
- Natural language interface agent
- Communication agent
- Network traffic management agent, etc.

It is possible to hybrid two or more agents' methodology for application that uses multiple diverse functionalities. The following section presents the design of a hybrid agent to achieve two diverse functionalities such as mobility and user interface.

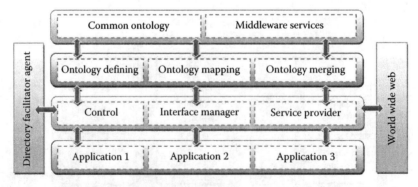

Figure 11.13 Multiagent system for ontology management.

11.6 Hybridization of mobile agent and interface agent: A case for personalized content representation

11.6.1 Mobile agents: Characteristics and working

Mobile agent has an ability to cooperate with heterogeneous network environment. There are specific predefined techniques to impart mobility to an agent. As a result, the agent behaves only in predefined way. To impart other features besides mobility that helps in interfacing the destination network to complete the intended job, a mobile agent needs to be incorporated with additional functionalities. One of such functionalities is the ability to access local user profiles, preferences, and other resources as well as other local agents to present information in user's context. To meet this demand, hybridization of mobile and interface agent that facilitates development of customized application is discussed in this example (Sajja 2011).

A mobile agent is often described as software that can travel from machine to machine in a heterogeneous network. Harrison et al. (1995) highlighted some desirable characteristics of mobile agents:

Efficiency: If an agent can move across networks to the location where resources reside, then network traffic can be reduced since the agent can preprocess data and decide the most important information to be transferred.

Persistence: Once a mobile agent is launched, the agent should not depend on the system that launched it and should not be affected if that system fails. Furthermore, a mobile agent does not require continuous network connectivity.

Peer-to-peer communication: As stated earlier, a limitation of the client–server paradigm is the inability of servers to communicate with other servers. Mobile agents are considered to be peer entities and, hence can adapt the most appropriate action according to the needs of users.

Fault tolerance: In a client-server relationship, the state of the transaction is generally spread over the client and the server. Loss of the connectivity during a request causes problem. However, since mobile agents do not need to maintain permanent connections and their state is centralized within themselves, failures are generally easier to deal with.

Besides the aforementioned characteristics, a mobile agent is equipped with methods of security, authentication, validation, and other restrictions that exist within domains. The major mobile interactions are as follows:

1. *Selection of domain where agent can migrate*: The mobile agent can then use the list of all possible domains to determine an application domain. This can be done by checking the domains that offer a set of information resources which are compatible with its own goal set. The list can be prepared dynamically.
2. *Authentication of mobile agent*: Mobile agents are authenticated by an electronic signature that they carry. This signature may be encrypted for the additional security. To avoid encrypting and passing keys all the times, a heuristic approach can be considered for the same. For example, one possible heuristic (practical idea) is to use predetermined password string between a given pair of sender and receiver. This fix string is used to encrypt documents every time when there is need of communication between these parties. At the receiving end, the string can be used in conjunction with the transaction type and date. This eliminates the use of sending password every time.

3. *Nonreliance on the host domain*: As stated earlier, the mobile agents possess the characteristic of persistence and do not reliant on the host domain that launched them. Because of this virtue, continuous connectivity from host domain to the application domain is not required.
4. *Cooperation*: Mobile agent needs to communicate with other local agents or third party software/services to complete the intended tasks and to satisfy the requirement of local and environmental information of the other domains.
5. *Interaction*: To transmit the results and messages and to control the actions of a mobile agent, frequent interaction and reporting mechanism to the host domain/users need to be guaranteed.

The mobility of a mobile agent can be achieved through three different aspects such passing code or passing whole agent with the status. Mobile code mechanism deals with the extraction of software from remote systems and transferring the software across a network in order to execute the software on a local system without explicit installation by the recipient. Examples of mobile code include scripts (JavaScript, VBScript), Java applets, ActiveX controls, flash animations, shockwave movies (and Xtras), and macros embedded within office documents. Mobile agents are autonomous and independent entities embedding task and other instructions to move in various heterogeneous networks. On request, any network may demand the facility of an agent. For a valid request of an agent's utility, a ticket is generated and a copy of an agent with ticket is sent to the guest network. The ticket contains password string in encrypted form, destination information, and optional tasks list to be executed on remote network. The guest network authenticates the data and allows agent to work in its environment. The network connectivity is required only to pass the request for an agent and to pass a copy of agent and appropriate ticket. After that the connectivity can be broken. There may be multiple requests from different networks for a common facilities/agent.

11.6.2   Hybridization of a mobile agent with an interface agent

As stated earlier, the mobile agent has a virtue or mobility but cannot exhibit the virtue of interacting in friendly fashion with the network it traverses. To effectively deal with the hosting environment where the mobile agent travels to and performs, there is a need to identify the users' interests and preferences. If the agent is context aware and possess some information about the environment and users, anticipation and predication of users need can be done effectively. "Knowing" the users always increases the ease of operation and increases quality of deliverables to the users. The task of interface agent is similar to these. Hybridizing this virtue of an interface agent with the mobile agent serves the purpose of mobility as well as friendly user interactions. By taking advantage of such contextual data, hybridization of mobile and interface agents can proactively travel, search, filter, and present information, which is not only relevant, but also useful to the user current activities and goals.

Typically, an interface agent hybridized with a mobile agent performs the following tasks:

- It launches mobile agents on behalf of the user and keeps track for agent's execution progress and position.
- It facilitates and controls (authenticates) communication with agents. This includes reorganization of agents output in suitable format for users, retrieval, filtering of information, etc.

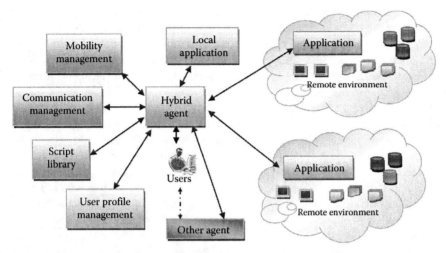

Figure 11.14   Hybrid mobile and interface agent.

- It supports security and failure management at local level.
- It maintains history/log of the execution.

The hybrid agent's structure is shown in Figure 11.14. The hybrid agent described here has functionalities that facilitate mobility as well as communications between agents and users. The mobility can be managed through set of tickets containing list of destinations and tasks to be executed at remote network along with the authentication information. A ticket is generated with the encrypted authentication and sent to the destination along with the keys for decryption. Once ticket is approved by the destination, either the code of agent or the full agent with its execution status is passed to the destination.

   To know the user and satisfy their requirements at best, registered users' profiles are maintained by user profile module. The user profile includes basic information regarding users such as name, location, type of job, etc., as well as dynamic information such as purpose of surfing, pages visited so far, etc. The objective of maintaining such user profile is to increase the degree of customization. A sample profile (Sajja 2010) file containing user profile information structure is given in the following:

```
< profile class="user_profile">
    <user_name = "myname"/>
    <user_age = "myage"/>
    <user_jobtype = "myjobtype"/>
    <user_mail = "mymail" />
    <user_purpose = "mypurpose"/>
    ...
    ...
</profile>
```

The user profile is compared with the agent information as a final verification. It also helps in managing history and temporary results. The stored user profile helps in predicting users' requirements early and presents the content in more effective form.

   Along with such user profile, an indicator matrix can be designed. The indicator list is manually set by checking different categories of documents by administrator for a group of users. The indicator set enlists typical interest and preferences of a group such as purpose of surfing/using the system (research, teaching, learning, problem solving, etc.), level information needed (highly technical, conceptual, mixed, etc.), and media preference (type of document such as text, code, video, etc.). Some of these indicators like research interests and level of information needed are approximate and do not represent rigid range/values. Hence, they are bit vague or fuzzy. Other indicators like media preference are static values directly obtained from users group. With the help of user profile and indicator matrix, the hybrid agent finds appropriate information to be presented to the users. There may be some fuzzy rules designed to match these user's requirements with the indicator matrix and user profile. Agent uses these rules to determine a set of candidate recommendation and suggests appropriate content. For this, the agent performs a small search on the repositories of the documents. Two mechanisms are possible to avoid such frequent searches. The first one is to consider the count of usage (showing how many times the document is referred) and index the comment master according to the usage count. Another mechanism is to manage a log having details as document identification, date of use, beginning time, end time, etc.

Component called communication management manages the interface activities such as input/output queuing, parsing, querying, and presenting information in desired format. The script library contains necessary codes and tasks to be executed by the agent.

11.6.3   *Personalized content representation through the hybrid agent*

Rapid growth of ICT and emergence of knowledge era have increased the quality and scope of education. Different models of teaching and education such as classroom technology and distance learning having their own pros and cons are in use. ICT has great potential as a support tool for learning. Such tools may provide the possibility of affordable, individualized learning environments. The ideal situation is a learning model, which can be considered as a clever teacher that able to communicate knowledge to individual learner in customized fashion. It is observed that most of the e-Learners are adults either working or professionals in related domain. The younger ones looking for parallel learning opt for such learning with their main stream learning for technical enhancement to meet their career objectives. Above this, the paradigm shift from formal graduation to lifelong learning is also observed. Learners' basic requirement is content (domain knowledge) that makes them to learn some fruitful knowledge. First important thing that determines the credibility of such system is the domain knowledge and content offered by the system. However, the domain knowledge represented in the system cannot be utilized in its full extent if the delivery and timely services are not accompanied with the system. The timely presentation of suitable knowledge; useful services like presentation of material with concepts and examples; questions and answers; practical hints for problem solving; help and interface for interaction; validation of input; facility to back up, copy, and document play an important role in increasing scope and acceptability of the system. All learner needs can be summarized in three components, namely, quality domain knowledge, efficient location-independent delivery on request, and efficient representation.

Personalized learning (p-Learning) can be considered as a hybrid model of education reform, which has the following common themes:

- Learners are given prime importance
- ICT is utilized as a key enabler
- Anytime, anywhere, and lifelong learning
- Ease of usage, documentation, and collaboration of communities

Major objectives of the system are as follows:

- The system should support multiple functionalities for different user groups like administrator, learners, and instructors. These functionalities include storage, retrieval, filtering, and presentation of learning material in reusable form.
- The system should support presentation of material considering user access rights and contents such as purpose of the use, media type required, habit, history of the users, etc.
- Different functionalities of the system need to be developed as autonomous and reusable on distributed platform. Some of the functionalities (such as presenting learning content according to user's context) need mobility and friendly interface with the help of fuzzy linguistic variable.
- The system architecture should be generic so as to utilize for other domains using infrastructure such as mobile and personal computers.

Considering the aforementioned objectives and need, the hybrid agent discussed in Section 11.6.2 can be utilized to implement the p-learning system. The general architecture of the system is given in Figure 11.15.

Considering the dependencies of different functionalities, the architecture is divided into three basic tiers, namely, resource tier, service tier, and application tier. Such partitions are logical and required to group and support agents exhibiting common functionalities. For example, the firewall management, antivirus patches, and other third party software as well as middleware services are not part of system and can be changed according to the need and availability of the services. These services are generic, reusable, independent, and may be readymade. The source of these services is different than the local environmental data. Hence, these facilities and agents are kept in separate layer. Similarly, the location-based data and user profiles are different and vary at every location. These location-dependent functionalities should be grouped in different layers. The agents that contribute to domain knowledge acquisition and general problem solving strategies should be kept in separate tier. With this information in mind, it is decided to divide the system architecture into three layers, namely, resource tier, service tier, and application tier. The

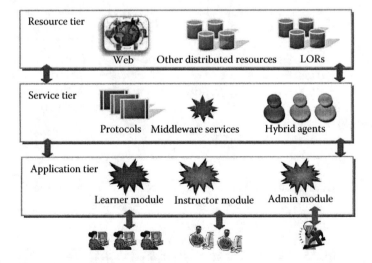

Figure 11.15 Architecture of p-Learning system.

resource tier consists of databases on the Web, local data and information, and mainly a learning object repository (LOR). An LOR is collection of different reusable components of independent items, called learning objects, used for learning a given course. Learning objects are small independent digital resources that can be combined, shared, and reused in different educational contexts. Optionally, an LOR may contain path/reference to the learning objects instead of the object themselves if objects are not available at single place. These LORs can be prepared from physical courses available in the area. For different regions and courses, separate reusable repositories are designed and used at the resources tier. The service tier contains protocols and middleware services along with one or more hybrid agents discussed so far according to the purpose. Institutional firewall and learning object metadata standards with the typical network protocol work here. The agents are kept at this layer as they are thought as independent reusable generic services that used to travel from this layer to application layer to accomplish their intended job. The application tier consists of different modules such as learner module, instructor module, and administrator module. The mobile agent defined into the service tier travels into appropriate module to present content according to the requirement.

The discussed p-learning system promises to provide a learning experience that accommodates the two distinct learning styles of classroom learners and distance learners in most sophisticated and personalized fashion. Such system reduces the cost of execution and maintenance once developed and implemented. Instructor-led courses are clumsy and costly as they require time and infrastructure. The reduced cost of globally publishing material, assisting users worldwide in personal way, and efficient distribution accelerates the development and use of such p-learning system. The p-learning system also offers individualized instruction and assistance that print media cannot provide. By using personalized learning style, p-learning can target individual learning preferences and hence, increases the scope and effectiveness of the system. Additionally, p-learning system offers independent self-learning. Advanced learners are allowed to speed through or bypass instructions that are redundant according to their style and preferences. The number of beneficiaries is conceptually unlimited as per the design of the system. However, such p-learning system may be restricted to limited number of registered users on a local environment.

The p-learning systems are suitable for majority of courses like technology (programming languages, tools practice, etc.), arts topics (like literature and history), and commercial (tax saving advises, investment, etc.). The advances of ICT enable the developer to create a virtual classroom/laboratory where training/experiment can be carried out through a simulated environment.

Commercialization of p-learning framework is possible. With empty course files and user profiles, architecture along with different agents can be prepared. This can be called as p-learning shell. To store and update course and other information in this shell, there is a need of interactive editor that enables noncomputer professionals to easily update the "knowledge base" of the shell.

11.7   Case study

In this section, we will present four cases of advanced agent-based systems.

11.7.1   Multiagent system for oil company

Decision support-integrated operations can be used to support operators at plants. By getting the right information to the right people in right time, people involved can come to a good decision faster. Imagine there is defect pump on one of the platforms of an oil company. One of the operators has not enough information to solve the problem. He needs support to make the right decision. He knows that it is only a few couple of people who have expertise about the pump. By using mobile equipment, he can transfer information, like pictures of the pump, to an expert team. The members of the team can be situated all over the world. Integrated operations provide the needed information and gather the team in a virtual environment. The expert team can discuss how to solve the problem and give the operator essential support by using the received information combined with manuals of the pump.

In this scenario, MASs could be used to predetermine when the pump needed to be changed. They could continuously receive data from the pump during operation. Some of the agents in the system could then have analyzed the incoming data, and when the pump started to show signs of wear out failure, the MAS could inform the operator that the pump had to be changed. To avoid disruption of operation, the MAS could suggest for the operator an appropriate time to change the pump. The agents could base their suggestions on production and delivery information. To make a decision, information from different sources need to be handled and analyzed. Some of the agents in the system could have been information seekers. These agents could have cooperated with analysis agents to find the right information. Together, they could have served as a link between humans and the rest of the system. If the failure of the pump was emergent, and there was a need for an expert team, the agents could have been used to search for people with needed skills. The team could also have been composed by both agents and humans. The agent–team could have cooperated and handled the information from the operator and other agents, to find the best solution. Agents with different roles in the system could meanwhile investigate the options for getting a new pump and decide how it could be delivered in accordance with other events. The MAS makes it possible to prepare the operator about the situation and gather appropriate knowledge for decision making. By using the MASs, possible disruption of operation can be avoided. The operator is able to act proactively instead of reactively. Handling of unexpected critical situations–integrated operations are about working faster and better. This applies to both normal and irregular situations. In critical situations, time plays an important role.

11.7.2 *RETSINA calendar agent*

Next case deals with a calendar agent, which works symbiotically with Microsoft's Outlook 2000 and the semantic web (Payne 2002). The *RETSINA Calendar Agent (RCAL)* is a distributed meeting scheduling agent that can navigate semantic web content to collect and reason about events. For an agent to act as a convenient meeting scheduling assistant, it should be able to automatically schedule meetings that are suitable for its user, without continually requesting extra information. To achieve this, the agent maintains an up-to-date model of the user's current activities. RCAL improves this dependency by automating the acquisition of schedules from the Web and other heterogeneous agents. RCAL works synergistically with a commercial personal information manager (PIM). It retrieves appointments and contact details from the PIM and uses these to reason about available meeting slots. It can also negotiate with other RCAL agents to determine mutually available time slots for meeting requests. This approach, based on the contract net protocol (Smith 1980), seeks meeting times from every agents involved, and evaluates the responding bids to conclude a suitable meeting time, which is then transmitted back to the other agents. Schedules and contact details found on the semantic web can also be imported into the PIM via the semantic web schedule browser [e.g., the user specifies a uniform resource locator (URL) of a conference program and then selects specific talks to attend at a conference], or by automatically obtaining and importing new schedules shared by a community of agents (e.g., receiving seminar notifications, etc.). Concepts defined by the iCal ontology are used to mark up the schedule illustrated in the following schedule on the semantic web containing two calendar events. The Dublin Core ontology is also used to provide metadata about the schedule, such as title, description, and author. This schedule illustrates how information can be distributed across different documents, and how concepts can be reused.

```
<foaf:Person rdf:ID="tomwood">
<foaf:name>Tom Wood</foaf:name>
<foaf:mbox rdf:resource="mailto:twood@npl.no"/>
<foaf:workplaceHomepage rdf:resource="http://www.npl.no/~twood"/>
<foaa:RCalendarAgentName>tom_ieee.org-CalAgent</foaa:RCalendarAgentName>
</foaf:Person>
<ical:VCALENDAR rdf:id="WIMS12">
<dc:title>Web Intelligence, Mining and Semantics 2012</dc:title>
<dc:contributor rdf:resource="#tomwood"/>
<dc:date>2012-06-13</dc:date>
<ical:VEVENT-PROP
rdf:resource=" http://www.ucv.no/Wims12.rdf#PainInNEC"/>
<ical:VEVENT-PROP>
<ical:VEVENT rdf:id="IndustrialKeynote">
<ical:DTSTART>
<ical:DATE-TIME><rdf:value>20120615T145000</rdf:value></ical:DATE-TIME>
</ical:DTSTART>
<ical:DTEND>
<ical:DATE-TIME><rdf:value>20120615T150000</rdf:value></ical:DATE-TIME>
</ical:DTEND>
<ical:LOCATION rdf:resource="#HPlaza"/>
<ical:ATTENDEE rdf:resource="http://www.npl.no/people.rdf#ks"/>
<ical:ATTENDEE rdf:resource="http://www.npl.no/people.rdf#yn"/>
<ical:DESCRIPTION>Presentation: keynote</ical:DESCRIPTION>
</ical:VEVENT>
</ical:VEVENT-PROP>
</ical:VCALENDAR>
```

It contains two events (via the property VEVENT-PROP). The first event is referenced by the resource "http://www.ucv.no/Wims12.rdf#PainInNEC", whereas the second, "IndustrialKeynote", is defined within the document itself. In addition, the location of the event (i.e., the Conference Hall, Hotel Plaza) is also defined in a different place. As concepts are often referenced by a resource URI, they may also include other information that may be of use to the user. If these properties are known to RCAL, then additional services are offered to the user when the user selects a concept. These properties can also be used to query service providers (i.e., other agents) via a discovery infrastructure. RCAL constructs request for services based on the properties of the selected concept and return a URL of a web page that can then be presented to the user. For instance, the LOCATION property refers to a Gene Expression Omnibus (GEO) concept, HPlaza, which includes properties describing the latitude and longitude of the Conference Hall at Hotel Plaza. These requests can then be submitted to a middle-agent, which returns the advertisements for the matching services. These services can also be offered to the user; if the user selects a service, a query can then be sent to the selected service and the results displayed.

11.7.2.1 OpenStudy.com

OpenStudy is a large-scale open social learning community (SLC) that promotes effective social presence, cognitive presence, and teaching presence online through state-of-the-art Web 2.0 technologies. OpenStudy is built on top of an open source framework called, Lift.* It does a lot of the heavy lifting for OpenStudy. It also uses an actor framework from the Akka[†] open source project.

In this system, there is collaboration among geographically distributed users. As given in Figure 11.16, the parallelism and collaboration are implemented using the actors in the Akka distributed framework model. The Akka framework runs on Amazon EC2 cloud. Actors (Java) provide the following:

- Simple and high-level abstractions for concurrency and parallelism
- Asynchronous, nonblocking, and highly performant event-driven programming model
- Very lightweight event-driven processes (create ~6.5 million actors on 4 GB RAM)

In OpenStudy.com, an actor per topic for a study group and an actor per user are defined. OpenStudy's key features are focused on providing this interaction: who is online, ask question, join discussion, study together, thank a user for help, and "real-time" chat.

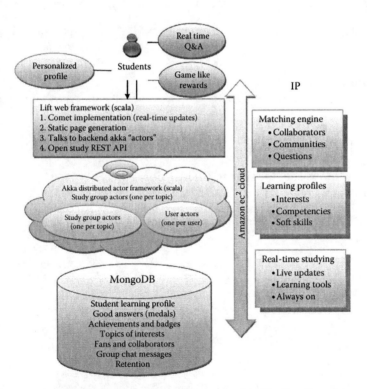

Figure 11.16 Parallelism and collaboration amongst geographically distributed users.

---

* http://liftweb.net/
† http://akka.io/

11.7.2.2   Cobot

Collaborative social search involves different ways for active involvement in search-related activities such as use of social network for search, use of expertise networks, involving social data mining, or crowd-sourcing to improve the search process (Sahay and Ram 2010). The search agents perform multiple tasks of finding relevant information and connecting the users together; participants provide feedback to the system during the conversations that allow the agent to provide better recommendation temporally in the conversation.

Cobot is an information agent with memory, categorization, and learning modules to remember, understand, and improve recommendations over time for the user. The system architecture for Cobot is given in Figure 11.17.

- Different conversation facets (topic, message, asker, presence, and time of asking) should have different metrics for comparison to provide for search criteria beyond query relevance
- Ability to reformulate relevant queries from conversational sentences and paragraphs
- Ability to understand the progression of conversation context to determine suitable interference points
- Critique-based feedback in search results (e.g., ability to like different facets) to support personalization of results
- Support for quick access to past conversations (ability to re-find information)

In Text Analysis and Processing Engine (TAPE), The agent's task is to use the submodules for extracting meaningful queries from conversations, classifying messages into relevant categories, and calling the right combination of algorithms for retrieving candidate recommendations.

Following features are defined for the message classification problem while generating message labels:

- Position of the message thread
- Length of message
- Number of responses of the user for that forum
- Emotive features (vector of words and testing for binary presence)
- Question words (vector of words and testing for binary presence)
- Previously responded in the forum or not

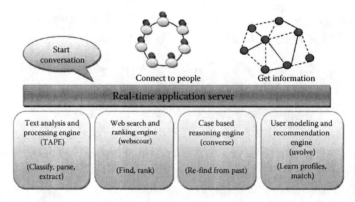

Figure 11.17 System architecture of COBOT.

- Number of previous responses
- Response time windows
- Words in the thread (high information gain 5950 words vector from the corpus)

Eventually, *Cobot* provides three types of recommendations. It recommends and notifies relevant people who may be interested in joining conversations. It provides topic-specific web recommendations, and it also suggests past similar conversations from the system.

11.8   Conclusion

Agents have great potential for design and engineering web applications. Since web supports a variety of businesses in all fields, multiple functionalities can be conceived in the form of independent and reusable agents. In other words, the Web can be thought as loosely coupled network of independent functionalities that can be developed and used in parallel. With such modular approach, the security can be enhanced by providing access rights or tickets to the appropriate agents. Also, the Web becomes more transparent as all the functionality might not be available to all. The core services and application services are kept separate, which aids better control and management of web-based systems. Besides the development of such agents, necessary protocols are also to be designed and developed.

Some of the business applications of software agents have raised a number of issues about personal privacy. Suppose a software agent recommends new iPods to a customer. To do this, the agent builds a personal profile of the customer, collecting demographic information and information about the types of music the customer likes and the iPods that she has purchased in the past. Derived from this information, the agent compares the customer's profile with the profiles of others. It then generates recommendations by finding the profiles of people like that customer and seeing what they have purchased but that this customer has not. Intelligent agents of all types are not only accessible to consumers' personal profiles, but also to their personal actions. An agent has the potential of knowing where a user has been and where the user is likely to go. Providentially, commercial suppliers of agent technology are nowadays aware of the privacy issues. For instance, Firefly, which was one of the early companies that tried to bring "recommendation" agents to the Web (now part of Microsoft's Passport system), proposed a series of standards such as P3P (the platform for privacy preferences), which makes individual control and informed consent the key operating principles of software agents.

Agents can be used to outsource knowledge from the semantic web. They can use their reasoning abilities to extend and enhance their knowledge bases. In a mature semantic web, agents can be used to decide, which resources are reliable and relevant. Agents can build societies to share experiences and knowledge. The society will be build upon trust and understanding. Agents in the society need to understand the knowledge obtain from other agents. Trust indicates which of the agents are known for using reliable sources. The standards are continuously being considered by the W3C (w3c.org) and by the Web community at large. Only time will tell how valuable these standards will be.

Exercises

11.1   Choose a domain that you are familiar with, and write a Percepts, Actions, Goals, Environment (PAGE) description of an agent for the environment. Characterize the environment as being accessible, deterministic, episodic, static, and continuous or not. What agent architecture is best for this domain?

11.2 (Project) Design and implement different agents with internal state. Measure their performance. How close do they come to the ideal agent for this environment?

11.3 Explore various characteristics of learning (i.e., intelligent) agents.

11.4 Use Internet to find various standards for software agents. Are such standards needed for improving communication, collaboration, and use? Justify your answer.

11.5 Once you have visited an online bookstore, the store keeps track of what you have viewed and purchased and uses the data as a basis for recommending new items for your consideration. Intelligent agents that provide such services are called recommendation systems. There are two key functions of such systems: profile generation and maintenance, and profile exploitation and recommendation. Investigate examples of intelligent agents that provide these recommendation services.

11.6 Write a short note on multiagent negotiation in e-commerce.

References

Harrison, C. G., Chess, D. M., and Kershenbaum, A. 1995. Mobile agents: Are they a good idea? IBM Research Report, IBM Research Division, Yorktown Heights, NY.

Maes, P. 1994. Agents that reduce work and information overload. *Communications of the ACM* 37(7):31–40.

Padgham, L. and Winikoff, M. 2004. *Developing Intelligent Agent Systems: A Practical Guide.* Chichester, U.K.: John Wiley & Sons.

Payne, T. R., Singh, R., and Sycara, K. 2002. RCAL: A case study on semantic web agents. Paper presented at the *First International Conference on Autonomous Agents and Multiagent Systems,* New York.

Sahay, S. and Ram, A. 2010. Conversational framework for web search and recommendations. Paper presented at the *Workshop on Reasoning from Experiences on the Web (WebCBR-10),* Alessandria, Italy.

Sajja, P. S. 2010. Multiagent knowledge-based system accessing distributed resources on knowledge grid. In *Knowledge Discovery Practices and Emerging Applications of Data Mining: Trends and New Domains,* ed. A. V. Senthilkumar. Hershey, PA: IGI Global Book Publishing, pp. 244–265.

Sajja, P. S. 2011. Personalized content representation through hybridization of mobile agent and interface agent. In *Ubiquitous Multimedia and Mobile Agents: Models and Implementations,* ed. S. Bagchi. Hershey, PA: IGI Global Book Publishing, pp. 85–112.

Simon, C., Nader, A., Marcus, T., and Takeshi, O. 2001. Enhancing e-communities with agent-based systems. *Computer* 34(7):64–69.

Smith, R. G. 1980. The contract net protocol: High-level communications and control in a distributed problem solver. *IEEE Transactions on Computers* C29(12):1104–1113.

chapter twelve

Web security

12.1   Introduction

There are many common misconceptions on the objective, efficiency, and use of security on the Internet in general, and the Web in particular. This has directly contributed to the lack of real security in applications and services in the past. Well documented vulnerabilities and attacks have undermined the average user's confidence in the Internet. This trend will continue until better security tools are made available and safer computing is practiced by administrators and end users.

The Web is a client- and server-based concept, with clients such as Internet Explorer, Mozilla Firefox, Opera, Google Chrome, and others connecting to web servers such as Internet Information Services (IIS) and Apache, which supply them with content in the form of HTML pages. Many companies, organizations, and individuals have collections of pages hosted on servers delivering a large amount of information to the world at large. This makes use consider issues such as information security and privacy. Web servers often are the equivalent to the shop window of a company. It is a place where you advertise and exhibit information, but this is supposed to be under your control. No one on the Internet is immune from security threats. In the race to develop online services, web applications have been developed and deployed with minimal attention given to security risks, resulting in a surprising number of corporate sites that are vulnerable to hackers. Unfortunately, web servers are complex programs, and as such have a high probability of containing a number of bugs, and these are exploited by the less scrupulous members of society to get access to data that they should not be seeing. And the reverse is true as well. There are also risks associated with the client side, for instance web browser. There are a number of vulnerabilities, which have been discovered in the last year, which allow for a malicious website to compromise the security of a client machine making a connection to them.

The steps involved in connecting to the Internet and then to the Web are very detailed even if it does seem to be smooth from the user end. So what happens for real when you just want to get into a website? Assuming you are already connected to the Internet, here are the steps that occur in the following order:

1. You open your browser.
2. You type in the uniform resource locator (URL) (website name).
3. Website name saved in history cache on the hard disk.
4. Your computer looks up the name of the address to your default domain name server (DNS) server to find the Internet protocol (IP) address.
5. Your computer connects to the server at the IP address provided at the default web port of 80 transmission control protocol (TCP) if you used "HTTP://" or 443 TCP if you used "HTTPS://" at the front of the web server name (by the way, if you used HTTPS, then there are other steps involved using server certificates, which we will not follow in this example).
6. Your computer requests the page or directory you specified with the default often being "index.htm" if you do not specify anything.

7. The pages are stored in a cache on your hard disk. Even if you tell it to store the information in memory (RAM), there is a good chance it will end up somewhere on your disk either in a PAGEFILE or in a SWAPFILE.
8. The browser nearly instantaneously shows you what it has stored. Again, there is a difference between "perceived speed" and "actual speed" of your web surfing, which is actually the difference between how fast something is downloaded (actual) and how fast your browser and graphics card can render the page and graphics and show them to you (perceived). Just because you did not see, it does not mean that it did not end up in your browser cache.

This chapter deals with several issues related to web security and privacy. We shall also discuss the contributions of intelligent techniques for web security.

12.2 Web vulnerabilities

The simplicity of giving someone something that they ask for is made much more complex when you are in the business of selling. Websites that sell to, companies selling products, bloggers selling ideas and personality, or newspapers selling news require more than just HTML-encoded text and pictures. Dynamic web pages help you decide what to ask for, show you alternatives, recommend other options, and up-sell add-ons. When we log on to any web application, we are in a whole new world of security problems. Figure 12.1 illustrates different vulnerabilities associated with the Web.

12.2.1 Scripting languages

Many scripting languages have been used to develop applications that allow businesses to bring their products or services to the Web. Though this is great for the proliferation of businesses, it also creates a new avenue of attack for hackers. The majority of web application vulnerabilities come not from bugs in the chosen language but in the methods and procedures used to develop the web application as well as how the web server was configured. For example, if a form requests a zip code and the user enters "jihif", the application may fail if the developer did not properly validate incoming form data. Several languages can be used for creating web applications, including common gateway interface (CGI), hypertext preprocessor (PHP), and active server pages (ASPs). These terms are introduced in the following:

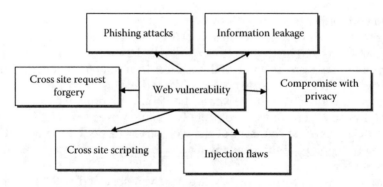

Figure 12.1 Web vulnerability.

CGI: A CGI is a standard way for a web server to pass a web user's request to an application program and to receive data back to forward to the user. CGI is part of the Web's hypertext transfer protocol (HTTP). Several languages can be used to facilitate the application program that receives and processes user data. The most popular CGI applications are C, C++, Java, and PERL.

PHP: PHP is an open-source server-side scripting language where the script is embedded within a web page along with its HTML. Before a page is sent to a user, the web server calls PHP to interpret and perform any operations called for in the PHP script. Whereas HTML displays static content, PHP allows the developer to build pages that present the user with dynamic, customized content based on user input. HTML pages that contain PHP scripting are usually given a file name with the suffix of ".php".

ASPs: It is a specification for a dynamically created web page with an .ASP extention that utilizes ActiveX scripting—usually VBScript or JScript code. They utilize ActiveX scripting, usually VBScript or JScript code. When a browser requests an ASP, the web server generates a page with HTML code and immediately sends it back to the browser—in this way, they allow web users to view real-time data, but they are more vulnerable to security problems.

12.2.2   Understanding communication

Today's web applications are often vulnerable to attacks. There are several reasons why many web applications contain vulnerabilities. It may not come as a surprise that web vulnerabilities cannot be prevented completely. However, one must be aware of the mistakes and vulnerabilities that are present, and adapt his web applications to minimize the chance that they are compromised.

To understand why *input validation* is necessary, it is essential to understand the communication between a browser and a remote server. The communication starts by the browser issuing an HTTP GET command to the server:

```
GET /members/tmrf/fun/ HTTP/1.1
Host: tmrf.in
```

The server then responds with

```
HTTP/1.1 200 OK
Date: Wed, 20 May 2010 10:22:31 GMT
Server: Apache/1.3.33 Ben-SSL/1.55 (Unix) DAV/1.0.3 PHP/4.3.10
Last-Modified: Wed, 20 May 2010 10:22:35 GMT
ETag: "6e000e-7f-47273155"
Accept-Ranges: bytes
Content-Length: 127
Content-Type: text/html
<HTML>
<HEAD><TITLE>Exercise</TITLE></HEAD>
<BODY onload='alert("Battery is down!");'>
<H1>Hello World</H1>
</BODY></HTML>
```

The response is interpreted by the browser in following three steps:

1. The browser reads the header:
   ```
   HTTP/1.1 200 OK
   Date: Wed, 20 May 2010 10:22:31 GMT
   ```

```
Server: Apache/1.3.33 Ben-SSL/1.55 (Unix) DAV/1.0.3 PHP/4.3.10
Last-Modified: Wed, 20 May 2010 10:22:35 GMT
ETag: "6e000e-7f-47273155"
Accept-Ranges: bytes
Content-Length: 127
Content-Type: text/html
```

2. The browser reads and displays the HTML code:

```
<HTML>
<HEAD><TITLE>Exercise</TITLE></HEAD>
<BODY onload='alert("Battery is down!");'>
<H1>Hello World</H1>
</BODY></HTML>
```

3. The browser interprets and executes scripts in the content:

```
alert("Battery is down!");
```

Input validation is the part that requires the maximum care and effort when implementing security in an application. For instance, in ASP.NET, good input validation prevents SQL injection and cross-site scripting (XSS) attacks. SQL injection attacks are particularly dangerous and are often looked for by malicious attackers. XSS vulnerabilities are very common and are some of the most upsetting. Input validation helps prevent these two types of attacks.

The reason that input validation requires more commitment is that input validation is different for every application. Thus, there is no standardized library or built-in functionality that can be used as the input validation subsystem. Certainly, regular expression functionality greatly simplifies implementing input validation; however, it does not offer a plug and play component. The input validation subsystem has to be designed and implemented from scratch particularly for the given application. The quality of the input validation routines will play a significant role in determining the overall security level of the application.

12.2.3   Injection flaws

Injection flaws are common in web applications. There are many types of injections, for instance SQL, LDAP, XPath, XSLT, XML, and OS command injections. Injection flaws occur when user-supplied data are passed to an interpreter as part of a command or query. The most common type of injection flaw allows for SQL injection. Structured query language (SQL) is a computer language designed for the retrieval and management of data in relational database management systems, database schema creation and modification, and database object access control management.

A typical SQL query looks like

```
SELECT field FROM table WHERE condition;
```

For instance, if we have a table of all students and their grades, we might want to issue the following command to list all those students whose grade is below 6.

```
SELECT student FROM allstudents WHERE grade<6;
```

A classic way to verify a username and password provided by a user is to search the database for that username/password. If the database returns a nonempty set, the user has provided a valid pair and passes authentication. A common way to do this is to access the database from a PHP script using the following code:

```
$sql = "SELECT * FROM table WHERE username = '" . $user . "'
AND password='" . $password. "';";
$result = mysql_query($sql);
```

A simple SQL injection that would allow access to the website could be to provide admin as username and 'anypassword' OR '1'='1' as password. Giving such values would result in the following SQL query being executed:

```
$sql = "SELECT *
FROM table
WHERE username = 'admin'
AND password='anypassword' OR '1'='1';
```

The latter part of the injection (OR '1'='1') ensures that the WHERE clause is always satisfied. This would allow the attacker to pass the authentication mechanism and login to the system without knowing a valid username/password combination.

Although passing the authentication scheme is undesired, much more damage can be done by exploiting the fact that SQL queries can be composed using a semicolon. For instance, the following input for password would add a user "Kim" to the database with password "9876".

```
anypassword' OR '1'='1'; INSERT INTO table VALUES ('Kim',9876);--
```

Since the values of $user and $password are entirely under the control of the attacker, any malicious input can be passed onto the database.

Any application that allows users to input data, which is subsequently passed onto another system is potentially vulnerable to injection flaws. The main solution to this problem is to sanitize the data (for instance by disallowing certain characters in user input), before passing it onto another system. SQL injection has been at the center of some of the largest credit card and identity theft incidents. Today's backend website databases store highly sensitive information, making them a natural and attractive target for malicious hackers. Names, addresses, phone numbers, passwords, birth dates, intellectual property, trade secrets, encryption keys, and often much more could be vulnerable to theft. With a few well-placed quotes, semicolons, and commands, entire databases could fall into the wrong hands.

12.2.4   *Cross-site scripting*

XSS allows the attackers to execute scripts in the user's browser. This may result in hijacked user sessions, defaced websites, hostile content in websites, phishing attacks, and hostile browser takeovers. The malicious script is usually JavaScript, but may be any scripting language that is interpreted by the victim's browser. XSS flaws occur whenever an application takes data, which originates from the user and does not validate the user input.

The attacks are usually implemented in JavaScript, which is a powerful scripting language. Using JavaScript allows attackers to manipulate any aspect of a rendered page, such as adding a login box that forwards credentials to a hostile site. Another possibility is to perform a phishing attack on the user. The evolution of JavaScript malware, finding its way into more and more attackers' toolboxes, has made finding and fixing this vulnerability more vital than ever.

XSS attacks can be protected against by validation of all incoming data ("whitelist validation") and appropriate encoding of all output data. Validation allows the detection of attacks, and encoding prevents any successful script injection from running in the browser.

12.2.5   Cross-site request forgery

A cross-site request forgery (CSRF) attack forces a logged-on browser to send a request to any website of the attacker's choice, which then performs the chosen action on behalf of the victim. The attack works by including a link into a web page that accesses another website to which the user has logged in. The attack allows attackers to make an HTTP request to, for example, the victim's bank, blog, or web mail. The following tag in any web page viewed by the victim will generate a request to the web page that logs out the user:

```
<img src="http://www.example.com/logout.php">
```

If an online bank allowed its application to process requests without explicitly verifying the user's credentials, the following code asks for a transfer of funds:

```
<img src="http://www.example.com/transfer.php?toIBAN=123
&toBIC=456&amount=500">
```

Although XSS flaws are not required for CSRF attacks to work, any website that is vulnerable to XSS attacks is also vulnerable to CSRF attacks. When building defense against CSRF attacks, eliminating XSS vulnerabilities in a website is essential, since such flaws can be used to get around CSRF defense mechanisms.

The only protection against CSRF attacks is that applications do not rely on credentials that are automatically submitted without the user's knowledge.

12.2.6   Phishing attacks

Phishing is an attempt to criminally and fraudulently acquire sensitive information by masquerading as a trustworthy entity in an electronic communication.

The first phishing technique was described in detail in 1987. Phishing was first applied on a large scale in the early 1990s. While early phishing attempts were targeted at large groups of users, recent phishing attempts are becoming more and more targeted at individuals using additional information of the user that is attacked.

In a phishing attempt, the attacker tries to spoof a legitimate website, with the aim of obtaining data the victim would normally supply to the original website. This data could be usernames and passwords or credit card information.

The first part of a phishing attack is to fool the user into visiting a malicious website. Common techniques are to make the anchor text for a link appear to be valid, while the link actually goes to the malicious website. Another common technique is to use misspelled URLs, the use of subdomains (e.g., http://www.tmrf.ac.in or http://www.tmrf.in.ac when the attacker possesses resp. the domains ac.in or in.ac), or the use of IP addresses instead of URLs. Another, more dangerous attack involves poisoning the DNS cache of the user. If the attacker succeeds in poisoning the DNS cache of the user, the user will be redirected to the wrong server.

After fooling the user into visiting the malicious website, the attacker might try to alter the address bar. He can either use JavaScript to alter the address bar, place a picture of a legitimate URL over the address bar, or close the original address bar and open a new one with the URL of the legitimate URL.

In general, phishing attacks are performed through e-mail or instant messaging communication.

12.2.7 Information leakage

Applications can unintentionally leak information about their configuration, internal working, or violate privacy through a variety of application problems. Examples of such information are developer comments, user information, internal IP addresses, source code, and software version numbers. While information leakage itself does not have to be a problem, the information may be used by an attacker to launch, or even automate more powerful attacks. Examples of information leakage are given as follows:

- Detailed error handling such as failed SQL statements or other debugging information.
- Functions that display different results based on different inputs. For example, a failed login should display the same message (e.g., "login failed") irrelevant of whether username, password, or both were incorrect.

12.2.8 Browsers compromising privacy

The websites with cascade style sheet (CSS) can be used to violate the privacy of the user visiting the website. The website uses the fact that the browser stores a history of visited pages. Depending on whether a user has visited a page that is linked to from a browser, the color of the hyper link is changed. The following two websites show whether a user visited a page or not:

http://ha.ckers.org/weird/CSS-history-hack.html
http://ha.ckers.org/weird/CSS-history.cgi

The second website shows how a hostile website may abuse this information: it includes an image if and only if the user has visited the page. In doing this, the browser essentially tells the website which pages have been visited.

12.3 Web server protection

12.3.1 Firewall

Firewalls originally were fireproof walls used as barriers to prevent fire from spreading, such as between apartment units within a building. The same term is used for systems (hardware and software) that seek to prevent unauthorized access of an organization's information. Firewalls are like security guards that, based on certain rules, allow or deny access to/from traffic that enters or leaves an organization (home) system. They are important system safeguards that seek to prevent an organization's system from being attacked by internal or external users. It is the first and most important security gate between external and internal systems.

Firewalls are generally placed between the Internet and an organization's information system. Standard firewalls are designed to restrict access to certain ports, or services that an administrator doesn't want unauthorized people to access.

Web Application Firewalls are often called "Deep Packet Inspection Firewalls" because they look at every request and response within the HTTP/HTTPS/SOAP/XML-RPC/Web Service layers. Some Web Application Firewalls look for certain 'attack signatures' to try to detect a specific attack that an intruder may be sending, while others look for abnormal behavior that doesn't fit the websites normal traffic patterns. Web Application Firewalls can be either software, or hardware appliance based and are installed in front of a webserver in an effort to try and shield it from incoming attacks.

The firewall just like a security guard cannot judge the contents of the information packet; just like the guard allows all persons with a valid identity card irrespective of nature of the persons, firewall allows entry or exit based mainly on IP address and port numbers. Hence, an entry or exit is possible by masking IP address or port. To mitigate this risk, organizations use intrusion detection system (IDS), which is explained in Section 12.3.2.

There are various kinds of firewall depending on the features that it has, namely, packet filter (operates on IP packets), state-full firewall (operates based connection state), or application firewall (using proxy).

Example of a firewall rule could be Block inbound TCP address 200.224.54.253 from port 135. (An imaginary example); such rule would tell a computer connected to Internet to block any traffic originating from the computer with an IP address 200.224.54.253 using Port 135. Important activities relating to firewalls are initial configuration (creating initial rules), system maintenance (additions or change in environment), review of audit logs, acting on alarms, and configuration testing.

12.3.2   Intrusion detection system

IDSs help information systems prepare for and deal with attacks. It is accomplished by collecting information from a variety of systems and network sources, and then analyzing the information for possible security problems. Let us consider in a university campus with security guards. How will the guards detect entry of unauthorized persons? The university authorities would install burglar alarm that will ring on entry of unauthorized persons. This is exactly the function of IDS in computer world. Firewall (security guard or fence) and (IDS, burglar alarm or patrolling guard) work together; while firewall regulates entry and exits, IDS alerts/denies unauthorized access.

Intrusion detection provides the following:

- Monitoring and analyzing of user and system activity
- Auditing of system configurations and vulnerabilities
- Assessing the integrity of critical system and data files
- Strange activity analysis
- Statistical analysis of activity patterns based on the matching to known attacks
- Operating system audit

Let us see how IDS is helpful. Just like burglar alarms, IDS alerts the authorized person (alarm rings) that an authorized packet has entered or left. Furthermore, IDS can also instantly stop such access or user from entering or exiting the system by disabling user or access. It can also activate some other script; IDS can, for example, prevent or reduce impact of denial of service by blocking all accesses from a computer or groups of computer. IDS can be host based or network based; host-based IDS are used on individual computers while network-based IDS are used between computers. Host-based IDS can be used to detect, alert, or regulate abnormal activity on critical computers; network IDS is similarly used in respect of traffic between computers. IDS thus can also be used to detect abnormal activity.

There are three key components of the IDS:

- Network intrusion detection system (NIDS) performs an analysis for a passing traffic on the entire subnet. It works in a promiscuous mode and matches the traffic that is passed on the subnets to the library of known attacks. Once the attack is identified, or strange behavior is sensed, the alert can be sent to the administrator. Example of the NIDS would be installing it on the subnet where firewalls are located in order to see if someone is trying to break into your firewall.
- Network node intrusion detection system (NNIDS) performs the analysis of the traffic that is passed from the network to a specific host. The difference between NIDS and NNIDS is that the traffic is monitored on the single host only and not for the entire subnet. The example of the NNIDS would be, installing it on a virtual private networking (VPN) device, to examine the traffic once it was decrypted. This way you can see whether someone is trying to break into your VPN device.
- Host intrusion detection system (HIDS) takes a snapshot of your existing system files and matches it to the previous snapshot. If the critical system files were modified or deleted, the alert is sent to the administrator to investigate. The example of the HIDS can be seen on the mission critical machines, which are not expected to change their configuration.

12.4   Security and privacy

Generally, security communications are the processes of computer systems that create confidence and reduce risks. For electronic communications, three requirements are necessary to ensure security:

1. Authenticity: This concept has to do with ensuring that the source of a communication is who it claims to be. Web authentication enables data security, detect theft protection and a secure user experience. The strength of an organization's Web authentication method should match the value of the information and resources opened for access.
2. Integrity: That a communication has integrity means that what was sent is exactly what arrives and has not undergone alterations (voluntary or involuntary) in the passage.
3. Nonrepudiation: If the conditions of authenticity and integrity are fulfilled, nonrepudiation means that the emitter cannot deny the sending of the electronic communication.

For example, suppose a netbank website sends instructions to the main bank office requesting a change in the balance of an account. If the main bank office is not convinced that such a message is truly sent from an authorized source, acting on such a request could be a serious mistake. The form used to assure authorization from a website are called an electronic certificate. Maintaining the conditions of security gives us tranquility in our electronic communications and allows to assure the principle the privacy in the cyberspace.

The communications are considered to be safe when the web address URL changes from HTTP to https, this change even modifies the port of the communication, from 80 to 443. Also, in the lower bar of the navigator, a closed padlock appears, which indicates the conditions of security in the communications. If you put mouse on this padlock, a message will appear detailing the number of bits that are used to provide the communications (the encryption level), which as of today, 128 bits is the recommended encryption level. This means that a number is used that can be represented in 128 bits to base the communications.

A security protocol called secure sockets layer (SSL) enables websites to pass sensitive information securely in an encrypted format. It is based on the RSA Data Security's public key cryptography. One can recognize web pages that use SSL because the URL says "https://" and the web browser will show some type of lock or other icon to denote that the connection is secure.

Phishing scams attempt to trick people into providing sensitive personal information. In order to avoid these situations, the authenticity of the site should be verified and checked that the communications are safe (https and the closed padlock), and to the best of your knowledge, it verifies the certificate.

Most websites receive some information from those who browse them—either by explicit means like forms, or by more covert methods like cookies or even navigation registries. This information can be helpful and reasonable—like remembering your book preferences on Amazon.com and, therefore, in order to ensure security to the person who browses, many sites have established declarations of privacy and confidentiality.

Privacy refers keeping your information as yours—or limiting it to close family or your friends, or your contacts, but at the most, those who you have agreed to share the information. No one wants their information shared everywhere without control, for that reason, there are subjects declared as private, that is to say, that of restricted distribution.

On the other hand, the confidentiality talks about that a subject's information will stay secret, but this time from the perspective of the person receiving that information. For example, if you desire a prize, but you do not want your information distributed, you declare that this information is private, authorize the information to a few people, and they maintain confidentiality. If for some reason, in some survey, they ask to you specifically for that prize, and you respond that if you have it, you would hope that that information stays confidential, that is to say, who receive the information keep it in reserve. We could generalize the definition of confidentiality like "that the information received under condition of privacy, I will maintain as if it was my own private information." It is necessary to declare the conditions of the privacy of information handling, to give basic assurances of security.

Also, it is recommended that you read the conditions established by the website you visit in their privacy policy.

12.5   Contributions of AI for security issues

The world of web applications is growing fast in importance and size, but in parallel it raises increasing concerns about security, which will not be solved adequately within the present paradigm of web security.

AI-based approaches potentially offer a way to address the multiple threats associated with web security, without having to rely on an increasing list of changing rules or security procedures for diagnostic and recovery procedures. If security tools were expert systems, which could not be abused as easily, the situation would be very different. Ideally, they would understand what users are trying to do and make sure that this is what is happening. They would develop a sense of "situational awareness," from which they would be able to tell malicious activity from legitimate ones. They would be able to make context-dependent determinations.

If AI means introducing intelligence in an automated system, there is no doubt that the future of web security lies in AI. The limits of the possible with AI are not known. The limits of the capabilities of AI are a moving frontier. In a "post biological intelligence" world (Davies 2010), the division between natural and artificial intelligence will be blurred.

We are still far away from that world, but it is not too early to envision it. And the question is how AI should be introduced in the world of web security with maximum effect in the short term. Should we have a vision of AI-based web security as a cyber equivalent of what happens with the immune system during biological evolution? That is of the creation over time of a large and complex organ inseparable from the rest of the organism? Should the first-phase attempt to build the equivalent of a rudimentary immune system, with the vision of an eventual large and sophisticated one? Or should the search be more random and based on trying to introduce more intelligence in security tool whenever possible and wherever possible? In fact, the two approaches differ only on paper. The immune system must have developed out of a random search as we are told the rest of biological evolution, leading in the long run to high levels of organization.

To what extent does AI in its present state provide a framework to start building such a system? It is impossible and not useful here to try and describe a field like AI. On the one hand, it is a large body of academic knowledge (Russell and Novig 2003). When it comes to its applications, it looks more like a vast and fragmented field. Through expert systems, AI has found applications in numerous fields from medical diagnosis to helping manufacture to finance management to fault analysis to advanced optimization and to a very limited extent to web security.

Of the many techniques used in AI, when it comes to anomaly-based intrusion detection, the techniques, which seem the most natural, are either "statistics based" (Mitchell 1997) or "knowledge based" (Akerkar and Sajja 2010).

The whole area of machine learning tends to make heavy use of statistics. Statistically based machine learning traditionally needs huge amount of data. This may turn problematic in many situations of interest for intrusion detection. It points to the fact that there are fundamental cognitive differences between human beings and machines. Human beings need much less data to "learn" than machines and get a better power of discrimination. One implication of that remark is to invalidate partially the assumption that what human beings can do, machines will also be able to do.

Still an approach based on statistical learning in web security is not hopeless, quite the opposite. But this suggests that the best use of AI may not be to try to find a way to have machines replicating what human beings do.

An alternative to statistical learning is knowledge-based system (KBS) (Akerkar and Sajja 2010), although that approach raises also challenging issues. KBS tends also to be specialized. The system can acquire its knowledge in a variety of ways. It can be made to learn.

A lot rides on the way knowledge is stored and represented. Those systems can reason and make inferences. In principle, they could be used to make autonomous determination of whether a malicious attack is unfolding.

In practice, AI and data management techniques can be called upon to create an environment for network security management without increasing the burden on the network administrator.

Other approaches used in AI may turn out quite powerful in web security. Intrusion detection has some features in common with problem solving. Techniques using formal logic and theorem proving may turn out to be quite useful. If it were possible to reformulate the problem of intrusion detection as solving a logical problem, we would know better what the limits of the possible are.

As of now probabilistic reasoning seems to be the most natural and easiest way to introduce AI in intrusion detection, but this may not be the only one in the long run.

In the context of web security, AI applications could take several forms. But it is clear that to be useful, any AI will have to be used intensively. Even if the processing power of computers is increasing impressively, one has to be concerned by the potential CPU overhead associated with any intensive AI technique. Considering that there is hardly any alternative in the long run to AI in web security, one has to be prepared to see web security to be part of the rest of cyber in the same way as the immune system is part of the animal's organisms. Instead of being a protection added at the end, it will be an integral part of the system, and as is the case with the immune system, it could be made "dual use," that is, its function may not be limited to protection.

Exercises

12.1 Open up google and type in "inurl:search.asp" or "inurl:search.php". With any of the websites that come up, attempt to type in the following in the search field <script>alert ("hello")</script>. What happens? Try this for several sites.

12.2 Knowing the types of security mechanisms, a web application may have, open your favorite, interactive website and try to identify if it has security mechanisms, which conform to any of the Risk Assessment Values (RAV) classifications.

12.3 Commonly discussed web vulnerabilities are XSS and SQL injection. What are they and how does an attacker use them to steal data or information from a web application?

12.4 Are both firewall and IDS required in an organization for securing its information system? If yes why? If not, why not?

12.5 Give an example of a specific use of firewall rules that is applicable to the front desk person in a school; does she need to access Internet? If not, how will the rule be enforced?

12.6 Review the conditions of privacy of worldwide suppliers of WebMail, Google and Hotmail, and of manufacturer like General Motors (http://www.gm.com/privacy/index.html). Are they equal? Of those, who will share the information that I give? What measures will I be able to take if they do not observe these rules?

12.7 Go to http://cve.mitre.org and go to search for CVEs. Enter the name of a web server (i.e., Apache) into the search field. When did the latest vulnerability get released? How often have vulnerabilities come out (weekly, monthly, etc.)?

References

Akerkar, R. A. and Sajja, P. S. 2010. *Knowledge-Based Systems*. Sudbury, MA: Jones & Bartlett.

Davies, P. 2010. *The Eerie Silence: Renewing Our Search for Alien Intelligence*. Boston, MA: Houghton Mifflin Harcourt.

Mitchell, T. M. 1997. *Machine Learning*. New York: McGraw-Hill.

Russell, S. and Norvig, P. 2003. *Artificial Intelligence: A Modern Approach*. Upper Saddle River, NJ: Prentice Hall.

chapter thirteen

Human–web interactions

13.1   Introduction

The Internet and web have significant effect on how people function both at work and at home. These technological virtues support activities such as learning, entertainment, applying for job, composing an academic paper, and shopping for holiday gifts. These tools have become the world's most widely used research vehicle too. The interaction with the Web can be done by expert, professional, or common man. The successful website must handle and satisfy these users.

Since its establishment, the World Wide Web has flourished. While advances have been made in the technological aspects like web organization, web data structure, searching within the Web, etc., little attention has been paid to the development theories of human–web interaction (HWI). HWI is defined as the processes that take place when humans interact with a system on the Web in order to access and retrieve content. It can also be defined as study, plan, and design of what happens when a user navigates with the Web. Nature of the Web makes this procedure a little bit challenging. An exponential growth of the Web (in terms of the number of available websites and applications on it) has been observed since last few decades. However, the design of an effective website that meets user needs still remains a challenge. The goal of the HWI is to meet this challenge and to produce usable and safe web-based systems and applications. For this, the developers of such systems must attempt to understand the tentative users; develop tools and techniques to enable building suitable systems; and achieve efficient, effective, and safe interactions.

This chapter initiates with the discussion of features of a good website considering content, look, information organization, performance, and interaction design. It further discusses interaction, interaction styles, models, and related parameters. The usability of the system is also discussed with issues such as learnability, efficiency, and memorability while discussing the detail methodology of interaction design. Methods like activity-centered design, contextual design (CD), focus group, iterative design, user and usage scenario, etc., are introduced to facilitate the design of interaction.

Resources on the Web include documents, models, services, and techniques. To manage the vast pool of resources on the Web, some intelligent support is required. Artificial intelligence (AI) methods and modeling techniques are gaining increasing attention in this context. The usefulness of such methods is significant, since the nature of the Web is unstructured, heterogeneous, and dynamic. To manage and facilitate applications like browsing, searching, mining, filtering, managing traffic, and other interactions, AI methods are useful. The chapter further illustrates the support of AI methods and techniques for effective and quality utilization of resources on the Web. These methods include searching, filtering, mining, and knowledge management using AI for the Web. Many R&D areas are also listed at the end that may be considered to carry out independent research in the area of HWI.

13.2   Features of a good website

It is observed that some people believe restaurant food is to "dine" and not to "eat." If they really want to "eat" good food, they prefer home-made food. And we all know that the restaurants are chosen according to their ambience for formal dining. According to Nathan Shedroff (www.nathan.com), interaction to a website is what ambience is to a restaurant. It is probably the most important aspect to websites. However, it helps in attracting the audience initially. A very good-looking website many times gives the impression of lower quality content. The good design should also include parameters such as content, information design, performance, compatibility, and visual design besides interaction design. These parameters are shown in Figure 13.1.

The characteristics illustrated in Figure 13.1 are discussed in the following in detail.

13.2.1   Content

The best domain content is one of the prime necessities for a good website. The content must be fair, reliable, and of good quality, and should not be contradictory. One must see the expiry date of the content. Many websites with excellent look may not offer fresh content. Many government and university websites still show retired employees, expired deadlines, and outdated information. The site must have some objective instead of miscellaneous patches of gathered information, which are poorly related with each other. Many unnecessary things can be hidden for ordinary user's category and level.

13.2.2   Information organization

The site must look clear, organized, and easy to navigate. Customized navigation path can be designed for different types of users. It is to be noted that at every click, users must be provided sufficient information. Too many clicks and less amount of information increase the burden of webpage administration within network and generate poor content effect.

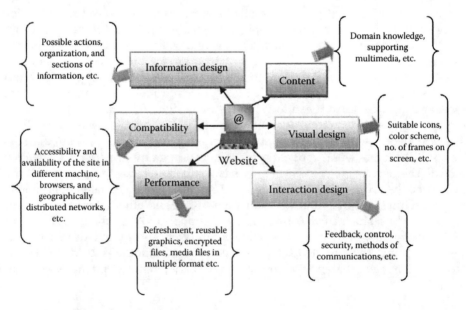

Figure 13.1 Parameters of good website.

13.2.3 Performance

The website must be quick enough to load and refresh. The heuristic like multiple formats of same file may be kept ready at background. Alternatively, reusable graphics file, encrypted or portable documents with reduced size, and some quick format tags can be used to increase the performance of the website. Speed of the website also depends on who watches your site. Audience like old age people and very young kids may not be as fast as school children.

13.2.4 Compatibility

Different types of platforms, operating systems, and browsers are available to view the developed website. It may be arranged that the website automatically identifies the configuration of the workplace, and appropriate version, which fits best to the configuration, can be loaded automatically.

13.2.5 Visual design

The site must look attractive. It is observed that the good sites are often visually less attractive and reverse is also true. The site must be appealing to the target audience. It is obvious that you cannot please everybody all the times; however, the important people to your business must be identified prior to design a visual interface of the site. The visual design of the site must complement your business.

13.2.6 Interaction design

The site must have means to interact with users. For user information acquisition, for password and other inquiry, and for feedback and comments, the site must have efficient mechanism. Furthermore, there may be different gateways on a page of content (site) according to the level of the users.

13.3 What is interaction?

We are used to many interaction processes and instruments such as telephone, reservation of tickets, online shopping, personal organizer, bank ATM, watch, VCR, weighing scale, etc. Some devices are very friendly such as weighing scale and telephone. As these devices are old, they eventually evolve to have good design interfaces with years of experience. However, there are systems such as new versions of personal organizer, forms that transfer money to the e-commerce website, and VCR, with which we may have to spare a lot of time to get them into real work. Many of these tasks (which gave us trouble) might not have been designed considering users ease in mind. Web content is not exception of these examples. Many times we have had difficulties with locating (and executing) some applications as well as finding information from a website. A website or any content on the Web is designed considering the users in mind like other products. In general, the Web must allow users the gateways of better interaction. As stated in the introduction section of this chapter, the HWI is defined as the set of processes that take place when humans interact with a system on the Web in order to access and retrieve the content. It can also be defined as study, plan, and design of what happens when a user navigates with the Web. There are three main components of these procedures, namely (i) the user, (ii) the Web, and (iii) the process of navigations.

13.3.1   Common interaction styles

The common interacting styles to deal with the Web are command line arguments, mouse clicks (point and click), voice inputs, natural language, images, through remote location via wire, and menus. These parameters are shown in Table 13.1.

Most of the web applications use a combination of some of the techniques mentioned in Table 13.1. A common combination is windows, icons, menus, and pointers (WIMP). It has become the default style for a majority of interactive computer systems. Other techniques such as touch screen are also available for users who are physically challenged or not literate in given languages. Also, there are special techniques available which are compulsory for some application. Section 13.3.2 discusses 3D interfaces in brief.

13.3.2   Three-dimensional interactions

In this technique, human interacts with the Web through 3D space. It has its roots in virtual reality. It uses the techniques of virtual or augmented reality. In this kind of interaction, user can virtually move into the system and perform interaction in three dimensions. Users can experience very real and actual feeling of presence within the system and have better understanding of how information interchange takes place just as in the physical

Table 13.1 Common Interaction Style

Interaction style	Characteristics
Command line interface	It is the way of expressing instructions and data to the computer directly using function keys, single characters, abbreviations, words, or a combination of these It is suitable for repetitive tasks carried out by computer literate professionals
Pointers	It is the way to select an entity of interest through mouse without much effort. One need to just point out on entity such as icons, pictures, labels, location of map, etc., and click to invoke it
Menus	Set of options displayed on the screen in attractive and visual form using icons, pictures, and labels. These options can be selected through function keys, arrow keys, mouse pointer, or combination of them It is easier to use for noncomputer professionals Often the related options grouped in meaningful way
Query interface	It is an interactive way to pass the structured query (like SQL) to get some response from the Web Generally, it is used in conjunction of database as well as the Web It may use natural language for ease of use
Natural language	It is more familiar to user; however, it is complicated to deal with as users are giving vague, incomplete, and partial information Keyboard, text files, and other multimedia inputs are allowed
Form filling	Standard forms with space to provide or select information are provided to the user to get data These fields at back end may have some scripts for validation and preprocessing Forms can be designed through any front-end tool like. NET framework, spreadsheet, and interface such as SQL forms
3D Interfaces	Three-dimensional interface allows browsing, exploring, and interacting with web applications in a virtual 3D environment It requires more space and specialized techniques

world. Scenarios, texture, sounds, and speech can all be used to augment 3D interaction. The 3D interaction techniques involve selection, manipulation, navigation, and system control techniques. Furthermore, the navigation technique uses techniques such as way finding and traveling. The travel techniques are further classified into the following five categories:

- Physical movement—user moves through the virtual world
- Manual viewpoint manipulation—use hand motions to achieve movement
- Steering—direction specification
- Target-based travel—destination specification
- Route planning—path specification

Techniques that support system control tasks in three dimensions are classified as follows:

- Graphical menus
- Voice commands
- Gestural interaction
- Virtual tools with specific functions

There are tools and products available to use these techniques for various applications. Edusim is one of them. Edusim (http://edusim3d.com/) is a 3D multiuser virtual world platform and authoring toolkit intended for classroom interactive whiteboard. This tool can be used to create guided 3D tours using concepts of virtual reality to historical places, scientific labs, and futuristic demonstrations. Besides the Edusim, a variety of tools are available for 3D file visualization, 3D windows manager, 3D search interfaces, and 3D browsers. Some of these tools are presented in Table 13.2.

13.4   *Interaction design and related parameters*

Interaction design is the art of effectively creating interesting and compelling experiences for others. It applies to all forms of interaction, all products, and all media including the Web content and applications. Interaction design includes navigation strategy, look of the site, information organization of the site, and interface to the users to work in ease. Interaction design must consider some products and process to facilitate better and effective interaction between the system and its users. As far as support from standard models and set of technique concerns, the interaction design is more art and less science. Scope of including lots of creativity is there while designing good and comfortable interaction mechanism. Interaction, in general, can use any material to pass messages, such as smoke signals that the Red Indians and tribals used, Samuel Morse telegraphic code to pass information, punch card to old computers, telephone and mobile interfaces to talk and hear, different types of input/output devices that work with computers and other machines, etc. Interaction design is related to fields such as human–computer interaction (HCI), sound design, visual design, industrial design, users interface design, information organization, and users' experience design. Interaction design for the Web that is HWI design primly considers the content of website, its users, information organization, navigation strategy, and visual look of the site. For example, public phone interface and railway reservation interface are to be designed considering public. In the case of railway reservation, one can remember to/from (departure and destination) stations and date of journey instead of train numbers. The train number should be automatically inserted as user selects the train

Table 13.2 3D Interaction Tools

Interaction style	Tool	
3D file system visualization	Tactile3D	Tactile3D (http://www.tactile3d.com/) is a next generation 3D desktop program that allows users to organize files and directories in a 3D space. Users get the impression of exploring a vast virtual landscape, with each directory being a new world in which they can roam around and place objects where they want
	XCruiser	XCruiser (http://xcruiser.sourceforge.net/) is a 3D file system visualizer for Linux. It allows users fly through their file system as if it were interplanetary space. Directories are represented as galaxies, files are represented as planets (whose mass is determined by the file size), and symbolic links are represented as wormholes
	File system visualizer (FSV)	FSV (http://fsv.sourceforge.net/) produces a 3D rendering of a file system. FSV is modeled after file system navigator (FSN). It lays out files and directories in three dimensions, geometrically representing the file system hierarchy to allow visual overview and analysis. FSV can visualize a modest home directory, a workstation's hard drive, or any arbitrarily large collection of files, limited only by the host computer's memory and graphics hardware
3D process visualization	LavaPS	LavaPS (http://www.isi.edu/~johnh/SOFTWARE/LAVAPS/index.html) represents OS process activity as blobs, with size that is proportional to memory usage, movement that is proportional to CPU usage, and color that is based on the program name and the time since the program last ran
	Bubbling load monitor	Bubbling load monitor (http://www.nongnu.org/bubblemon/) represents CPU and memory load monitor as a vial containing water, whereby the water level indicates how much memory is in use; the color of the liquid indicates how much swap space is used, and the system CPU load is indicated by the rate at which bubbles float up through the liquid
3D window managers	3DTop	3DTop (http://www.3dtop.com/) is an extension for windows that represents desktop icons in 3D, letting users to fly around desktop, change the shape of the icons, and rearrange them in 3D by dragging and dropping actions
	CubicEye	CubicEye (http://www.cubiceye.net/) organizes windows into a navigable 3D cube. Cubes can be arranged by thematic or functional subject matter, and can be explored either individually or collectively as part of a more comprehensive structure of multiple cubes representing various areas of interest
3D search interfaces	Pansophica	Pansophica (http://pansophica.sourceforge.net/) is an intelligent web search agent that presents results in a dynamic and interactive virtual reality. Pansophica organizes and personalizes websites and searches

(continued)

Table 13.2 (continued) 3D Interaction Tools

Interaction Style	Tool	
	3DTopicsscpe	3DTopicsscpe (http://www.topicscape.com/) is an organization assistance that helps users map concepts by visualizing details about documents and their relationships using a 3D Mind Map. Users search for keywords, phrases, and intuitive concepts by flying around the 3D landscape
3D browsers	Clara	Clara (http://www.spatialknowledge.com/) is a 3D web browser that lets you walk, fly, or jump through a virtual world where all the objects are usable, interactive web pages. You can read the pages just as you would in 2D, that is, scroll them, click them, or hear them
	SphereXPlorer	SphereXPlorer (http://www.spheresite.com/spherexplorer. html) is a 3D web browser that shows a new way of exploring the Internet. It provides easy manipulation and navigation browsing facilities

time and other information (train name) of the train. Different types of users have different usage, understanding, and perception of the same system. According to user's level, there may be more than one interface to the same system.

13.5   Usability

One common thing in all the systems developed in the world is that they are developed for users. If a system is efficient to use, easier to learn, and satisfactory to the users, it is acceptable. The system can be website, standard single user system on a dedicated machine, electronic machine, or even a noncomputer–nonautomated system like book or any product. ISO norm defines usability as "the extent to which a product can be used by specified users to achieve specified goals with effectiveness, efficiency, and satisfaction in a specified context of use." Usability is associated with the functionality of the product/system. The parameters associated with usability are learnability, efficiency, memorability (when users return to the system after a long time, it must be easy to recall the systems' functionalities and ways of working with the system), error handling by the interface, and satisfaction of the users. Usability can be planned with the interface design. Usability includes considerations such as main users, user's general background, their objectives to use the system, data required from the users, speed of providing deliverables to the users, trouble shooting help if required, how to test usability, and what are the acceptable standards regarding the usability. Different perspectives and consideration regarding usability are described in Figure 13.2.

The design of the system and/or interface of the system must be tested for the degree of usability it offers. The typical steps to test the design for acceptable usability are as follows:

* Evaluate the existing approaches for its strong and weak points.
* Test various alternatives.
* Identify different users and their objectives, method to use system, style and habits along with crucial requirements.

Figure 13.2 Different perspectives of usability.

- Also identify the typical errors that users are prone to make. Specify the remedies and cost of such errors.
- Make quick mock-ups, prototype, and simulation to train users to test new ideas about new design of interface. Go for enough iterations to revise these ideas.
- Compare the resulting design against standards and objectives.
- Implement, inspect, and collect postimplementation feedback.

The knowledge of usability helps developers to know about the users and the patterns they usually deploy to surf websites. The relative importance of search and navigation pattern is that it can easily be identified and used to develop useful systems. Such knowledge contributes to combining web presence, search, navigation, and content into a pleasant user experience that makes people happy.

13.5.1　World usability day

World usability day was founded in 2005 as an initiative of the Usability Professionals' Association to ensure that services and products important to human life are easier to access and simpler to use (http://www.worldusabilityday.org/). World Usability Day is celebrated annually on the second Thursday of November. In 2012, it falls on November 15. Each year, on this day, over 200 events are organized in over 43 countries around the world to raise awareness for the general public, and to train professionals in the tools and issues central to good usability research, development, and practice.

13.6　Process of interaction design

The aforementioned parameters including usability are considered to develop interaction design, which is useful and appealing. The process of interaction design starts with identifying users and objective of the interaction with the specified system/website. The process involves conceptualization, planning, specifying requirements, designing, evaluating, and implementing the design. Many developers follow discovery, design research, reporting, designing framework of interaction, and follow through phases to develop desired interface. Many undergo ad hoc approaches such as trial and error or iterative mechanism. In general, the process of interaction design involves basic phases as follows.

13.6.1 Know your users, their requirements, and identify the objective of the system

The very first activity in this phase is to identify the target users. When it comes to a specific product or website, there are always some target users in mind. Referring to mass and identifying the target users as just "anybody" shows that not enough importance is given to the target audience. After finding proper target audience, determine what content can be offered to them and how it will be presented so that it can appeal them. Unnecessary information can be hidden for clean and secure presentation of the content. The usability of material can also be defined here. The content presented must be usable, safe, efficient, complete to apply, and having some utility. Utility is defined as extent to which it can solve user's problem. The users experience goals that are also to be defined here. The usage of systems' experience must result in some learning, problem solving, entertaining, motivating, and rewarding.

13.6.2 Check the feasibility and cost–benefit ratio of different alternatives

To meet the goals and requirement mentioned earlier, multiple design solutions are available. Each solution considers parameters like effort, resources, and processes required in comparison with tentative expected benefits. From multiple such alternatives, one of the alternatives can be finalized.

13.6.3 Build selected alternatives considering content

The selected model can be built by finalizing the content and revising the information organization, navigation processes, interface, and look of the system. Library of ready-made code, graphical user interface (GUI) images, text blocks, arrows, and boxes can be used for development.

13.6.4 Test the developed interaction design

This phase involves testing the individual components as well as a full-fledged integrated system. The parts can be tested on various browsers, machines, and networks for different user groups. These components or system may be communicated to some actual users for further testing (beta testing) or implemented on selected locations.

13.6.5 Conduct postimplementation review and update if required

It is important to evaluate the users' experience and usability of the website through survey or any fact finding like observation, placing counters, comments, etc. The negative feedback helps a lot in improving the system. This process is illustrated in Figure 13.3.

13.7 Conceptual models of interaction

A conceptual model of any activity/entity is a high-level description of the abstraction of ideas and concepts about behavior, look, and actions of the entity. This is purely logical and also be called as mental model. Many models designed for human interaction have a foundation in psychology, cognitive science, and/or information technology. Such frameworks and models are important in the context of research activity. The starting point of

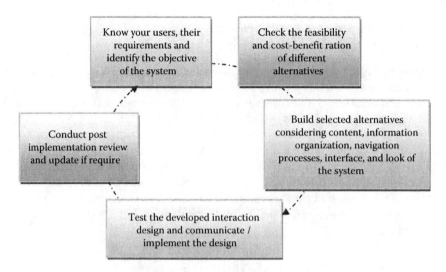

Figure 13.3 Phases of interaction designs.

Figure 13.4 General framework of conceptual model.

any interaction model is its goal. As far as website is concerned, the goal can be information finding, carrying out transaction, shopping, or entertainment. Based on the goal, the methods and tools are selected in order to achieve the goal. The goal must be translated into some actions. The way it should carry out different actions to meet goal is nothing but strategy. Carefully planned strategy when implemented leads to desired results. These results are evaluated and generic strategy can be learned. After thorough testing, these strategies may be refined, used iteratively, and becomes well-established generic schema. These general steps are described in Figure 13.4. These general steps are concluded from various models used for interaction design.

Most of the interaction models are based on the cognitive model proposed by Neisser's (1976) perceptual cycle. The model represents a cyclic procedure of real-life entities/model explored through a model by following a particular strategy/schema, which samples some objects. Repetitive occurrence of these processes modifies the model/schema. It is a cyclic procedure involving real-life entities, strategies, and schema.

13.8   Interface

Interface design or interface engineering is designing application that facilitates the interaction between instruments, processes, and users with the focus on user's requirement and interaction. It is also known as user interface. Good user interface facilitates ease of using system in a transparent way. That is, the working of the interface must not disturb the users or system rather it should help user in exploring and using systems' components. It may use multimedia input and output, allows preprocessing while accepting data from users and other sources, and passes important messages to the users. Interface can be developed for noncomputer professionals, considering a particular target audience in mind, or can be developed for different machines such as electronic microscope, cars, and mobile phones, and platforms such as the operating system UNIX.

Designing is one of the crucial fields in software engineering that deals with how system components are conceived, developed, and implemented. Software engineering field provides some useful methods and guidelines for the development of interface. Some of the important methods are described in the following.

13.9   Interface design methods

13.9.1   Activity-centered design

Instead of focusing on goals and objective of the user's interaction process as a complete process, the activity-centered design focuses on behavior of users performing a particular task. The behavior can be learned by typical fact-finding methods such as observation, interview, record reviews, questionnaire, etc., as well as specialized knowledge acquisition methods such as conceptual mapping and sorting (where concepts are documented formally and mapped or sorted according to actual problem solving activities while observing experts). By mapping users' activities and tasks, the designer may notice any contradiction, redundancy, or missing important tasks for the activity. It is always better to prevent errors or catch them early, failure in which makes the error handling costlier. Documenting the activity design helps in evaluating and cross-verifying against the goal set. Often, the activity-centered design is similar to scenario design, where a scenario is considered and design is developed for it.

13.9.2   Body storming

Body storming concerns with setting up a scenario and let participant users acting in it. This can be in the studio or outside location with or without props. This method is based on brainstorming techniques and forces the users to believe that they are playing some role in virtual, simulated, or prototype scenario/product/website. The participant users generally check the look, usability, working, and other factors of the product. They may suggest some creative ideas based on their experience. This method can be considered as a physical version of the brainstorming method. This is why it is identified as body storming. This approach allows us to investigate different qualities that an idea may have when applied in a physical setting. Body storming encompasses the following subtasks:

- Scenario setting and briefing
- Roles playing by users
- Idea sheet writing
- After role playing review

Acting within the real-world environment helps in clearing ideas about the product/services and encourages idea generation process. It helps participant to become familiar with the product/services very quickly and increases the understanding of the problem and the context in which it resides. This method also allows quick feedback that may improve the overall quality. However, the comments and ideas received through this process may not be realistic; they need to be reviewed thoroughly. It is a bit costly as it involves setting up a complete working environment for a selected subtask.

13.9.3   Contextual design

CD is a user-centered design (UCD) process developed by Beyer and Holtzblatt (1998). It incorporates ethnographic methods for gathering data (such as observation) relevant to the product/service via field studies, rationalizing workflows, and designing human–web or human–computer interfaces. CD can be seen as an alternative to engineering and feature-driven models of creating new systems. This method involves collection of data through contextual inquiry, interpretation, data consolidation, visioning, storyboarding, user environment designing, and prototyping. The generated prototype is then evaluated, and necessary revisions are considered.

13.9.4   Focus group

A focus group is a form of qualitative research where a dedicated group of users are asked about their perceptions, opinions, beliefs, and attitudes toward a product, service, or concept. Questions are asked in an interactive group setting where participants are free to talk with other group members. The process can be formal or informal. The focus group generally consists of 6–12 members. Small groups with 3–5 members can also be formed. Such small focus group is called mini focus group. There are different types of focus groups as given in the following:

- *Two-way focus group*: One focus group observes another focus group and discusses the observed interactions and conclusion.
- *Dual moderator focus group*: A focus group has two moderators. The first moderator ensures the session progresses smoothly, while another ensures that all the topics are covered.
- *Dueling moderator focus group*: The two moderators as mentioned in previous technique take opposite sides on the issue under discussion and encourage discussion.
- *Respondent/client moderator focus group*: One of the respondents or client is asked to act as the moderator temporarily.
- *Online focus groups*: Computer (or any electronic such as telephone) network is used to enable the connectivity between the focus group members.

13.9.5   Iterative design

Iterative design is a design methodology based on a cyclic process of collecting requirements, generating working model, testing, analyzing, and refining a product/service. This process is intended to improve the quality and functionality of a design. In iterative design, an interaction with the designed system is used as a form of research for informing and evolving a project, as successive versions of a design are implemented.

Iterative design is also used in the development of human–computer interfaces. This allows designers to identify any usability issues that may arise in the user interface before it is put into wide use. Many times the designed interface for the entity may not be perfect according to user's perspectives. The interface to the product/service must be checked against desired quality parameters. Typical steps of iterative design in user interfaces are as follows:

- Collect the preliminary requirements
- Complete an initial interface design

- Present the design to several test users
- Note any problems the test user had
- Repeat and refine interface to account for/fix the problems till the design is accepted

Iterative design in user interfaces can be implemented in many ways. One common method of using iterative design in computer software is software testing and collecting feedback. Website design may follow the same approach while designing their interfaces. Their tester may be the actual users. The website interface may be modified by recommendations from visitors to the sites. There is one more concept that follows the principles of the iterative design with little variation. This approach is rapid prototyping. Rapid prototyping is the quick, automatic, and iterative construction of entities. The emphasis is given on quick as well as automatic generation. The prototyping in general can follow one of the approaches, namely, experimental, evolutionary, and exploratory.

13.9.6   Participatory design

Participatory design is a cooperative approach by involving different types of users such as employees, partners, customers, citizens, and end users in the design process. The objective is to ensure that the designed product meets their needs and is usable. It is a collaborative as a way of creating environments that are more responsive and appropriate to their inhabitants' and users' cultural, emotional, spiritual, and practical needs. Participatory design is an approach, which is focused on processes and procedures of design and is not a design style. It can be considered as an approach with political dimension of user empowerment and democratization. A variant of the participatory approach called distributed participatory design also follows the similar principles. However, the users and resources in this approach are distributed in nature. Alternatively, this system may use advanced computing facility such as GUI.

13.9.7   Task analysis

Task analysis is the analysis and description of how a task is accomplished. It includes description of both manual and mental activities, task and element durations, task frequency, task allocation, task complexity, environmental conditions, necessary clothing and equipment, and any other unique factors involved in or required for one or more people to perform a given task. Task analysis may further extended to the tasks modeling. Roots of task analysis are in applied behavior analysis. Information from a task analysis can then be used for many purposes, such as personnel selection and training, product design, interaction design, equipment design, and procedure design.

13.9.8   User-centered design

The design of service/product/website is developed keeping users' perception in mind. UCD is also called as pervasive usability. It is a consortium of activities that evaluates a design's usability at every stage of the design process, keeping in mind the goals of the project and the users' needs. UCD can be characterized as a multistage problem solving process that guides the designers to foresee how users are likely to use a product. The difficulties and limitation of the design can be foreseen here and can be repaired earlier. The main difference from other product design philosophies is that UCD tries to optimize the product around what users want and how they would use the product. It involves three broad steps: analyzing and collecting requirement, conceptualizing the design, and implementing the design.

13.9.9   Usage-centered design

UCD is an approach to user interface design based on a focus on user intentions and usage patterns. It analyzes users in terms of the roles they play in relation to systems and employ basic design task analysis. It derives visual and interaction design from abstract prototypes based on the understanding of user roles and task cases. Many times this method uses models like unified modeling language (UML) workflow and task analysis models. UCD shares some common ideas with activity-centered design.

13.9.10   User scenario

In computing, a scenario is a narrative description of foreseeable interactions of type of users and the service/product. Scenarios include information about goals, expectations, motivations, actions, and reactions. Scenarios are planned attempts to interact with the selected entity considering the way in which it will be used in the context of daily activity and different roles of users. Scenarios are helpful tools for the system development process. Scenarios are written in plain language such as structured English, with minimal technical details, so that the end users such as designers, usability specialists, programmers, engineers, managers, and marketing specialists can have a common example, which can focus their discussions. Scenarios are also used to define the required behavior of software: replacing or supplementing traditional functional requirements. Vannevar Bush's "As We May Think" essay first published in The Atlantic Monthly in July 1945 is a famous example of a scenario that served as a vision piece. It was the user scenario that presented the idea of hyperlinks and illustrated the value of hypertext. It described the (fictitious) Memex machine that inspired Douglas C. Engelbart to see the potential of the personal computer, and enabled him to secure the funding necessary to design the computer mouse and first GUI in 1968.

13.9.11   Value-sensitive design

Value-sensitive design (VSD) is an information system design methodology emphasizing the values of direct and indirect users. It was developed by Batya Friedman and Peter Kahn at the University of Washington starting in the late 1980s and early 1990s. Designs are developed using a tripartite investigation consisting of three phases: conceptual, empirical, and technological. These investigations are intended to be iterative, allowing the designer to modify the design continuously.

13.9.12   Wizard of Oz experiment

The term Wizard of Oz (originally Oz paradigm) has come into common usage in the fields of experimental psychology, human factors, ergonomics, linguistics, and usability engineering to describe a testing or iterative design methodology. Here, an experimenter (the "wizard"), in a laboratory setting, simulates the behavior of a theoretical intelligent computer application (often by going into another room and intercepting all communications between participant and system). Sometimes this is done with the participant's a priori knowledge.

13.10   Tools for human–web interaction

This section presents some tools that employ to some extent AI techniques for HWI procedures.

Bloodhound: Bloodhound is a simulation-based tool, which automatically analyzes a website to produce a usability report and help the designer to identify navigability problems. The major inputs of this tool are user-given keywords and uniform resource locators (URLs). It outputs high-traffic pages, success per tasks, and number of wrong pages traversed.

Messa: This tool outputs mean navigation time and simulates user's processes in a cognitive model by taking URL and other keyword-related information.

ACWW: ACWW considers user goal, detailed description of user's goal, webpage details like regions, and other links to produce mean predicated links, navigating problems such as weak scent or unfamiliar headings. The underlying model of this tool is cognitive walk-through.

ISETool: This tool also considers detail information regarding keywords and URLs to produce interactive tabular report as well as reports navigator problems.

CoLiDeS+: Links, headings, keywords, region of webpage, etc., are considered by this tool to produce simulated cognitive user processes.

CogTool-Explorer: This tool uses free text, URLs, and website design components to predict task time and provides simulated cognitive user processes.

AutoCardSorter: AutoCardSorter text description of content-item and outputs best-fit categories through card sorting.

13.11   Interaction evaluation methods

Evaluation of the interaction methods begins in parallel with the design of interactions. When interaction design is in developing phase, it should be evaluated in laboratory against the objectives and expectations of the target audience. When implementation of the interaction is done, it must be tested in live environment. There are some methods to evaluate interaction designed. Some of these methods are given here. Interaction design can be automatically and formally designed through software.

13.11.1   Cognitive walk-through

Cognitive walk-through evaluates the design of interaction against different aspects such as usability in a website (or any software). It is usually performed by the expert in cognitive psychology. The expert walks through and explores design to identify potential problems using psychological principles and evaluates design. Generally, the expert considers aspects like usability, impact on users, learning, and fulfillment of goals. The errors encountered during the walk-through are considered for solution. After finding out proper cause of the problems, revision on design is proposed. This method is a low-cost method to test interaction design while design is still under developing phase.

13.11.2   Heuristic evaluation

Heuristic evaluation depends on general and practical rules/situation, which may not be successful every time. They are "rule of thumb" and do not offer specific guidelines. In the case of heuristic evaluation of interaction design, experts are setting usability criteria and test the design accordingly. The usability criteria set by the expert must not be violated.

The visibility, user control, error handling, user help, documentation, and efficiency of use can be considered by the expert to evaluate the design.

13.11.3   Review-based evaluation

Designed rationale and existing guidelines/literature can be used to check the interaction design. This is also known as model-based evaluation of interaction. Cognitive models are used for this purpose. Cognitive modeling uses formal model to estimate the time required to perform a given task. Models like parallel design, Goals, operator, methods, and selection rules (GOMS), and human processor model can be used here. Parallel design involves several experts creating and testing initial design from the same set of requirements. GOMS model, which is a family of techniques, analyzes the user complexity of interactive systems. Goals are what the user must accomplish. An operator is an action performed in pursuit of a goal. A method is a sequence of operators that accomplish a goal. Selection rules specify which method satisfies a given goal, based on context. Human processor model considers how human brain processes information.

13.11.4   Evaluating through user participation

In-house or on-site participation of user is required to evaluate design here. In-house testing takes advantages of well-established environment of laboratory and can assure secure environment for testing. However, users must have to come to the place. More users cannot be accommodated in restricted environment of in-house testing. For on-site testing, it may need proper setup and environment to test. The site preparation, equipment setting, responsible personnel, etc., are key factors that should be kept ready before testing begins. On site, many times secure environment and laboratory facility/equipments are not available. However, it is possible to accommodate more number of users in their familiar environment. Obviously, it is costly and difficult as several users may test the design/system in parallel in a new environment. Furthermore, in any method, the users need to be aware of the context and objective of the evaluation.

13.11.5   Evaluating implementations

Implemented design of interaction/system requires an artifact or working model of the system. One may use simulation or prototype. A set of test cases, hypothesis, and expected outcome lists, scenarios, etc., are also prepared before actual testing begins. In case, error or exceptional situations are reported, they may be analyzed and necessary revisions have to be implemented. The implemented interaction design/system must be tested against the parameters such as usability, compatibility, navigation scheme and information organizations, security, and performance. Different tests can be developed to test the implementation such as unit/component test, integration test, usability tests, load/stress test, and user acceptance test.

13.12   Human–computer interaction and human–web interaction

The field of HCI deals with the study of the interaction between humans and computers with the general aim of developing more humanly acceptable technology. Many different models, theories, and techniques contribute to this area. Many psychological models, mental models, cognitive theories, linguistic theory, social science, computing theories, and models (such as software engineering) help in fulfilling the objectives of the development of better HCI. HCI involves study, plan, design, and implementation of interaction between human and computers. The study of HCI includes software as well as hardware. Due to the multidisciplinary nature of HCI, people with different backgrounds contribute to its success. HCI is also sometimes referred to as man–machine interaction (MMI) or computer–human interaction (CHI). Internet and web are two important aspects that facilitated a special kind of systems in distributed environment. While dealing with the Web, these HCI techniques and concepts can be applied too. They may be extended further with specific application in mind according to need. In one way, the HCI is generic and super set of the HWI.

13.13   Issues in human–web interactions

The Web is ubiquitous and hence generic. Dealing with environment like the Web, some important issues may arise. Some of the issues are listed in the following:

- General issues like security, customized utilization of web applications, and facilitates offered to explore the Web may have significant effect on web interactions.
- Development methodology also needs consideration as there are no strict guidelines available for the development of system that appeals the mass of users. It is an art that considers how interaction with web applications can be developed, implemented, and tested that meet developers concerns.
- To cope up with new and continuous advancements in technology, the technical problem such as hardware compatibility and adaptability to deal with new platforms must be considered to make system more flexible and useful.
- Organizational issues with the Web such as locking of sites (e.g., social networking, share market, and news sites), security and firewall, backup, log management, etc., are also need to be considered. Also, one has to consider structure of organization, team for development, and measuring quality of web interaction system, etc., before enabling the web application.

13.14   Support of AI for human–web interactions

Support of practical, useful, and intelligent techniques are needed to intelligently utilize huge, rich, unstructured, and shared web resources and services in effective as well as efficient ways. Consider the application of searching. Even though we write a program and/or take the help of search engine, it is practically impossible to search every piece of the content on the Web. The main reason is, during the process of the search, many new pages are uploaded. Another problem deals with complexity of the search mechanism that we need to employ. The Web contains heterogeneous and unstructured documents dynamically increasing fashion. To search from such undisciplined resources, we need to develop really very complex program that takes care about variety of ontologies and structure, media, and tools. Many such problems arise while working with the Web. The use of AI techniques is helpful in avoiding these problems and to support the Web management and utilization more effective. The nature of AI solution is to provide practical and acceptable solution within a given time. The solution offered by AI may not be optimum or perfect. However, such solutions are worth and acceptable to get working solution. Many real problems are not worth to go for optimization. For example, to purchase a car, one may not spend months in searching. Probably when the search is finished, some new car models might have come in market. Normally, we consider fuel efficiency, price, engine, and driving comfort to purchase a car. Web has become one of the major supports to acquire information and solutions for day-to-day business transactions, research, and entertainment. Most of the business requires good acceptable solution in practical time frame, instead of working hard to get optimum solution in infeasible time. Application of AI techniques for web allows us to find solutions from the Web and help in web management activities by imparting intelligence. This section presents some ideas that can be considered application of AI for improving quality surfing and managing the Web.

13.14.1   Searching, retrieval and filtering, and semantic search

One of the most popular purposes to access the Web is to search for required information. Web search engine provides thousands of documents in fraction of second. These web pages are ranked according to the search engine strategy. However, this ranking is based on generic formulas, and usually lacks searching and ranking in customized fashion. The AI support in this field can be abstracted as follows:

- The techniques of heuristic search may be used in conjunction with the typical search engine. The added component along with typical search considers a practical rule ("rule of thumb") as a function to determine which documents are to be considered first that meets the solution criteria.
- AI techniques can be used to determine the rank of the searched information according to user's perspectives and based on which the searched content is sorted and presented.
- Two or more searching mechanisms can be employed in parallel and results are compared, ordered, and presented. This concept is known as metasearch engine.
- AI techniques can also be used to dilute Boolean functions such as logical AND. As we know that search engine works on the keywords provided by users. Logical ANDing of these keywords restricts many important and useful search outcomes. That is, the use of AND restricts the content very tightly. Instead, if logical OR is used to filter the searched outcomes, the resulting content covers a broad spectrum. There is a need to dilute the AND and strengthen OR. By developing Fuzzy AND and OR functions, one can do this. That is, the "Boolean" retrieval of information can be upgraded with fuzzy functions.
- Instead of searching based on keywords, that is syntax-based search, semantic (meaning) of the keywords can be considered and search mechanism can be developed using the same. Semantic search searches the domain based on the context. Syntax-based search engine considers keywords supplied by users and searches the physical occurrence of the keywords in the content. However, the semantic search considers the context and searches relevant documents that do not have the keywords mentioned in the content. For example, if you search for "credit" card schemes, the semantic search might retrieve content mentioning "debit," "petro," and "master card" along with some e-commerce scheme that offers handsome discount on such card shopping. Semantic search is powerful; however, it cannot replace the syntactical search engine. The better use of the semantic search is to use it on the basis of syntax-based search.
- The content offered by semantic search engine can be categorized in classes such as images, news, web results, and creditable sites as done by hakia

(http://www.hakia.com/), which is a general-purpose semantic search engine. Hakia handles synonyms, generalizations, and natural and unambiguent language and handles morphological variations.

- Furthermore, the retrieved result of syntactic search can be summarized using some intelligent techniques. For example, sensbot senses the purpose of the retrieved documents and summarizes the search results based on it. It uses text mining and multi-document summarization to extract sense from web pages and present it to the user in a coherent manner.

13.14.2   Native language interface and fuzzy logic for web applications

Applications on the Web may use linguistic parameters and native language for comfortable and friendly usage of the applications. Especially, noncomputer professionals are very comfortable with such interface. The special utility of interface works between users and the system as a facilitator that accepts fuzzy and native phrases such as *"please set the warm temperature."* It de-fuzzifies the "warm" temperature into specific crisp value given a mapping function. This function is known as fuzzy membership function. The membership function helps in determining the fuzzy term into appropriate crisp value through the process of de-fuzzification. When machine/system wants to communicate with user, the same fuzzy membership function is again used to convert the crisp output to fuzzy value, with which user is comfortable. The interface needs to be very generic to allow a number of users from different fields.

For web applications, an interface is planned which allows user to input some keyword/phrase or query. The first step after getting the input is cleaning the noise from the input. The punctuation marks, spelling mistakes, and other stop-words are removed from the input. In the second step, the cleaned input is parsed and tokens are separated from it. Third step involves matching the tokens with appropriate set of synonyms. With the help of such synonyms, back-end database, files, and web pages can be explored. The system may guide the possible completion of the query while entering input. This concept is also applicable to generic search engine. The popular examples are Ginseng, guided input natural language search engine, Querix, natural language processing (NLP)-Reduce, Semantic Crystal, etc., which uses the similar approaches to query semantic web. NLP-based web application requires a set of dictionaries and relationship besides the software for the application. Optionally, the NLP is implemented by purchasing a natural-language search engine and carrying out the implementation of the dictionaries and relationships. Besides search engine and other application, the NLP as well as fuzzy interface can be designed for browsers also.

13.14.3   Knowledge management and knowledge representation on the Web

The Web is a large-scale repository of information as well as knowledge that supports transactions of lives. The amount and type of knowledge make the management of the content difficult and challenging. The typical knowledge management cycle includes knowledge discovery, knowledge documentation, knowledge use, and knowledge share. Like the size, structure, and nature of the Web, there are other drivers that make knowledge management of the Web a trivial activity. These parameters include requirement of uncertainty handling, discovery of new knowledge, improving quality, documentation of knowledge in more machine understandable form, and intellectual asset management. Knowledge discovery is supported by tools and techniques such as meetings, presentations, interview, profiling, and information audit. Discovered knowledge is documented using authoring tools, taxonomies, metadata, thesaurus, and specifications in structured English. Typical AI-based knowledge representation techniques are also useful here. For example, the taxonomies may be fuzzy and uses linguistics parameters. With the help of Internet platform and the Web, the documented knowledge is shared and used with portal, websites, and knowledge centers, groups, or forums on the Web.

13.14.4   Agent-based systems

The Web consists of different documents, models, techniques, and services to facilitate large amount of content to its users. At a time, all the users must not need and access these facilities. Many times unnecessary entities should be hidden for effective and transparent utilization of the Web resources. For every different utility, an agent can be conceived and posted on the Web itself. Different agents developed under this consideration are search agent, query agent, ontology mapping agent, etc. These agents are discussed in Chapter 11. The functionalities that have multidisciplinary nature can employ hybrid agent or multiple agents in a framework. These agents can communicate with the agent's communication language such as ACL and knowledge query and manipulation language (KQML).

13.14.5   Modeling users experience and usability for better web interactions

User experience, many times abbreviated as UX, is a term used to describe the overall experience and satisfaction of a user while interacting with the web application. To measure the user experience and degree of usability of the application, different test mechanisms can be developed. To test such a system, guidelines can be taken from software engineering and AI. Furthermore, some expert systems can be designed to guide integrated development of the web application, to provide test metrics, for workflow management, for user's motivation and ergonomic advisories, aesthetic advisors for visuality and look of the application under development, and expert system that works on customized taxonomy for modeling and measuring the user experience and usability, etc. AI can also support for predicating web usage and guiding users for web interaction.

13.14.6   Intelligent web mining

The objective of the typical data mining technique is to mine patterns and hidden perspectives from large databases and data warehouses. The Web is also a dynamically growing pool of content from which useful content is to be retrieved by users through variety of services. With little modifications, the data mining techniques can be applied on the Web or semantic web. Web content mining as well as web usage mining processes can be strengthened by employing AI search mechanism such as hill climbing and heuristic search methods, genetic algorithm, and classification rule mining.

13.14.7   Interacting with smart environments

The mobile phone has assumed an exclusive role in the context of HCI for smart environments. It is so vast and well known and enables a wide range of usage scenarios for mobile phones beyond making phone calls. The fact that mobile phones nowadays provide a very powerful computing platform with built-in networking capabilities makes them an ultimate platform for prototyping ultramobile interaction devices. If the phone is just used as a mobile display with a keyboard, its small screen and limited input capabilities have to be accounted for by an appropriate interface design.

Many interactions in smart environments involve multiple devices. Indeed, in several cases, the actual user interface is distributed over different devices, taking input from one device and feeding output through another. It is a challenge to structure, develop, and run such a multidevice user interface in a reliable and stable way, and the coordination of multiple devices in such a way is often managed in a middleware layer. In smart environments, the computing power of the environment encompasses the physical space, in which the user actually lives. Thus, it becomes exceptionally essential to investigate the user's perspective of these interactive environments.

While in PC-type interfaces, the interaction bandwidth between the human and the computer is relatively low (limited by the use of mouse, keyboard, and screen), this bandwidth requirement is much higher for interaction with smart environments. The human user can interact using her or his body and multiple senses. Units of information can occupy the same space the user actually lives in. This situation makes the transfer of classical UCD and development methods, but also evaluation much difficult, since interaction becomes rich and highly context dependent.

With constant increase in computing power and stepwise improvement in the look of new sensing technologies, entirely novel input technologies and concepts will inevitably emerge. From the human point of view, it will always be important to be able to form a coherent mental model of the entire interaction possibilities. The understanding of physicality is deeply rooted in human life from early childhood on. It, therefore, provides a very promising candidate for skill transfer and as a basis for such a coherent mental model.

13.15   Case studies

This section presents a collection of examples for various interaction concepts in smart environments. This collection neither asserts to be comprehensive nor to represent every group, which has worked in this area.

13.15.1   MIT intelligent room

The computer science and artificial intelligence lab (CSAIL) designed the concept of "intelligent spaces" and set up an intelligent room in the early 1990s. The room contained mostly conventional PCs of that time in different form factors (projection display on the wall and table, PDAs as mobile devices, and laptops on the table) and a sensing infrastructure consisting of cameras and microphones. This allowed using speech input and computer vision besides the conventional PC interface devices. Applications in this room include an intelligent meeting recorder, which would follow meetings and record their content, as well as a multimodal sketching application. For further details, refer to the website www.csail.mit.edu.

13.15.2   MediaBlocks system

Perhaps, one of the initial tangible user interface prototypes was the MediaBlocks system (Ullmer et al. 1998), in which simple wooden blocks act as placeholders for information bins. The information is not physically stored in these blocks, but it is conceptually associated with them by physical operations. A MediaBlock can be inserted into a slot on a screen and then the screen's content is conceptually transferred to the block. In the other direction, when a block is inserted to a printer slot, the contents of that block are printed. On a block browser device, the block can be put onto trays of different forms and all of its contents can be browsed by scrolling a dial and seeing the contents on the screen. These operations make excellent use of our sense of physical interaction, and they seem very intuitive, once the concept of the block as a placeholder for information is understood by the user.

13.15.3 PhotoHelix

The PhotoHelix (Hilliges et al. 2007) is an example of a category of interfaces, which lies between tangible user interactions (UIs) and purely graphical UIs on an interactive surface. Envisage a graphical widget on an interactive tabletop with interactive elements, such as buttons, sliders, lists, etc. Also, imagine one of its interactive elements not being digital, but physical, for example, a wooden knob on the surface instead of a slider to adjust a specific value. This physical object is part of the entire widget, and the graphical and physical parts are undividable.

The presence of a physical part in this hybrid widget has several advantages. For one thing, real physical effects, such as inertia, can be used in the interface. Then, it also becomes very simple to identify multiple users around a digital tabletop. If each user owns their own physical input object, it can unfold into the full hybrid widget as soon as it is put down on the table, and then is clearly assigned to the owner of the physical part. This solves the identification problem in collaborative input on a desk surface, and also allows adjusting the interface toward the respective user.

The PhotoHelix is the right hybrid interface. It unfolds into a spiral-shaped calendar, on which the photos of a digital photo collection are arranged by capture time. The physical part is a knob, which is meant to be held in the nondominant hand and when it is rotated, the spiral rotates with it and different time intervals of the photo collection are selected. Scrolling far can be achieved by setting the knob in fast rotation and then letting it spin freely, thereby harnessing a true physical effect in this hybrid interface.

13.16   Research applications

Besides the aforementioned area, some R&D applications in the area can be listed as follows:

- Development of customized taxonomy
- Application of swarm intelligence for web searching
- Intelligent crawling
- Wisdom web
- Development of web analysis tools
- Pattern discovery for web transactions
- Web application development model and web engineering
- Development of quality tests, protocol, and standards for the Web
- Web services repository management including identifying and automatic binding of services on need
- Virtual organization on the Web
- Traffic management and load balancing on web processes
- Web application security

- Development of tools that measures web usage
- Web server management
- Interaction on small screens, etc.

13.17 Conclusion

Any software (application) and/or hardware entity must supply proper mechanism to utilize the entity. Application on the Web must be generic for ubiquitous and meant for easy use by noncomputer professional. To manage large and complex pool of information, the Web must be handled intelligently. AI techniques understand users' need and habits, search and present information in customized way, and support web content management in more effective way. The most important thing in these operations is to facilitate the interaction between users and the Web in meaningful way. Not only the Web but also semantic web is benefited by AI techniques. Besides increase in effectiveness and quality of solutions offered by employing AI techniques, there are some points that require consideration. The AI techniques are identified as weak method as they do not guarantee the solution. Furthermore, employing such technique may be costly in terms of effort and cost. Application of human-like intelligent technology in HWI provides bridges between cognitive modeling research and web design practice and helps in improving the usability of web applications.

Exercises

13.1 Examine skilled and trainee operators in a well-known domain: for example, expert and novice game players, or expert and novice users of a software application. What differences can you detect between their behaviors?

13.2 Find out all you can about natural language interfaces. Are there any popular systems? For what applications are these most suitable?

13.3 What influence does the social environment in which you work have on your interaction with the computer?

13.4 Experiment with any hypertext system if you have access to one. As you work through the system, depict a map of the links and connections. Is it clear where you are and where you can get to at any point? Justify your answer.

13.5 (Project) Conduct a survey on video search interfaces.

13.6 Scenarios and personas are being increasingly used in industry as part of a user-centered design approach but people have diverse approaches and different opinions. What are the fundamental arguments surrounding the use of scenarios and personas?

13.7 Conduct a usability evaluation of the program that you use to read, send, and archive email. You have to identify five usability problems, and see if you can use the results of your analysis to suggest design changes that would fix these problems.

13.8 (Project) You are a design team given the task of producing a new breakthrough in mobile phone design. Find at least three people and interview them individually for up to 30 min each about how they feel about their current phone and what they would like improved. You will need to plan what to ask them in advance. During the interview, have them demonstrate what they think are the best features, letting them talk you through it as they do so. Record what they say, with an audio or video recorder (with their permission). Write up your findings, including the method you used to get the information, how good it was, and how useful the information might be.

References

Beyer, H. and Holtzblatt, K. 1998. *Contextual Design: Defining Customer Systems*. San Francisco, CA: Morgan Kaufmann.

Hilliges, O., Baur, D., and Butz, A. 2007. Photohelix: Browsing, sorting and sharing digital photo collections. Paper presented at the *2nd IEEE Tabletop Workshop*, pp. 87–94, Newport, RI.

Neisser, U. 1976. *Cognition and Reality*. San Francisco, CA: W.H. Freeman & Co.

Ullmer, B., Ishii, H., and Glas, D. 1998. Mediablocks: Physical containers, transports, and controls for online media. Paper presented at the *25th Annual Conference on Computer Graphics and Interactive Techniques*, pp. 379–386, New York.

Index

Printed by Publishers' Graphics Kentucky